Nurture Your Spiritual Path

Nurture Your Spiritual Path

Exploring the Rainbow of Belief

John L. Young

Compassionate Futures Books
Mill Valley

Nurture Your Spiritual Path: Exploring the Rainbow of Belief
Copyright © 2022 by John L. Young

Compassionate Futures Books
John L. Young
40 Camino Alto, The Redwoods, Apt. 11305
Mill Valley, CA 94941
415 640-7463
johnlyoung43@gmail.com

Book Production by Cypress House
Cover design by Kiersten Hanna

Permissions

Excerpt(s) from AWAKENING INTUITION by Frances E. Vaughan, copyright © 1979 by Francis E. Vaughan. Used by permission of Doubleday, an imprint of the Knopf Doubleday Publishing Group, a division of Penguin Random House LLC. All rights reserved.

Hymn #446, "Calling the Directions," from the Unitarian Universalist Association's *Singing the Living Tradition*, is reprinted by permission of the estate of Joan Goodwin.

Excerpt from *The Irony of American History* by Reinhold Niebuhr, copyright © 1952 by Charles Scribner's Sons, is reprinted by permission of the estate of Reinhold Niebuhr.

Publisher's Cataloging-in-Publication Data Block
Names: Young, John (John L.), author.
Title: Nurture your spiritual path : exploring the rainbow of belief / John L. Young.
Description: First edition. | Mill Valley, CA : Compassionate Futures Books, [2022] | Includes bibliographical references.
Identifiers: ISBN 9781735950105 (trade paperback) | ISBN 9781735950112 (ebook/ePub)
Subjects: LCSH: Religions. | Spirituality. | Devotional exercises.
Classification: LCC BL80.3 .Y68 2022 (print) | LCC BL80.3 (ebook) | DDC 200--dc23

Library of Congress Number: 2021901056

Printed in the USA
2 4 6 8 9 7 5 3 1
First Edition

For Rahul, Leela, and Kathleen

Creative endeavor without possession,
action without aggression,
and development without domination.

—Lao Tzu

Table of Contents

Preface

This book is for the many millions of people who consider themselves spiritual but not necessarily religious, and for millions more who might not think they are spiritual, but endeavor to live lives of integrity, conscience, and principle, striving to transcend selfishness and greed. It's also relevant for the more than 2 billion humans who identify with one of the world's historic religions but remain tolerant of and interested in other faiths. Some have read the primary texts of other religions; others have tried some of their practices, and still others have integrated one or more of these practices into their lives.

Most adults choose to remain believers in and practitioners of their inherited faiths. I'm not suggesting that readers adopt either my personal spiritual practices or my chosen religious communities. Rather, I invite them to broaden their own religious perspective and to open themselves to the wealth of wisdom embedded in historic religious scriptures and the empowering insights they'll discover through the practices and celebrations of other spiritual traditions. By doing this, they will integrate the best of the world's contemporary insights with the elements of historic religions that touch their spirits and inform their life choices.

This book begins with a summary of the development of humanity so we can start from a shared understanding of how the various historic religions and a sample of modern faiths evolved. The second section contains descriptions of the world's primary historical religions. Each chapter begins with a short overview of that faith, followed by a longer history of its development, and then a brief discussion of my concerns and insights about that tradition. Section 3 contains brief chapters that discuss more recent spiritualities that have achieved worldwide participation. The chapters in the concluding section examine the nature of the sacred—for others and for me; how ethical foundations of the major religions differ and have evolved; how human experiences have been examined and categorized into conceptual systems.

A final chapter summarizes how the world's religions and other institutions continue to evolve as they're challenged by new experiences. A primary intent of this book is to help readers grasp the power of integrating spiritual practices into their lives, which can help them continue to mature throughout their lives and find lasting happiness, fulfillment, and peace of mind and spirit. By sharing my own life's evolution, I remind readers that this process of living our values is enhanced and empowered by how we blend rituals that we find satisfying into daily spiritual practice. This is followed by suggestions for how to discover and establish your own spiritual practices.

Our future on this planet must be based upon sharing, cooperation, nonviolence, and partnership. We can attain this only by becoming religious pluralists—spiritual seekers, learning to embrace the Earth as our home and the human future as our time.

Acknowledgments

My wife and partner, Kathleen Moran, has been my patient editor, advisor, and guide throughout the decade of writing this book. It would have been impossible without her and her daily support. In addition, the book would never have assumed its final form as a publication without the great work of the Cypress House staff and its professional guidance; a special thanks to publisher Cynthia Frank and infinitely patient copy editor and permissions specialist Joe Shaw.

Many of the countless mentors I have had during my seven-plus decades of spiritual discovery have been mentioned in this book, but I would like to particularly mention my parents, Ruth and Cy Young, the El Dorado Great Books group, and Zita Long who guided and supported me throughout my first eighteen years; Professors Emory Lindquist and John Millett from my undergraduate years; Professors Malcolm Sutherland, Bob Tapp, and Peter Baldwin from my seminary years; Professor Diana Eck from Harvard; my first wife, Madhavi, for her introducing me to India and the world in so many ways, as well as for her loving support and wonderful parenting of our children throughout our twenty-eight years of marriage; and the countless ministerial and clergy colleagues and fellow spiritual searchers in the course of my spiritual journey.

Japanese Tea Ceremony, Konkokyo, Japan.

Section I

Chapter 1
A Shared Perspective of Human Development

M odern humanity has an increasingly shared perspective. Our 21st-century world compels us to develop a common reality that allows us to share scholarship, collaborate in scientific discoveries, and use technologies and electronic innovations to communicate and cooperate. A generation into the 21st century, we are rapidly becoming a global society. It is increasingly difficult to remain contained within an isolated family, tribe, or one small community, geographic region, or monolithic group, and unlikely that most individuals either believe in or practice only one ideology or particular version of a single faith.

Since the world is now within the electronic grasp of billions of people, almost daily they see, read, or hear about countries, cultures, and peoples different from themselves. We observe strangers who are being loving, brilliant, and brave. We are regularly confronted with virtuous, faithful people who believe in and practice views of reality and/or faiths other than our own. It is apparent that we can learn useful things from almost everyone, that each of us has some of the truth, but that no one has all of it, and that no individual, group, faith, or nation knows all the important things we will need to know to survive and flourish.

Billions globally are adapting to explosive technological changes: new foods, products, and media entertainment from around the world. Many of us have neighbors, colleagues, and helping professionals from entirely different cultural backgrounds. Millions are immigrating or traveling globally. Twenty percent of US citizens are not now members of any religious congregation; 50 percent of members have changed their religions during their lives, and 25 percent of marriages are interfaith unions. Many countries have a variety of religious communities and life ideologies living together. The largest democracies, India and the U.S., are religious salad bowls.

Life is a continuing series of experiences. We have an experience; then try to make sense of it, connecting that one with others to form patterns and stories. As we mature, we develop intuitive wisdom and explanatory conceptual systems, receiving insights from people and from what we read, experience on electronic media, and share in communities. Those receiving formal educations are introduced to tools and methods that communities have developed to shape their experiences into worldviews and faiths. All cultures have treasured stories, legends, and icons that help individuals develop faiths they can believe in. Daily, everyone uses and depends upon both their intuitive-imaginative-mystical wisdom and their rational-empirical-scientific understanding.

Things don't always work out as we hoped. Everyone has disappointments, even dark nights of the soul. When a new experience does not fit with our understanding, we either must deny that experience or adjust our beliefs. "I thought he loved me"; "I believed I was doing a good job"; "My prayers (hopes) have often been answered"; "I dedicated myself to that scientific, economic, political theory, or religious faith, but now I'm not sure." If you believe that a certain ideology or faith is evil, but then someone with that ideology or faith saves your life, helps your family, or becomes an ally with your cause or nation, you are likely to change your opinion and moderate your distrust.

Everyone has some core beliefs; has faith in something. They use these central beliefs to express their actions. In that sense, everyone is spiritual. Most people also participate in groups and communities that share some beliefs. These groups celebrate together, using rituals and expressing allegiance to and enthusiasm for those beliefs. In that way, most people are religious. In the course of their lives, many people change their faith, discarding some childhood beliefs or ancestral traditions, or have transformative experiences that dramatically change their lives, make them think differently, and inspire them with awe, ecstasy, or expectation. For some people, their deep, careful thinking is as profound and reverential as others' meditations; one culture's songs, dances, music, or arts may be as heartfelt and respectful as another culture's prayers.

Generally, people believe that our universe has some ultimately benevolent foundations, humans can be good, societies are capable of justice, groups can be fair, and individuals may act with love. Almost everyone realizes that it's not enough to simply believe in or regularly repeat their foundational laws. Like the Good Samaritan in the New Testament, courageous Buddhist nuns, or a humble follower of Confucius' admonitions, we need to do things that help our neighbors and the world. No one stands alone. We are all dependent upon powers in nature and society external to us, and we try to remain connected with those powers. Humanity generally shares certain ideals—like being patient, kind, fair, and just, striving for peace and love—and we test our truths with these ideals.

We cannot do justice to spirituality without considering the cosmos, the natural world, and both our empirical and intuitive perspectives. The cosmic dimension reflects our comprehension of ultimate reality or truth. Much of our aged and vast cosmos remains mysterious and unknown—gigantic changing spaces packed with dark energy and dark matter. Most people today agree that the cosmos appears largely insensitive to and neutral about us as individuals, even perhaps to humanity. With cosmic truths, 21st-century humanity tends to accept the most current scientific and scholarly knowledge, which advocates for the most likely (most probable) explanations. They recognize that people need to understand nature's evolving patterns and strive to proceed in ways that sustain, and whenever possible, enhance, our changing natural environments. The earliest religions attempted to make magical connections with the heavens to please nature. Now we know more about nature's evolving processes, but we're still dependent upon those natural processes, and we continue to struggle with how to live in harmony with nature and maintain a healthy balance between our human desires and nature's unfolding wonders and needs.

We all use both our empirical and intuitive processes in searching for appropriate behavior. This is a lifelong path of trial and error. As we seek the sustainable within ourselves and our societies, we simultaneously try to minimize nature's and humanity's tendencies to disintegrate, do nothing, or become excessive (entropy, inertia, or violation). People hope they are guided by some ultimate truths—a worthy character, spirit, or soul (our immanent dimension), and that these immanent insights and actions will

3

nurture connections with ultimate meaning and value with nature and the cosmos (our transcendent dimensions).

For much of history, most people depended upon oral communication to share and remember their histories, stories, and rituals. People are considered literate when they can read, write, and calculate. The earliest discovered written scripts are from about 3500 BC in Egypt, 3000 BC in Mesopotamia (now Iraq and Syria), 1200 BC in China, and as early as 900 BC in lowland Central America. It's also likely that people of the Indian subcontinent had early manuscripts, but those dates lack scholarly consensus. The Canaanites had the earliest known consonant alphabet by 1550 BC; Greeks added vowels by about 750 BC; the far-sailing Phoenicians used the first sequential alphabet thereafter. Only a few in any ancient culture were literate or had access to the few handwritten manuscripts available. Citizens of some Greek city states and Roman citizens at that empire's peak may have been literate, but these populations' majorities (women, slaves, other noncitizens) remained illiterate.

As the Roman Empire declined, so did literacy, becoming a rarity in the Christian world. In most other cultures, literacy also remained the preserve of a tiny elite concentrated among religious leaders and scholars who also controlled the contents. This remained largely true until the 15th century, when Gutenberg's printing press began to publish, and not until the mid-19th-century industrial revolution, when paper and book production became more affordable, did mass literacy become feasible within any population. General education, even for males, was not the norm in the U.S. and Western Europe until the late 19th or early 20th centuries. For most of the rest of the world, general literacy was achieved during the 20th century—and only then did a majority of the world's people become capable of understanding and interpreting their religions for themselves.

Until 1800, the average human lifespan was about thirty years. Thereafter, medical advances, sanitary practices, and technological and organizational improvements were introduced into a more industrialized world. Still, by 1900, the average lifespan was only twenty-six in Africa and Asia, and only forty-seven in the industrialized areas of Europe and North America. By 1950, the average had advanced to a range of thirty-five to sixty-five, depending upon region; by 1970 from forty-seven to seventy-two, and by 2012 from fifty-eight to eighty. Only since 1980 has most of humanity begun to reach what most contemporaries consider the prime years of productivity and accomplishment. This has affected how spirituality is perceived and how religions evolved. Before 1900, half of children worldwide died before they reached age five, and many women died in childbirth. No one received disease inoculations; people understood little about infections; and medicine was generally nonexistent or rudimentary. Radical differences remain between the richest and poorest areas. In 1845, if a child survived to age five, she could be expected to live an average of fifty-five years; by 2012, that average was up to eighty-two. Relatively few women die in childbirth now, childhood diseases are more under control, and on average, women are likely to live several years longer than men. A growing proportion of people have far less tragic lives; they live longer and remain heathy enough to have the time and peace of mind to reflect more upon life's meaning, potentially allowing individuals to adjust their spiritual paths.

For most of history, people lived in small, isolated groups. They shared their experiences only with their families, neighbors, and tribal members. Most were consumed by daily survival, and left scholarship and belief leadership to spiritual specialists whose task it was to understand and direct their group's spirituality. These specialists interpreted the heavens, explained the changing Earth, and assigned value or warnings concerning their tribes' ideas and actions and their beliefs and deeds concerning outsiders. Their valued stories grew into myths, and as writing was invented, these myths became the foundations for their scriptures.

These stories' most virtuous characters became their heroes and heroines. Some evolved into ideals—a few were considered divine. Spiritual specialists became prophets, seers, or healers. Some holidays were celebrated as holy days; a few rites became sacraments, and occasional teachings morphed into unquestionable dogmas. The evolution of stories into cultural myths, and myths into scriptures, was a gradual process, controlled by spiritual elites until the early 20th century, a practice that continues in sizable areas of the world today.

Yet, each of us has friends or neighbors who, without any official badge of faith or high social status, perform everyday miracles and do repeated good deeds; we intuitively recognize them to be of good character-soul-spirit.

Likewise, many human activities can become spiritual practices, though almost any ideological ritual or religious practice can be exaggerated into perversions that both betray their practitioners and diminish humankind.

Spiritual specialists mirror our human foibles. Religious scholars and bureaucrats have their own shortsighted agendas. So, as we consider religious material, we need to combine our own deepest spiritual insights with the best available scholarship and scientific understandings. No existing scripture has arrived to us unaffected by time or unchanged by circumstances. Many individuals and cultures have added to, subtracted from, and interpreted scriptures before we heard or read them. It is imperative that we connect what we hear, read, or study with our own cultural collective unconscious and deepest experiences to help us grasp the archetypes and foundational myths combined in these scriptures. Though they have endured tests of time and circumstance, and often deserve our attention and respect, they are not sacrosanct, unquestionable, or unchangeable. We must not mistake these scriptural menus for our spiritual meals. We need to experience spirituality for ourselves. Organized religion can help, but it can only provide tools and communities that enable us to understand our experiences and offer guidelines and support structures that we may use to test our choices. We need to do the living ourselves by having the experiences and making the choices that reveal and demonstrate our spiritualities.

Religions in the World Today

No one religion dominates the world. Of the 7 billion-plus people in the world, more than 2 billion identify as Christian, of whom 1.2 billion are Roman Catholics. More than 1.5 billion are Muslim, and more than 80 percent of them are Sunni Muslims. One billion are nonreligious; most reside in Communist countries, but there are growing proportions in Europe, the U.S., Canada, Australia, and New Zealand. One billion are Hindu, most of them in India. Half a billion practice an indigenous, ethnic faith. At least 400 million of those are Chinese traditionalists (many practicing combinations of Confucianism, Buddhism, and/or Taoism). Almost 400 million are Buddhists—most in Asia. There are 23 million Sikhs, mostly in India's Punjab state. There are 14 million Jews, the majority of whom live in the U.S. and

Israel. There are 4 million Jains, most in India. Many Japanese make use of both Buddhist and Shinto traditions and practices. There is also a mélange of newer, syncretistic faiths that often mix traditional systems with newer ideas.

People's ideas about the true, beautiful, and good vary incredibly. Their beliefs about what is worthy of respect and reverence are even more diverse. Because this is so, we need to understand the wisdom in ancient myths and scriptures, the imagination of our collective unconscious, and the deep wisdom not only of our own cultures but also of all the world's cultures. One culture's assumptions are often not another's predominant suppositions. Millions of us might not believe that God intervenes in human history or that there is or will be a human savior. Millions of practicing Buddhists, Jains, Confucians, and Taoists, and many in other religions, do not necessarily pray to a God who influences history; neither do they believe in a savior or expect salvation. It's not enough to say no to things that initially appear to threaten us, particularly when we sometimes have little or nothing to say yes to or are unsure whether our assumptions solve life's dilemmas.

Sixty years ago, scholar Huston Smith made a useful geographic generalization in *The World's Religions* about the historic religious traditions. Western traditions had concentrated upon a material universe with a single male deity engaged in human history, while the East Asian traditions concentrated upon the unity of heaven, Earth, and humanity, complementing them through prudent societal arrangements; and the South Asian traditions focused upon the connections humanity could have with the divine through individual liberation and cosmic evolution. Some ancient Western thinkers sought understanding about how people's minds influenced their behaviors or analyzed social relations, but most westerners concentrated on manipulating the physical world through analysis and experiments. East Asian sages focused on people's behaviors, and South Asian seers explored conscious and unconscious minds; 2000 years ago, Buddhists had already discovered many varieties of unconscious behavior.

Aspects of our lives do lend themselves to empirical observation and to scientific method and analysis, but no one can make it through a single day without having experiences and using their intuition. Our lives and emotional satisfaction depend upon how we interpret our experiences in ways that are not, and probably cannot be, understood by rational analysis or scientific experimentation alone. Most who embrace a religion or dedicate themselves to spiritual practices believe not only in interactions among body, emotions, and mind but also in the existence of characters-spirits-and/or souls. They perceive their spirits to be the aspects of humanity that continue striving to understand and cooperate with ultimate realities and enduring values. They believe their spiritual lives help them to discipline their bodies, mold their emotions and minds into character, and connect them with the laws of nature and the overarching cosmic purposes. We need to focus on finding healthy balances between mind and body, individuality and community, soulful fulfillment and ethical behavior.

Spirituality is not something you acquire or lose; it's not a fixed possession, but a dynamic quest. Every human has depth dimensions and cosmos-connecting aspirations, and we all practice them, if only intermittently and imperfectly. Everyone is faithful and flawed, saved and searching. We all have some strong beliefs, but everyone also has periods of profound doubt, even episodes of despair. Jesus urged people not to judge lest we be judged. Globally, ideological hubris-spiritual pride is recognized as the preeminent human weakness—sin. Muhammad said: "The ideas of the scholar are more sacred than the blood of the martyr."

Few of us can deny that some people believe in and practice life philosophies that challenge our own deepest beliefs and practices, yet we often love, cherish, or respect these relatives, friends, neighbors, colleagues, or strangers, though they believe and live in ways that appear to contradict our own faith. I propose that we find the viable, valuable, and respectable in a wide array of life practices that can benefit us from their accumulated global wisdom. This process is more deeply understood by recognizing that just as every individual changes and evolves, so each spiritual tradition and life philosophy changes and continues to evolve.

I'm not an optimist, believing all will be well, but am hopeful. I think we humans must learn to evolve beyond our inherent selfishness and stretch our tribal boundaries beyond intimates, family, sect, ethnicity, or nation into a more planetary perspective. We need to put into global practice the mutual respect, concern, and empathy that a vast majority espouses and seeks. If we fail to do so, it is unlikely that our descendants can survive or thrive. We cannot afford prejudices that claim that those who are different are not fully human and can thus be justly oppressed, or that entire communities can or should be abused or even wiped out.

Within any community, there appear to be individuals who concentrate upon or are even obsessed with bodies or emotions or minds. Once we realize that every person uses empirical observations and scientific and logical analysis, and has experiences and intuitions, we are better able to grasp both our shared humanity and our surprising individual variety. Sane people agree there is a real world, but also that both individuals and cultures only imperfectly perceive and understand reality, so it is honest, prudent, and realistic to forsake obsessive quests for the one and only truth, the single answer, or the final solution, and resist clinging to an unchangeable faith. Certainly, it is desirable to use reliable sources of information, to practice habits that make us more reliable, and to invest ourselves in dependable communities, including intimate friends, beloved family, a spiritual community, meaningful work, and larger groups that make sense to each of us. The cocoons of self and/or of "tribal" ethnicity, class, or intimate circles are too narrow and limited to afford us either adequate enduring wisdom or the breadth of perspective we need to evolve and grow adequately in the 21st century.

During the last century there occurred a dramatic liberation of the individual spirit, growth in human understanding, organization, and cooperation, and a universalization of values. While traditional ethnic boundaries and traditions were being transformed, millions of people were also avidly exploring their own spiritual nature, absorbing wisdom not only from their own cultures and groups but from elsewhere in the world. People are often actively cooperating to develop more universal rules of behavior, mutual respect, and understanding, and effective ways of nurturing ethical systems that better serve global populations.

Chapter 2
My Life and Spiritual Path

In some ways, my life has been typical for my generation; but I've also been blessed with special opportunities and advantages. My parents grew up in Wichita, Kansas, during the early 20th century. Dad didn't graduate from high school; mother did, but missed graduation delivering her first child. They struggled through the Dust Bowl and Great Depression, with father changing jobs often, and my parents and two daughters moving frequently. In contrast, by the time I was born (1943), my father had become a federal employee, and I grew up in El Dorado, Kansas, (pop. 12,000). We lived in the same small house until I graduated from high school. I shared a bedroom first with an older sister and then my younger brother. Mom was a full-time homemaker. Most of our extended family lived nearby in Wichita, where we visited regularly. I attended local public schools, and from age ten had part-time jobs. To supplement scholarships during my university years, I worked at janitorial and construction jobs, as a Chicago airport U.S. Immigration agent for one summer, and as a Germany factory worker for another. After marriage, I began my career as a Unitarian Universalist minister, and we co-parented our two children. In retirement, my second wife and I moved close to the children and are active grandparents.

Although I grew up in a largely Protestant town in a region where most attended church, no one in my birth or extended family were regular churchgoers. My father had disliked his evangelical Christian upbringing, and he criticized religion. My maternal ancestors were Episcopal and then Methodist; my maternal grandparents donated generously, but rarely attended. My father revered classical music, jazz, and opera on records and radio, and greatly respected philosophers and good writers, while my mother was a nature mystic. They shared devotions to music and culture, and intensely discussed ideas and current events. Their spirituality focused on people and nature; a dictionary lay on our dining room table rather than a Bible. Our summer trips and my father's fascination with geography and world events introduced me to global thinking at an early age.

At ten, I began to attend church regularly, not as a believing participant but as a paid musician, playing piano both for the Episcopal Sunday School and the Christian Scientists' Wednesday evening healing service. I became the substitute Episcopal organist and choir accompanist. Confronted with weekly Bible lessons, sermons, and testimonials, I read through the Bible twice, and my parents quizzed my reflections on services. I became the well-versed inquirer about Christianity but didn't join a church until college.

My personal spirituality began in my mother's lap. She conveyed that the natural world was a beautiful and awesome place worthy of reverence, that life had a unique role for each person, and that we need to live in harmony with nature and treat other people fairly and with love. My parents instilled in me a veneration for beautiful music, great art, good literature, and innovative ideas, and taught me to stand up for my beliefs and to be a proud nonconformist. My mother's practical kindness to my classmates and others who were poor or mistreated, and both parents' awareness of social injustices, pointed me to an activist path.

I grew up with people of color, new immigrants, and poor people among my playmates, friends, and mentors, including our immigrant trash collector and Anne, a fiftyish African American caretaker on my maternal grandfather's ancestral Georgia farm. My parents gave me the run of El Dorado; I made adult friends through after-school jobs and frequent trips to the library. At thirteen, a neighbor gave me Mohandas K. Gandhi's *Experiments with Truth* and Claude Bragdon's *Yoga for You*. I've practiced yoga daily since. Gandhi and Martin Luther King Jr. became my spiritual heroes, demonstrating that nonviolent actions were more effective than violation, courageous activism was necessary to become ethical, and that being socially responsible was empowered by inclusive spiritual practices. Since my youth, these have always been spiritual practices for me, not just a political tactic or an exercise routine.

An older sister, Nancy, and her family had become Unitarian Universalists (UU). When I began college in Wichita, I began to attend its UU church and soon joined. A Western faith as old as the beginning of the Protestant

Reformation, UU continues to protest and evolve with a changing world. UUs are more concerned with people's deeds than their creeds, with their affirmations rather than their prohibitions. My second year there, I taught their early teen class "Church across the Street," studying a different denomination one week, attending their service the following weekend, and gathering the class the next Sunday to discuss our experiences, thus attending my first Roman Catholic, Jewish, and evangelical services.

I grew up relatively privileged: A white, lower-middle-class male in a small town with a close and loving family. Many individuals and institutions supported and encouraged my enthusiastic, inquisitive nature. I had a variety of friends, including several adult mentors who aided my success at school, piano, wrestling, track, Scouts, and jobs. My maternal great-grandfather had started a Wichita bank, and my maternal grandfather was a VP there. He also served as Wichita's mayor when I was a teen. That extended family wealth and status provided a safety net that many families never have. It permitted my family a yearly car vacation. My parents taught me to save my earnings; as a young adult, I became a modest investor.

I had a full fellowship for graduate work in political science at Washington University, in St. Louis, and was granted a tuition scholarship and inexpensive housing while I attended Meadville Seminary and the University of Chicago, and a fellowship at Harvard in midcareer. As a Unitarian-Universalist minister, I flourished in a career that I loved. Those congregations provided my family and me with built-in-communities. UU ministry permitted me opportunities to lead, teach, and be my inquisitive-generalist and volunteer-activist self. As a minister, I negotiated more vacation for less pay in order to travel the world, do research, and write books and poems that few find the ambiance or have the energy to do.

I've been blessed with love and patience from two wives, a series of close friends, congregants, colleagues, my children, Rahul and Leela, and now my four grandchildren. Madhavi Pandya, my first wife, was an Indian from a prominent Mumbai industrial family. I proposed as an about-to-be college professor; then, after I failed my doctoral exams, partly because of my campus activism, she graciously accepted my sudden change from prospective professor to seminary student. Madhavi gave me access to the wonders of India. Her mother's hospitality allowed for research on the

Gandhian movement, and Indian religions guided my life. Madhavi was a loving mother, and a stimulating and challenging companion. After twenty-eight years, our different emotional natures eventually divided us, and we divorced. Two years later, I married Kathleen Moran, who has since given me twenty-three years of love and shared adventures. She became a good companion to my daughter, Leela, as she finished her secondary education, and is now the beloved grandmother we all depend upon.

My years at the Meadville Seminary and the University of Chicago were a combination of intimate dialogue at the seminary and with world-renowned professors at the university. It was a time of turmoil in Chicago and the nation, and I participated in civil rights, student power, and disarmament efforts, served as a hospital chaplain, as an intercity organizer (leading a successful three-week grade-school student/parent boycott), was the religious education director and youth minister for a Chicago UU church, and then their interim minister during my final seminary year, while I wrote my dissertation. My third seminary year, I received a research grant that enabled me, for eight months, to study the Gandhian movement in India, as well as a to spend a month in Japan studying Konkokyo, a neo-Shintoist group's unique counseling techniques.

My forty years of ministry were generally successful. At times, some congregants in Chicago, New York City, Bloomington, Indiana, Paramus, New Jersey, Sacramento, California, and Jacksonville, Florida, gave me more care and wisdom than I was able to provide them. I spent many hours in Unitarian Universalist denominational work and in local and regional volunteer activism. The summer after seminary graduation, I served as the summer director for the UU's legislative office in Washington, D.C., and a later summer as minister at NYC's famed Community Church. The six years in Bloomington, Indiana, was stimulating work for a largely academic congregation. We doubled our facilities and started new programs. I helped lead local antipoverty and nonprofit efforts, and participated in ecumenical antiracism training throughout Indiana, and our son was born. My fourteen years in New Jersey were central to our children's upbringing and provided me with many satisfactions. The congregation published a book of my sermons, *A Graceful Minority,* and a since much-reprinted pamphlet on UU. I led the UU's United Nations office and, through IARF, U.S., UU ecumenical efforts, including a study tour in India. I directed the anti-homeless activism for a Bergen County ecumenical effort involving many denominations and more than 200 congregations.

My years in Sacramento, California, were filled with growth and achievements within the congregation and the larger community, including lobbying for gun control and against domestic violence in the California legislature and a Sacramento ecumenical antiviolence campaign. I was, however, the only minister for eventually 700 area UUs, and the changes, both in my personal and our congregational lives, ended in my resignation. Kathleen saw me through some tough months during which I sometimes doubted myself. My final ministerial congregation was in Jacksonville, Florida (1999–2009). The church flourished, and I could again be more fully a pastor to a smaller congregation. I helped start a peace group and a UU group at the University of North Florida and was active ecumenically in the community. I also taught nonviolence, Indian religions, spiritual practices, liberal religions, and truth and reconciliation at the state University of North Florida, including co-teaching with Nobel Peace Prize laureate Archbishop Desmond Tutu. I published *Creation Songs,* a book of my poetic interpretations of the Old Testament psalms and wrote the biography *Fred Schultz: The Gift of Public Service.* Schultz was an outstanding Jacksonville community activist, Florida legislator, and philanthropist. The book received a City of Jacksonville award. This decade of activities completed my ministerial career.

Kathleen and I have been retired since July 2009. We live in a small apartment in San Francisco, grandparent weekly with both families, and are active in the San Francisco UU Society. Kathleen has led their scholarship program for the last six years. I have led services, adult education series, ecumenical efforts, and the economic justice working group, and served as chair of their Social Justice Council. Kathleen and I hike, bike, travel, attend concerts, and savor one another's and our families' and friends' company.

As an undergraduate political science major, I took a World Religions class. Since I was already a civil rights and disarmament activist, I did my term paper on religious attitudes toward peace; I interviewed the Roman Catholic bishop, a rabbi, two ministers, and Chinese Buddhists and Confucians in San Francisco. During my doctoral studies at Washington University in St. Louis, I became good friends with Jews, Asians, and a rainbow of ethnicities, not only as a student but as an activist and in my social life. I attended my first Seder with a Jewish girlfriend, had my first serious Buddhism discussions with a Japanese American classmate, and experienced both my own and her racism differently with an African American girlfriend.

I began seminary as a '60s activist and completed it as a global citizen committed to embracing the best of the world's wisdom and to helping others integrate contemporary knowledge with ancient wisdom. I was predominantly a secular person when I began seminary, and left it as a spiritual mystic, a Jesusian, as much a Buddhist as a westerner in my spiritual practices, fascinated by Hindu and Oriental insights, inspired by Buber's humanistic Judaism, and tempered by Reinhold Niebuhr's and Martin Luther King's faithful Christian activism.

Chapter 3
Useful Conceptual Systems

People have experiences. We think about and organize them logically-analytically through education and training, which provide us practical skills and rational knowledge. We also experience them intuitively as we live in our cultures, articulate our ideologies and faiths, and do our social and spiritual practices. Through stories, myths, ceremonies, and celebrations, intuitive thinking helps us integrate our collective consciousness with our individual experiences and learning, which provides us experiential wisdom. Throughout our lives, we discover conceptual systems, ways of thinking that we find particularly useful and insightful and adopt and use them as we continue to develop. Chapter 1 addressed patterns of thought presently shared by a growing majority of the world's people. Now, I introduce a few conceptual systems that have been particularly important in my social life of ministering, teaching, and activism and in my own evolving spiritual beliefs and practices.

As earlier scientists had revealed that our Earth was a single planet in a gigantic, evolving universe, so Charles Darwin's *Origin of Species* revealed that humanity has evolved from our continually evolving Earth through the process of natural selection. People are a small and recent twig on an enormous and luxuriantly growing tree of life. Darwin's subsequent *Descent of Man* argued that prosperity of our social groups depends upon their altruistic cooperation. As Darwin complemented his scientific revolution with spiritual and ethical insights, so Einstein relativized the universe without abandoning the sacred. The world made sense and ultimately was an evolving harmony. Science cannot teach us to be moral; any attempt to reduce ethics to a scientific formula fails. In his *Credo,* Einstein said that as we comprehend portions of this beautiful and mysterious world, we realize that we are each an element of a complicated web of interrelations within a single whole, both spectators and actors in the great drama of existence, as Lao-Tse and Buddha had also taught.

Informed by science, 21st-century truth is contextual and situational; it looks hard at the data, but recognizes that it is always human beings looking at those data, and that data is inevitably affected by who and why, when, and for how long it has been studied. We know more, but there is immeasurably more to know. Among some of the most knowledgeable scientists and the deepest spiritual and secular thinkers/seekers, there is camaraderie, for they share intents to know as much as they can about life and the world's great mysteries while they continue to be awed by the mysteries remaining. Their enlightened realism and sense of mystery, awe, wonder, and reverence have grown, rather than diminished. They realize that the scientific method comes at a price: it can only validate itself by an unconscious process of exclusion. Science, like all human enterprises, remains a mixture of fact and value, truth and falsity, knowledge and power.

My philosophical perspective is a combination of pragmatism, existentialism, and the realistic rationalism of UC Berkeley philosopher John Rogers Searle. My pragmatism is the hopeful practicality of John Dewey, which embraces meaning and value, freewill, consciousness, and purpose. My existentialism is closest to Martin Buber's, embracing a humane and cooperative future, discovering the divine in "the between," nurtured by intimate interactions between individuals and within societies. My realism, like Searle's, holds that reality does exist independently of human representation; statements are true or false depending upon the extent to which they correspond to what they refer to, and both global objective and intersubjective criteria need to be used to appropriately judge any understanding.

Psychology studies how people develop behaviors. I agree with Carl Jung that adult development is a process of *individuation* by coming to grips with the shadow side of one's personality and learning effective methods to cope with our and others' crises and transformations. A significantly individuated person eventually embodies humane values and develops a practical understanding of human nature and the world, practices freedom and justice, and sees each person as a splinter of deity with psychic processes that we can only partly direct. We depend on our collective identities and organizational memberships, but also need to learn how to differentiate ourselves from others, take responsibility, and realize the good and evil we're capable of. I also agree with Marie-Louise von Franz who, in *Man and His Symbols*, said that individuation has four stages: physical; romantic; keeper of a tradition; and wise guide to spiritual truths. Whenever we think we've solved cosmic riddles, we are likely to lose control.

My psychological stance is healthy human functioning to encourage practical education, which embraces conscience, social influences, and religion. My humanistic psychology believes that people cannot be reduced to components—the whole is greater than its parts, and exists within a cosmic ecology and a human context; that we are aware of ourselves and others, have choice and responsibility, and are intentional with goals that affect future events. Because people vary significantly in their personalities, behavioral scholars have developed categorical systems explaining these globally shared variations. Many individuals may appear to largely fit into one type or at one end of a spectrum, but most are a mix of characteristics.

The most prevalent of these analytical psychological systems is the Myers-Briggs Personality Indicator (MBTI) created by the mother-daughter team of Katherine Cook Briggs and her daughter Isabel Briggs Myers. The MBTI grew out of Jungian ideas that were based upon Hindu concepts. Myers-Briggs places people in four categories: extrovert-introvert; sensing-intuitive; thinking-feeling; and judging-perceptual. Extroverts interact easily with other people, while introverts are more self-oriented. Those on the sensing end are practical and base decisions on sense experiences, while intuitive people tend to be more imaginative and make decisions based more upon their intuition. Thinkers focus on logic and analysis, while those at the feeling end of the spectrum are more swayed by their own and others' feelings. Those on the judging end like to come to clear decisions, while those on the perceptual end prefer to keep their options open.

Other spiritual-path organizing systems that, like MBTI, I've used in congregational adult education courses, separate and connect people by their personality types in other ways. Some favor directions—hand (vision, principled actions), head (understanding, structure-doctrine), heart (personal relationships, practical service), and mystic (awe, intuitive, meditative), whereas UU minister Rev. Fred Campbell's four liberal spiritual divisions are: humanists (societal, ethics); naturalists (scientific, stewardship of nature); theists (creative energy, faith-belief, divine purpose); and mystics (mystery, intuitive, spiritual experiences).

Spiritual Experiences: More Intuitive than Empirical

Both empirical and intuitive understanding use both empirical and intuitive reasoning and consciousness. The tools of reason—firsthand observation, logical analysis, and scientific experiments—tend to pick things apart, hold one variable constant, and manipulate life, while the tools of consciousness or intuition strive to put things together, seek cooperation, and favor unity and equanimity. Throughout our lives, many of our ethical choices and most of our faith decisions depend more upon intuition than empiricism. Empirical tools are often excellent aids to testing our intuitions, faith choices, and ethical decisions, but spirituality and daily life mostly entail using consciousness and the tools of intuition rather than resting only on scientific experiments or confirmed empirical data.

Everyone uses the way of knowing called intuition, but it's sometimes repressed or underdeveloped. Portions of the brain, especially the left hemisphere, are predominantly rational, linear, and verbal; other parts, especially the right hemisphere, are largely intuitive, holistic, and oriented toward imagery and story. Intuition gives us access to both our conscious and unconscious knowledge, so we can use our analytic logic but also portions of the collective unconscious or world's intuitive wisdom we've digested. Meditation, receptivity, and reverie can improve intuition. Those who deepen their intuition are able to accept the serendipitous and paradoxical, and continue to consider options without becoming stuck in or possessed by them. They use more of themselves, have greater access to life, and are less likely to become imprisoned in a single way of understanding their experiences.

Mysticism

Mystics are focused on having their own direct spiritual experiences, discovering, and then practicing, the art of direct union with the most sacred aspects of reality. Mysticism is found in all the historic religions. While some mystics certainly hold conservative religious views, mystics tend to challenge aspects of their traditions and oppose some tenets of religious orthodoxy. Some non-mystical religious practitioners and leaders feel challenged by mystics within their religions and even by their own mystical tendencies, as do some secular individuals. While most traditional believers tend to remain focused on theologies, scriptures, dogmas, rituals, and rules—upon being religious through intermediaries, many others by adding mystical experiences are granted fresh spiritual vitality. Since I'm urging people to open themselves to global religious and spiritual traditions and systematically develop their own spiritual practices as a central aspect of their lives, I'm enthusiastic about people owning their mystical experiences and empowering their mystical practices.

Mystics seek to experience an ultimate beyond a solely sensual reality, via direct experiences of deity or sacredness and through contacts between the individual self and larger-than-self realities. They intuit dimensions of reality not ordinarily perceived and seek cognitive awareness of life-changing profundities. They have traditionally named the stages of their mystical experiences *awakening, purgation, surrender, illumination,* and *union,* or, as stages of initiation, *preparation, testing, illumination,* and *return.* Some mystical traditions have become institutionalized, including Hindu bhakti sects, yogic schools, Sufi orders, Buddhist and Christian orders, and Jewish mystical traditions, but most mystics have long pursued, and eagerly continue to pursue, their individual, sometimes isolated and lonely, mystical experiences.

In *Mysticism East and West* Rudolph Otto, a German Protestant, perceived two main approaches to mysticism: an introvert path that retreated into one's own soul, researching consciousness, clearing away the ego self to fulfill the *atman,* or deeper self; and an extrovert path that embraces all, perceiving the entire universe and/or humanity as one with our essential self. Otto emphasized the *numinous* as that which persists beyond the transitory. He argued that we need to move toward the identification of the perceiver and the perceived.

In *The Perennial Philosophy,* Aldous Huxley says mysticism recognizes a divine reality substantial to the world and our lives, a psychology that finds in the soul something similar to divine reality, and an ethic that places our final goal in the knowledge of the immanent and the transcendence of all being. Mystics learn to detach themselves from emotions and egotism to discover that they are both creator and created and surpass their egos to become fulfilled. They work to transform temptations and distractions into opportunities for spiritual advance, convert challenges into discriminative taste and sacramental awareness, and transform each act into service. Poets, nature lovers, and aesthetes are granted mystic glimpses, but unless they grow beyond egotism, they remain incapable of knowing the divine in its fullness. A principal cause of suffering and wrongdoing is the intensity of craving. For example, Rumi suggested that charity casts out fear, vision replaces hope, and selflessness ends both complacent reminiscence and remorse. Societies are held together not primarily by fear but by faith in others' decency and the world's reasonableness and trustworthiness. Do not become idolaters of feelings. Test habits, ceremonies, and beliefs by the extent to which they remind us of the true nature of things and fit our most harmonious relationships within the sacred aspects of life and the world. Hindus say: as a bee gathers honey from many flowers, so a wise person accepts different scriptures' essence and the good in all religions.

D.T. Suzuki, a Japanese American Zen Buddhist, wrote in his book *Mysticism: Christian and Buddhist* that a world consciousness is unfolding that restores the individual's humanity while empowering our communion with the universe. Suzuki believed that God's Old Testament self-identifier, "I am that I am," is the most profound utterance of any religious experience. Religious consciousness is confronted by a network of contradictions running through our lives, demanding practical experiences that enable contentment and relate to the infinite while serving the finite with grateful acceptance.

Myths

Myths are not falsehoods. They are the tested cultural metaphors of our societies, the truths that our experiences have confirmed for us.

Mircea Eliade, a professor at the University of Chicago with whom I studied, set the agenda for religious scholarship during the second half of the 20th century in his *History of Religious Ideas*. He saw religious behavior as actual participation in and with the sacred, systematically tracing parallels and unities globally from the earliest human history to now. People often recount their sacred experiences as distinct from normal existence or linear history.

Eliade was concerned that secular people cocooned themselves in anxiety by attempting to do without the sacred. He searched for the myths that had become models for understanding the archetypes of human imagination. By revealing how people dealt mythically with the paradoxes of their experiences, he sought to show how myths help us reconcile the creative and destructive, actual and potential, benevolent and terrible aspects of existence and ourselves. In spirituality and religion, we simultaneously bare our most intimate selves, celebrate our peak experiences, and articulate our worldviews. Myths are episodes from our experiences that become transparent indicators of the truths we have discovered to have integrity and provide fulfillment. We build myths out of familiar stories, but also continue to discover additional myths that resonate with our experiences. Myths become both bridges to the evolution of civilization and enhance our own peak experiences.

For Carl Jung, psyche and soul became synonymous. We need religion and myth to realize our whole self. Myths can nurture psyches resistant to unhealthy and destructive impulses within and outside of ourselves and help us continue to evolve and to maintain abundant energy while we grow more definite and mature. Dreams are natural responses to our self-regulating psychic systems. Our unconscious is an essential helpmate to our rational selves. The unconscious has both individual and collective components that carry the memories of what humanity has learned throughout its shared existence. Together, individual and collective unconscious can become agents of intuitive receptivity far exceeding our analytic mind.

Jung defined myth as what is generally believed throughout history. People need to understand the myths they are living. Myths are the public version of our collective unconscious, and provide an existing and available second psychic system for everyone that complements our rational, analytical mind. Archetypes are the norms of myth that inherently express our shared needs, instincts, and potentials. The unconscious is compensatory to consciousness; its products are not only corrective but also prospective. Through analyzing the unconscious, we can come to know our shadow sides, the less-accepted aspects of ourselves—for many men their feminine side, for many women their masculine side. Myths and the collective unconscious give form to our psyches, providing the archetypes behind our behaviors.

23

American Joseph Campbell became a household name in the late 1980s when Bill Moyers interviewed him for a TV series, *The Power of Myth*. A rather secular and skeptical person, Campbell thought every human being could and should become a potential heroine/hero of her own mythic dramas. Don't take myths literally; that would be like seeing roast beef on a menu and eating the menu, because myths are not literally true, yet they are sometimes more important than facts because they contain truths inadequately conveyed by statistics or formulas alone. Each of us should discover, follow, exuberantly live our bliss (the endeavors that make us fulfilled), and remain involved in a determined mythic quest.

For Campbell, myths serve four functions: Individual centering; harmonization of the individual with the community; cosmological ordering of humanity's place in the universe; and relating individuals to the mysteries in ourselves and in all things. In our era, the individual has become the center of his/her own mythology, so we must learn to have the courage to credit our senses, honor our decisions, name our virtues, and claim our visions of truth. Today's religion cannot be focused on a single denomination or any one traditional faith. Today's world culture needs to remain open to our broad experiences of reality, finding myths new to us and shaping myths together within our increasingly global world.

Lifelong Development

Until recently, people tended to believe that our personalities developed in childhood, and once we became adults we were fully developed and didn't change much. This was no doubt true through much of history, when the vast majority of lives were short, illiteracy was common, and people lived at a subsistence level; but since more people lived longer, learned to read, and began to develop means that enabled them to live above a subsistence level, humanity has increasingly been able to more fully explore the world around and inside themselves.

I approach scriptures as vital, but as mythic and mystical, and access individuals' spiritual practices within the context of enlightened intuitive consciousness and adult psychological development. With my seminary's counseling professor, Peter Baldwin, I studied adult development psychologists like Abraham Maslow and Erik Erikson, which provided me a framework for understanding how we continue to change as adults.

Jean Piaget, a Swiss psychologist of thought development in childhood and youth, and five American theorists of adult development—Maslow, Erikson, Kohlberg, Gilligan, and Fowler—identified sequential stages of adult development. Piaget concentrated on stages of children's thought development: from infants' growing sensory capacities to the development of intuition and the practice of concrete skills; then on to youthful stages of thinking abstractly and logical reasoning; and while finishing secondary school or beginning adult life, cooperating within formal institutions.

Abraham Maslow began with an early childhood foundation of health and safety. As children grew through parenting and school, they developed into acceptance through love and belonging. In youth, they developed goals, skills, and eventually some disciplined masteries. As adults matured, Maslow believed they could *self-actualize* through increasingly complex searches for truth. The most mature individuals sought to have their quests for truth affirmed by peers, approximating society's moral ideals, and creating aesthetic expressions that harmonized with nature and society. Events and circumstances might force any individual back into focusing on health, security, or adequate mastery, but with good fortune, mature people can increasingly concentrate upon more socially constructive goals.

Erik Erikson, in *Childhood and Society,* expanded human psychological development into eight stages from infancy to old age, and perceived each stage as an inevitable struggle between positive and negative faith elements: trust vs. distrust, autonomy vs. shame, initiative vs. guilt, industry vs. inferiority, identity vs. role confusion, intimacy vs. isolation, generativity vs. stagnation, and finally, integrity vs. despair. People evolve and mature through these inevitable struggles. Infants need a dependable, trustworthy world. Without it, they are likely to become distrustful. A growing child needs increasing autonomy; without growing independence, a child tends to act shamefully. As children grow up, they take initiative. Failing to do so, they develop guilt. Preadolescents need to become skillful and industrious; failing to do so they feel inferior. Adolescents need to form separate identities; otherwise they remain confused. Young adults need to develop intimacies with others, or they become isolated. Middle-aged people want to make a difference in others' lives, as spouse, parent, teacher, worker, or artist; failing to do so, they feel stagnant. In the face of diminishing flexibility, health, and inevitable death, we elderly put our lives into perspective and either find integrity or give in to despair.

Lawrence Kohlberg, in *The Psychology of Moral Development,* outlined seven stages of moral-ethical development, and Carol Gilligan added a necessary critique from a feminist perspective. For infants, the good is what I want and like. Childish materialism is full of punishment or obedience. The third is an ethic of hedonism and reciprocity—"I'll scratch your back, if you'll scratch mine." The fourth develops interpersonal mutuality: friendships and in-groups. The fifth maintains social orders with fixed rules and set authorities. The sixth develops social contracts, utilitarian lawmaking, and higher social consciousness. At Kohlberg's most elevated level of ethical maturity, he found individuals who practiced forms of universal justice and were sensitive to integrity for self, friends, and strangers. Carol Gilligan pointed out in her *In a Different Voice* that from an early age girls become oriented more toward an ethic of care than an ethic of achievement; they are directed more toward nurturing relationships and communities than to individual power and accomplishment.

In *Stages of Faith,* theologian James Fowler explicitly turned humans' maturation into stages of spiritual development. The first stage is that of infantile mutuality, based upon trust of the caregiver parental figures, with anxiety about separation. Early childhood is a faith of intuition and projection. Using stories, gestures, and symbols, children develop their imagination, creating enduring powerful images. A third stage may remain a primary faith in which their emerging logical thinking allows them to develop a sense of cause and effect and to accept a mythical-literal faith. Fowler called adults caught at this stage mythical-literalists. The adolescent stage remains many adults' primary faith, a synthetic-conventional one that shapes diverse self-images into an emotional group identity and a solidarity that sometimes remains unquestioned. The fifth stage is an individualistic-reflective faith in which individuals reflect upon their values and come to understand themselves as responsible parts of social systems, with commitments in relationships and vocations. A sixth stage that may develop in middle-age embraces life's contradictions, is alert to paradox, and realizes that ideas and symbols are metaphors. Fowler's last stage develops for some in midlife or old age; it's a universalizing faith connected with the powers of being. Their commitments free them for a passionate yet detached spending of self in love, dedicated to overcoming division, oppression, and brutality.

Lifelong Stages of Development

Piaget	Maslow	Erikson	Kohlberg	Fowler
Sensory	Health & Safety	Trust or Distrust	Want and Like	Infantile Trust
Intuition	Love & Belonging	Autonomy or Shame	Obey or Punish	Imaginary Powers
Competence	Goals, Skills & Achievements	Initiative or Guilt	Selfish Reciprocators	Mythical-Literal Faith
Reason	Disciplined Mastery	Industry vs. Inferiority	Mutuality of Groups	Synthetic-Conventional Faith
Cooperation	Complex Searches for Truth	Identity or Confusion	Social Order	Individual-Reflective Faith
Responsible	Quest to actualize moral ideals and/or creations of beauty in harmony with nature and society	Intimacy or Isolation	Contracts & Higher Law	Paradoxical-Metaphoric Faith
		Generativity or Stagnation	Integrity & Universal Justice	Passionate, Detached Service
		Integrity or Despair	Gilligan combined an ethics of care with an ethics of achievement	

As you proceed through the following chapters on the world's historic religions, use these conceptual systems to consider both how to better understand the various religions' evolutions and to discover how you might usefully apply their teachings and practices in your own life and spiritual development.

Each historical religion has practitioners who reflect the full spectrum of personality types and emphases; each involves intuition and mysticism; uses myths; and represents the entire spectrum of psychological, ethical, and spiritual adult development. As you come to understand these religious traditions, I believe you'll realize, as I have, that you have soulmates in each of them, both historically and today, and that you'll see how certain beliefs, practices, and traditions may impose unnecessary hardships on individuals who do not reflect the currently dominant personalities, beliefs, and practices of their tradition's or group's rules. Individuals may find themselves fully embraced within some religious communities, and practically outlawed, or at least deprecated or marginalized, in others.

After a brief chapter on pre-historic religions, each of the historic world religions' chapters proceeds in the following manner: 1. Major suppositions, tenets, and practices; 2. Its historic evolution including major leaders, scriptures, and sects; 3. Elements that I find troubling; and 4. What I've found inspiring or particularly interesting and relevant that I believe could benefit readers in developing their global spiritualties.

Notre Dame Cathedral, Paris, France.

Srivangan Hindu Temple, Tamil Nadu State, India.

Standing Buddha, Bangkok, Thailand.

Section II

Chapter 4
Prehistoric Religiosity

Millions of years ago, humanoid species most likely appeared first in Africa and eventually spread across the globe as hunter-gatherers. By 30,000 years ago, diverse agricultural communities had evolved almost worldwide. They lived in settled groups that practiced artistic endeavors and shared rituals of hope, grief, remembrance, and celebration. In these geographically isolated communities, women and men were sometimes relatively equal; old people were usually respected and honored. These groups rarely built impressive monuments to hierarchical or military leaders; instead, they often practiced a more "live-and-let-live" attitude toward strangers as long as they did not invade others' settlements, and appeared to be more oriented toward peace and cooperation than war or power.

This early evidence of the human race reveals that they wrestled with some of the same not fully answerable questions that we still ask today, and developed religious practices that helped them cope with the multitude of unknowns in their lives. Among the best known were the people of ancient Crete; they, and other pre-historic Eurasian agricultural peoples were popularized in Riane Eisler's *The Chalice and the Blade,* in which she argued that, at their best, these pastoral societies presented less militant or hierarchical and therefore "more civilized" cultures than many of the warrior cultures that later conquered and replaced them.

Until the twentieth century, however, most Western intellectuals claimed that *civilization* arose first in Mesopotamia and Egypt, and only later spread slowly out to the rest of the world. Churchill popularized Orwell's aphorism that "the victors write the histories." It seems this aphorism was generalized to "civilization." As scholarship, however, revealed that other early cultures had arisen not only in Mesopotamia (Iraq-Syria) and Egypt but also in the

Indus Valley (India-Pakistan), the Yellow River (China), and somewhat later in Iran, the Asian steppes, North and South America, and Ethiopia. "Earliest civilizations" were only credited to have become civilized when they were controlled by male-dominated warrior cultures with hierarchical class systems empowered by an elite, literate priestly class who had evolved written languages.

Scottish anthropologist James G. Frazer wrote rather differently about the development of preliterate spirituality in *The Golden Bough,* connecting the relationships among their myths, rituals and cults, and drawing parallels with historic religions and modern ideologies. He divided ancient religiosity into preliterate and classical pagan forms and argued that preliterate religiosity dominated human existence for countless ages. These religions varied but had several shared elements, including ancestor worship, rites of purification, sacrifice, and death memorials, animism, magic, and divination. Most were polytheistic, with a pantheon of goddesses and gods connected with the forces of nature dominating aspects of human life. A great goddess was often central, representing the Earth and the powers of fecundity in nature as well as women's ability to bear and nurture progeny. Holidays and rituals focused on seasons, the stages of the agricultural cycle, and of life—birth, childhood, youthful responsibilities, physical maturity, sexuality, family life, the wisdom and frailty of aging, and death. Most archaic religions were also animistic, endowing all living things and even inanimate objects with spirits and power that humans might, through proper connections, knowledge, sacrifices, or rituals, access and use for good or evil purposes. Some objects, places, situations, and people evolved into being considered either taboo, forbidden, or instead became sacred.

Spiritual specialists developed within these cultures. Many were believed to have magic powers that connected them with divine forces, and were given positions of leadership, though they rarely became either military or political leaders. Instead, they were usually credited with being capable of healing or threatening others, divining the future, or manipulating natural forces. As Frazer enumerated, the prevalent forms of magic included fetishism, which used the powers of inanimate things; shamanism—spirits conjured into or out of a person through bewitching or exorcism; and magic, either aversive, which transferred guilt to a scapegoat, or productive magic, such as rain dances and sacrifices. Divination was practiced, in which these specialists gained rapport with spirits to reveal secrets about life's mysteries or predict the future.

Until recently, classical pagan religious scholarship focused on the ancient Middle East and Europe before the advent of Zoroastrianism, Judaism, Christianity, and Islam. Egypt developed an elaborate cult of the dead, life after death, an emerging national ethic, and, briefly, monotheistic sun worship with the Pharaoh Ikhnaton as its human representative. Babylonia had a great mother goddess, Ishtar, and under Hammurabi developed a patriarchal code of law, including the tendency to blame evil on women. They perceived the world to be a continual battle between the powers of darkness and of light under the god Marduk.

Early Greek religion rested upon Hera, a great earth goddess. By the 12th century BC, Greeks also worshipped Zeus, the great sky god who ruled a pantheon of goddesses and gods on Mount Olympus and made Hera his wife. The Romans adopted much of the Greeks' belief system, added Roman names, and created more organized, military elements. Both Greek and Roman traditions were influenced by mystery cults introduced from Asia.

Western Europe's Celts were expansive nature worshippers who practiced some human sacrifice. The Druids' maypole dances continue to this day in Britain. The Teutonic traditions centered upon a world tree and hopes for a better world. Their queen mother goddess, Frigg, and Balder, the kindest, gentlest of the gods, emphasized an annual cycle of birth and extinction. Odin and the Valkyries added battle dimensions. The Slavs worshipped a sun god and had both a giver of life and wealth and a devil figure.

Chapter 5
Hinduism

Hinduism's Central Beliefs and Practices

Hinduism is the world's oldest continually practiced major religion. Hindus believe that each individual soul relates to the universal Creator in a single transcendental reality named *Brahman,* or Creation. Within each of us there is also an ultimate personal reality, an immanent reflection or microcosm of Creation itself, called *atman,* the God within, the invincible soul. Their chanted expression for the *Brahman-atman* is the mystical sound AUM, or OM, which implies the liberation of knowing that we can be one with the infinite spirit. Hindus believe that when we spend our lives celebrating the miracles of our existence and of the universe, do our best with what we've been given, and practice disciplined joy and empathetic love, then we and Creation are one.

Hindus ascribe reality to many aspects of life. Life produces innumerable twists and turns, and people exhibit many differences, so they embrace innumerable goddesses and gods as manifestations of their divine unity, the Brahman-atman, often represented as a three-faced deity including images of Brahma (the creator), Vishnu (the evolving preserver), and Shiva (the source of fertility, doer of justice, and divine symbol of yogic spiritual seekers). Hindus often identify themselves as primarily followers of either Shiva or Vishnu, since Brahma is perceived as less approachable, yet they also believe in a united divine force behind these images, understanding that this spiritual unity continues evolving within each person and within the entirety of Creation. Most individuals, families, and groups have their favorites, and though male gods often appear as dominant, Hindus share the belief that behind every god, an accompanying goddess possesses his *Shakti,* the foundational cosmic energy.

Life is the sport or play (*lila*) of the deities, as our human grasp of Creation is necessarily partial and imperfect. Their word *maya* reflects our illusive understanding of and control over Creation's powers. Time remains cyclical; Hindus generally expect to be reincarnated after death, acknowledging a failure to spiritually progress enough to gain freedom from *karma,* which makes clear that our actions have enduring consequences, as people often impede their own quest toward *moksha* (enlightenment). Hinduism concentrates upon individual spiritual development, influenced by their circumstances, personality, and stages of life. Their vocations, roles, and duties—their *dharmas*—change according to these myriad influences and are guided by each person's spiritual choices. An individual's evolving dharma is her practiced spiritual choices, actualizing the atman within her chosen disciplines, or *yogas.*

Hindus developed four primary spiritual yogas, each expressing a human personality type: reflective, emotional, active, or experimental. The reflective path, *jnana yoga,* is for people who live primarily in their heads, like Socrates. *Bhakti yoga,* the love path, is for those usually in their emotions, like Jesus. *Karma yoga* is the path for activists focused primarily upon their work, like Gandhi. *Raja yoga* is the path of psychophysical experimenters in search of life's infinite Creative powers, people like Carl Jung. No one is only one of these, but most lean more toward one than the others. Jung based his personality types upon this Hindu typology, and the Meyers-Briggs personality tests were based upon Jung's work, so Westerners are indebted to this ancient Hindu wisdom. It has special relevance for religious pluralists, who believe there are many integrative paths to human understanding and reliable faiths, and who believe individuals choose their paths because of their different personalities and experiences.

Hindus also divide human lives into four sequential stages: a student stage, when one is dependent and primarily learning; the householder stage, when one takes charge and practices sexuality, ambition, and acquisitiveness; a retirement stage (usually after the first grandchild is born), when people change their life's primary emphasis from experiencing to reflecting; and the fourth stage, during which people hopefully learn to let go of their former obsessions.

India is filled with Hindu temples, from immense complexes visited by millions to roadside shrines seen by a few locals. The sacred center of Hindus' spiritual lives is, however, neither a community nor a temple but their home shrine. This place of worship might be a shelf in a slum hut, a corner in an apartment, or a prayer room in a larger home. They usually include several divine images, photos of chosen gurus/spiritual teachers and deceased relatives, and devotional tools such as prayer beads, bells, incense, and an oil lamp. Most Hindus perform daily devotions there. Since a majority still live in multigenerational settings, Hinduism continues to be practiced largely within a family context. The most devout may also go to a temple regularly, but only when they choose. Priests go about their own routines, apparently oblivious to the comings and goings of visiting laity. Religious festivals do attract huge crowds, but even in these mass gatherings, Hindus essentially perceive themselves as personally striving to connect their particular atman with the cosmic Divine.

Hinduism has always had a safety valve for individuals who could not cope with their ordinary lives: they could renounce life to become *sadhus* and seek spiritual liberation. Hindu society has generally made room for them. Most fail to become socially prominent, and many might not find spiritual fulfillment, but there has always been an acceptable alternative to normal life within Hinduism. A few of these spiritual seekers do become the gurus and god-folk of legend. During my visits to India in the 1980s, I met several, including the then most prominent male and female Hindu holy people, Sai Baba and Anandamayee. Probably the most famous god person today is Amma, the hugging woman saint, whose organization, MAM, in Kerala attracts millions of visitors and has substantial financial assets.

With a thousand others, I went to an audience at Sai Baba's ashram near Bangalore, and sat with a group of villagers who had walked several hundred miles over two weeks to perform *darshan,* the Hindu devotional practice through which a person achieves significant karmic merit simply by being in the presence of a great soul. With hundreds of others I received some ash that appeared magically from his hands. I have no explanation for how he managed to distribute literally bushels of ash on that occasion. While I felt his magnetism, it seemed packaged, even a bit predatory; however, he told a wonderful story about being caught by our desires. Monkeys are often caught when they see something desirable in a big pot with a small mouth. They reach into the pot but are then unable to take their hand out without letting go of the desired object, which they are often unwilling to do. Sai Baba said that in this big pot of the world, with its sometimes seemingly narrow mouth, people are tempted by its pleasures, get lost in their involvements, and believe that someone or something else is enslaving them. In fact, only we are responsible for being caught by our desires. When we can let go of our cravings and detach ourselves, we gain more freedom.

When I met Anandamayee, who had given *guru dakshina* (a sort of instant spiritual connection) to Indira Gandhi and other prominent Indians, this humble woman saint said nothing of consequence, and we did not physically touch. She performed no miracles; she simply embodied a quiet and peaceful soul, but I felt an overpowering feeling of emanating love and goodness. I gather "hugging Amma" conveys similar feelings to her devotees. Hinduism's holy people do run the gamut from con artists and power freaks to people of startling power and transparent goodness, and each personality and practice is attractive to certain people.

Weddings are often held in a secular setting, but usually officiated by a priest. Hindu dead are ordinarily cremated on a wood pyre, traditionally at a *ghat* by a local river, performed by the deceased's male relatives, but now also at modern crematoria.

Hindu holidays fill the year. I celebrated many with my Indian family and friends. These holidays are usually jubilant, sometimes ecstatic, almost always multifaceted, and generally family affairs; but the "families" may include teachers, friends, colleagues, neighbors, and gurus. Here are aspects of three important holidays: *Dussehra, Diwali,* and *Holi,* which are celebrated nationally in India, and about which I led celebrations for the UU congregations I served.

Dussehra explicitly recognizes the righteous strength needed to overcome evil power. Goddesses are the central divine images celebrated, including Creation's terrifying powers. People's tools are honored: trades and professions, vehicles, weapons, and tools of learning. Young people are taught the alphabet as a necessary tool to access the power of knowledge. The powers of security and government are acknowledged as legitimate and necessary.

Diwali is a celebration of constructive energies. Lamps and fires are lit; light and fire are recognized as central to human progress, but it is also recognized that fire can destroy cities, and that light can blind rather than enlighten humanity when too narrowly focused. People pay respects to their bosses or professional seniors by visiting them at their homes. In my American congregations, Diwali became an opportunity to talk about light and the power it brings to enlighten and draw people closer, and how we find ways to work together to use power wisely. Brothers and sisters, genetic and chosen, tie string bracelets onto one another.

Holi is a jubilant spring festival, best known for its celebrants' throwing colored powders on one another to breach status barriers—tenants dusting their landlords, students their teachers—and for dancing and partying across social divisions. Lord Krishna is honored as a lusty, flute-playing youth who consorts with the local milkmaids. Holi is an unbridled celebration of love. My congregational Holi celebrations gave us opportunities to consider love's many forms: erotic, romantic, friendship, and love for the greater good and longer future than our own.

The Emergence and Historic Evolution of Hinduism

There have been human settlements in the Indian subcontinent for at least 100,000 years. By 2300 BC, there were two large cities, Harappa and Mohenjo-Daro, thirty miles apart along the Indus River (now in Pakistan), where residents tended fowl, water buffalos, and cows, irrigated crops, produced cotton textiles, and likely had built dams. Hinduism's roots were practiced there, including a Shiva-like yogic seated figure along with evidence that yogic meditation was their most revered spiritual practice. Fertility symbols (lingam and yoni) were also worshipped, and females were already the cosmic powers' guardians.

About 1500 BC, Aryan warriors (from near the Black and Caspian Seas) conquered this Indus River civilization, probably after their dams had been destroyed by floods and their populations decimated by famine. The Aryans brought their language, Sanskrit, a patriarchal and patrilineal family system, and a four-caste hierarchical social structure based upon skin color, with a priestly caste on top ("white" mouths), a warrior caste next ("red" arms), a caste of landed farmers ("brown" thighs), and finally a peasant caste ("black" feet) at its base. At first, Aryans ruled only in the northwest, but gradually conquered to the southeast.

As they integrated with the indigenous peoples, Aryans developed the Vedic scriptures, the oldest scriptures still in use by millions, far older than any Hebrew scripture. The oldest of the four Vedas, the *Rig Veda*, contains 1,017 poems, hymns, incantations, and commentaries. They are still usually spoken in Sanskrit, a language now rarely understood except by priests at ceremonies. The Rig Veda provides visions of divine light often associated with Surya, the sun god, but also including Vishnu, who periodically redeems the world from chaos. Unfortunately, the Vedas also reinforced the four-color caste system.

Beginning with the Aryans, the Indian subcontinent has been invaded repeatedly, usually by culturally inferior peoples with superior armies. These sequential invaders gradually integrated with the more numerous resident Indian peoples and built an evolving civilization based largely upon the indigenous culture but adding some of the invader's unique cultural elements. Each conquering wave was then replaced by an imperialistic Hindu ruler who increased Hindu unity to the south and east. By the 6th century BC, there were sixteen major kingdoms in North India, along with countless smaller ones dividing the subcontinent, characterized by a steadily growing reaction to priestly domination and caste divisions.

Two of the small kingdoms in the Himalayan foothills spawned major Hindu reforms that eventually became separate religions, Jainism and Buddhism. The reforms were led by former princes who abandoned their political positions to pursue lives of yogic retreat and meditation, and challenged caste division, with its emphases on priestly rites and warrior power. They advocated instead on behalf of lives of personal purity, peace, and compassionate service. Hinduism continued to become more diverse, with paths that emphasized social action, personal devotion, or philosophic dialogue.

The Primary Hindu Epics: the Mahabharata and the Ramayana

Heroic stories are at the heart of religions. The ancient Greeks had *The Iliad* and *The Odyssey,* the Jews Genesis and Exodus, and the Hindus have two primary spiritual epic poems, the Mahabharata and the Ramayana. The Mahabharata presents a picture of Hindu life in northern India in about 1000 BC. Its most famous portion, the Bhagavad Gita, was added about 100 BC. The Mahabharata's present form took shape by AD 200. The Ramayana was first standardized in the 5th century BC by the poet Valmiki. Its story takes place in southeastern India and Sri Lanka. These epics transmit Hindu ideals, articulating the best life paths (dharmas) which indicate appropriate life choices concerning vocation, family life, friendship, and conflicts. They spread Indian culture not only throughout India, but in later centuries to Indonesia and Southeast Asia. They remain universally beloved and revered by Hindus and are, like all successful myths, essentially unconstrained by time or place.

The *Mahabharata* tells of the rivalry between two different branches of the Kurukshetra family, the Pandavas and the Kaurvas. The Pandavas' mother had her children with gods, so while the Kaurvas, with their earthly father, are older and would thus have precedence, the epic depicts a mythic struggle between the Pandavas, representing dharma and good, and the Kaurvas, representing chaos and evil. Its 100,000 verses are often didactic. Its theological centerpiece, the Bhagavad Gita, is the story of the Pandava brother Arjun's dialogue with his charioteer, the God Krishna, a reincarnation of Vishnu. Although the Kaurvas win the kingdom at dice, they then try to also possess the Pandavas' shared bride, Draupadi, yet it is the Pandavas and Draupadi who are exiled. Having completed their exile, they return to claim their promised kingdom, but the Kaurvas refuse to keep their bargain, and a battle ensues. Is the Mahabharata simply a dualistic battle between good and evil, like the Iranian Zoroastrian myth, or rather an example of the periodic struggle that ensues when the world becomes too chaotic and needs to be brought back to dharma, or a just order, beginning a new cosmic cycle?

The Ramayana's 48,000 verses tell the story of King Dasaratha who had three wives and four sons, and his neighbor, King Janaka. Janaka had raised a girl he discovered in a furrow. He named her Sita, and she grew up to become a beautiful and talented woman. King Janaka possessed a bow from Shiva and vowed that he would only allow Sita to marry whoever could string Shiva's bow. It was King Dasaratha's son, Rama, who strung the bow and was made his father's heir; however, Dasaratha's youngest and favored wife, Kaikeyi, persuaded the king instead to make her son the heir and have Rama and Sita sent into exile, where Rama's half-brother, Laksman, joined them. Sita was then kidnapped by the demon Ravana, king of Sri Lanka. Aided by Hanuman, the monkey god, Rama and Laksman conquered Sri Lanka. They rescued Sita, and Rama was proclaimed king. Sita was, however, initially rejected as impure because she had lived in Ravana's home while married to Rama. Mother Earth intervenes to prove Sita's purity, and she and Rama ruled happily. In the Ramayana, the demon becomes a personification of unbridled ego, Sita a symbol of purity and intellect, brother Laksman a representation of filial devotion and focused attention, and Rama a personification of soul, or atman.

Persian and Greek Invasions

Cyrus the Great led a Persian army into northwest India by 518 BC. His armies brought Zoroastrian ideas about ongoing wars between good and evil, reinforced the holiness of fire in religious rituals, and presented a Hittite war god, Indra, whom the Hindus reshaped into a manifestation of Shiva. After the Persians returned home, the Hindu kingdom of Magadha seized power until Alexander the Great invaded in 326 BC and thrust far into the Indian subcontinent.

After the Greeks left, Chandragupta (324–301) became a great Indian emperor; he unified much of India, controlled a million government soldiers and bureaucrats, took 25 percent of all crops as taxes, and ruled 50 million Indians (about one sixth of that era's world population). He eventually resigned and became a Jain monk, and his son, Bindusara, ruled. Then, Bindusara's son, Ashoka (269–232 BC), became perhaps the greatest of Hindu monarchs. After winning a mammoth but horrific battle, Ashoka felt so heartbroken that he became Buddhism's most effective political advocate. He remained Hindu, but nurtured a kingdom based upon law, duty, and responsibility; he tolerated all religions, and urged lives of compassion and truthfulness. He also took great interest in Buddhism. He hosted a global Buddhist council, had 84,000 Buddhist stupas built, and constructed large pillars, engraved with Buddhist wisdom in the farthest boundaries of the subcontinent. This Mauryan dynasty ruled for 140 years and represented the first great unification of India.

During the next five centuries, India was fragmented into many Hindu and/or Buddhist kingdoms, but also had expansive international trade and cultural exploration. Its varied kingdoms developed different languages and cultures, and Hinduism emerged from concentrating upon Brahmin priests into a religion focused on individual devotion and continuing to grow in strength throughout India and beyond. Simultaneously, Buddhism evolved from remaining focused upon monks seeking enlightenment toward a people's religion urging laity to practice *bodhisattva* ideas of compassionate service. Christianity was also introduced into India, perhaps with the arrival of the Christian Apostle Thomas ("doubting Thomas") on the southwest Indian coast soon after Jesus' death. Several Jewish communities were founded in major ports. As we proceed through other religions, you'll see that global trade often spread new religions to other areas of the world, and that even small communities with "foreign" religions influenced their new cultural contexts. We can wonder how the Indian stories that Cyrus' and Alexander's soldiers brought back to Persia and Greece affected their cultures, as we can trace how each invasion and settlement brought new ideas to India.

The Upanishads

The 112 Upanishads are the most philosophic of Hindu scriptures. These mystical discussions were dialogues in which all the participants expected to learn from one another. They were written between 800–400 BC. The two longest are about one hundred pages each. The shortest, and one of the most important, the *Isa Upanishad,* has only eighteen verses. Altogether, the Upanishads are about the length of the New Testament. My favorite translation is by Juan Mascaro who compares the Upanishad's message with the Christian words "The kingdom of God is within you." God is not only universal and transcendent, but also immanent within every human being; perhaps, in Christian terms, closest to the Holy Spirit. Brahman is Creation itself in all its evolving complexity; atman is the holy within you, me, and everyone, the essential self that we spend our entire lives trying to actualize. Much of life inevitably remains illusion, but that doesn't suggest that life is not precious and genuine; instead, it emphasizes that we humans are easily fooled, seduced, or mistaken.

Life is a process of unique and individual duties, callings, and opportunities. We may live up to these challenges and opportunities poorly and/or splendidly. People build their own destinies, and the results are not limited to one life. From good, joy arises, and from evil, suffering happens; thus, cosmic evolution flows on toward fulfillment. Discovering life's miracles and the love expressed and received through our relationships gives each person their ultimate experiences of truth and fulfillment. Early in the Isa Upanishad, it says that those who see all beings in themselves and themselves in all beings lose all fear. Those who know both knowledge and action, with action overcome death, and with knowledge reach immortality. The *Katha Upanishad* proposes two attractive paths: joy and pleasure. The wise choose a path of joy; the foolish take a path of pleasure, for the childish, the careless, and the deluded go from death to death. To get through to the Atman, you must abandon evil ways, find rest among your senses, concentrate the mind, and find peace in your heart. Without these actions, the deepest knowledge is useless. As our desires, so are our faiths; as our faiths, so our works; and as our works, so we become. A person's persistent actions represent their life's conclusions.

The Bhagavad Gita

The sixth book of the Mahabarata is the Bhagavad Gita (Song of the Lord), written about 2,100 years ago. With 125 pages and eighteen teachings, it is considered the "sermon on the mount" among Hindu scriptures. My favorite translation was done by Barbara Miller. Arjuna is about to begin a great battle, a justified and necessary conflict, but he will be fighting his relatives and teachers. He fears battle and death, struggles with the ambiguities of politics and wars, and is horrified by the prospect of killing his own relatives and teachers, or being killed by them. He faces an existential crisis, perceiving himself a professional warrior, but conflicted by the complexities of reality.

Fate forces few of us to kill or be killed by our families, but everyone faces hard choices about how to live with integrity.

This primary principle of the Gita is found in the second teaching: "Be intent on action, not on the fruits of action," like the idea that virtue is its own reward. If you choose paths of virtue, good means, then those chosen means become your primary reward. Gandhi found the Gita persuasive because it took the most repellant human duty, i.e., civil, even familial war, and demonstrated that even that most problematic of life's possible tasks might conceivably be done with integrity. People do not always reach their life goals, but when they proceed toward those goals with virtuous methods, they can remain upon solid ethical and spiritual foundations.

The Gita says it is better to be yourself, even with your mistakes and blemishes, than to try to be someone else. It presents three common paths to despair: craving, anger, and greed. We need instead to learn to transform our cravings into understanding and empathy, turn our anger into fair actions and loving enthusiasm, and change our greed into graciousness and generosity. Since people become easily addicted to wealth, pride, stubbornness, or selfishness, we must master ourselves and learn how to live responsibly with our intimates, and within the human communities we depend on. It presents three additional life tools: humble submission, asking questions, and service. When facing death, natural disasters, or overwhelming odds, humble submission may be the best course. We can usually get closer to truth by asking the right questions and listening and responding to people's answers, and since service provides the foundation of faith, it should remain our intent.

The Gita's closing pages have a useful contrast among three ways of living: the ways of dark inertia, passion, or lucidity. In the way of dark inertia, people become obsessed with a single thing as if it were the whole of knowledge. Unconcerned with consequences, they grow lazy, undisciplined, vulgar, stubborn, dishonest, and depressed and mistake anarchy for duty. People who live by passion see themselves as separate from others. As egotists, they strive almost exclusively to satisfy their own desires, anxiously seek results, and remain greedy, prone to excitement, grief, even violence, and often fail to discern right from wrong. In contrast, the way of lucidity perceives in all creatures a universal existence. The lucid person acts without obsessive craving and without hatred; is satisfied with the act itself, not requiring rewards to be at peace. The lucid are neither manically egotistical nor decimated by the flux of failure and success, but instead remain resolute and energetic. They distinguish bondage from freedom, act bravely in the face of fear, distinguish wrong and choose right, and are at home with both activity and rest.

Hinduism's Development Between 332 BC and AD 1300

The central scriptures added during the early centuries of our era were the Yoga Sutras of Patanjali (3rd century), The Law Code of Manu, which codified the caste system and caste duties, and the Puranas, vivid tales of superhuman gods and goddesses. Lord Shiva became Hinduism's preeminent symbol for striving to reconcile life's extremes of erotic passion and ascetic renunciation, violence and peacefulness, encapsulated in the story of Shiva leaving his wife and going off to practice ascetic renunciation and meditative calm while she produced a son before his return. Delighted to be coming back, Shiva vowed to sacrifice the first living thing he encountered upon reaching home. His young son runs to meet his father, and Shiva must fulfill his vow, so he chops off his son's head. Then, realizing his tragic error—and being a god—he kills a nearby elephant and places the elephant's head upon his son's body to revive him. Thus was born the elephant-headed god, Ganesh, symbol of both wisdom and joy, who welcomes guests at the main temple door. Vishnu, the preserver God, also became more popular—embodying goodness, peace, and joy, particularly in his reincarnation as Krishna, the flute-playing God, a youthful cowherd who sports with his female companions. Mother-goddess stories were widely told: Brahma's bride, Saraswati, patron of the arts; Lakshmi, Vishnu's consort, manifesting good fortune and wealth; the benevolent Parvati; even malevolent Kali and Durga, embodiments of death and destruction.

The next great Hindu unifiers were the Guptas (AD 320–550), particularly Chandra Gupta II, who reigned from 375–415. He reunited North India, including Himalayan Kashmir, eliminated corporal punishment, charged a water tax for irrigated land, and provided remarkable personal freedom and tolerance for Hindus, Buddhists, and Jains alike. The vertical, highly sculptured Hindu temples built during his rule became India's classical architectural symbol. The great Hindu poet and playwright Kalidasa, India's

Shakespeare, became Chandra Gupta's court poet; seven of his works survive today. There were Hun invasions, but most of India remained free of foreign rule. In Southern India, there were multicentered powers, particularly the Pallavas, Pandyas, and Cholas, each of which ruled large areas between 600–1200. In the mid-700s, in eastern-central India, Dantidurga and his son, Krishna 1st, ordered the great Kailasa temple of Lord Shiva to be carved out of solid rock at Ellora. Along with the nearby Buddhist caves of Ajanta, it remains among the foremost monuments of India.

As India became a dominant trading power in Southeast Asia, Hinduism spread through the region, reaching Borneo by the 4th century. Its influence on the spiritualties of Southeast Asia continues into modern times. Hindu deities and temples stand today within the vast temple metropolis of Angkor Wat in Cambodia. A gorgeous stone retelling of the Ramayana adorns a temple near Jogjakarta, Java. There are many Hindu images that retell the Hindu epics throughout SE Asia. When we visited Vietnam in 2013, a Hindu temple in Hoh Chi Minh City was packed with young women, few of them Hindu, for it had become "the favored location to assure pregnancy." The Indonesian island of Bali is permeated with a unique version of Hinduism, which has evolved advanced forms of ritual dance, carving, and artistry that imbue Bali with a palpable spiritual aura of joy and transcendence that embodies many Hindu ideals.

From 900 to 1400 there emerged many distinct schools of Hindu thought: Vedic fundamentalism; yogic efforts at self-mastery; intellectual analysis; techniques for liberation by separation of soul from body; efforts to reconcile divergent elements with the Upanishads; and Vedanta, which eventually became dominant among Hindu intellectuals. Two leaders with enduring influence were Shankara (780–820) and Ramanuja (1017–1137). Shankara made the Brahman-atman central, established religious schools, and urged all Hindus to visit four geographically disparate places of pilgrimage, which helped Indians increasingly to perceive the subcontinent as their nation. Ramanuja rejected illusion, emphasized intense meditation and devotion, and popularized the Bhakti movement of devotees intoxicated by their reverence for deity. Before the Muslim invasions began to dominate Indian history, two traditions became particularly important to Hindus: tantric practices and understandings, and bhakti devotions.

Tantric ideas were established by the 8th century, became prevalent by 1000, and remained the dominant tendency within both Hinduism and Buddhism for the next five centuries, particularly in the northwestern and northeastern border areas of the subcontinent. Tantrism rejected the supremacy of the Vedas and was anti-ascetic and anti-metaphysical, accepting life in all its diversity. Tantra did not perceive the body as an obstacle but rather as a vessel for receiving the powers of the divine. Rather than shun the energies of sex and anger, they could be channeled into positive social interactions that could provide windows into, and revelations of, the holy. While some took notice only of the extreme lovemaking positions among the tantric sculptures on the magnificent temples at Khajuraho, or the occasional "black magic" practiced by some Tantric adepts, millions of Hindus and Buddhists were empowered by the relative equality of the sexes, enthusiastic life affirmation, and cultural progress Tantrism evidenced.

By the 11th century, Bhakti devotion became dominant among the Hindu masses; it slowly permeated increasing aspects of Hinduism throughout the following centuries and impacted the practices of other religions in India. They used the Purana stories (often slighted as unfit for scriptures by Vedic fundamentalists), because these stories humanized Hindu deities, placing them into helpful human relationships, and lifted up all who practiced virtue, regardless of their social status. Some singers of bhajans, their ecstatic prayer songs, were outcaste women. Bhaktis considered temple worship inferior, and priests became less important than the guidance of a guru or teacher. Some bhaktis worshipped a particular god or goddess, while others emphasized Vishnu, Shiva, mother goddess incarnations, or even a formless divine. Chanting their divines' names was the foundation for their worship.

Islamic Invasions

Islamic empires had perceived their conquests before India as jihads or holy wars, and converted most of their conquered peoples to Islam; however, in the tenth century when Islamic-controlled Turkish and Afghan slave armies first invaded India, Muslim invaders began to learn that they could neither convert nor destroy most of India's people because of its huge population, cultural diversity and sophistication. Although they looted temples, defaced monuments, and killed thousands of indigenous Indians, Muslim invaders learned to cooperate with the Hindu masses and to rule by tolerating local Hindu, Buddhist, and Jain leaders. At first, Hindu Rajput warriors of the Punjab and Rajasthan made a spirited defense, so it was not until 1202 that North India was largely under Muslim control.

While in most of their earlier conquests, the conquered peoples were forced to convert to Islam, die, become slaves, or pay a special 6 percent tax in order to continue practicing their own "religions of the book." In western Asia and North Africa, Jews, Christians, and Zoroastrians already paid that tax, though Islam had also been much deepened and enriched by these older, more sophisticated cultures of the Syrian, Turkish, and Persian empires. In the Indian subcontinent, Muslim empires were themselves transformed by the other religions that already flourished there, and Muslims, Hindus, Buddhists, and Jains learned from one another. A significant minority did convert to Islam, especially many lower-caste Hindus and pre-Hindu tribal peoples. Now, South Asia has the four largest national Muslim populations: Indonesia, Pakistan, and Bangladesh, which are largely Islamic, while India, being 14 percent Muslim, has the third largest Muslim population.

The Delphi Sultanate lasted for 320 years from 1206 to 1526. Shams ud-Din Iltutmish (1210–1236) and his daughter, Raziya al-Din (1236–39), exemplified their rule of persuasion and tolerance, increasingly relying upon indigenous leaders, bureaucrats, and soldiers, political decentralization, and economic self-sufficiency. The Delhi Sultanate reached the height of its power under Ala ud-Din Khalji (1290–1316) who forbade hoarding and inflicted a 50 percent tax on his subjects. A terrible drought and famine occurred from 1335 to1342, and the sultanate also had to resist Mongol invasions from the northwest.

Islamic mysticism (Sufism) gradually dominated the Islam of the Indian subcontinent and continued to do so until nearly the end of Muslim rule. Sufis concentrate upon direct union of the individual believer with God, so Indian Sufis reflected much of the same spirit as Hindu Bhaktis and other spiritual mystics—God-intoxicated people. The Muslim ruler Firuz (1351–1388) abolished torture and built many Islamic institutions—including forty mosques, thirty colleges, a hundred hospitals, and 200 new towns—while fighting off the invasions of Tamerlane in the northwest. The Muslim ruler

Sikandar (1489–1517) had a Hindu mother and a Hindu wife; he created new mystic schools and sponsored a religiously diverse group of mystic teachers. Among them was Kabir (1440–1518), a Muslim weaver and poet who urged Indians to abandon sectarian identities in favor of a syncretic path of love for God. Kabir's poems continue to attract millions. By the dawn of the 16th century, the subcontinent was fragmented politically and divided spiritually into many religious and philosophical camps. The king of Kabul, Babur (1483–1530), whose father descended from Tamerlane, and his mother from Genghis Khan, founded the Mughal Empire, which ruled the subcontinent until the British took control.

Babur's grandson, Akbar (1556–1605), whose mother was Persian and who married a Hindu Rajput princess, won cooperation by ending the poll tax and stopped the slaughter of cows. He maintained control of most of North and Central India with a talented indigenous bureaucracy who stopped taxing afflicted districts during periods of drought or famine, allowed conflicts between Hindus to be resolved by Hindu law, and nurtured a population of 100 million in which the average Indian was better off than south Asian peasants would again be until the mid-20th century. The textiles of the western state of Gujarat then clothed most of Africa and Asia. In his new capitol's hall of private audience, Akbar sponsored interreligious discussions, asking provocative questions from his balcony perch. While he made Persian the official language, he also became a patron of Hindi literature, like the Tulsidas Ramayana. Hindi functionally became India's national language. The witty tales of Raja Birbal, Akbar's poet laureate, are still told today. Confounding Muslim orthodoxy, Akbar sponsored portraits and miniature paintings including Hindu divines, arguing that God, controlling all, could scarcely be repelled by any human beauty or art. Akbar's empire became the world's strongest; the population of his capitol, then the world's second largest city, was twice London's.

European Traders and the Impacts of the British Colonial System

In 1498, the voyage to India of Portuguese explorer Vasco da Gama yielded a 3000 percent profit. European colonial powers thereafter competed for the Indian market. The British East India Company made its first voyage in 1608. By 1700, the Child brothers and their John Company had settlements and factories on both coasts, and envisioned "a future of English business, civil, and military power throughout India." A 1770 famine in Bengal starved one third of that state's population. By 1784, Lord Cornwallis had taken British government control of most of India. His Cornwallis Code abolished India's own courts and administrative units, destroyed their traditional village cooperative farming system, and mandated private land ownership, which destroyed the ability of India's peasants to control their food supply. Using local landlords to heavily tax the population, the British replaced indigenous institutions of self-government and entrepreneurial enterprise with young English bureaucrats who arrived to succeed at their careers and entrepreneurs who came to make their fortunes. England exported Indian opium to China, took Indian raw materials to England, and returned them to India as manufactured goods that Indians were forced to purchase. Each transaction produced massive British profits. Entrepreneurial imperialism was one of the most effective parasitic strategies ever devised.

The British policies fueled revolts. The Indian Mutiny began in 1858 when Hindu and Muslim soldiers arose in what became the bloodiest war ever fought on Indian soil. Any Indian suspected of rebellion was shot or hanged. In the generations that followed, Englishmen seized large agricultural estates to grow export crops, ship raw materials to England, and otherwise maximize the colonial withdrawal of India's wealth to England. Except to keep the military forces strong and the high taxes paid, indifference became the standard colonial policy.

Gradually, many Indians did receive an English education. As they learned about democratic and Western moral ideals, they began to advocate, successfully, that Indians too were worthy of self-respect, human rights, and self-government. This is an inherent weakness in any colonial system. It becomes dependent on educating enough of its indigenous population in the colonists' "superior" ideals that makes the oppressive system vulnerable to the natives' adopting those ideals and applying them to their own population while also pointing out the grievous injustices of any colonial economic and political system. The Congress Party began in the late 19th century. Although the British used their standard colonial "divide and conquer" policy, abetting Muslim suspicions of this largely non-Muslim Congress movement, criticism of and activism against colonial rule steadily strengthened. The British grew ever more dependent upon Hindu and Zoroastrian Parsee colonial bureaucrats and indigenous military forces disproportionately manned by India's religious minorities.

Ram Mohan Roy (1772–1833) created the Brahmo Samaj, a modernist Hindu movement whose theology was based upon a strictly monotheistic formless Divine. The Brahmo Samaj also adopted British reforms such as ending slavery, child labor, and widow burnings (*sati*), and argued that Indians should be involved in governing their own country and could adopt both the best of their Hindu heritage and of English innovations. The Tagore family was Brahmo Samaj, and Rabindranath Tagore received the Nobel Prize in Literature in 1913. His writings introduced many Westerners to Hindu mysticism, and emboldened colonial Indians to realize they could become leaders within a global culture.

Ramakrishna (1834–1886) was a traditional Hindu mystic who was proclaimed modernity's Hindu master guide. He encountered the mother goddess Kali, and found union with the Atman; however, he also married, abandoned traditional food taboos, revered both Jesus and Allah, and selected Swami Vivekananda to broaden his work. Vivekananda gained widespread attention at the Chicago Parliament of Religions in 1893 and popularized the Ramakrishna Mission. In the U.S. and Europe, he established Vedanta Societies that taught a universalistic and activist Hinduism to thousands of Westerners. In India, the Ramakrishna Missions provided a dynamic modern version of Vedanta that urged Hindus to reform caste and lift the common people through lives of selfless dynamic activity and involvement with the world.

The Vedanta Centers became the first of a growing variety of Hindu centers created by diverse Hindu teachers arriving to help Westerners with their spiritual regeneration. These centers have continued to proliferate as a spectrum ranging from Hare Krishna devotees to Gandhian activists and from weekend meditation schools to Hindu communes. Today, millions of Westerners practice yoga, many not only as an exercise routine but also as a spiritual practice. Since British colonists in the 19th century had transported groups of Indian peasant workers to other colonies, Indians constitute a major segment of the population on the Caribbean island of Trinidad and the South Pacific island of Fiji, and remain a vital element of the middle classes in South Africa and areas of East Africa. In 1963, changes in US immigration policies have attracted more than a million Hindus to become American citizens. Per capita, Hindus now constitute the wealthiest and best educated among US religious populations, and are prevalent among leading professionals throughout the world.

After World War I, the capital was moved to New Delhi, major indigenous heavy industries like Tata Iron and Steel were established, and vastly different political movements arose. Muhammad Ali Jinnah (1876–1949) established the Muslim League—the Islamic movement that eventually became the independent country of Pakistan (slicing off both the western third and an eastern piece of the Indian subcontinent where Muslim populations predominated). Mohandas Gandhi (1869–1948) transformed the Congress Party from an elite club to a mass national movement that actively worked to include Muslims, Sikhs, untouchables, and ethnic minorities. From 1920 to 1939, Gandhi led mass movements of nonviolent noncooperation that stirred millions of activists to boycott non-Indian goods, refuse British titles, and mobilize interest groups throughout the nation. WWII unified India's nationalist movement and further empowered its industrial infrastructure, but also shattered any hopes for reconciliation between the Muslim League and the Congress Party. In 1948, the Indian subcontinent was divided into Pakistan and India; there was a wrenching migration of Hindus out of Pakistan and of Hindus and Sikhs into India. Millions were killed or died in transit; many millions more were displaced and had to establish new lives in new places.

India Today: The Largest, Most Culturally and Religiously Diverse Democracy

In 1950, India established a highly democratic constitution, significantly organized by Dr. Ambedkar, a Western-educated Hindu untouchable. He led the creation of a federal system of state governments, a bicameral national parliament with a strong prime minister and a relatively titular president, outlawed caste discrimination, guaranteed religious liberty, and set up affirmative action for discriminated peoples. By 1951, India, with 173 million people, was already the world's largest democracy, but 80 percent of the population were illiterate and impoverished. It was not until 1955 that there began to be specific penalties against caste and religious discrimination. Jawaharlal Nehru, India's first Prime Minister (1947–1964), established a social democratic economic system and directed a series of five-year economic plans that succeeded in modernizing much of the country's economy and agriculture, educating a much greater proportion of India's population, and producing research institutions and private enterprises that have made India among the most rapidly modernizing of nations. Nehru also applied Gandhi's policies of nonviolent activism internationally, transforming a version of the Jain ethics of *pancasila* (truth, nonviolence, self-restraint, non-stealing, and non-possession) into the five principles of peaceful coexistence among nations: 1) Respect for territorial integrity and sovereignty; 2) eschewing armed attacks on other nations; 3) noninterference in their domestic affairs; 4) maintaining equality and mutual benefit in trade and commerce; and 5) tolerance for diverse ideologies among nations. Like human rights or democratic institutions, peaceful coexistence has not been practiced consistently; nonetheless, it continues to represent a prudent standard for relationships among nations.

There are a billion Hindus in India, about 80 percent of the population. India also has the world's third largest Muslim population, a growing 14 percent; 2 percent are Christian, about 1.7 percent are Sikh and then, in descending order, less than one per cent are Buddhist, Jain, or Zoroastrian (Parsee). For most of India's independent history, the Congress Party dominated Indian politics, and worked at being religiously inclusive, with a Hindu prime minister but often with a president from a different religion or minority group.

Elements of Hinduism that I Find Troubling

I'm dismayed by the continuing potency of the caste system in Hinduism today. I don't understand how Hindus can simultaneously assert that ultimate spiritual potency resides with women yet continue to practice widespread gender inequity and violence against them. Hinduism's philosophy is more tolerant and inclusive than those of most religions, yet religious violence is still prevalent. Cow worship appears to be a fetish in a society that is routinely merciful to neither its domestic animals nor its fellow humans. Modern India was in large part created by Gandhi's nonviolent activism (*satyagraha*), so it's ironic that Indian politics seems to oscillate between a sort of high-caste neocolonial administration, and angry and violent outbursts of caste, sectarian, and religious division, mutual distrust, and open hostility against its neighbors. Far too many Hindus still passively accept grave injustices in ways that betray their own potential, undermine an equitable distribution of resources and opportunities, and continue to hinder progress in their great nation, the birthplace and vibrant home of Hinduism.

Sixty-five years ago, the Indian Constitution wisely outlawed caste discrimination and established affirmative action with quotas for disadvantaged castes in education, bureaucratic positions, and legislative seats. These quotas have given many millions access to better education and jobs, middle-class status, and increased political power; however, instead of disappearing as a source of discrimination, caste continues to be reinforced within the political arena, and remains the number-one characteristic by which voters choose their candidates. Fully two thirds of India's population is still at the bottom of its economic and social hierarchy. The caste system today can be broken down as follows: the highest caste, Brahmins, represent 5 percent of the population; Kshatriyas, 10 percent; Vaishyas, 23 percent; Sudras (peasants), 40 percent; Dalits, 16 percent (Hindus beneath caste, "untouchables" because caste Hindus were not supposed to be touched by them); and Adivasi, 6 percent (non-Hindu tribal indigenes). As the world's second largest population at 1.2 billion, this means that many millions of people are affected by this socially and economically stratified system, and that the top one third of the caste population controls most of its wealth, property, and economic and political power. Caste continues to dominate marriage, still usually arranged by relatives. Urban areas have more inter-caste marriages but are primarily limited to a liberal urban middle- and upper-class minority. The caste system is slowly breaking down in cities, but most Hindus still live in rural villages, where caste divisions continue to rule daily life for the majority, often reinforced violently when individuals don't conform.

Independent India has produced many powerful and successful women, and progressive social policies do provide many girls with educational opportunities, jobs, and political advancement. Male children, however, are still preferred to such an extent that millions of "illegal" abortions are done each year to avoid the birth of a daughter, and men now outnumber women by several million. Daughters are perceived to be a burden because their fathers must provide a dowry (outlawed but still pervasive) and an expensive wedding. Upon marriage, a daughter becomes a member of her husband's family, and provides no further economic benefit to her birth family. Married women are often mistreated by their husbands' families; domestic violence is prevalent, and if a married woman fails to produce a male heir, her life is still sometimes in danger. Widowhood remains extremely difficult. Marriage remains so important in Hindu society that millions of women who become well educated and professionally trained leave their non-household jobs behind once they marry.

Now, a Hindu nationalist prime minister, Narendra Modi, is in power, and traditional Hindu preferences and priorities appear to be dominating the government's religious agenda. The division of the subcontinent into India and Pakistan, and the subsequent division of Pakistan into Pakistan and Bangladesh, has nurtured generations of war, suspicion, and mutual hostility. Current Islamic fundamentalism and terrorist militancy reinforce old prejudices and mutual fears. Most of the time, Indians of different religions do cohabit peacefully; millions have good friends and neighbors of other faiths, but when an incident of violence toward one religion or another happens, too often the response is mob violence. Religious affirmative action in the military, politics, and bureaucracy have usually kept intolerance under control, but Hindu sectarianism, like any ideological sectarianism, needs to be disrupted and undermined by the people themselves. For an American looking at India, a nation one third our size but with four times our population and as culturally diverse as all of Europe, it is tempting to be dismayed, but my experiences make me hopeful that Indians can surmount their multiple difficulties.

Albert Schweitzer criticized Hinduism as life-renouncing. I've not found that to be true, but I do think that caste prejudices, reincarnation, karma, and the cultural acceptance of "renouncing life" make it seductive for Hindus to passively embrace economic, political, and social status quos. I am allied with activist Hindus who wish to preserve the many aspects of Hinduism that can be spiritually fulfilling and religiously inclusive, while continuing to embrace modern life and value other religions.

Elements of Hinduism that I Find Particularly Relevant

My first trip to India was in 1969; by 2005, I had visited India nine more times. I soon discovered that for Hindus there really was divine immanence to be nourished within each of us. Hindus' eye-to-eye, hands-pressed-together greeting, *namasté,* conveys that they "see the God in you." In the course of my life, I have found that the Brahman-atman conception best fits my comprehension of the Divine because I perceive God as Creation—a process of evolutionary cosmic energies unfolding in the universe and on the Earth, within human history and within each of us. I have also gained a deep appreciation that humans often need more identifiable images of the Divine.

My favorites among the Hindu pantheon are Vishnu, the Divine who incarnates in evolving forms when the Earth and humanity need help to reassert order and nurture progress—from his first incarnation as a fish, to his eighth as Krishna, the ninth as Buddha—and who will continue to incarnate as needed, perhaps, for instance, as Jesus or Gandhi. My favorite Hindu goddess is Saraswati, an embodiment of culture—music, arts, beauty, the consort of Brahman itself. There are times when I identify with the justice-doing or meditative Shiv, or even with the emotional Kali. If the Divine is the All, and we are aspects of that All, then, life-reality is not only sweetness but encompasses the entire emotional repertoire.

Yoga has long been a central aspect of my spiritual practice. From adolescence, I grasped yoga's insight that people could not only stretch their muscles and joints but simultaneously learn to carefully stretch their breathing, thinking, compassion, research, action, silence, and speech.

Hinduism's recognition and celebration of each person's uniqueness, and recognition that spiritual paths and life journeys will vary, has been of great help in my life and ministry. People differ; circumstances change; we each evolve. As Krishna says in the Gita, "When devoted people sacrifice to other deities with faith, they sacrifice to me." We need to be tolerant of each other because we are all partly in error, yet each of us is a unique and irreplaceable portion of Creation, of what is most real and holy.

Like others, I'm not purely dedicated to a single yoga. Sometimes in my head, other times in my heart, occasionally lost in my body, often an experiential experimenter, but usually a *karma yogin,* like Gandhi, a person dedicated to my chosen actions. Most of us will evolve a primary spiritual path as we age but will also integrate other aspects during our lives. Many activists become more philosophical. Teenagers, often prone to experimentation, reach middle age and focus more upon devotion. Some feel stuck in middle age, and return to school, or embark upon a new career, or become activists for a new cause or devotees of a new faith. No one model works for everyone, but Hindus' spiritual roadmap can be amazingly useful in the 21st century.

In maturation, the fortunate develop a witnessing consciousness that grows beyond ego and even thinks of futures beyond the individual's own life. Those who have lived primarily in their minds may have largely attempted to "understand" God; in their devotions, everyone wants to experience God, to love, to adore the objects of their devotion, but hopefully we all learn that emotions too need training and tempering. A Hindu prayer reflects this emotional growth: "You are everywhere, but I worship you here. You are without form, but I worship you in many forms. You need no praise, yet I offer you these prayers. Forgive these sins that are due to my human limitations."

I found the four traditional Hindu life stages (student, householder, grandparent-supporter, and old-age seer) helpful, both in my personal life and in serving congregations. Our Western model traditionally has a single climax. One works into middle age to develop talents and skills and to succeed at work, with a spouse, children, and to gather wealth; then one simply doubled down on all these achievements, anxiously dreading inevitable failures or declines. Not everyone achieves all these or is able to hold on to them. I spent a fourth of my life primarily as a student, a generation raising a family, and two generations in satisfying vocations. Now my work is reflection and writing, being an active spouse and grandparent, and volunteerism. I'm doing my best to share what wisdom I have and to continue savoring the gifts life blesses me with, while bearing life's tragedies with integrity when they appear. Too often, we seek and have the ambition, lust, and greed that are natural for the householder stage of young adulthood and young middle age, but fail to evolve beyond them, even as our passionate excesses increasingly become burdensome to us and detrimental to others. Now many of us live into old age, and we need to discover how to transform our youthful obsessions into truly living for others and on behalf of futures in which we will not be present.

The Hindu concept of dharma has been of central importance to me. It's tempting to forget that our responsibilities also need to evolve. You can fulfill your own chosen responsibilities in life right up to your last day. It works best to do so mindful of your unique personality and special experiences, the realities of the present stage of your life, and the practicalities of your life's situation. I won't be tolerated long if I act like a child or as an adolescent when I'm an adult. I need to put away most of my childish things. If I act as though I am rich when I'm poor, I'll go bankrupt and my enterprises will fail. If I act as though I'm poor and needy when I have resources, then I squander those resources and waste myself, refusing to do the good that my well-being empowers me to share. We each proceed with special perspectives. By identifying the nature of our thinking and choosing, we may reason more clearly and choose more wisely. How, as Jung asked us, can we explore our shadow sides and fulfill our own wholeness in ways that nurture the wholeness of the world?

Along with my chosen spiritual communities, which I return to routinely, I have also, through the years, periodically found spiritual teachers and spiritual centers that became life-changing, extremely helpful, and deeply challenging. I admire Hinduism's tradition that people grow best spiritually by finding appropriate teachers or gurus, spiritual communities, special religious celebrations, and pilgrimage sites that they find inspiring.

I agree with Western scholars like Mircea Eliade and Joseph Campbell who perceive tantric philosophy and practices as climactic developments within Hinduism. Many individuals' experiences of love are among their most transparent spiritual experiences. Tantrism grasps this complexity: that in partially losing oneself in devotion to another or others, one comes nearest to reaching those connections with life's essential truths and deepest realities; in exuberantly loving another or others, we embrace the infinite within ourselves.

Unlike most other religions, which evolved into masculine-centric doctrines, Hinduism still has many powerful goddesses and significant women gurus, and its philosophical foundations for power are significantly female. Power remains both attractive and scary for humanity. Gandhi did much to break bondages for women and helped millions of men to understand that power could be used most effectively when it combines both traditional female and male qualities. This Hindu recognition of female power could become a useful support for 21st-century feminism, which I believe can do more than anything else to liberate humanity.

Hinduism, with its ancient continuity, diversity, and embracing philosophical inclusiveness, offers opportunities for building a global spirituality. Reality is too complex and fluid for any individual or group to grasp its full meaning. Our lives can become living hells of obsessive craving, anger, and acquisitiveness, or we can use the karma of our challenges and opportunities to live our unique and sacred lives, our dharma, through disciplined desire, assertive participation, and cooperative enterprise. Hinduism helps us realize that we have many points of access and connection with the infinite and enduring, which I call Creation and many call God. It is not only the transcendent in the world but the immanent within us. In your daily spiritual practices, always be prepared to change and adapt to life's changing realities, and have the courage and patience to put your beliefs into daily practice through your love for your intimates and in your responsible commitments to your chosen communities.

As Kalidasa proposed:

> Look to this day! For it is life, the very life of life. In its brief course lie all the verities and realities of your existence. The bliss of growth, the glory of action, the splendor of beauty. For yesterday is but a dream and tomorrow is only a vision, but today, well lived, makes every yesterday a dream of happiness and every tomorrow a vision of hope. Look well, therefore, to this day!

Chapter 6
Jainism

Central Jain Beliefs and Practices

In brief, Jainism is concerned with conquering oneself. Central Jain doctrines include truth, nonviolence, nonattachment, not stealing, and sexual control. Acts of asceticism are necessary to reduce the burdens of human error. Truth is inevitably both relative and transitory, so tolerance is necessary and pluralism desirable. Taking personal responsibility for our own actions is the central human duty. Only then can individuals progressively evolve, and culture matures through compassion. Gandhi was strongly influenced by Jainism, particularly *ahimsa* (nonviolence), which became the foundation for his practices of nonviolent activism. Jainism's initiator, Parshva, taught that people's deeds are deposited upon their souls by the laws of karma, but that a person can gradually diminish most of his karma through asceticism. Parshva and Mahavira, another founder of Jainism, almost certainly perceived themselves as Hindu reformers rather than as creating a new religion, for both rejected the centrality of the Vedas, priestly Hindu dominance, and the rigidity of caste divisions and barriers, and continued to embrace Hindu doctrines like karma, dharma, and reincarnation.

The Jain religion is philosophically atheistic, i.e., there is no overarching deity. In their basic nature, people are essentially identical. We remain eternally separate, and never become one. We neither arise from nor return to a common source or larger state of consciousness or bliss. We are likely to become bound up in material existence, so Jainism's spiritual goal is to free the soul from its material bondage. All knowledge is relative and transient. Any truth has many aspects and perspectives; no proposition is either true or false; truth, right, and goodness are inevitably relative, partial, and impermanent. Thus people need to practice tolerance and acceptance, minimize aggression, and endeavor to shelter and nurture others so that they too may enjoy what they learn and earn. Jain methods of self-conquest include self-sacrifice, compassion, and love. They seek to avoid possessive attachment to objects, to people, even to ideas. To make compassion and love possible, we must be nonviolent, speak the truth, and realize that we are responsible for our own thoughts and deeds, shaping our futures with positive ideas and actions. Jains do not conquer others; they conquer themselves. In vital ways, Jainism is a model for philosophical liberalism, both by its insistence that truth is relative and multifaceted, and in its willingness to accommodate all possible viewpoints, even those of rival philosophies and faiths. Self-reliance and individual efforts alone are responsible for any person's liberation. Jain philosophy has remained unified through the centuries and had major impacts upon Hinduism and upon India's cultural development and variety.

Jainism's Historic Evolution

Vedic Hinduism slowly spread throughout India during the early half of the first millennium BC, but Hinduism's pre-Vedic foundations were already flourishing in much of India much earlier. Pre-Vedic Hinduism was a religion of nature gods and goddesses and fertility rituals, but also of vigorous yoga disciplines and the universal opportunity to renounce ordinary life in search of spiritual enlightenment. Those who renounced life focused instead upon shedding the accumulated weight of previous unwise actions in this and earlier material existences and concentrated upon unity with ultimate truth. This was particularly so in the lower Ganges River valley (Uttar Pradesh, Bihar, and adjoining Himalayan areas), where prosperous town-based tradesmen patronized non-Vedic teachers who accepted cycles of rebirth and sought escape from these karmic cycles through asceticism and introspection. Some more philosophical teachers theorized about the constituent elements of the universe and of the individual soul and strove to establish spiritual disciplines based upon this inner knowledge.

The most prominent of these was Parshva (872–772 BC). A prince of Varanasi, he married, had a daughter, and then, at age thirty, renounced life. After years of asceticism he reached enlightenment and shared his ideas during the remainder of his long life. He advocated living an ascetic life without recourse to deities, while practicing nonviolence, interpersonal tolerance, and taking full responsibility for one's own life. Some 250 years later, Mahavira, Jainism's central figure, popularized Parshva's teachings into an enduring spiritual movement.

Jains believe that Mahavira was the twenty-fourth and last *Tirthankara,* or self-conqueror. Parshva was the twenty-third, and countless eons before, there had been previous self-conquerors, Adinath the first of them. The twenty-four liberated souls stand as ageless examples whose enlightened existences demonstrate that purity, truth, and nonviolence are possible, and that one can eradicate one's karma. These eons of mythic history are a way to assert that Jainism represents an indigenous, pre-Aryan and pre-Vedic spirituality. As Hinduism evolved in the middle centuries of the first millennium BC, rebellions arose between the priests and the two castes directly below them, the warriors and bureaucrats, and business and tradespeople, who were gaining economic and political power in opposition to the priestly caste's sense of cultural superiority. Mahavira and Buddha were two nobles whose reactions to the increasingly rigid Hindu caste system became historically and spiritually important. Mahavira lived a generation before Buddha. Both were sons of regional kings in Northern India. Their Hindu reformations became two separate religions, Jainism and Buddhism.

Mahavira was born a prince in Bihar about 599 BC. His parents were followers of Parshva, and their kingdom favored Parshva's teachings. Mahavira grew up, married, had a daughter, and became the ruler, but then, like Parshva, at age thirty, Mahavira renounced life, and after thirteen years of asceticism and meditation reached enlightenment. Thereafter, he traveled widely to teach Jainism's doctrines. He attracted many thousands of lay followers and persuaded 14,000 men and 36,000 women to become monastics who took five vows: nonviolence, non-stealing, non-lying, chastity, and non-possession. Mahavira eventually went about completely naked as a symbol of absolute non-possession. Jain monks and nuns not only refrain from killing people and animals but try to avoid even stepping on or inhaling tiny creatures, sometimes by wearing masks over their mouths or carrying brooms to sweep ahead of where they walk. Jainism popularized a vegetarian diet. Many Jains not only abstain from eating meat or fish but also don't eat eggs or even those botanicals that require one to kill the entire plant to consume it.

German philosopher Karl Jaspers labeled this first eon BC the Axial Age and celebrated the number of seminal people who revolutionized human thought during the period. In his book *The Origins and Goal of History*, Jaspers pointed out that in addition to Mahavira and Buddha, Mahavira's Jain predecessor, Parshva, the Indian monarch Asoka, who spread Buddhism, the Persian Zoroaster and the later Persian monarch Cyrus, the Hindu writers of the Upanishads, Lao Tzu and Confucius in China, the Hebrew prophets Isaiah and Jeremiah, and a panoply of ancient Greeks from Homer and Heraclitus to Socrates, Plato, Aristotle, and Thucydides, lived during these centuries that transformed human consciousness. The Axial Age concept initiated a fervent academic discussion that endures today, with Robert Bellah's and Hans Joas' compilation, *Religion in Human Evolution from Paleolithic to the Axial Age* a recent installment. Whether one accepts Jasper's thesis that these varied figures laid spiritual foundations for humanity in an almost divine synchronicity, or is more inclined toward Bellah and his colleagues' arguments that these innovations were analogous responses to the spread of written language and urbanization, it is certain that these centuries were filled with intellectual evolution and spiritual flourishing.

The sequential invasions of the Indian subcontinent were culturally overwhelmed or at least significantly changed by the rich social and spiritual traditions of India's indigenous peoples. Heinrich Zimmer reinforces this view in his *Philosophies of India*. In reference to the Greek invasion, he says:

> The village life of India was little modified by the rise and fall of dynasties… even the Greeks soon recognized the virtues of the native way of being civilized. Alexander adopted as his spiritual advisor the Jain saint Kalanos, whom he invited to fill the vacancy of his old boyhood tutor Aristotle.[1]

After Mahavira's death in 527 BC, Jainism's teachings were transmitted orally for at least 200 years. During that time, several councils were held to establish their scriptural canon. Toward the end of the third century BC, Jainism was patronized by India's ruling monarch, Chandragupta, who eventually abdicated in favor of his son and became a Jain monk. Also, during this period, because of famine, a large group of monks had migrated south to the Karnataka region. When they returned years later to Bihar, they discovered that the more northern group had taken to wearing clothes and had decided that women could also attain the highest enlightenment realizations. These and other, lesser, differences led to an irreconcilable split between what became the two primary Jain sects: *Digambara,* or sky-clad, whose monks go naked, and the *Svetambara,* whose monks and nuns wear white clothing. A small third sect, the *Sthanakavasis,* have no images or temples at all.

Among the 6.5 million Jains today, the Digambaras live mostly in South India; their monks perceive women as their greatest temptation. Their best-known symbol is the fifty-seven-foot statue of the Tirthankara Gomateshvara in Mysore State, visible from fifteen miles away. The largest sect, the Svetambaras live mostly in Gujarat and Mumbai in western India. Their most famous pilgrimage sites are Mt. Abu and Palitana in Gujarat State. I took the Palitana pilgrimage, a moving experience. I joined a host of other pilgrims climbing barefoot up thousands of steps to an arid mountaintop with hundreds of white marble temples honoring the Tirthankara.

Jains are generally united about their scriptures and philosophy. The extant Svetambara canon consists of forty-three texts, chief among them the eleven *angas,* which are sermons and dialogues of Mahavira and other Jain monks and philosophers. The most ancient are the *Acaranga Sutra,* or *Book of Good Conduct,* and the *Sutrakritanga.* Other texts are considered subsidiary; they have five divisions and contain biographies of the self-conquerors. They were written in vernacular languages. Jains do not consider their scriptures to be the literal words of their founders or as inherently sacred, but rather as adequate records of those who have achieved enlightenment. Jains are a literate and informed group of people whose writings have had a significant impact upon the many regional Indian languages. Jain libraries have been historically and culturally significant and have consistently included the texts of many religions and philosophies. Ancient literary figures like Kundakunda and Mallinatha, as well as more recent figures like Yashovijaya, are important to Indian literature. Mallinatha became the foremost commentator on the poetry of the Hindu seer Kalidasa.

Here are some ideas characteristic of the Jain scriptures:

Mahavira was without love or hate, endured hardships and natural disasters with fortitude, kept the rules of penance, and became indifferent to pleasure and pain. For two thirds of each year, he traveled daily from one village or town to another.

People should strive to live without attachments, avoid killing, take only what is given freely, and curb false speech because those who lose themselves in worldly pleasures are reborn repeatedly. The faithful remain free from greed, calmly exert themselves, practice forbearance, and embrace meditation as a welcome duty. Jains avoid meditating upon causing injury or being unpleasant and concentrate upon positive focused meditation.[2]

Jains advocate nonviolence and are thus unlikely to become farmers or soldiers. Like Western Puritans and Quakers, the nonviolent and ascetic lifestyle has enabled Jains to become disproportionally rich and powerful, despite their philosophical disdain for those very aspects of life. Many Jains are wealthy business owners or successful professionals; most are well-educated. Even though Jainism is a theologically and historically distinct religion, many Hindus honor it as a Hindu sect. Many Jain temples contain some Hindu images in addition to their own self-conquerors, and Jains may happily celebrate Hindu holidays. Generally, Jains are embraced by India's predominantly Hindu society, and rarely perceive themselves a challenged minority.

Elements of Jainism that I Find Troubling

I don't believe in the transformative power of asceticism, don't wish to renounce life, and don't believe that extreme doctrines or spiritual disciplines are usually effective or fulfilling. I've seldom killed the animals I've eaten, except for a few fish on the occasional camping trip, and would find it difficult to do so. I don't fully understand the distinction between killing animals and killing plants, which also would likely prefer not to be eaten. Nonetheless, we must all kill or accept killing to survive. I honor Jains and others who restrict their diets for ethical reasons. I've found lust a challenge since adolescence, but am persuaded by both my own experiences and intimate knowledge of a host of congregants, friends, and colleagues, that for many, sexuality is one of the best avenues to the rewards of intimacy as well as to insights into spiritual depth and wisdom. I believe in gender equality and women's empowerment, and don't perceive women as challenges but rather as allies with and models of effective spirituality.

There are inherent dilemmas in practicing non-injury, nonattachment, and non-possession. I embrace the need for the effective use of power. People who accomplish things and lead will inevitably injure others as they do so. Injuries need to be minimized and deserve to be constantly monitored, but there will remain situations when force will be preferable to inaction. Tough love is often better than neglect or inertia. My life has been a series of lessons in passionate attachment, in seeking how to effectively practice love without disabling those to whom I'm devoted. I reject the notion that complete non-attachment is a superior ethical position. I certainly don't want to become possessed by my possessions, and realize that it's tempting and easy to do so, but few people can live without possessions. Many who try become dependent upon unworthy people and institutions and bear some responsibility for their sponsors' missteps.

I can't even entirely embrace some of Gandhi's adaptations of foundational Jain doctrines. I would, for instance, argue not for Gandhi's goal of "continual meagerness" in consumption and possession, but would instead strive for moderation in those matters; nor strive for chastity in mature marriage, but instead for mutual fulfillment with a chosen spouse. I greatly honor Gandhi's and other great nonviolent activists' examples in matters of nonviolent action, but my studies of their lives have led me to believe that sometimes, by too obsessively focusing on such nonviolent leadership, they failed to take sufficient care of their family responsibilities and participated in disreputable personal behaviors (Gandhi's treatment of his wife and children and King's infidelities).

Elements of Jainism that are Personally Relevant

I embrace Jainism's central insights: that truth remains inevitably relative and transitory, only more or less probable or likely, and that all aspects of reality continue to evolve. It's impressive that Jains discovered these truths 2,500 years ago. A major proportion of any person's spiritual journey needs to remain patiently focused upon overcoming their own unwise impulses and exaggerations. I passionately agree that humanity needs to become as nonviolent as possible, to remain tolerant of others' opinions and practices, and to live lives that combine diligent effort with enduring humility.

Jainism was introduced to me through my former wife, Madhavi, my Indian mother-in-law, Lilyben Pandya, and her family, who were prominent Jains in Mumbai. Lilyben's father had started a wholesale cloth business when all of India's raw cotton and wool had to be exported to Britain as colonial policy. The British made these raw products into cloth to be sold primarily in the Indian and other colonial markets, particularly ironic since India had had spinning and weaving enterprises for eons. When Gandhi told Indians to stop buying British cloth, Grandfather Shah sold his business and put his wealth into gold, which happily multiplied in value. After Independence, he founded and directed textile factories and a factory that built textile machinery. During the fight for independence, he became one of Gandhi's financial backers, including his "salt march," and taught astronomy to Gandhi during one of Gandhi's prison stays. By 1969, when I first visited India, Grandfather Shah was dead, but his widow, a devout and traditional Jain, was pleased that I was an enthusiastic Gandhian and spiritual devotee with whom she could share her late husband's extensive library.

I learned much from my mother-in-law, who kept a Jain Tirthankara as the central focus of public reverence in her home. For me, Lilyben became a model of those individuals who can be thoroughly in the world yet maintain a witnessing consciousness and a modicum of emotional detachment from it. She had barely survived childhood typhoid to become a youthful athlete. She went against tradition by marrying a Hindu. When he died in a car accident, Lilyben fought to become a board member of the large engineering firm her husband had helped to found. She also became a local elected political leader, serving on the Bombay City Council for nineteen years. Despite her Hindu father-in-law's initial opposition to their marriage, Lilyben never wavered in her support and generosity for both the Hindu and Jain branches of her extended family. For most of her adult life, she remained a widow, celibate and intimately solitary, yet with many devoted friends and a great love for life. She regularly managed to transform her anger into effective action. Lilyben was certainly a very liberated Jain but retained essential elements of its clear thinking and ethical living.

Madhavi also embodied some Jain tenets. She became warmly attached to our children and was devoted to her birth family and youthful friends. Madhavi could let go of physical and emotional intimacy—even with those she was closest to—in ways that I've never even wished to master. She was quietly nonviolent in word and deed, and I suspect could have foregone sexuality entirely had it not been necessary for the creation of our children. She often seemed to be an old soul—much further along in gaining a dispassionate connection with life than I.

Another Jain who had a strong influence on my spiritual development was Gurudev Chitrabhanu, with whom I became acquainted during my years in New Jersey. Gurudev Chitrabhanu had been a Jain monk for twenty-nine years when he attended a spiritual conference at Harvard Divinity School and then decided to leave monkhood, married, and thereafter led Jain meditation centers in New York City and elsewhere. He spoke at the Paramus, New Jersey, congregation that I then served. I recommend his book, *Realize What You Are: the Dynamics of Jain Meditation*. Chitrabhanu presents Jainism as a spiritual practice and way of living that emphasizes relativity in thinking, nonviolence in action, and a realization that every person is a portion of the cosmic energies. He represented these energies as the invisible vibrations that make up all elements of the universe including us.

His meditation practice begins with investigation, continues into awareness, and evolves into transformation. In its practice, you learn to let go of your ineffective mental and emotional habits through quietly and silently figuring out whom you really are and are not, to cherish the many graces and gifts already in your possession, and to shed shackles of your mind and bondages of your desires. He used the traditional Hindu conceptual trinity: *Sat, Chit, Ananda*—truths that continue, are conscious, and blissful. The steps of his meditation practice are: gradually relax your entire body; breathe deeply; discover who you are and are not, and thereby grasp enduring, effective, and creative realities. Meditation takes time, patience, and continuing practice, and cannot be accomplished without some sacrifice and suffering.

Learn to be at home within ourselves. Become a witnessing consciousness; concentrating on one thing at a time, like using a magnifying glass to cause a flame because our bodies, concepts, and egos are like candlewax, and our essential natures are like a candle flame. Our suffering is a necessary debt to be paid, and then we need to learn to leave our suffering behind. Concentrate upon the abundant light you already possess, for this is your genuine nature. He embraces the use of *mantras,* simple Sanskrit words filled with deep meaning and universal energy. First, say them aloud, then, simply feel the word on your breath, and finally, bring it into the center of your consciousness. Eventually, like a flash of lightning, you are at home in your true self. A mantra I learned was: *veerum* (being brave), inhale on the first syllable, exhale on the second; *sohum* (combining life's extremes), *kohum* (who am I?), *nahum* (I am not that), and return to sohum. Repeating this mantra has helped me toward that genuine reality that we are part of. He compares reality and our essential natures with a symphony. Our task is to become in tune, harmonious, join the rhythm of the universe, find the music of our souls.

This lifelong process provides us with a mother's heart, making ever-widening circles of contribution, patiently listening to others so that they may become able to hear. By patching the holes in our consciousness made by our boundaries, resentments, projections, judgments, and expectations, we move beyond categories and labels to realize that we are a microcosm in the macrocosm, and can recover from our wounds by understanding what we need to discard as outworn or no longer useful. By learning to leave behind our mental and emotional junk, we regain our essential nature, and realize that we still have worthwhile things to do with our lives, for within each of us is a universe of beauty and truth, energy and bliss.

In the context of usual Western thinking about religion, Jainism is revolutionary. All truth is relative and transient. There is no overlord divine. Jain seers are not saviors but models; we honor them by acting like them. Each person is on her own and needs to conquer herself in order to become spiritually free. This must be done through a lifetime of progressive self-understanding and self-discipline, genuine sacrifices, and nonviolent actions. All these make sense to me. I share the Jain belief that the universe is a living entity that continues to evolve and change forms and is made up of common elements that do not die, and I hope, along with the Jains, that our souls contain elements of the universe's global and eternal spirit so in that sense we too remain eternal.

Jains can inspire us to confront the powers of evil in ourselves and in the world and to better avoid idolatries of mind and spirit. Truth is not certain, only probable or improbable. We must remain open to multiple perspectives and embrace pluralism in our social lives. Your fulfillment in life is your personal responsibility; you must conquer yourself, no one else can do it for you. The path there involves practices of disciplined sensualism that seek simplicity, patience, and humility. It advocates living as nonviolently as possible, realizing that it is not only the harm that we choose not to do but even more the good that we manage to do, which becomes our enduring life legacy. My embrace of Jainism is significantly modeled on Gandhi's adaptations of this ancient and wise spiritual tradition.

Chapter 7
Buddhism

Central Buddhist Beliefs and Practices

The Buddha's teachings can be summarized in his four noble truths: 1) genuine suffering—life's tragedies; 2) craving, self-created, unnecessary suffering; 3) we need to overcome craving; and 4) this is accomplished by practicing the noble eightfold path. Life is tragic, bad things happen, life won't be all happiness and light. Most suffering is needless because the sufferers themselves create it through psychological and social frictions and by emotional bad habits, including learned inabilities, death phobias, remaining caught in what one dislikes, or being separated from what one loves. Buddha is focused upon the consequent needless suffering produced by the illusory aftermaths of life's tragedies.

Buddha did not believe that anyone could shed all desires, but that we all must learn to control our cravings by refusing to isolate ourselves within our egos and to refrain from fighting unwinnable battles. Most of us will fail as often as we succeed, either by not reaching some goal or by not trying in the first place. There will be disappointments, pain, and suffering, but we can reduce them to bearable proportions if we learn how to understand and convert the cravings that chronically take possession of us, dilute our satisfactions, destroy our peace of mind, and all too often ruin our lives. We transform our cravings by practicing the eightfold path. As often happens with philosophical or theological efforts, this "single answer" contains many useful steps summarized by eight admonitions:

Appropriate views – We need to use our reason, to think affirmatively, practically, and critically, particularly about both our own limitations and potentials.

Intent – We need to make up our minds, actualize our hearts' commitments, for "sitting on the fence" nurtures lost souls. Become invested in what you are doing. No form of mastery or excellence can be achieved without passionate commitment.

Speech – Our words need to meet two standards: truthfulness and compassion. Deceit reduces our very being. Compassionate speech is not just trying to avoid violence or defamation, but means being tactful, avoiding comments that leave scars or belittle others.

Conduct – The Buddha sought not only to minimize the killing of human beings but also other creatures. He wanted us not only to avoid stealing possessions but also ideas. He urged us to avoid self-defeating lust and admitted that controlling his own sexual urges had been his most difficult inner battle.

Right livelihood – People need to choose occupations that promote life and sustain the future. One's livelihood is a means rather than the primary purpose of one's existence. A livelihood is not just your job but any course of action with a sense of vocation, embodying who you really are or hope to become in the course of your life.

Effort – The path to understanding and virtue requires persistence and steady, patient effort. It is naive to believe that once we reach a certain level of knowledge, achievement, or power that we can then behave however we wish. The wise realize that they need to continue to strive throughout their lives.

Mindfulness – To become progressively aware of our own delicate strength and tenderness toward others; to develop a witnessing consciousness and a conscience that can be in the world but not caught by it. To become nonreactive, especially toward our own moods and emotions; to take control of our senses and impulses rather than be driven by them. To be able then to face even our worst tragedies and overcome our fears and aversions by coping with life's inevitable dilemmas. We can aspire to being filled with compassion and lovingkindness, and patiently put them to work, not only with intimates but with all who surround us.

Concentration – To focus on what is important. By minimizing delusions, cravings, hostilities, and obsessions, we can awaken and be filled with the bliss that already exists in our lives, the compassion that flows to and through each of us and can grow among people, and embraced by the love that can fill our own and others' hearts.

The dual goals in Buddhism are to gain enlightenment through practicing the eightfold path so one's life, made mostly free of false cravings and fears, can be spent in compassionate aid to our fellow humans. The Buddha was concerned that many wander aimlessly through their lives and wanted to help them live intentionally, awaken to what is real within, and become effectively compassionate beyond their narrow egos.

The foundations that make the eightfold path possible are *appropriate associations,* for health is as contagious as disease, virtue as catching as vice, cheerfulness as infectious as morosity, so we need to spend our precious lives keeping company with people who arouse the best in us. Therefore the Buddha believed passionately in the *sangha,* the monastic community, and why I believe passionately in congregations and other intimate spiritual communities. We should strive to spend our time with those who help us and our intimates awaken to our own best inclinations, for this enables us to concentrate on what is truly important, to become virtuous by being universally compassionate. Buddhism continues to flourish because it promotes the importance of spiritual community, which is most often found within family, congregation, and spiritual practice group.

Many Buddhists appear to worship various images and teachers of Buddhism, go to temples, and participate in forms of worship common in other religious traditions, but the Buddha did not want or expect to be worshipped. Instead, he wanted people to wake up to the truths he had discovered. The word "Buddha means" awake. The Buddha almost certainly perceived himself as a Hindu reformer, not as someone starting a new religion. He did, however, want to radically reform Hinduism; he denounced a Vedic, priest-centered religion and dismissed the importance of caste divisions. For him, the Hindu concepts of karma, dharma, and reincarnation were still relevant and true, but he perceived them through the lenses of individual meditation and community compassion.

The Emergence, Historical Development, and Spread of Buddhism

The Buddha

The Buddha was born Siddhartha Gautama around 563 BC in Nepal, near the Indian border. His father was a minor king, comparable to a European feudal lord. Soothsayers told the king that his son would either become a great king or an outstanding spiritual leader. Because his father wanted him to become a king, he sheltered his son from the negative and tragic aspects of life. Siddhartha was a handsome, intelligent, and strong youth; he married an exemplary bride when both were teenagers, and they had a son, Rahul. Though surrounded by luxuries and blessed by close relationships, Siddhartha still felt incomplete. His emotional unrest is recounted in an iconic story about four experiences he supposedly had in a single day during which he observed for the first time a frail old person, another full of disease, a dead person, and a monk who appeared untroubled by these challenging experiences.

Siddhartha was shocked by life's tragic realities, but inspired by the monk's equanimity, so he decided to renounce his comfortable life. He abandoned his family and wealth, exchanged his clothes for a servant's, and disappeared into the forest. For six years, he participated in the austerities practiced by Hindu and Jain holy men. Outstanding in his self-denials, he attracted his own disciples, but ultimately, asceticism too proved unfulfilling, so he sent his disciples away and decided to simply meditate until he came to a better understanding of what life demanded. This is said to have taken place in Gaya, near Patna in India, and is immortalized in Buddhist stories as a weeklong period during which Siddhartha meditated in isolation under a peepul tree (a traditional Hindu village's community gathering place). The Buddha experienced many temptations, somewhat analogous to Jesus' temptations in the wilderness. The powers of evil tempted the Buddha with sexual desires, luxuries, wealth, and amazing powers. Having surmounted these, he then faced his ultimate challenge: how to translate what he had come to understand into words, practices, and deeds that others might comprehend. He concluded his meditation by deciding his efforts could be worthwhile because some would learn to understand and be able to live his insights.

Unlike Jesus' three-year ministry, Buddha had forty-five years of sharing his insights after his spiritual breakthrough. For three quarters of each year, he traveled through the Indian subcontinent teaching people, and then, during the monsoon months, he withdrew with his growing community of monks. His daily schedule combined listening to and teaching others along with three periods of solitary meditation. His teachings and practices evolved over these forty-five years of leadership. He made clear that he was neither a god nor a saint, only a person, saying simply that he was "awake." His was a middle way, neither unbridled sensuality and freedom from all restraints nor a world-renouncing life of asceticism. He had experienced both sensual excesses and severe austerity and discovered that neither brought him peace or fulfillment. Although many associate Buddhism with withdrawing into an ascetic, monastic life in order to achieve individual enlightenment, it was the Buddha's intention from the outset to create practices that would lead to fulfillment for ordinary people in everyday life.

Early Buddhism in Nepal and India

After the Buddha died in 483 BC, his reformation of Hinduism gradually evolved into a family of faiths, organizations, and religious practices that sometimes focused more upon the Buddha than upon his insights. Ideologies, religious or secular, tend to evolve in that manner when there's a central, strong individual or individuals who come to exemplify and dominate the tradition; the human leaders progressively become endowed with superhuman and mythical qualities. During the next two centuries in India, the number of Buddhist monks, nuns, and their communities of discipline grew significantly while the number of lay Buddhists, especially among social elites, multiplied even more quickly. Buddhism's historical development began with centuries in India, but then gradually spread throughout Asia. These historical developments varied significantly according to geographic and political factors, as well as a proliferating variety of Buddhist sects and teachings.

In 273 BC, the emperor Ashoka came to the Indian throne, becoming one of the great rulers in world history. A grandson of Emperor Chandragupta, who had overrun Alexander's Indian garrisons, Ashoka united much of India, significantly expanding his kingdom; however, after he caused the deaths of hundreds of thousands during his conquest of Bengal, Ashoka felt great remorse and began to spread Buddhist ideas. He issued thirty-five edicts of Buddhist teachings, inscribed on pillars across India in its regional languages, and did his best to rule with gentleness and patience, regulated the slaughter of animals, and exhorted people to live together peacefully.

The Buddha had argued against continuing to use the Sanskrit language, already not widely spoken by most people. Buddha used his own language, Pali, which became the primary language for Buddhist scriptures. As Buddhism spread geographically, Pali also became a language mostly known by monks rather than by common people. Ashoka was the ruler who organized Buddhism as a world religion and ensured that Buddhist principles were shared with practical applications among the populace. He invigorated Buddhism, sending missionary-ambassadors who reached Sri Lanka, Southeast Asia, and even Syria, Egypt, and Greece.

After Ashoka, Buddhism enjoyed great prestige throughout India for the next 800 years. Just forty years after Ashoka's death, however, the Hindu Gupta regime took power in central India. For the next five centuries, India was fragmented into many Hindu and/or Buddhist kingdoms in which Buddhism, Hinduism, and Jainism all evolved somewhat differently. Buddhism gradually changed from being focused upon a relatively few monks seeking enlightenment toward a much broader people's religion that encouraged Buddhist worship among the laity and urged them to practice Bodhisattva ideals of compassionate service, and many who became monks remained monks for only for a youthful period.

The geographic center of Buddhist influence gradually shifted to northwest India, increasingly dominated by Greco-Bactrian cultures. By the first century AD, Kushans, central Asian nomads, overran that region; their greatest king, Kamisha, whose capital was Peshawar, was religiously pluralistic. Kamisha became a patron of Buddhism, nurtured new forms of

Buddhism and Buddhist art, and hosted the fourth Buddhist Council, which had representatives from eighteen distinct Buddhist sects.

Impacted by Hinduism's bhakti movement, a major shift was taking place in Buddhism: it argued that the Buddha was to be revered as a divine being, that there had been earlier Buddhas, and there would be future Buddhas. These divinities could help Buddhists realize the latent Buddhahood within them. Some of our knowledge of Buddhism in India during these centuries comes from a visiting Chinese Buddhist monk, Fa Hsien (c. AD 400) who encountered four different highly developed Buddhist philosophic systems in India, two Mahayana and two Theravada, living side by side with thousands of monks in vigorous debate.

In Theravada scripture, the Buddha is presented as a human who achieved enlightenment, or nirvana, by his own effort. Upon his death, he received complete liberation and had no further contact with the world. Those who follow his eightfold path may themselves also achieve liberation. For Mahayana Buddhists, it seemed inconceivable that the Buddha would cease to be. They perceived instead a transcendent Buddha with innumerable manifestations. They acknowledged the Theravada Pali scriptures, but argued that the Buddha had shared other ideas with his closest disciples that had remained secret during his lifetime. These became the "greater vehicle" of Mahayana, the Mahayana Sanskrit scriptures. They presented the Buddha as turning back after enlightenment, postponing personal salvation until all sentient beings could become enlightened. This bodhisattva ideal was incarnated in countless past and future helpful Buddhas. Every Mahayana Buddhist becomes, prospectively and in principle, a bodhisattva, with many progressive stages gradually elaborated to fulfill various bodhisattva ideals.

Theravada Buddhism

The original, strict, monastic, Pali canon-based Buddhism, Theravada, became increasingly dominant in Sri Lanka and Southeast Asia, as well as continuing among many Indian Buddhists. Theravada Buddhism focused upon the unreality of the ego and denied any enduring personal self. It emphasized the transient and sorrowful realities of the world and perceived the goal of the faith as the quest for individual enlightenment through meditation that transcended the egotistic mind, and idealized monastics. In subsequent centuries, Theravada's purity of focus on solitary meditation seems somewhat belied among many Theravada Buddhists, with their apparent worship of the Buddha, reverence for historic relics, stories of predecessor Buddhas, and hopes in future Buddhas.

In Southeast Asia, many young Buddhist men still spend some months or a year or more as monks before proceeding with their secular lives. They beg daily for their food, which puts monastics and laity into regular interaction; then, after their often-temporary monkhood, they reintegrate with the public. For instance, our Cambodian taxi driver-guide at the Angkor Wat temple complex had been a Buddhist monk for nine years, including two years in Thailand, before choosing a secular life so he could earn enough money to afford a wife and children.

Southeast Asian Buddhist history had two distinct but overlapping periods: centuries of "Indianization" followed by varied national developments. Buddhism was first introduced during the 3rd century AD, and this combination of Buddhist geographic expansion and cultural Indianization continued until the 13th century. Hindu deities and Buddhist images spread throughout the region and were widely adopted by both local elites and the common people. Most became Theravada Buddhists, focused on monks' communities, but gradually added Mahayana elements among the laity. Vietnam's northern region was often under Chinese control and received more Mahayana influence from Chinese monks. By the 13th century, Buddhism and Hinduism were waning in Indonesia, which was becoming predominantly Islamic, except for Bali, where a unique Hindu-Buddhist synergy thrives today. Elsewhere in Southeast Asia, Theravada Buddhism became the primary religion, except among the Chinese Mahayana Buddhist communities that increasingly emigrated throughout the region.

Theravada Buddhist Scriptures

Buddhist teachings were initially shared orally, memorized by the monastics, and taught to the believers. Three months after the Buddha's death, a council of disciples gathered to remember his teachings and rules. They approved them as authentic and classified them into the *Tripataka*, or three baskets: monastic rules, discourses, and supplementary materials. The discourses most directly share the Buddha's teachings along with an important moral treatise, the *Dhammapada* (verses on the dharma or law). The *Jataka*, a collection of 500 story poems, purportedly shares the Buddha's recollections of his twenty-four previous incarnations. The original post-Buddha leadership included his cousin and loving companion, Ananda, Upali, and Kassapa, who became the next great Buddhist organizer. At the end of the 4th century BC, at the second Buddhist Council, a split developed between monks wishing to maintain traditional practices (fortnightly public confessions, no meal after midday, abstinence from liquor, no valuables or comfortable beds), and another group who sought more privacy, comfort, and flexibility. The stricter group temporarily won out, making their ideas the "Elders'" teachings.

Here, from *What the Buddha Taught*, translated by Sri Lankan Walpola Rahula, are some central Buddhist teachings from Theravada Buddhist scripture:

> Do not practice either of two extremes: indulgence in sensual pleasures or devotion to self-mortification—ours is a middle path. Avoid lust, hate, and delusion. Become contented through a simple livelihood, sensual control, and discretion, living without impudence and without becoming greedily attached. Avoid: fetters of false ideas of self, skeptical doubt, or attachment to certain observances or rites. If a cloth is soiled, it appears dirty even when dyed with the brightest colors, while a clean cloth, like a pure mind, remains clear, reflecting beauty. Evil actions are done from motives of partiality, enmity, stupidity, or fear. Avoid friendships with those who are rapacious (giving little—expecting much), who only pay lip-service or are flatterers.[3]

> The Dhammapada: Hatred is not appeased by hatred, only by love. By endeavor, diligence, discipline, and self-mastery the wise person makes an island that no flood can overwhelm. Fruitless are words of those who fail to practice wisdom. Do not follow mean things, dwell in negligence, or embrace false views. Health

is the best gain, contentment the best wealth, a trusty friend the best kin, and enlightened compassion is the supreme bliss.[4]

Mahayana Buddhism

The newer Sanskrit Buddhist texts became the scriptural foundations for Mahayana Buddhism. This more inclusive, laypeople-based Buddhism grew explosively, first in what is now northwest India, Pakistan, and Afghanistan, as well as among some of the Indian Buddhist schools, then gradually spread north and east throughout Asia. Mahayana Buddhism evolved into a more traditional religion that increasingly emphasized Buddha's superhuman qualities. It argued that since Buddha had been without blemish, he must have come from heaven, and surely had predecessors. Mahayana Buddhists made nirvana no longer simply an individual achievement of the meditating self, but instead a salvation process substantially aided by the examples and worship of varied divine beings, with vast knowledge and power, who were eager to share their wisdom and help the faithful.

Through the following centuries, Mahayana Buddhism was more easily integrated into the existing animistic and other spiritualties that existed in Pakistan and Afghanistan, and later in China, Mongolia, Korea, and Japan. It sought more of a balance between the two primary Buddhist goals of enlightenment and compassion, with the bodhisattva becoming the Mahayana ideal. A bodhisattva is any person who achieves enlightenment, but then steps beyond personal nirvana to apply his/her wisdom in ordinary life to help a suffering world. Bodhisattvas are spiritual people who discover truth, show compassion to others, and nurture peace in their larger communities. Monasteries remained important in Mahayana, but their monks were perceived as teachers and models for the populace rather than elites separated from ordinary life in order to achieve personal liberation.

Mahayana Scriptures

Different Mahayana schools emphasized different essential concepts within the Mahayana sutras. Among the most important: the classic formulation of the *Heart Sutra*—all is emptiness. To practice emptiness is to be content with whatever comes, to not lean on anything, and have no need for fame. In the *Diamond-Cutter Sutra,* the emphasis is on patience (especially honored by the Japanese Zen schools). Suchness is another central Mahayana quality, which is simply the "way things are." Mahayana also has a meditative tradition analogous to Theravada's Vipassana meditation: *dhyana paramita.* A thought cannot see itself, so whatever its practitioners' circumstances, they should remain calm, contented, frugal, and without distraction. In the *Lotus Sutra,* Mahayana Buddhism becomes devotional, bowing to Avalokiteshvara, the bodhisattva of compassion, who destroys all sorrow, fear, and suffering and is always available to teach or rescue.

Mahayana Buddhism Spreads to China and Korea

Buddhism first arrived in China about 75 AD, but China was then dominated by Confucian ideals for an ordered and harmonious society, and their focus upon family, humanistic optimism, and love of life made a monk-centered and world-renouncing religion unacceptable. During the following centuries, however, which were filled with invasions by Central Asian nomadic tribes, the public mood shifted toward the mystical consolations and naturalistic quietism of Taoism. Since neither Confucian nor Taoist traditions provided much of a vision of life after death, and Chinese folk traditions taught that the living remained dependent upon their continued rites and reverence for their deceased relatives, Mahayana Buddhism, with its many images of heavenly Buddhas with vivid heavenly stories with saving powers, had great appeal.

By the 4th century AD, the Chinese were becoming a mixed people, and Buddhism was becoming a dominant faith, particularly in northern China, much impacted by invaders, some of whom brought a Mahayana faith with them. Buddhist growth took longer in southeastern China where Confucian and Taoist traditions were still dominant and well organized and whose populous often considered Buddhist ideals to be un-Chinese. Some Confucian or Taoist rulers even persecuted Buddhists, like the T'ang dynasty ruler Wu Tsung who in 845 had thousands of Buddhist buildings destroyed, their images melted, and forced monks and nuns into secular lives. Generally, however, Buddhism continued to spread. By the 7th century AD,

Buddhism reached its climax of Chinese influence, claiming converts among all elements of Chinese society, from the imperial family to peasant farmers, in every region. Chinese monks traveled to India as pilgrims, and to Korea, Japan, and Vietnam as missionaries; they decreed that Buddhahood was open to everyone and emphasized faith and devotion to Buddhas and compassion for all.

Mahayana practitioners began to diverge into various traditions, practices, and scriptures within the "Greater Vehicle" of Mahayana Buddhism. The T'ien-t'ai school emphasized the idea of emptiness—since all the Buddhas are present in a single grain of sand, and phenomenal life is part of the absolute, the life of a layperson can also be the life of the Buddha. The Hua-yen school focused on the interpenetration of the absolute and the everyday, using playful tricks to open their followers to their own Buddha-natures. The Ch'an school highlighted the potential in each person through a combination of elaborate philosophy and simple meditation, while discounting the reciting of sutras, worship of images, or performance of rituals that were important in other schools. The Pure Land tradition stressed worship of Amida Buddha, which could lead its practitioners directly into the delights of the Western heaven, even erasing evils they had committed.

Buddhism was introduced in Korea in the 4th century by a Buddhist monk named Sundo. Korea's indigenous spirituality had been largely animistic. By the 6th century AD, Buddhism had become Korea's official religion, and its emperor sent Buddhist missionaries to Japan.

Buddhism in Japan

(Nation-centered forms of Japanese Buddhist history appear in a subsequent chapter.)

The first Korean Buddhists arrived in Japan in AD 552. Emperor Kinmei received them, but Buddhism made little headway there until 588, when Shotoku Taishi became regent. An ardent Buddhist, Kinmei sent Japanese scholars to China to study Buddhism and learn the Chinese system of government. He built temples and monastic schools, but also erected hospitals, dispensaries, and houses of refuge, demonstrating that Buddhism was good for the whole society. By the 8th century, Buddhism was the dominant religion. From the 8th to 11th centuries, Shinto and Buddhist principles and practices became more integrated. During this integration, Shintoism almost succumbed to Buddhism. A 400-year period of feudal strife followed until the end of the 16th century, during which pietistic spirituality elaborated new forms, which emphasized a third period of "Buddhist time," believed to have begun after the Buddha's death and be characterized by vice and strife.

At the end of the 16th century, a *shogun* of the Tokugawa family unified Japan, beginning its long reign from 1600–1867, and there was a Shinto renaissance. There followed the Meiji era until after WWII. During that era, Buddhism was again attacked as foreign, but Buddhism and Shinto were now so firmly intermingled that a national return to pure Shinto was as unlikely as trying to separate Japanese culture from its multitude of Chinese roots. Most Japanese continued to practice elements of both, often with a home Buddhist altar and Buddhist death ceremonies. The Constitution of 1889 promised religious liberty, but this was government-controlled freedom. Most Japanese believed they were an integral part of a gigantic cosmic organism permeated by divine nature.

The Multiplicity of Buddhas

For Buddhists in China, Korea, and Japan, Mahayana Buddhism offered the good news of a multitude of divine assistants whose central desire was to lessen their suffering. These varied Buddhas are categorized into three primary types: *Manushi*-Buddhas, Bodhisattva Buddhas, and *Dhyani*-Buddhas. Manushi-Buddhas are saving-teaching Buddhas who, like Gautama himself, have entered Nirvana and are no longer accessible to prayer. Bodhisattva Buddhas have postponed their entrance into Nirvana to help others. In Theravada, the only Bodhisattvas are Gautama before his enlightenment, and Maitreya, the Buddha who followed him; while in Mahayana, Bodhisattvas include Maitreya, Manjushri, the law giver, and the all-important Avalokiteshvara, who personifies compassion and is called the Jewel of the Lotus, as well as innumerable lesser Bodhisattvas, often with different names and even forms that varied from one nation to another. Dhyani-Buddhas achieved Buddhahood in nonhuman forms before the

Buddha. Like Bodhisattvas, Dhyani-Buddhas can respond to human needs and prayers. Among them are Bhaisajyaguru, the healing Buddha, Amida, who presides over the Western Land of Bliss, and Amitabha, the Buddha of infinite light, considered greater than Buddha himself because he assures both present happiness and future bliss.

Kwan Yin is the most revered Asian goddess and the primary Buddhist goddess. Kwan Yin began as a male Bodhisattva, Maitreya, the Buddha of the current age. Since ancient times, China has had female deities. Taoism had an earth mother whose all-creative womb was the cosmos, and the Divine Feminine has never been rooted out of Confucian patriarchal society. After three centuries, he was resurrected as Kwan Yin in China, Kwan Seum Bosal in Korea, Kannon in Japan, and Quan Am in Vietnam. Kwan Yin comforts human beings and saves them from disaster. One traditional image of Kwan Yin has her seated astride a tiger and holding a sword—which seems odd for a figure representing compassion and nonviolence.

For me, this version symbolizes the difference between ineffective and effective compassion. Too often, sympathetic persons neither do effective self-care nor truly resolve others' deep problems because codependence is not effective compassion; instead, it produces anger for everyone involved. Effectively compassionate people need to become brave and creative, asserting power in what some call *tough love*. For many Western Buddhists Kwan Yin has by choice become symbolic of an effectively compassionate person, more accessible than a patriarchal god, but certainly no less an enlightened being. She helps people practice spirituality without getting lost in patriarchal rules or rights, instead emphasizing attributes of intimate interaction and patient caring, which are required to become effectively compassionate.

The Varied Schools of Mahayana Buddhism

Five distinct sects of belief and practice developed within Mahayana Buddhism: The *Pure Land* sects believe that by only worshipping Amitabha and repeating his name believers can reach a heavenly state. All who faithfully call upon his name would after death be brought to his Pure Land paradise whence Nirvana would be easy.

The *Intuitive* sects of Zen (Chinese version Chan) seek enlightenment through disciplined intuitive insight, purging the mind of false ideas through years of meditation and/or *koans*, or word puzzles, offered by one's teacher (e.g., What is the sound of one hand clapping?). Nirvana is identical with the original Buddha-nature and is inherent in everyone. Enlightenment is the eventual discovery of the unity of understandings of "I" and "not-I," and depends upon the individual's meditative efforts. Zen has two primary branches: *Soto Zen*, founded by Dogen, advocates sitting meditation and chanting to gradually approach enlightenment; and the more intellectual *Rinzai Zen* argues for achievement of sudden enlightenment through koans and sitting and walking meditation. Many samurai adopted Renzai Zen.

Rationalist sects such as *Tendai* believe in long, disciplined meditation, but assert that emptying the mind does not necessarily produce intuitive enlightenment. Instead, once the mind empties of nonsense, people need to gradually refill their purified minds through the study of scriptures and with philosophical forms of meditation. Tendai Buddhism came to Buddhism through Dengyo Daishi, beginning in 805. He wanted to reconcile Buddhism with Shinto and Japanese aesthetics. *Kami* (Japanese deities) are more sacred than Buddhas; the phenomenal world need not be incompatible with Buddhist dharma. Aesthetic contemplation can lead to enlightenment, which is inherent in all things and is attainable by everyone.

The *Mystery* or *True Word* sects such as *Shingon* believe repetitive chanting of certain holy words and doctrines can by themselves trigger enlightenment. Shingon Buddhism arrived in Japan with Kukai in the 800s, emphasizing the tantric side of Buddhism. Truth is expressed directly through inner experiences, not easily attainable intellectually, but readily comprehended through rituals like mantras and mandalas that provide access to the "womb" realms.

Sociopolitical sects, such as *Nichiren* argue that effective Buddhism requires social and political activism, which has at times led to aggressive patriotism. The primary scripture of Nichiren Buddhists is the Lotus Sutra. Nichiren, who lived in the 1200s, emphasized a new Buddhist age. Everyone could be enlightened by simple acts of faith in the Lotus Sutra and a recitation of *Nam myoho renge kyo,* or "Glory to the marvelous teachings of the Lotus Sutra." Nichiren Buddhists argue that if everyone adopted Nichiren Buddhism,

Japan would become both a peaceful nation internally and a spiritual light to the world.

Buddhism in India Since the 13th Century

While Buddhism gradually gained power in most of Asia, it lost potency in India, partly due to continued invasions from the northwest that destroyed many Buddhist centers, but mostly because of Hinduism's ability to adopt elements of Buddhism and incorporate Buddha himself into Hinduism as a reincarnation of Vishnu. By 1193, when Muslim invaders reached the last of the Buddhist strongholds, there were relatively few practicing Buddhists left in India. Buddhism remained a minor religious community until the 20th century when it had a renaissance due to three factors: 1) repair and reconstruction of historic Buddhist monuments by Buddhists from other countries, with support from many Buddhist sympathizers among Indian citizens; 2) the immigration of hundreds of thousands of Tibetans escaping Chinese aggression; and 3) Dr. Ambedkar, father of India's Constitution, urged India's untouchables (Dalits) to convert from Hinduism to Buddhism to avoid caste discrimination and express their Indian pride. More than 7 million former Dalits are now Buddhists, which has given contemporary Indian Buddhism a strongly egalitarian and social and political reform agenda. India is the tenth largest Buddhist population, with 8 million participants, 90 percent of whom are Dalits, but Buddhists remain a tiny proportion of India's population, though millions of other Indians do revere the Buddha.

Tibetan Buddhism: Vajrayana Buddhism

There is a third major branch of the historic Buddhist family tree: Vajrayana Buddhism, the Diamond Way, usually identified as Tibetan Buddhism. Because of its geographic isolation and the demonology of Tibet's Bon deities, Buddhism did not arrive in Tibet until 630, when Song Tsan Gampo, a Tibetan prince, established a well-organized state in Lhasa, and introduced Buddhism to Tibet, primarily because his wives, from China and Nepal, were already practicing Buddhists. Buddhism continued to fail among ordinary Tibetans until the mid-700s, when a Bengali Buddhist teacher, Padmasambhava, vigorously spread a particular Buddhism then widely practiced in northeast India. Strongly influenced by medieval Hindu tantric doctrines, this Buddhism perceived the universe in terms of energy forces and the pervasive power of Shakti, the foundational energies. Padmasambhava argued that natural forces reveal a spiritual connection of male and female elements striving for union. Devotees are urged to meditate as they use their energies and learn to rise above their passions as they learn to expend them spiritually. Their iconography includes a multitude of male and female characters, often united in passionate sexual union. Its general sense of spirituality is the disciplined expression of passions rather than any rejection of passion. In Tibet's harsh, dangerous natural environments, this tantric Buddhism fit the necessities of living fully rather than rejecting life.

Tibetan Buddhism evolved into the worship of five celestial Dhyani-Buddhas who represented the directions along with their original Buddha-essences. The Dhyani, however, felt inaccessible to most Tibetans, and so became surrounded by a multitude of Bodhisattvas, each with a female consort, or Shakti, called *Taras,* and Tibetan Buddhists identified with one or more of them. Tibetan Buddhist spiritual practices include periods of fasting and prayer, repeated utterance of mystic mystery syllables, and monk-led rituals involving body movements, gestures, and sounds. These disciplines are practiced to visually evoke the divine person(s) and hopefully to merge with them, which became the Tibetan way of entering Nirvana. Thus, secret energies that are stored in each of us gradually become accessible, and then, in "thunderclap moments," may be released in mystical unions with ultimate reality.

Among Buddhists, the Tibetan way is unique in arguing that Nirvana can be achieved in a single lifetime. Tibetan images, even the benevolent ones, can appear hideous and frightening, which is intended to scare off demonic energies and protect positive ones, which causes the cowardly to hesitate and challenges the courageous to proceed. Ritual elements particular to Tibetan Buddhism include prayer wheels, mandalas, streamers, and prayer flags. Their preferred Sanskrit phrase is *om mani padme hum* (Praise to the jewel in the lotus).

In 2005, I spent a month in Nepal and a week in Tibet where I saw many of the primary Tibetan Buddhist sites and rituals. Tibetan Buddhist monuments and monasteries are filled with prayer flags and streamers, long lines of prayer wheels (carved vertical barrels filled with prayers and blessings, easily turned by anyone passing, which allows them to achieve spiritual merit). People fortunate enough to watch the creation of a sand mandala become mesmerized by their intricate and colorful designs. Mandalas are created, savored, then swept away and deposited in a nearby stream—a potent symbol for the transience of all material things. The amazing and sometimes melodious chants of Lamas can put even those ignorant of Buddhism into a blissful state. Many Tibetan lay-Buddhists have obvious calluses upon their foreheads and knees from repeated prostrations as they make long pilgrimages or repeat the three pilgrimage circles around the Potala, the former residence of the Dalai Lamas in Lhasa. My family and I made that several-mile circuit along with thousands of pilgrims, and were deeply moved by the experience, filled with prayer, meditation, and jubilation.

Tibetan monks are called lamas, or superior ones. Monks had monasteries that kept them protected and warm. Because of Tantric teachings, most monks married in the early centuries, and in many monasteries, sons followed fathers as their monastery leaders. During the 9th century, the monks' power was greatly increased when a Tibetan king gave the monasteries land grants and acknowledged their right to collect taxes from the tenants on their lands, thus unwittingly handing them political power. Centuries of civil strife followed, but by the 13th century, a Chinese Mongol Emperor had appointed one of the monastery's head lamas as Tibet's ruler. In the 14th century, after the fall of the Mongol Empire, the great Tibetan monk Tsongkhapa, the first Dalai Lama, organized his Yellow monasteries (the color of their hats and girdles) into the rulers of Tibet. He "purified" Tibetan Buddhism by declaring celibacy for monks, discouraged sensual excess, and made Buddhist practices and public rituals more rigorous. Subsequent lamas were chosen by colleagues through a process "discovering" his reincarnation—a child born close to the time of his death who appeared to have physical marks and personality traits similar to those of the recently deceased—using spiritual rather than genetic connections. Successive Dalai Lamas continued as Tibet's spiritual and political rulers for more than 600 years, until China retook power in 1951.

The Dalai Lama

The present Dalai Lama, Tenzin Gyatso, was born on July 6, 1935. The son of a farmer in northeastern Tibet, he was "discovered" at age two and enthroned at age four. He was educated with both Tibetan and Western learning, granted full political and spiritual power when he was fifteen. At nineteen, after some 80,000 Chinese military invaded Tibet, he negotiated with Chinese leaders, and at twenty-one visited Nehru in India and held joint talks with Chinese and Indian leaders. By 1959, however, Tibetans were in armed revolt against their Chinese conquerors; Lhasa exploded in demonstrations, and the Dalai Lama escaped to India along with more than 100,000 other Tibetans. The Chinese ruthlessly crushed the revolt, killed hundreds of thousands of Tibetans, destroyed most monasteries, murdered thousands of monks, and began to absorb Tibet, transforming it into a Chinese province with an emigrant Chinese majority. Many Tibetan Buddhists, including the Dalai Lama and much of the Buddhist leadership, now live in India and Nepal. Today, the Chinese government maintains a Tibetan police state; they imposed fake lamas and resettled Tibet with Han Chinese immigrants. Despite pervasive Chinese attempts to destroy, marginalize, or trivialize Tibetan Buddhism, it still burns brightly among indigenous Tibetans, and continues to bravely exemplify a proudly separate people.

Tibetans in India and Nepal have their own schools, handicrafts, and culture, and are busy making economic and political progress in their adopted countries. The Dalai Lama has helped establish Tibetan Buddhist centers throughout the world. He is one of the world's most respected spiritual leaders, revered even by many outside of his own religious community. He has helped exiled Tibetans evolve into a democratic, upbeat, and devoted people who model a variety of Buddhist virtues. In 1989, the Dalai Lama received the Nobel Peace Prize, which he accepted "on behalf of oppressed people everywhere and for all who struggle for freedom and work for world peace, and on behalf of the people of Tibet." He still hopes that Tibet will be liberated "with truth, courage, and determination as our weapons. Our struggle must remain nonviolent and free of hatred."

In *The New York Times Magazine*, Pankaj Mishra wrote that there were then 6 million Tibetans in Tibet, another 3 million in China, and 150,000 in India.

At age eighty, the Dalai Lama abandoned his temporal leadership and now addresses himself not only to Tibetans but to a nondenominational worldwide audience. He says that people must be realistic: If Buddhist scriptures are disproved by science, they should be abandoned. He urges people to go beyond religion and embrace principles of secular ethics of selflessness and compassion, which he points out are rooted in the fundamental Buddhist doctrine of interconnectedness.

Western Buddhism

James Atlas wrote in *The New York Times* that more Americans convert to Buddhism than to Mormonism, and that Buddhism is the fourth largest American religion. There are now at least 5 million American Buddhists; more than half of them, along with many thousands in Europe and elsewhere outside of Asia, are not ancestral Buddhists but instead spiritual seekers like me. Those who self-identify as Buddhists have found Buddhism their most useful spiritual practice. For some, this simply means their quest for individual peace through meditation, but for most of us it combines disciplined meditation to focus our minds and keep our minds and hearts balanced as we learn to express compassion more effectively.

Present Western influence on Buddhism is considerable and has a great impact on how it is practiced outside of Asia, as well as on how spirituality is generally perceived and practiced globally. Mindfulness meditation sessions are being sponsored by thousands of Westerners. Neurologists have demonstrated that human brains have extensive neuroplasticity (they continue to develop throughout life). Repeated research has shown that meditators significantly change their brains; they reduce blood flow in areas involved with anxiety while they increase flow to regions responsible for planning, decision-making, and empathy. Regular meditation increases practitioners' immune responses, improves emotional stability and sleep, and enhances creativity. It also makes people happier and healthier and helps them to remain more flexible. Professor Erik Braun believes that mindfulness meditation shapes people into systems thinkers, and that globalization is now producing revolutionary changes throughout the world: Americans and

Europeans are as often changed by non-Western ideas as the rest of the world continues to be changed by Western ideas and practices.

Mindfulness meditation originated in the early 20th century under Myanmar monk Ledi Sayadaw. His *Manual of Ultimate Truths* translated Theravada texts into a lay-based mass movement that he believed anyone could master in four months. His ideas swept through South and Southeast Asian Buddhist communities. Then, his disciple, Pa Auk Siyanda, argued that while even momentary concentration could produce results, more traditional doctrines were needed to gain genuine enlightenment, and proposed forty objects of meditation that would allow his practitioners to consider their present, past, and future lives.

The Insight Meditation Society (IMS) trained Americans Jack Kornfield, Joseph Goldstein, and Sharon Salzburg. Goldstein summarized Insight Meditation as becoming deeply aware of what's happening without inner commentary or external interference. Since the only power that our thoughts have is what we give them, it becomes vital to discern what power we give each thought. We must attend to our emotions without allowing them to turn into melodramas and be at home with them without being overwhelmed by them through the practice of daily meditation and periodic retreat from our daily routines. In *Lion's Roar,* Kornfield writes that love is the source of all our energies to create and connect. At a UUA General Assembly, Salzburg said that people need to redeem the word "faith" by having spiritual experiences themselves: They must question, examine, experience, and practice what they know and have tested deeply. My niece, Rebecca Reagan, began to practice Insight Meditation fifty years ago when she lived in Nepal; she had a long career as an English teacher abroad, and has led both an online and a local group from her home near Kansas City. Insight Meditation is at the center of her life.

One significant emphasis in Western Buddhism is upon *engaged Buddhism,* which uses the wisdom and serenity found in meditation to effectively go to work in healing the world. Engaged Buddhism has increased the intensity of Buddhist social and political involvement; it has shifted Buddhist compassion toward practical, long-term social change, and has helped activists to have more humility about their own ideas and practices. Engaged Buddhism places great emphasis on practicing reconciliation and nonviolent conflict resolution. An excellent book about engaged Buddhism is *The Path of Compassion,* edited by Fred Eppsteiner. Kornfield's essay therein distinguishes between the Buddhist virtues of love, compassion, and equanimity, and their "near-enemies": attachment, pity, and indifference. Love appreciates, while attachment tries to grasp and control. Compassion is empathetic, while pity is feeling different from but sorry for. Equanimity embraces the world while keeping one's own internal balance, as opposed to indifference, which is withdrawal from and failing to care for others. Joanna Macy's essay states that there is no self to defend and we can help to empower reality's evolution. Power is not a zero-sum game but a win-win process like the energy found in synergies, neural nets, computer webs, and ecosystems.[5]

Elements of Buddhism that I Find Troubling

I consider it a mistake to turn the Buddha into a deity with magical abilities or mythic histories; I prefer to revere human beings who have managed to become exemplary in certain ways or who've had persuasive insights. Pieties of whatever sort, including Buddhist ones that focus primarily upon gaining one's personal enlightenment as a separate being, seem practically sacrilegious to me. We are more likely to become spiritually mature and ethical human beings by remaining actively engaged with others, including intimate relationships. Mahayana Buddhism's emphasis on compassion and being a hopeful and life-affirming person regularly engaged in ordinary life and service to others is attractive, as is Tibetan Buddhism's emphasis on the integration and transformation of energies not only within us but between and among people and communities. I identify with engaged Buddhism, as opposed to isolated or solitary Buddhism.

The overwhelming tendency in contemporary culture is to commercialize and trivialize almost everything. This certainly makes countless options available for those with discretionary income and time, but it also often cheapens and dilutes them into meaninglessness. This is happening with spiritual practices as well. The *Financial Times* (2/17) reported that there were 1,300 apps devoted to mindfulness and meditation, and the Global Wellness Institute estimates that the mindfulness industry is worth about $1.7 billion. Choices, access, and availability can be valuable, but to take responsibility, to be persistent, and to continue humble daily practices remains foundational to any fulfilling spiritual life.

Reincarnation remains a central concept explicitly or implicitly embraced by most Hindus, Jains, and Buddhists. All religions address human concerns about a physical afterlife. I find it likely that our individual spirits do continue in some fashion after our physical deaths from our present bodies, but I don't believe that any living person can be assured about the form post-death existence will take. Given present knowledge, it's unlikely that earlier religious visions about heaven or paradise were true. Humans often have feelings of "much yet to accomplish"; such feelings make reincarnation attractive. I've fantasized about returning as a faithful dog, a free-flying cliff swallow, a woman, or some other future person, to finish my spiritual journey. Who doesn't have visions of an afterlife connected with our present lives and intimates? For me, such visions appear intellectually untenable. What seems probable is that we become one again with the world's energies, and in doing so, are "reborn" within reality to complete "our" journey as embodied energies, but perhaps not as individual beings.

Elements of Buddhism that I've Found Particularly Relevant

Buddhism has been and continues to be central to my spiritual understanding and practices. Our son is named Rahul for the Buddha's son, and for a Hindu mythic hero who retrieved the Sun. After I graduated from seminary, I added Zen meditation to my spiritual practices; I learned it from two extraordinary members of the Bloomington, Indiana, UU Church: Esther Robinson, a psychiatric social worker in her sixties who led the meditation group, and Dr. Julia Thom, a retired physician in her seventies who lived at her rural Christmas-tree farm. Our Zen meditation group sometimes comprised only the three of us, and I wouldn't have persevered without the patient witness and instruction of these amazing women. If they could maintain an uncomfortable position for forty minutes at their ages, unfocused eyes upon the exterior world while intent upon penetrating their own consciousness and searching for its connections with spiritual realities, surely I should have the fortitude to do so, and I did eventually learn to sit still and quiet my mind, though meditation sessions felt like time and effort

I could hardly afford. After about six months, however, there was an occasion when the bowl of my consciousness finally stood sufficiently cleared of unnecessary turmoil so that, for moments, it filled to overflowing. As others who've experienced a spiritual breakthrough will relate, you never forget those moments, and hope the rest of your days to experience comparably intense insights and fulfillments.

Thich Nhat Hanh

I seek a spirituality that helps me become meditative *in* the world, not separated from it. I want spiritual practices that empower me to become a gentle but effective activist. In 1987, I read Thich Nhat Hanh's *Being Peace,* and in 1989 I attended a weeklong silent retreat with him and his companions at the Omega Institute in Rhinebeck, New York. Hanh coined the term "engaged Buddhism." He wrestled there with how to be in the world without becoming totally addicted to and possessed by the illusions of everyday living. As a civil rights and antiwar activist, I was attracted to this activist monk who appeared to combine the best of Buddhist efforts to search for inner enlightenment while simultaneously trying to express compassion in a world exploding with conflict and turmoil.

Hanh was born in 1926, near Hue, Vietnam, became a Zen Buddhist monk, editor of a Buddhist magazine, initiated a Buddhist university, and founded Youth for Social Service (SYSS), which trained monks, nuns, and laypeople to become nonviolent peace workers who would voluntarily go into rural areas throughout Vietnam to establish schools, healthcare clinics, rebuild villages being decimated by the war, and sometimes put their bodies between conflicting soldiers in that civil war. In 1965, his organizations asked the opposing forces to stop the war and live with mutual restraint; he left for the U.S. and was not allowed to return to Vietnam until 2007. In 1969, he became a delegate to the official peace talks and peace accords, which were finally signed in 1973. Since then, he has led efforts to rescue refugees from piracy and mistreatment, and founded a spiritual community, Plum Village, in southern France, as well as establishing other monasteries and teaching centers.

Hanh focuses on *mindfulness,* arguing that people are like a TV set with many channels. If we turn on compassion and insight, we are those; turn on sorrow and anger, then we are those, so we cannot permit one channel to dominate our consciousness. No one can eliminate life's basic hindrances, including sensual excesses, anger, laziness, agitation, scruples, and doubt, so instead we need to learn to convert them into more positive and effective energies and actions. A person who is mindful meditates on suffering without rejecting the world, on the homeless nature of truth but continues to orient toward the good, on the quandaries of reality while still acting responsibly, and meditates upon transcendent possibilities while embracing interdependence.

When we meditate on our achievements, we come to understand that they are not really ours alone. Countless people and events have made them possible; we are part of communities of achievement. While we acknowledge our failures, we need to recognize that we have often done the best we could in that time and those circumstances. If we cannot learn to have compassion for ourselves, how can we do so for others? We must not remain wedded to our past experiences or former truths but become truly open to new truths and wisdom from other people and traditions. Thich Nhat Hanh urges us to consider using any routinely repeated action as a possible form of meditation. Since I was a teenager, I've usually cleaned the dishes after meals. Hanh helped me realize that washing the dishes was already one of my spiritual practices, that I could wash the dishes with deep attention, even joy, as a source of peaceful satisfaction. Try taking a few deep breaths before you respond to any electronic stimuli, to linger with any source of frustration until you can turn it into a smile, and to reflect upon your anger until you can transform it into loving understanding and effective action.

In his book *True Love,* Hanh says that love contains four basic aspects: loving-kindness, compassion, joy, and equanimity. Loving-kindness provides full and honest presence, really listening and then responding kindly but honestly. Compassion is the realization that another person is suffering; that recognition frankly conveyed allows the sufferer to not be alone in her suffering. If we make room, there is joy in even the bleakest situations. Help people reawaken to the daily miracles that surround us. Always do what you do with a portion of joy. Equanimity is getting back in balance within yourself and as a member of communities so you may find fulfillment, act responsibly, and become fully able to live with joy.

Throughout their lives, all human beings are simultaneously engaged in two continual struggles, one with the world, and the other with themselves. People tend to concentrate on their struggles with others, but much of our despair, confusion, and doubt stems from our internal struggles with the different facets of our own being. This struggle *within* is what Buddhists have concentrated on for 2,600 years. Meditation's task is not to chase away or suppress the energies of anger, jealousy, and fear, but instead to transform these potent energies into insight and love.

The Dalai Lama

A portion of my daily spiritual practice is to consider spiritual mentors; I summarize each with three short phrases. For the Dalai Lama they are: to overcome anger; face limitations; and find happiness through equanimity. Few people have faced as many provocations to anger or limitations as he. Anger, for him, represents an exaggerated desire for separation from someone or something he is unable to bear or wants to harm. Realistic analysis is his favorite form of meditation. If we recognize our interdependence and acknowledge that we all struggle, we realize that we share the human condition. If we listen and communicate, we can get our anger in perspective. Change needs to happen through our own forgiveness to move past our anger. We need to learn to control our words and gestures to transform anger into compassion.

The Dalai Lama tells the story of a child who often got angry, so her parent gave her a hammer and a bunch of nails and asked her to pound a nail into a fence every time she felt angry. First day, thirty-seven nails, but finally a day came when she pounded none. Pleased, she went to her parent, who praised her for overcoming her anger and told her that each subsequent day she had without anger, she could remove one nail from the fence. After many days, she had pulled all the nails. Again, her parent praised her for learning to overcome her anger. They go to the fence. See, you have done well, but look at all these holes. The fence will never be the same. When you say things in anger, they leave scars in people just like those nail holes. You can put a knife in a man and draw it out, but no matter how many times you say I'm sorry, his scars will remain. It is better to feel regret and ask for forgiveness for your anger than not to do so, but better yet not to let your anger loose in the first place.

The person with equanimity tries not to possess or control the objects of her love. You can't become effectively compassionate unless you learn how to be fair without self-condemnation. Happiness is the primary object of life; we find it when we overcome anger, face our limitations, and continue to do our best to live with equanimity.

In 2010, the Dalai Lama visited the high-tech hub of San Jose, California. As a leader of a Bay Area interfaith group, I had the privilege of sitting with him. He argued that there are four levels of mind: encounter; analysis; contentment; and love. He believes that shared faith in realistic analysis and an energy-based universe provides powerful connections between the scientific and intellectual communities and realistic, life-affirming spiritual communities. Many scientists have made mystical connections while dedicating their lives to reason and scientific experimentation. I share the Dalai Lama's confidence that these shared spiritual understandings can become more explicit between scientists and other intellectuals (who reached their mystical senses of wholeness and enlightenment primarily through scientific experiments and sustained analysis) and with dedicated spiritual seekers (who may have found their mystical connections to energy through traditional spiritual practices, but who are also happily science-based and thoughtful, embracing human beings). Like him, I seek happiness by transforming anger into effective compassion, acknowledging life's limitations, and approximating equanimity through an enthusiastic embrace of scientific method and spiritual practice.

My own journey in Buddhism includes not only my own experiences and practices, and those of many congregants I served, but also my children. Both have Buddhist images in their homes and at times practice Buddhist mindfulness and compassion more effectively than their father. I treasure a memory of my daughter, Leela, who at age three was guided by a Tibetan monk in completing a tiny portion of a Wheel of Time mandala at the Museum of Natural History in New York City. We can't know how what we do will "stick," but when I'm with Leela's daughter, Stella, now ten and passionately engaged in some project of her own imagining, I wonder whether she intuitively grasps the sacred evolving transience of all Creation. When my son, Rahul, was a Stanford student, he spent six months in Japan where he occasionally visited a Zen priest who kept several tricycles that he rode exuberantly around the temple courtyard. For Rahul, this conveyed living fully in the present moment.

Chapter 8
Taoism

Ancient Chinese Religion and the Central Beliefs and Practices of Taoism

In Asia, the old is seldom cast away; its enduring truths are usually integrated into present cultural traditions. In Hinduism, Jainism, and early Buddhism, the focus of spiritual discoveries was upon the illusory and transient aspects of both the natural world and human civilization. Many of their spiritual seekers tried to escape everyday reality to gain spiritual liberation. In contrast, the Chinese tended to focus upon the practical, realistic, and concrete, affirming nature and ordinary human existence. They wanted to prolong life and extend human powers harmoniously with nature and culture. The Chinese less often conceived the spiritual to be opposed either to nature or human relationships. Philosophically, the Chinese are both humanists and naturalists. In their scheme of things, from ancient times, humans, nature, and ultimate reality (Heaven) were thought to be interdependent—continuously impacting each other. Not only do nature and the ultimate powers shape human lives and civilization but humans also affect nature and even heaven. For while they are unequal in potency, they are mutually interdependent.

Taoism came to represent a strongly naturalistic faith, and Confucianism a clearly humanistic faith, both with roots in Chinese indigenous folk religions. As in other cultures, the Chinese gradually evolved from earth-centered to heaven-centered worship and from animistic beliefs (where everything was alive) to distinguishing the living from the dead and the organic from the inorganic. The earliest Chinese believed that a giant first man, P'an Ku, created the world out of chaos (in a role somewhat analogous to that of the Hindu god Vishnu). P'an Ku eventually transformed himself into China's five sacred mountains: Hua in the west; T'ai in the east; Sung in the center; one Heng in the north; and another Heng in the south. They believed that eons ago there had been a Golden Age in which ancient emperors shared the blessings of civilization: Fu Hsi domesticated animals, taught people to hunt and fish, and invented musical instruments; Shen Nung taught agriculture and medicine; Huangdi, the Yellow Emperor, helped people learn how to make buildings, use silk, and invented a calendar and money. Also ancient was the preeminent Chinese symbol and its philosophy of Yang and Yin, with its consorting tadpole-like shapes: one white with a black eye, the other black with a white eye, together filling a circle. Yang is the Sun, white, full of light, masculine, warm, dry, procreative, and positive. Yin is Earth, dark, female, wet, mysterious, and negative. Yang's growth and success has a strong internal tone of *shen* (good spirits), while Yin's failure and decay contains internal *kwei* (bad spirits). No other people have been as obsessed with good and evil spirits and energies as the Chinese, except for the ancient Zoroastrians in Persia (modern-day Iran).

Ancestor worship was central to Chinese indigenous religion; it is still important and prevalent among millions of Chinese worldwide. The Chinese perceive the dead to be dependent upon the living because the living may, through appropriate respect and rituals, help ensure their ancestors' peace and harmony. Relatives who abandon or betray their families become "hungry" (lonely, needy) ghosts when they die. In turn, the dead may continue to aid the living through advice, thus continuing to promote their living family members' health and prosperity. Early Chinese rulers set up a vassal system to collect taxes and promote public order. By the 2nd century BC, a strong spiritual hierarchy developed in which richer and more powerful people had their separate rituals, while common people were limited to worshipping their ancestors and household guardians.

Lao Tzu

Lao Tzu is the acknowledged author of the *Tao Te Ching*. He may have been the archivist in a western area. Confucius may have been a contemporary, but we have no evidence that they met. Lao Tzu means old boy or grand old master, probably an honorary name. Our knowledge about him is a mosaic of myths. Best known is that as he grew old, he was so saddened by people's disinclination to cultivate the natural goodness he had advocated that he left home to seek solitude. Riding on a water buffalo, he headed westward toward Tibet. The Han Kao Pass gatekeeper sensed Lao Tzu's deep wisdom and persuaded him to share it, so he paused and wrote the *Tao Te Ching: The Way and Its Power,* his only book, and then disappeared. This little book and amazing mythic figure are Taoism's foundations.

The *Tao Te Ching* has only 5,000 linguistic characters or words, and is divided into eighty-one poems, the shortest with four lines, the longest less than a page. Mystical and naturalistic, they portray a deep wisdom that often seems to speak directly to our unconscious. For eons, they have guided, sometimes governed, millions of Chinese. In recent generations, they have also influenced, inspired, and transformed millions of other lives worldwide.

Taoism's central concept is the Tao, which has three distinct sets of meanings. Tao literally means path or way. The first set of meanings is that the Tao is the way of ultimate reality, the ground of being, what transcends, making the Tao the womb from which all life springs and to which it all returns—clearly ineffable, far too vast for any definitive human definition. This is reflected in the classic Taoist saying, "Those who know don't say; those who say don't know." The second set of meanings of Tao is: the way of the universe, the ordering and integrating principles of the world, the driving power of nature, the eternal laws, the immanent, the Mother of the world. The final set of meanings are the habits of human living that mesh with the Tao; that is, when humans' good lives reflect, connect, and are "in flow" with the ultimate reality and with the laws of nature. I have included some verses from the *Tao Te Ching* to illustrate this third set of meanings of *Tao.*

#24: You cannot stand steadily on tiptoe or run rapidly forever, and the arrogant are not respected.

#28: Have man's strength, while practicing woman's care, and remain honorable while maintaining humility.

#30: When you advise a ruler, counsel him not to use force, which only causes resistance, but rather to do only what needs to be done to achieve results.

#48: Effective power lets things take their course without interfering.

#52: Control your senses and life is abundant; rush around while always talking produces despair.

#61: Those who would conquer must yield.

#66: Leaders guide their people with humility so that they do not feel oppressed.

#67: From mercy comes courage, from economy comes generosity, and from humility comes leadership.

#68: A good fighter is not angry, a good winner is not vengeful, and a good employer is humble.

#72: It is disastrous to lack a sense of awe.

#79: Quarrels leave a residue of resentment, while a wise person keeps her half of the bargain without demanding that others do so.

#81: Forget possessiveness: the more you give or do for others, the greater abundance you will possess.[1]

Historical Evolution of Taoism

All three branches of Taoism that developed focused on different meanings of Tao: *popular* (magic) *Taoism, vitalizing* (energy) *Taoism,* and *philosophical* Taoism. Popular Taoism adopted most of traditional Chinese folk religion. It is filled with magic rituals and sacred texts to be uncritically accepted, transforms Lao Tzu and other Taoist sages into deities, and is populated by faith healers, shamans, and psychics. Its intention is to make cosmic power accessible to ordinary people by acting as a magnifying glass that focuses cosmic energies for the welfare of those in need of help; it represents a spiritual "magic."

Vitalizing Taoism

The goal of vitalizing Taoism is to increase the energy available to people by concentrating upon the Chinese concept of *Ch'i,* or vital energy. *Ch'i* means breath, but this breath represents the basic form of or metaphor for human energy. People learn disciplines to dislodge their internal blockages to energy and draw Ch'i from the world around them by eating specific foods and medicinal herbs, and through acupuncture. *Tai chi* and *Chi Gong* are central disciplines for Vitalizing Taoists: a synthesis of calisthenics, dance, meditation, yin/yang philosophy, and martial arts. They use a type of "yoga" much like Hindu raja yoga, with psychosocial experiments, including sexual disciplines, like the Tantric yogin, in which, for instance, the man, by internal manipulation, tries to keep his sperm within his own body during intercourse, based upon the theory that this allows him to absorb the yin of his female partner without dissipating his own yang energies. I see no reason why this wouldn't work in reverse for female partners.

Philosophical Taoism

Philosophical Taoism teaches that knowledge is power; that to live wisely is to conserve life's vital energy by not expending it in useless, draining ways. The world is interconnected, so wise people use their energy to connect with the world. The universe's divine forces interact effectively with each other rather than trying to impose their independent wills upon it. That's what people should also do to follow the Way. Philosophical Taoism is most relevant for many modern spiritual seekers, including me, so I'll concentrate on its evolution after briefly sharing the histories of magic-religious and vitalizing Taoism.

The Evolution of Magic and Vitalizing Taoism

By the 1st century AD, magic Taoism was the dominant form. Chang Tao-ling founded a secret alchemy sect in Western China. His son and grandson built the sect into a movement with hundreds of thousands of adepts who lived together on Dragon Tiger Mountain in Kiangsi province and considered Chang Tao-ling their celestial teacher. They probably borrowed ideas from Zoroastrians who had traveled from Persia. Other Taoist magic sects flourished until after 1100. For instance, the Yellow Turban sect also had hundreds of thousands of adepts and took political control over the length of the Yellow River valley during the 2nd century AD. In the 7th century, Emperor Li Shih-min, who established the great Tang dynasty, made Taoism China's official religion, partly so as to compete with the influx of "foreign" Buddhism. By 1012, Emperor Tsung, of the Sung dynasty, was losing northwest China to the Tartar hordes and announced that he was receiving celestial messages from a new celestial being, Yu Huang, whom he made the high god in a growing pantheon with obvious Taoist gods and goddesses, heaven and hell, and multiple paradises, both in the eastern seas (between China and Japan) and on the three isles of the blessed. Getting their ancestors out of hell became a major obsession for the Chinese populace. A Taoist trinity evolved: Yu Hua, Lao Tzu, and Ling Pao (the Jade Emperor).

Many pre-Taoist popular mythic figures were added to this celestial complex. Within this framework there evolved four perceived levels of cultivated practice or wisdom: 1) *human immortals* who had lived long, healthy lives and were good role models; 2) *earth immortals* who, like the Old Testament Methuselah, had lived an incredibly long time; 3) *spirit immortals* who live forever, some in their bodies and others as liberated spirits; and 4) *celestial immortals* who are deified, like Lao Tzu and Chuang Tzu, and considered manifestations of the cosmic energy of the Tao itself.

What fascinates me about this complex of evolving wisdom is that most of them, whatever their level, were believed to have lived as ordinary people: healers, scholars, bureaucrats, teachers, social activists, military commanders, entrepreneurs, or politicians. Some lived in solitude, others amid society. All shared three things: early interest in the Tao, shunned fame and fortune, and lived simple and unencumbered lives. Taoism strongly suggests that power corrupts, so it becomes critical to know when to withdraw from seeking or exerting your power in action.

The most popular figures in Chinese mythology are the eight Taoist immortals–figures who preceded Taoism by centuries and retain fallible personalities. Ching Liu Chuan: a famous general who saw past the illusions of power. Lu Tung-pin decided against learning any technique that would delude or harm people and pledged (like a Buddhist bodhisattva) not to enter immortality until he had helped all sentient beings return to the Tao. Zhang Guolao is an old man with a mule, a great magician who willfully disappeared, demonstrating humility's magic. Tsan Kuo-chiu is a hermit aristocrat who realized that the way to heaven is through our hearts. Ho Hsien-ku is a woman who awes everyone with her knowledge; she taught that the arts of immortality should not be abused by the selfish or power-hungry. Lan T'sai-ho is a wandering musician and cross-dresser, who is overdressed in summer and often naked in winter—like a medieval fool or minstrel. Han Hsiang is the faithful nephew—a symbol of the wise relative who guides his family members. The eighth immortal is Tieh-kuai Li, an expert at traveling out of his body. His servant mistakenly thought him dead while he was out of his body and had it cremated, so Tieh-kuai had to magically take over the dead body of an aged, crippled beggar who leaned upon an iron crutch. (Spiritual wisdom can get people into a fix). The eight Taoist immortals remain central to Chinese consciousness and mythology, with magic and fantasy, but are also diverse, idiosyncratic, and so very human.

Evolution of Philosophical Taoism

Philosophical Taoism argues that the primary ways human energies are dissipated are through friction and conflict. It urges us to avoid interpersonal aggression, intrapsychic self-defeating behaviors, and fruitless attempts to conquer nature or rebel against the inevitable. The way to power is the way of *wu wei,* creative quietude. In practice, Wu wei becomes effective actions that enable disciplined persons to allow the world's powers to flow through them. By aligning with the Tao in daily life, you learn to ride the boundless energy and delight of Creation. Active, relaxed, and supple, you become able to stop standing in your own light. You let go into true creativity, become part of nature's rhythm and ultimate reality itself, and reflect simplicity and freedom, now calm, increasingly selfless, and progressively able to shed dissipations. By getting in touch with Tao, you allow behavior to become spontaneous, realizing the way to do is to be.

Chuang Tzu

In the 4th century BC, Chuang Tzu became the great popularizer of philosophical Taoism. He wrote thirty-three brilliant essays, with witty anecdotes, allegories, and imaginative conversations. He challenged Confucian principles, and explained Taoist transformations in ways somewhat analogous to contemporary chaos theory, with objects originating in the whirl of becoming, and time having circular qualities, with seasons and phases that create and destroy each other. He argued that no human regime lasts. Those who arrive in the wrong time or circumstances are called usurpers, while those who come at the right time and place are called defenders of right. The final goal of human life was the ecstasy of absorption into the quietude and ultimate truth of the Tao. His anti-institutionalism went far beyond Lao Tzu's ideas. Like Rousseau, Chuang Tzu seemed to argue that institutions often confuse people's natural wisdom and sense of equality. He expected Chinese artists, poets, and musicians to try to convey in their arts the eternal Tao in nature. He also enabled the spread of magic Taoism by arguing that not only ancients but also contemporaries could become "immortal" through meditative trance, alchemy, or the consumption of odd substances.

Chuang Tzu told the story of Prince Wen Hui's cook, who could cut up an ox with a whisper. His secret was his awareness of the spaces between their joints, which afforded him the room that his blade needed. This was the secret of wu wei: seeking out life's and nature's empty spaces and moving through them. This takes disciplined training and great intelligence, but it permits effective people to appear effortless as they do their best work. People barely recognize their best leaders because they talk little, fulfill their aims, and their constituents think they have done the work themselves. Chuang Tzu's books helped people apply Taoism in their daily lives.

Chuang Tzu's Writings

In *The Middle Course:* Avoid fame when you are striving on behalf of others, avoid disgrace when striving for self. Pursue a middle course: keep a sound body and mind and fulfill your duties.[2]

In *Nature of God:* Knowledge is dependent upon fulfillment; fulfillment is uncertain, so how can we be sure that our divine is not too human or that our humanity contains divinity?[3]

Tao of God: The repose of the sage is not what the world calls repose. Nothing disturbs his equilibrium, like still water reflecting like a mirror.[4]

In *Confucius and Lao Tzu:* Gratitude, receiving, giving, self-censure, instruction of others are instruments of right. Only those who can adapt themselves to the vicissitudes of fortune without being carried away by life's tragedies and triumphs are fit to instruct others[5]

In *The Value of Hsi P'eng:* A true leader forgets the authority of those above him, and makes those below him forget his own authority by sharing his virtue with others.[6]

In *Nang Yung:* Model people share their food, but also the happiness of God, and refuse to join in censuring, plotting, or toadying. They remain prepared for the unexpected, and deferential to the rights of others. Inevitable calamities do not disturb what they have already achieved.[7]

Chuang Tzu emphasized that yin and yang were complementary. Human excellence requires long, patient training so our actions appear spontaneous, and requires us to retain the ability to remain open to new perspectives, for no point of view remains universal.

Elements of Taoism that I Find Troubling

I'm not attracted to magic or to vitalizing Taoism. I don't consider Taoist figures divine or, in many cases, even historically significant; rather, I view them as mythic images, relevant because of their admirable human qualities, not for any suspected or surmised magical powers or superhuman abilities. For me, the eight Taoist immortals convey simply a naturalistic and humanistic way of talking about the spiritual search. We have a beautiful embroidery version to remind us that the search is full of unexpected surprises.

I do not assume that the deceased can help me or others, though it is conceivable, but I do give daily, prayerful respects to my parents, grandparents, and other deceased relatives, teachers, mentors, and friends, not out of fear but out of deep gratitude for the love, guidance, and support they gave me. As I've aged, I find myself increasingly impressed with their character.

I'm skeptical of the vitalizing Taoists' attempts to find magical things to ingest or ways to take shortcuts to a life of power. I don't advocate attempts to gain without giving. I don't doubt, however, that T'ai chi, Taoist yoga, and acupuncture have wisdom to teach us if we have the patience and discipline to learn it. I find most of vitalizing Taoism too much like some Western New-Age solutions, shallow and shortsighted, at times manipulative and false, though occasionally profound.

Aspects of Taoism that I Find Particularly Relevant

My first encounter with Chinese culture was a landscape print placed prominently at my maternal grandparents' front door. It portrayed a magnificent mountain scene with a waterfall, a river, distinctive boulders, crags, and forest, a few flying and wading birds, and a deftly drawn tiny boat in the river, with an even smaller fisherman aboard. The painting reflected my boyhood understanding that nature was beautiful and vast, while our human imprint upon it often appeared insignificant. When, as a teenager, I was introduced, to Lao Tzu's *Tao Te Ching,* its nature-based mysticism represented the essence of my mother's naturalistic faith, which had also become my own. Before I graduated from high school, Lao Tzu's "creative endeavor without possession, action without aggression, and development without domination" had become my daily mantra. Other translations of that passage vary, but an aspect of the richness of great poetry and scripture is that similar ideas may be translated in different ways, each appropriate and with relevance for particular individuals in varied circumstances.

While much of Western art tends to be symmetrical, a charming aspect of much East Asian art is that it may initially appear to be unbalanced or focused on the odd or ugly, but upon closer observation reveals that the artist has perceived the inherent beauty in the ordinary or even in the grotesque, whether it is a broken branch, a crooked cat, or a frail old man. My first conversations with Chinese Americans were in San Francisco (1962), when I interviewed a few spiritual leaders about peace in the midst of the Vietnam War for a college report. They didn't trust me and were noncommittal. My first visit to Chinese territories was to Hong Kong in 1970. In 1997, Kathleen and I traveled for three weeks in the eastern half of China, including the Guilin area, its karst mountains so much like my grandparents' painting. In 2013, we made two visits to Taiwan, first to its western pilgrimage spots during the Chinese New Year, and later to its mountainous national parks, partly still inhabited by indigenous Taiwanese. We visited a variety of Taoist temples and shrines, in Lukang village with a million people on their biggest festival day.

Water, particularly waterfalls, have great spiritual significance for me. Water is the essential natural metaphor for philosophical Taoists. Nothing in the world is as soft and yielding, yet nothing surpasses water for dissolving the hard and inflexible. The soft overcomes the hard; the gentle overcomes the rigid. If we have the patience to wait until our mud settles and our "water" is clear, we will perceive reality more clearly. Can we remain unmoving till the right action arises by itself? If we come to understand the basic life forces, we realize that they will sustain us. Then we can stop flailing and let life support us as we float along. Since my young adulthood, waterfalls have put me into a nearly instant spiritual state, a feeling of direct connection with the universe's ultimate powers. Whenever I have the opportunity, I sit silently in meditation at a waterfall, and soon settle into a meditative state. These experiences have consistently been occasions of peace, and often embraced me in overwhelming feelings of transcendence.

Chuang Tzu's explanation of the cook's carving skills reminded me of having taught Boy Scouts as a camp counselor: two of my tasks were to supervise Scouts in the ax yard, helping them to learn how to chop wood safely; and how to properly carve a chicken. In both tasks, finding spaces, joints, and other natural separations made chopping and carving sometimes seem almost effortless whispers. As a nonviolent activist, like the philosophical Taoists, I strive to minimize aggression or cutthroat competition while I simultaneously strive to maintain appropriate humility. It's often the space within an apparently solid object that makes it useful—like the holes in a vessel, a door, or a window. Profit may accumulate from what is there, but usefulness often comes from what's not there. It is generally counterproductive to try to dominate nature. Taoist attitudes present a rather contemporary consciousness. As in their landscape paintings, humans remain a relatively small part of most realities, tiny in the beautiful vastness and complexity of nature, but we, with our journeys to make, burdens to carry, and hills to climb, are also part of the whole.

Confucians and even religious or vitalizing Taoists might want "ideal" responses that could be infinitely imitated with formality, show, and ceremony. These things leave philosophical Taoists cold; they avoid them whenever possible. For them, all values and concepts are ultimately relative to the mind that entertains them. Chuang Tzu dreamed he was a butterfly; then he awoke and found he was Chuang Tzu. Afterward, he wondered whether he was really Chuang Tzu who'd dreamed he was a butterfly, or a butterfly that was now dreaming it was Chuang Tzu. Life may wear us out with work and duties, but also gives us rest in old age and peace in death.

Philosophical Taoism is rather similar to contemporary mysticisms, which celebrate and savor life, doubt magical religion and quick salvations, but retain a strong sense of a graceful ultimate reality of which we are part, and revere the natural order at work in the world. These contemporary spiritual seekers also seek to learn how to be in flow with the way of Creation, to remain in rhythm with natural laws and cosmic unfolding, and to fulfill themselves as individuals while they help sustain the Earth and the common good. Taoism empowers my intuitions to be a creative steward of my gifts and a progressive who tries to act effectively while striving to resist temptations' attempts to overwhelm "my way."

Taoism also remains personally challenging. I still struggle with impatience and anger and continue to have occasional delusions of grandeur. Taoism's admonitions to be patient, empathetic, supple, and a careful listener remain important. Taoism urges us to seek nature's effective energies so we may flow spontaneously through life's turmoil with little wasted motion.

Taoism presents a spontaneous, transcendent naturalistic mysticism to balance the Confucian virtues, which are full of roles and responsibilities in human society. It argues that we need to pursue lives of voluntary simplicity, unencumbered by idolatrous goals or wasteful needs; that to become most effective, we need to focus our spiritual energies on generosity, kindness, integrity, and courage. We need to remain grateful for life while remaining aware of our illusions. The primary dilemmas are how to maximize our energies while deploying them in ways that not only develop and sustain us but also help to heal the world. For the philosophical Taoists, a good life includes the profundity of mysticism, the direct wisdom of empowering experiences, and productive connections with teachings and rituals.

Many of us are naturalists, our spiritualities grounded in ecology and evolution. We perceive ourselves as participants in and with the natural world. Taoism can help us become part of the benevolent and constructive powers of nature while it helps us minimize our futile attempts to "conquer" nature or struggle against the inevitable, and learn to shed self-defeating behaviors and minimize personal aggression. As Lao Tzu wrote: "Creative endeavor without possession, action without aggression, and development without domination." We can all benefit from regular quiet time amidst nature, meditating on what we can learn from the natural world. Then, in good Taoist fashion, we need to use those insights to reflect, empower, and sustain natural evolution and transformation. Perhaps then, as Lao Tzu said: "What the caterpillar calls the end, the rest of the world calls a butterfly."

Chapter 9
Confucians

Central Confucian Beliefs and Practices

Confucianism is based firmly upon the ideas and example of Confucius himself. His primary writing was *The Analects,* which Confucius wrote to teach people how to behave with each other. He wanted to improve the entire social order by helping people be fully human, which for him, meant becoming more altruistic. As you will see, many of his ideas are commonsense:

- What you do not wish done to yourself, do not do to others.
- Do not cherish resentments.
- Do not wish for quick results, nor seek unjust advantages.
- Practice what you preach.
- When you know a thing, realize that you know it, and when you do not know a thing, understand that you do not know it, and admit your ignorance.
- When you encounter worthy people, emulate them. When you encounter unworthy people, minimize your contact with them, but use their actions to examine your own character.
- Be intimate only with the virtuous.

Confucius

Confucius was born in 551 BC, north of Shanghai in Shantung province. His father died when Confucius was two; he was raised by his impoverished mother who managed to help him become educated. As a young adult, Confucius married, had a son and a daughter, and became a tutor, but judged himself as only moderately successful in these roles. He fervently wished to become a political advisor, but his candor and integrity threatened leaders. He was exiled from his province for thirteen years and wandered from state to state trying to be hired by a ruler. He was invited home only when he was too old to become a public official. He taught students and edited classic texts, and died at age seventy-two, still unknown by most Chinese.

Confucius' Ideas

As centuries passed, Confucius' editions of Chinese classics became the standard versions. His philosophical union of a hierarchical but benevolent family structure with parallel governmental structures served the powerful superbly, so his ideas came to dominate Chinese society. He lived in a time of great social and political turmoil when some of his peers (Realists) argued that force and violence were necessary or even desirable; others (Monists) believed that people should concentrate upon mutual love. Realists assumed that people were shortsighted, their baser impulses tending to dominate their nobler ones, so people needed clearly defined penalties and rewards. The Monists argued that Heaven loves the whole world and prepares all for human good, and people should therefore act with mutual love.

Confucius proposed a compromise between the Realists' cynicism and the Monists' romantic idealism. He argued that laws and governments backed by force can set limits but cannot generate love or companionship, and that while love is vital, it must be supported by social structures and a collective ethos. Neither governmental force nor personal commitment alone can produce peace and harmony. Asked if one should love one's enemies, Confucius replied: "Answer hatred and violence with justice and love with benevolence. Otherwise, you waste your benevolence." Confucius believed that ideas usually need to gain a level of general acceptance, and that is much easier if they can be connected with already cherished cultural traditions. However, if ideas are going to succeed, they must also work effectively in present circumstances.

Over the centuries, Confucius' translations and interpretations of Chinese classics were further shaped by later scholars. Teachers. students, bureaucrats, and citizens used his ideas to learn not only how to become literate but also how to think and cooperate. By emphasizing worthy aspects of China's ancient traditions, Confucius helped the Chinese create their "second natures." People become people by understanding, disciplining, and training their animal natures. They would and should gradually develop allegiances to larger and larger communities.

People can develop a social, even global, consciousness, capable in maturity of nurturing inner imperatives and a reliable personal moral compass. People are by nature good, but goodness is, at first, largely implicit, so it needs to be nurtured and renewed throughout life. Good practices need to be learned, and then regularly used by either individuals or societies to actually embody goodness within life's complications. Relationships are the essential tools for living, particularly family relationships. Properly understood, these become models for other relationships between friends, colleagues, employers and employees, leaders and citizens. Social disciplines and constraints also remain necessary for civilization to be preserved and nurtured. Practicing the habits of civility is a life-long discipline.

Five Central Confucian Virtues

Confucius' teachings had five central *virtues*: 1) *Jen* – human-heartedness: respectful to one's self and empathetic toward others; 2) *Chun Tzu* – gracious initiative, seeking not primarily what you can get out of others but what you can, with integrity, do to accommodate others; 3) *Li* – living with character and grace by carrying no pleasure to excess or trying to be gratified to capacity; 4) *Te* – the powers by which people are ruled; leaders need to overcome pride, anger, and vanity both in themselves and among their people, primarily through their own examples; then, a leader is like the wind, and the people become like grass; and 5) *Wen* – the arts of peace, believing that the aesthetic realm nurtures peace, teaches virtue, and improves human nature.

Confucius was no democrat; he didn't believe that most people could lead a government or run a bureaucracy. Like Plato, he believed that virtuous leaders were needed to harmoniously shape a virtuous citizenry. Confucius constantly sought the mean between unworkable extremes. Saintliness in isolation has no meaning. The self is simply a node of relationships, a meeting place where lives converge. Living life is like a bird adjusting her flight to air currents. Authority needs to be earned. Complicity in the face of unwarranted authority represents failure. A fully realized human expands empathy indefinitely.

The Swiss developmental psychologist, Jean Piaget, said that human maturation is a process of decentering. Confucius would have agreed that what needs to happen as people mature is that we should grow beyond self by strengthening our family, thus we transcend selfishness; then grow beyond family by nurturing our communities, thus we transcend nepotism; then grow beyond our communities by serving the nation, thus we transcend parochialism, and mature beyond nationalism to all of humanity, thus we counter chauvinistic nationalism.

Confucius concentrated on daily life and on humanity. He felt that the best way to honor one's ancestors was to take care of their living relatives and to prepare the world for their descendants. He did his best to change the emphasis in China from ancestor worship, magic amulets, and mystic ceremonies to mutual respect and a well-ordered society. He remained reserved about the supernatural, but did believe there was an ultimate force on the side of right. In traditional Chinese fashion, he thought humanity formed an evolving trinity with Earth and Heaven. While he said, "He who offends the gods has no one to pray to," he remained clear that people were good primarily by the practical good they accomplished and because of the tempting evils they avoided. This was to be managed through respect, generosity, empathy, and love in daily relationships. The 21st-century Neo-Confucian scholar Tu Wei-Ming writes:

> If we cannot go beyond the constraints of our species, the most we can hope for is an exclusive secular humanism advocating man as the measure of all things. By contrast, Confucian humanism is inclusive. Humanity forms one body with Heaven and Earth and enables us to embody the cosmos in our sensitivity.[1]

Like Socrates, Confucius could be called a one-person university; he taught by asking his students questions and discussing problems with them. What he added organizationally was the necessity of having wise teachers and lifelong students, saying that those who learn but do not think are lost, while those who think but fail to learn are in great danger. Confucius posed questions, cited classical passages, and interpreted them using apt analogies; then waited for his students to arrive at effective answers. He applied the classical Chinese disciplines of ritual, music, archery, chariot-riding, calligraphy, and calculation.

He concentrated on preventing people from destroying themselves by teaching them to leverage their natures to conquer the destructive aspects of their animal instincts. Through generations of trial and error, people had discovered certain ways of behaving that contributed to social well-being; those needed to be consistently applied. Good manners had to be learned in family intimacy, while the rituals of civility had to be learned in our larger social, organizational, and cultural settings. There were and always will be superior people, and they should be in charge, whether as the benevolent father in a family, the elder in a clan, or the emperor or Communist Party leader.

Confucius had high standards for all positions of authority. Reciprocal obligations needed to be practiced in each relationship, so cruel, corrupt, or dissipated rulers in a family, clan, or nation are not doing their jobs. Their improper expressions of power and lack of integrity will lead to tragedy and chaos. Power did tend to be disproportionate, so their obligations and their own and others' expectations also needed to be unequal. The male— older, more senior, and more powerful—might be in charge and rightly have expectations of cooperation from women, the young, employees, or ordinary citizens, but if there were failures, blame was appropriately placed upon those in charge, because they held the power. Integrity, character, effective communication, and ennobling and nurturing leadership were expected from the powerful in each human relationship.

Confucius Reorganizes the Chinese Classics

Confucius organized the classics that preceded him into five books: *Poetry (Shih Ching)*; *Rites (Li Chi)*; *Annals of Spring and Autumn (Ch'in Ch'iu)*; *History (Shu Ching)*; and *Divination or Changes (I Ching)*. For Confucius, the moral-ethical dimension was preeminent, and *Poetry* was the best text for developing moral-ethical understanding. *History* provided stories from life; *Annals* connected people with natural laws; *Rites* shared the successful trial and error of unfolding civilization; and *Divination* was a door to the realms of mystery and intuition. Here are passages from the books of *Rites* and *Poetry* that reflect Confucius' willingness to look unblinkingly at the tragic truths of life while also drawing out moral precepts for effective living.

From *The Book of Rites:* "Humanity is the heart and mind of heaven and earth…. truthfulness in speech and the cultivation of harmony are advantageous, while quarrels, plundering, and murder are disastrous."[2]

From *The Book of Poetry:*

> Compassionate heaven, why have you contracted your kindness, sending down death and famine….How is it that you seemingly exercise no forethought or care?….Why are people who have done no crime indiscriminately involved in ruin?….How vast is God, the ruler of humanity….but the nature it confers is not to be depended upon….All are good at first, but few prove themselves to be so at the last.[3]

Confucius' own ideas were gathered into three books: *Analects (Lun Yu); Great Learning (Ta Hsueh);* and *Doctrine of the Mean (Chung Yung).* These texts reflect his laser focus on ethical development as a process of empathetic broadening and deepening.

The Analects state: The superior person thinks of virtue, while the inferior person is obsessed with comfort; the superior person thinks of the sanctions of law, while inferior persons concentrate upon favors they might receive. In conducting yourself practice humility in serving superiors, respect in nourishing ordinary people, and kindness when directing people. Give the aged rest, grant friends sincerity, and treat the young tenderly. Reciprocity is the single word that could become a rule for all life practices. One should practice courtesy, generosity of soul, sincerity, earnestness, and kindness. The superior person honors the talented and virtuous; praises the good, pities the incompetent, and bears all.

In *Great Learning:* From the Son of heaven down to the mass of people, all must consider the cultivation of the person to be the root of everything else .... If you would become sincere, extend your knowledge and experience; if you would rectify your heart, become sincere in both thoughts and actions; if you wish to deepen your character, rectify your heart. Having cultivated your own character, you may then effectively regulate your family. Having effectively governed your family, you may lead. Proven an effective leader, you may rule a nation.

From *Doctrine of the Mean:* Show forbearance and gentleness in teaching others; do not practice revenge. Meet death without regrets. Seek equilibrium and harmony. Success depends upon previous preparation. Benevolence is the foundation for human character and the central exercise in benevolence lies in loving one's relatives. Righteousness is the practice of appropriate and effective actions with other people and in groups; its great exercise is honoring the worthy.

Confucianism's Historic Evolution

Confucius' paternalistic but responsible hierarchy of reciprocal social responsibilities provided an ethical framework for the realities of the Chinese social system, which made Confucius a central figure in their history. By 130 BC, Confucian texts were the foundation for training government officials. By AD 59, daily sacrifices were made to him in every school, and by the 8th century, temples had been erected in his honor throughout China. His ideas dominated the largest and most enduring empire in the world for over 2,000 years.

Mencius

Mencius (372–289 BC) was born about one hundred years after Confucius' death. Taught by a grandson of Confucius, Mencius became the most prominent writer in the Confucian school. He believed that all people were born with tender shoots of goodness, that heaven was benevolent and concerned with human welfare, but that goodness needed to be nurtured. People were born with awareness of others' suffering and dislikes, a sense of shame, natural deference, and a rudimentary sense of right and wrong. People needed to be taught and nurtured so mercy could become benevolence, shame could be transformed into righteousness, and deference would grow into propriety, so their embryonic sense of right and wrong could mature into moral wisdom. Mencius believed that some people labored primarily with their minds while others mainly used their strength, and that it was appropriate for the mind laborers to govern the strength laborers, and that most people accepted this division of responsibilities. He perceived a vast, flowing river of vital energy (chi) within each person, which needed to be nourished by uprightness. By doing so, people could avoid most injuries. He perceived nature primarily in terms of the natural energies within us, so a person's chi could evolve to pervade the whole space between Heaven and Earth.

Mencius recognized that people's environment and circumstances are crucial to their development. He felt that those born in difficult circumstances or bad times more easily abandon themselves to evil. People can be directed toward evil, but usually these tendencies are abetted by outside forces. Those favored by their times and circumstances are most likely to develop the moral courage and mental stamina to pursue the worthy within themselves, and are more likely to reach greatness, while those out of step with their times or oppressed by their circumstances tend to follow their inferior inclinations, committing evil and may even become inhuman.

Nonetheless, ordinary people are the most important participants in governments and should not be neglected. Existing paternalistic feudal systems, if administered on behalf of the populace rather than primarily for aristocrats, could become just governments. Since wars tend to destroy the very possibility of attaining good government, he consistently opposed state violence. He did not believe people could or should love everyone equally. Cultural norms of kinship and social structure were necessary because it was natural to pay more attention to one's family, friends, neighbors, and colleagues; but the interests of the innocents must be considered and responded to without allowing oneself to remain obsessed with only selfish or shortsighted concerns.

Xunzi

The Path is a fascinating book that I enthusiastically recommend as a deep dive into Chinese thought. Journalist Christine Gross-Loh and Michael Puett, Harvard historian and chair of its committee on the study of religion, climaxed their book with a chapter on Xunzi (b. 310 BC), who has recently received a renaissance of attention as a major Confucian thinker. He did not want people to gloss over other's less altruistic impulses and was long perceived as a sort of anti-Mencius. Xunzi's major contribution was his emphasis on what he interpreted "wei" to be, which he called artifice. The crookedness in human nature can be straightened through artifice, from which effective rituals emerge. Being natural or authentic is a kind of artifice. The belief that we should act naturally prevents us from recognizing better ways we could become creative, and neglects our responsibilities for the world around us. Human culture and society have arisen through countless acts of artifice. People have constructed the world between Earth and Heaven, and they can and should continue to change it for the better.

Hsun-tzu (298–238 BC) became another realist alternative to Mencius. Hsun-tzu was an important officer at the court; he even served as a magistrate until his death. Hsun-tzu rejected Mencius' cardinal assertions that human nature is innately good and that Heaven watches over Earth and humanity with personal concern. Instead, Hsun-Tzu asserted that humans are naturally bad and become good only if they constrain their unruly natures, learn the rules of propriety, and obey laws that compel them to respect the personal rights of others. He thought that Heaven was simply our name for the laws that operate from natural events, so people should not expect Heaven to respond to prayers. Winter won't be abolished just because people dislike the cold. People must learn to nourish themselves by exercising their bodies and faculties regularly and practice thriftiness to enrich themselves.

He believed that nothing supernatural happened during ceremonies, but thought they were helpful because ceremony introduced beauty into peoples' lives, cultivated their sense of propriety, allowed for a catharsis of their feelings, and provided repeated examples of beautiful and good actions. Reverence increases respect; faithfulness promotes responsibility and loyalty, and self-sacrifice nourishes love; each age should judge for itself what is useful within its traditions. Hsun-tzu produced an effective synthesis of Confucian principles for human relations and governmental and economic arrangements that allows us to function effectively within realist concerns about human flaws. People need to be guided by nature, but humans can't manipulate natural laws by ritual or magic. People must find their own ways through civilized living and meditative reflection upon nature's way. While the Tao does not evolve steadily toward a superior future, its impersonal ways do ultimately lead to good.

An outgrowth of this synthesis was the Legalists, who argued that everyone should be bound by laws and precedents that rewarded the law-abiding and punished the guilty regardless of rank or position. The Legalist wanted to strengthen the emperor and govern through bureaucrats, while weakening the regional nobility. Allowing common people to rise would undercut the nobles and decrease corruption. Their greatest successes were during the reign of Shih Huang-Ti, who united China by 221 BC and declared himself "First Emperor" (of the Qin Dynasty). He radically reorganized the Chinese bureaucracy, destroyed older public records, mandated a new Chinese scrip and currency, and built the Great Wall. Legalist realism reinforced a hierarchy of bureaucratic managers who followed legal precepts and manipulated the people from above, which has influenced China ever since.

During the following Han dynasty, its rulers instead nurtured a dreamy Taoist quietude during which alchemy, magic potions, and quests for immortality, or at least long life, became popular. Then, during the reign of the great Han Emperor Wu Ti, whose empire stretched from India's border into central Asia and penetrated Korea, it was Confucian scholar Tung Chung-Shu (179–104 BC) who provided another radical modification of Confucian teachings. He combined the Legalist idea that government needed religious backing with Confucian doctrine. Then, Confucian Wang Ch'ung (AD 27–100) attacked religious superstition and supernaturalism; he argued for a more empirical Confucianism, which was thoroughly naturalistic and humanistic. Wang Ch'ung even dared present Confucius as a fallible person.

Throughout most of the next 2,000 years, the major developments in Chinese religion involved growing syncretism among Buddhism, Confucianism, and Taoism, while significant elements of folk religion also continued among most Chinese. Between 220 and 570, political and social chaos made its rulers appear unable to provide either political safety or economic or social harmony. Taoism felt too passive; Confucianism too formal and bureaucratic, and Buddhism made great strides, for it was fresh, lively, and provided personal paths to enlightenment, peace of mind, even salvation. Leaders of each faith suggested various mixtures of the three religions. A Taoist, T'an Ch'iao (6th century AD) said the Tao tied the three together. Chinese Buddhists placed images of Confucius, Lao-tzu, and Buddha together on their altars. Wang T'ung (583–616), a Confucian, argued that the Doctrine of the Mean was the middle way shared by all three faiths.

Zhu-Xi

Zhu Xi (1130–1200) was the next major prophet of Confucian teaching. He declared Hsun-tzu's realism heretical and replaced it with Mencius' faith in both the inherent goodness of humanity and the benevolence of Heaven toward humankind. He accepted elements of Taoism and Buddhism as sound and argued that all things were brought into being by energy (chi) and by the law of rationality (Li). For Zhu Xi, the Great Ultimate was the Tao, but his Tao was neither static nor ultimately equalizing; instead, it was dynamic and differentiating. He was theologically agnostic yet believed in a *will* that ordered the cosmos. The Tao generates the chi to produce yang and yin and all material elements. All of nature reflects some aspect of rational law (li) of the Great Ultimate that works within it. In human beings, the Great Ultimate works as the inner guiding principles, in the form of Li embodied as mind and spirit, while the vital energies (chi) provide people's powers of action. The rational principle and the vital force interact in mutual dependence. To practice continual awe for the interconnectedness of cosmic being can keep people on a wise spiritual path.

Zhu Xi's own spiritual practice was essentially Buddhist silent meditation, which he saw as aiming our minds so that we can effectively concentrate on what is good, which enables us to practice the good with our actions. He argued that people need to develop reverential attention. By learning from our mutual dependence and concern, which we usually experience in our intimate relationships, we can train ourselves to care constructively for life, other people, and ourselves. We must learn to study wisdom intimately yet continue to question every teaching. We must develop the ability to see ourselves in others, while imagining them in their own circumstances. In these ways, we can manage and positively change our experiences of the world. Daily experiences become opportunities for concern about suffering, but we need to patiently build experiential wisdom in order to find effective ways to respond to suffering. By a century after Zhu Xi's death, his interpretations were treated as definitive, and from 1315 to 1905 were read and even memorized by almost all educated Chinese.

From 1200 until the 20th century, Confucianism tended toward a state cult. Most Chinese continued to combine folk religion and family rituals, often along with a primary allegiance to Buddhist, Taoist, or Confucian teachings and practices, while over the course of their lives, also connecting themselves with the other two religions to some degree.

Chinese Spirituality in the 20th and 21st centuries

After the 1911 Revolution, there was no emperor, and the new constitution contained a declaration of religious liberty, so Confucianism was no longer the official state religion. The Kuomintang Nationalists, however, took as their motto the Confucian virtues of loyalty, filial piety, benevolence, human-heartedness, fidelity, just attitudes, harmony, and peace. Their leader, Chiang Kai-Shek, made the four guiding principles of his newly inaugurated New Life Movement courtesy, justice, integrity, and self-respectful modesty.

Into the 21st century, Taiwan has retained an identifiably Confucian public temperament. When we traveled in Taiwan in 2013, we visited Tainan's temples on the southwest coast, and saw examples of folk religion, Taoist, and Confucian traditions. In the small town of Lukang, we joined a million people celebrating the Chinese New Year. There were dragon dances and special family rituals, and along with countless sticks of incense, people burned handfuls of fake paper money in the temple furnaces. The temple of Mazu, goddess of the sea, especially important to the Taiwanese, was the most mobbed. There were few non-Taiwanese present, and we were swept along in the crowd's bursting combination of joyful festivity and solemn reverence, as rituals seeking forgiveness, good fortune, and long life were celebrated. Huangdi, patriarch god of Chinese nationhood, Guandi, god of business, and Caishen, god of wealth and prosperity, were specially feted.

With the dawn of the People's Republic of China on October 1, 1949, mainland China became officially atheistic. The government declared that state and religion were now firmly separated and that religions were to be rejected as either feudal or colonial. During the 1966–67 Cultural Revolution, these antireligious policies were implemented brutally: thousands of places of worship and other revered ancient sites were destroyed; and countless religious leaders and devoted believers were killed or forced to renounce their beliefs and practices. By 1978, however, a new Constitution included a declaration of religious freedom, but its liberties were severely constrained since it did "not permit any disruption to public order, impairment of citizens' health, or interference with the regime's education system." In the 1980s, Taoism and Buddhism were again officially recognized as helpful to building a harmonious society. In 2006, China hosted its first Buddhist World Forum. Catholics, Protestants, and Muslims were also officially tolerated, but were often publicly shamed as arrogant and colonial. "Freedom" was circumscribed with Communist-appointed leadership for each permissible tradition, along with strict rules for what practitioners could and could not do. If they stepped beyond these limits, their religious expression was quickly controlled.

In 1998, my wife and I traveled in China for three weeks. In Hangzhou, we visited what I would characterize as a Buddhist theme park. It had beautiful concrete and plaster "restored" Chinese Buddhist historical monuments, conveniently located together for easy tourist viewing, and well attended, mostly by Chinese. We also visited Shanghai's famous temple of the Jade Buddha, which had a stream of worshippers, as well as the impressive Little Wild Goose Pagoda in Xian, and a beautiful ancestral temple in the southern city of Guangzhou. The religious monuments I found most moving were the Buddhist cave-temples in and around Guilin (perhaps also partly restored). We also encountered Taiwanese tourist groups proudly carrying Mazu boxes on their chests, Muslims praying publicly at an airport; also, we saw a few Christian churches. There were pervasive signs of ancestor worship—not only in rural areas but on Grand Canal barges and apartment balconies.

The dominant Han Chinese, now 91 percent of the Chinese population, treat the fifty-five official ethnic minorities as anthropological specimens and consider them inferior to the Han majority. Public religion is perceived as good public relations and its mostly reconstructed monuments and buildings as domestic and foreign tourist opportunities. Many Chinese are as disdainful of open religiosity as they are of non-Han peoples. Throughout the history of the People's Republic, it has been government policy to move Han people into minority areas so they gradually become either the local majority or serve as a controlling influence, whether in Guilin, Tibet, and probably now in the Islamic Uyghur area, where they also "re-training" the Uyghurs themselves. Government officials choose the bureaucratic leadership for all accepted religions, including a government-selected Dalai Lama, and continue to strongly regulate all public religious observance.

Despite the statistic that most of the world's officially nonreligious people live in the People's Republic, ancestor reverence, folk religion, and strong elements of Confucianism, Taoism, and Buddhism continue to pervade Chinese culture. *Economist* magazine (2/3/07) wrote that the Chinese leadership increasingly perceived organized religions to be necessary to ensure a harmonious society, and understood that faithful, energetic participants in religious communities could help provide traditional Chinese stability amidst social and economic flux. It stated that at least 100 million Chinese were Buddhists; there were 25,000 Taoist priests, and more than 100,000 identified places of worship.[4] The *Chicago Tribune* stated that lectures on contemporary Confucianism were the sensation of that TV season, that Confucius' *Analects* was China's best-selling book, and that then President Hu Jintao had incorporated Confucian emphases of unity and respect for authority into his call for a more harmonious society.[5]

Contemporary China has built the world's largest Buddha and its tallest pagoda and stupa. Throughout China there are many religious "theme parks" made up of restored sacred icons, monuments, and temple complexes. In 1998, we visited one above the Yangtze River called Ghost City Fengdu. Ironically, the people of Fengdu have since been displaced by the flooding of the huge Gezhouba dam. Ghost City Fengdu was a theme-park version of Earth, Paradise, and Hell. Earth was stately, with many bridges to cross; its idol of Lao Tzu bore no resemblance to the wise, humble man I'd come to know in the *Tao Te Ching*. Paradise looked like a carnival park with a white-faced God high on the hill. Hell, the most interesting, had the best view of the Yangtze, soon to rise many hundreds of feet above the flooding of the gorgeous lesser Yangtze gorges, which we visited before they disappeared. The underworld lords seemed almost benevolent with their obvious passions, though these enormous plaster guardians were demonstrating how the damned would be tortured eternally. Why do human visions of hell appear so interesting and fun to observers? Why do some people appear to secretly idolize or show such interest in what they officially abhor?

In 2010, research at Shanghai University research found that 31 percent of Chinese identified themselves as religious, with 56 percent practicing ancestor veneration, and two thirds of the religious identifying as Buddhists, 5 percent Christians, and 2 percent Muslims, the remainder being combinations of Taoism and folk religious elements. Buddhism is growing in popularity among younger and more urban Chinese. In many rural areas, Taoist clan organizations are still sometimes almost indistinguishable from the present political and economic power structures. A 2012 Chinese family study among twenty-five majority Han provinces found that while only 10 percent belong to an organized religious group, and 90 percent identified themselves as nonreligious, only 7 percent were fully nonreligious in practice; i.e., neither believing in gods or spirits nor practicing any rites or ceremonies. Confucianism is again growing in popularity among intellectuals and scholars, and Confucian and Taoist ideas and practices still pervade Chinese society. President Xi Jinping recently expressed hope that "traditional cultures may fill the moral void and fight corruption."

When Mao Tse Tung wrote his magnum opus. *Quotations from Chairman Mao.* aka *The Little Red Book,* it's obvious that, like the First Emperor twenty-two centuries earlier, he sought to choose among the Confucian virtues and radically reform classical Confucianism. While clinging to a moral code founded upon a family-based ethical system, he applied it to the relationship between himself as a paternal father-ruler with the Communist Party as the ultimate authorities for the Chinese people. Mao wrote: "Go to the people and learn from them; then, consider how to shape their ideas into practical programs which they will understand as fulfilling their heritage; then, return to the people, and implement these principles creating and maintaining a harmonious and unified society."

Elements of Confucianism that I Find Troubling

Political and cultural leaders in China have consistently used Confucian principles to justify their positions of power and dominance. This has remained true whether they were ancient emperors or now modern dictators, controlling husbands, fathers, and elders, and support currently favored classes throughout the many centuries of China's history. The Communist government in China does so now by treating the non-Han minorities as anthropological inferiors and by assuming that, if the government wants to act in certain ways in the global arena, their Chinese choices are naturally superior. Communist dictators continue to treat their own people as pawns, and too many Chinese feel they can bankroll the destruction of sharks, birds' nests, and African and South Asian mammals to possibly lengthen a few of their lives. If non-Chinese wanted to kill off pandas or other Chinese indigenous species for a similar purpose, the Chinese would of course be horrified. This Confucian conflation of religious principle with existing assertions of power and dominance represents my primary criticism about Confucian principles. Much like the political misuse of principles in other religions, such false and unjustified domination has rarely lived up to Confucius' own high standards of mutual sacrifice, for he justified domination only when extraordinary power was paired with extraordinary self-discipline, empathy, and self-sacrifice.

I'm no fan of divination, but I believe that human spirituality is significantly discovered, celebrated, and practiced in intuitive and mystical experiences. Not everything worthwhile in life can be put into a logarithm or statistic, nor dissected or replicated by scientific experiments. I do not support state sponsored religions. I embrace Confucius as a wise, ethical teacher, but certainly not as either superhuman or a perfect being. I credit him with being aware of many of his own limitations and generally demonstrating humility, but because of his ambition to become a political advisor to rulers, I believe he gave more credit to the ruling classes than I do, and certainly provided a more conservative embrace of traditional gender, family, and group structures than I would. The problem with any form of paternalism is that powerful individuals are left to control their own behavior. In my experience, the ambitious and successful are most likely to overreach and abuse. This happened with Shih Huang Ti and Mao Tse Tung. Social and political checks and balances must remain central to any social system to control the overly ambitious and power-hungry. The benevolent paternalism of Confucius needs to be controlled by the realization that chi exists in every person and by acknowledging that women and minorities have been routinely mistreated and undervalued.

I understand but don't agree with Mencius' idea that those born in difficult circumstances or bad times more easily abandon themselves to evil, while those who are favored by their times and circumstances are most likely to develop the moral courage and mental stamina to pursue the worthy within themselves. Neither do I believe that those so favored by birth or circumstance are more likely to become great, while those who are out of step with their times or oppressed by their circumstances tend to follow their inferior inclinations. Statistically, those born in fortunate circumstances are indeed more likely to succeed academically, socially, and economically by the standards of their times and cultures, but greatness actually seems to favor humans who face significant challenges presented by their environment, birth, or upbringing, but are nonetheless able to surmount these obstacles and then take advantage of the opportunities available to them. Some of our most creative people were ahead of their time and overcame disadvantages and tragedies in their lives to achieve greatness. Confucius and Mencius are excellent examples. Both failed their personal goals to become prominent advisors to a leading ruler, but found solace in scholarship, and only became famous after their deaths.

Elements of Confucianism that I Find Particularly Relevant

My focus is on this life and this world, and especially on how people cooperate and organize in groups, which made Confucianism attractive from my first youthful reading of the *Analects*. For Confucianism presents itself as straightforward principles for a moral life and ethical and political actions built on a foundation of universal human relationships between parents and their children, siblings, spouses, friends, and political leaders and their citizens. Within egalitarian and democratic boundaries, I find much worth embracing in Confucian teachings, both those of Confucius himself and other Confucians who followed, such as Mencius, Xunzi, Hsun-tzu, and Chu Hsi. Confucianism has much to offer to people with a humanistic and naturalistic philosophical and/or spiritual outlook.

I agree that becoming a mature human means becoming more altruistic. I resonate with his admonitions to not cherish resentments, to realize when you don't know something and admit your ignorance, to emulate exemplary people and to seek intimacy with the virtuous while using necessary contacts with difficult people to further your examinations of your own character. People need love, social structure, and participation in a collective ethos. Neither governmental force nor personal commitment can alone produce social peace and harmony. A more practical standard answers hatred and violence with justice, and love with benevolence. To become realities, ideals do need to gain general acceptance and to do so is more likely if these new ideas can become associated with elements celebrated from our culture's past. Any proposal needs to work effectively in the present to become a reality. I too have found poetry and music primary adjuncts to moral and ethical understanding, and often a direct way to put my spiritual experiences into action. Aesthetic realms serve me well spiritually, and often have been charmingly actualized by East Asian traditions. History provides useful stories from life; seasons help people get in touch with natural laws, and rites do reflect our human journey through trial and error into the wisdom of civilizations.

With Confucius, I believe that maturation implies allegiances with increasingly more global communities. Human goodness may be implicit, but it needs to continue to be practiced, and that requires self-discipline and social constraints. I find his five virtues useful: empathy; gracious initiative; moderation; that leadership requires curbing one's own pride, anger, and vanity; and that the arts of aesthetic peace nurture harmony and virtue. The self *is* primarily a node of relationships, and maturation does require decentering. We need to negotiate every encounter and situation to achieve practical shared resolutions between seemingly unworkable extremes.

For me, ethics does not imply that man is the measure of all things. Instead, I agree with the Chinese belief that we need to learn to work in harmony with the universe and with nature, to grow beyond our animal needs and selfish pride. Those with advantages should expect larger responsibilities and make greater self-sacrifices. People must become politically active in all their relationships. Negotiation, compromise, reconciliation, truth-telling, or tough-love, and forgiveness are as necessary in every intimate relationship and friendship group as within a community, city, nation, or global political arena. I admire Confucians' recognition of the need to nurture that sort of politics in their religious faith, for these truths have too often been at least partly lost in Western religions and philosophies.

In many ways, I find Hsun-tzu's realism truer to my understanding than Mencius' idealistic benevolence or Confucius' fervent hopes about both people and leaders. I disagree with Hsun-tzu that people are bad, but I do think that we need to learn how to be good. As Mencius suggested, goodness may be implicit at birth, but it needs to be continually nurtured. It's unlikely that Heaven routinely responds to prayers, or that people can manipulate natural laws, but like Hsun-tzu, I believe that spiritual practices help people to be good by introducing beauty into their lives, cultivating propriety, and allowing for a catharsis of their feelings. Ceremonies often provide people with repetitive examples of beautiful and good actions. Reverence increases respect, faithfulness often promotes responsibility, and self-sacrifice can nourish love. As Hsun-tzu argues, each age should judge for itself what is useful in its traditions.

I find Chu Hsi's reformed Confucianism attractive in its understanding of the universe as essentially energy governed by dynamic and evolving laws of rationality, and share his vision of an energy-centered, naturalistic Great Ultimate, which becomes embodied in humans as mind and spirit, its inherent energies providing people's powers of action. With Chu Hsi, I hope that the rational principle and the vital force interact in mutual dependence. Like him, I don't revere God as a super-person or believe that God routinely answers prayers by manipulating the natural order; rather, I perceive God as a cosmic ordering *will*, and that our human goal should be develop as much harmony with it as we're able. I resonate with Chu Hsi's perception that the goal of meditation is to help us effectively do good in our actions.

Like many global contemporaries, Confucians are humanists focused on this life and this world; however, they realize that humanism is actualized through intentional participation in communities and by stretching this connectivity and responsibility to a global scale. We can gain much by embracing this relational and community-oriented humanism. As Confucius urged: "To fit ourselves some tasks to do to well employ our days....to be fair to people when they err, when good your pleasure show, their faults be quick to understand, in judging them be slow."[6] Life becomes a continuing process of quiet self-criticism about our relationships and commitments followed by refreshed actions based upon our new insights, and then, again, reflection and meditation, followed by further actions.

Chapter 10
Shinto and Japanese Spirituality

Central Beliefs and Practices

For more than two eons, the Japanese have perceived themselves as a divine nation permeated by innumerable kami (goddesses/gods, spirits, sacred nature, supernatural powers). Shinto, their "way of the gods," has no historic human founder, official scripture, or fixed system of doctrines or ethics. Like the Chinese, the Japanese think of themselves (or humanity) as coequal with heaven and earth. Significantly informed and shaped by Chinese influences beginning in the 6th and 7th centuries AD, Japanese spirituality became an ever more complex tapestry of indigenous and foreign religious and cultural traditions woven together in unique Japanese fashion.

Japanese polytheism is practically limitless. Not only are the emperor and nobles divine but every Japanese individual is descended from divinities great or small. Any natural object—even any power or energy—may be considered kami. The enduring residual aspects of this blending of national patriotism and ethnic identity with spirituality and morality, called *kokutai*, makes it sometimes difficult to distinguish between what Westerners might consider patriotism or ethnic identity from what some Japanese consider their fundamental cultural and spiritual solidarity.

The ancient ancestors of the Japanese were a mixture of peoples who had invaded the Japanese islands from Korea, Mongolia, Malaysia, and the South Pacific islands. They intermixed with and eventually displaced the aboriginal Ainu, driving their remnants ever farther northward among Japan's islands. Until the late 19th century, Japanese history was largely shaped by intermittent internal warfare. In the 1st century BC, there were three primary centers of Japanese culture: a southwestern clan worshipping the sea kami, a western clan focused on the storm kami, and the Yamato clan, who lived at the northern edge of the Inland Sea and were focused on the sun goddess. The Yamato clan sealed its dominance by seizing the imperial throne and declaring their leader a descendant of the sun. Then they prudently combined the most prevalent myths into a single comprehensive way of the gods.

The core of Japanese myths is the belief that the primal male and female gave birth to Japan. Their last child was the fiery heat god who, during birth burned his mother badly. Ashamed of her distorted appearance, she descended to the underworld. Her husband tried to rescue her, but the prospect of him seeing her in a decayed state shamed her. This caused her husband to purify himself, and his acts of purification caused the birth of Amaterasu, the sun goddess. Aware of the world's disorder, she sent her grandson, Ninigi, to restore order. He ruled from Kyushu, and his descendant, Jimmu Tenno, Japan's first emperor, moved the capital to the main island. The most prominent Shinto shrine is at Ise. The central symbol of the sun goddess is a mirror, thought to be her embodiment, placed at the shrine about AD 260. In Amaterasu's myth, the other gods used the mirror to lure her out after she had darkened the world by isolating herself. They placed a mirror at the cave's entrance and made a commotion. Amaterasu looked out to see what was going on, saw herself in the mirror, thought she had a rival, and came outside to challenge her.

The following provides some Japanese character ideals.

Emperor Mimaki-iri-hiko-inie was wise, unassuming, reverential, and practiced self-restraint. He capably adjusted the instruments of government and worshipped the Gods of Heaven and Earth. The people's welfare was well-served, and the Empire was peaceful. Great Goddess Amaterasu wished to reside in the shrine at Ise where she had first descended from heaven. If you want to swim in the sea of Brahman, you must make many ineffectual attempts before you can successfully swim there....the mind when unrestrained luxuriates in idle thoughts, but when vanity and egotism drop away, Divinity manifests itself.[1]

These stories exemplify central themes in Japanese spirituality. Divine and human lives are full of conflict and disappointment unless people and kami are careful, disciplined, and live within their laws and customs. Early in their history, the Japanese accepted a religiosity led by a centralized, political-military elite. Spirituality meant learning to do the will of divine forces, but this required not only diligence and intelligence but also self-restraint. Shame was probable, so the need for purification was likely, and purification rituals became a central aspect of their spiritual practice. Religion became a process of rituals at shrines and prayers to meet life's crises. Japanese spirituality is clearly focused on a person's intuitive sense of her heart's feelings and intentions. Faith is how one feels and what one does or fails to do, rather than adherence to an ideology, dialectic, logical inference, or doctrines.

Historic Evolution of Japanese Spirituality

When the first Korean Buddhists arrived in 552, Emperor Kinmei received them. At first, Buddhism was popular only with the Soga clan, but by 588 their leader, Umako, had seized power and made his niece, Suiko, empress. She appointed her nephew, Shotoku, as regent. An ardent Buddhist, Shotoku sent Japanese scholars to China to study Buddhism and learn the Chinese system of government. He built the first Buddhist temples, monastic schools, hospitals, dispensaries, and houses of refuge. Other leaders became Buddhists and created public charities, demonstrating that Buddhism was good for both individuals and society. Chinese written characters allowed the Japanese to record their tradition, so by 712 there was a comprehensive version of the *Kojiki,* or *Chronicle of Ancient Events.* By the 8th century the capitol was moved from Nara to Kyoto, and Buddhism had become the dominant religion.

From 558 through the 12th century, the Japanese welcomed Chinese and Korean immigrants; they and their Japanese students and apprentices became an educated class of teachers, technicians, and bureaucrats. The Japanese accepted many Confucian traditions as well, including ancestor veneration, filial piety, and reciprocal rights and obligations between superiors and inferiors. These virtues were integrated into the Japanese clan-based, militarily oriented social system. Their leaders stressed Confucian virtues of uprightness, sincerity, and honesty, but the Japanese masses also embraced much of Chinese Taoism, with its Yin-Yang system and magic aspects such as fortunetelling, astrologers, and sorcerers. During this period, Buddhism continued as the dominant religion.

From the 8th to the 11th century, Japanese society formed three distinct classes: aristocrats, educated Japanese, and peasants and servants. Shinto and Buddhism became increasingly integrated. Shinto myths and rituals were joined with Buddhist organizations and practices to become *Ryobu,* the twofold way of the Gods. Buddhist priests had religious visions that Japanese deities were Buddhas and Bodhisattvas who had reappeared in Japan: the sun goddess a reincarnation of the Buddha; the war god Vairocana became the Bodhisattva Ksitigarbha. During this era of Buddhist dominance, Shinto almost succumbed as a separate religion. Japanese appropriation and adaptation of Buddhism continued until the 13th century.

The Medieval Era, 1192–1867

Between 1192 and 1867 there were 400 years of feudal strife, which began when Minamoto became shogun (military dictator), because under his aegis the imperial court separated itself from the warriors' political power, and established a new capital near what is now Tokyo. The power of the educated class and their ecclesiastical authority diminished while the relative power of clan warriors and their Shinto-based populace increased and Shinto apologetics multiplied.

The great Buddhist centers and schools lost much of their spiritual vitality but held on to their wealth. Pietistic spirituality elaborated new Buddhist forms, emphasizing a third and final period of "Buddhist time," when the world was characterized by vice and conflict. These new Buddhist sects often embraced faiths with simple, repetitive rituals for salvation, charismatic leaders, and clear solutions. Honen (1133–1212), founder of the Pure Land School, taught that Amida Buddha could save all beings, and believers only needed to chant "Amida." Nichiren (1222–1282) urged trust in the *Lotus Sutra,* and admonished followers to faithfully chant their faith in it. Two new forms of Zen Buddhism arose in the 13th century: Rinzai, systematized by Eisai (1141–1215), who taught with paradoxical puzzles (koans) and meditation, and Dogen (1200–1253), who systematized Soto and concentrated on practicing cross-legged meditation (*zazen*). Both Zen schools perceived no essential difference between life's sacred and secular dimensions and understood ordinary existence to be the essential arena of salvation.

These medieval Buddhist innovations continue to flourish today. During our October 2017 trip to Japan, we were able to visit the founder's hall (completed in 1636) of Nishi Hongwanji, and its adjacent temple, which is a thriving example of the Buddhist Pure Land School. My San Francisco colleague, Rev. Ronald Kobata, is the resident minister of the Buddhist Church. His daughter, Tabitha, is on the staff at their Kyoto international headquarters, and gave us a wonderful tour of their magnificent facilities. Unlike some Buddhist temples we visited, which seemed to have more tourists than regular participants, Nishi Hongwanji's Hall of Amida Buddha had a constant stream of worshippers, as well as an occasional Japanese tour group. It hosts a daily morning service and twice-daily confirmation ceremonies that certify active membership. We viewed an afternoon confirmation ceremony with a dozen adult participants.

Buddhisms of the Pure Land schools strive to convey that people need to remain aware that they are unable to do completely good acts like a bodhisattva, and that people also need to make constant efforts for the benefit of both oneself and for society. This self-awareness of both our human limitations and responsibilities can become the joy of being the object of the Buddha's salvific working, embodying the concept of a boundlessly compassionate Buddha.

The Rinzai Zen priest we visited with in Kyoto led us in a chant and meditation followed by discussion, and summarized Rinzai: Awake to formless (no ego) self, we rest on the standpoint of all mankind, and create a supra-historical history which stops worrying about the past and creates the future. Also, he cited Gandhi's seven social sins: politics without principles, wealth without work, pleasure without conscience, knowledge without character, commerce without morality, science without humanity, and worship without sacrifice.

When Japan faced a Chinese Mongol invasion in the late 1200s, a temporary movement toward national unity produced a brief imperial regime, but it was soon followed by a new feudal regime under the Ashikaga family, which held power from 1338 to 1573. They maintained power by acknowledging the hereditary property and political rights of the feudal lords.

During these centuries, there were repeated feudal wars as well as uprisings of disgruntled peasants and fanatical religious groups, and the people reacted against the previous emphasis upon faith. Neither Shinto nor the various Buddhist schools asserted much religious influence, except for the Rinzai Buddhist School, which the Ashikaga regime considered the de facto state religion. The era's religious innovation was the widespread adoption of Neo-Confucian learning. Rinzai Zen Buddhist priests were the predominant elite of learning and culture, and often were also involved in trade with China. They were convinced that their Buddhism and Neo-Confucianism could be unified, and that by incorporating features of Buddhism and Taoism into the Neo-Confucian religious-philosophical system, they could produce universal principles that transcended all cultural provincialism.

This Chinese system of *Chu Hsi* (*Shushi* in Japanese) combines concepts of physical science, psychology, ethics, and metaphysics, and Shushi had a strong, continuing impact on Japanese intellectuals. In the 15th century, the official training academy of the Ashikaga regime was a Neo-Confucian school with several thousand Zen priests. The Chinese Confucian scholar Chu Hsi (1130–1200) believed in humanity's inherent goodness and heaven's benevolence and embraced elements of Taoism and Buddhism. For him, all things were brought into being by energy (chi) and by the law of rationality (li). In his vision of the Tao, all things reflect aspects of rational law. Within humanity, the Tao works as reason embodied in mind, spirit, and energy, which produce our will and actions. Reason-Spirit and Energy-Action interact in mutual dependence. Chu Hsi's primary spiritual practice was meditation focused on discerning what is good so that people could act with ethical effectiveness.

From Isolation to Modernization

Reunification of Japan was finally achieved by Tokugawa in 1603 at Edo (now Tokyo), and continued until 1867. The leaders represented themselves both as shoguns and fathers of the nation. They redefined the family, and established neighborhood units composed of several households whose heads were then held responsible for both the behavior and welfare of their members. They also froze the occupational structure, virtually eliminating social mobility. Society was organized to support the warrior class, though richer farmers and merchants still exercised considerable power. The country was divided into some 270 fiefdoms. With earlier international trade, Christian missionaries, particularly from Spain and Portugal, had arrived, and thousands of Japanese had become Roman Catholics. A local rebellion in 1637 caused the regime to outlaw and persecute Roman Catholics and adopt a policy of strict national seclusion, which, except for limited trade with China, endured until 1853.

The Tokugawa shogunate empowered Buddhism while taking organizational control of its hierarchy; it required that every family secure a certificate from their local Buddhist temple, and depended on the temples for statistical knowledge of their people. The shogunate strictly controlled Buddhist schools and appointed Buddhist commissioners of religious affairs. The official guiding principles were firmly Neo-Confucian, guided by the systems of Chu Hsi and Wang Yang-Ming, both of which had avid adherents. Wang argued that most people intuitively know what their obligations were, so they should not act impulsively. People need experiences in order to know, but if they fail to act, but say that they know, then they really do not know.

Neo-Confucians created a Shinto revival during the Tokugawa period. Three scholars, Mabuchi, Hirata, and Motoori, were central to this Shinto renaissance, which took advantage of antiforeign sentiments and Japan's national isolation. Motoori, who was the most prominent, acknowledged former Japanese dependence on Chinese sources, but upheld Japanese superiority. He argued that since the emperor was the direct descendant of the gods, and since the Japanese people were themselves divine descendants, Japan naturally ranked above other countries and was without equal. Therefore the Japanese people were naturally upright and, unlike other nations, had no need for any moral or ethical code.

The Meiji Era and Forward

Isolation ended abruptly when U.S. President Fillmore empowered Admiral Perry, first in 1853 and then with a greater naval force in 1867, to "open up" Japan after two and a half centuries of isolation. This caused a revolution in Japan, which soon ended shogunate rule and produced an explosion of systematic modernization. The primacy of the emperor was reasserted, but emperors were now firmly controlled by a military-financial elite avid for modernization, industrialization, and eventually for Japanese imperialism. Initially, Buddhism was again attacked as foreign, but Buddhism and Shinto were now so firmly intermingled that a national return to pure Shintoism was as impracticable as trying to separate Japanese culture from its multitude of Chinese roots. Most Japanese continued to favor and practice aspects of both Shinto and Buddhism with their sometimes-distinctive Japanese versions. The Constitution of 1889 promised religious liberty, but this was a government-controlled version of freedom. A Department for Shinto Shrines was created, and a separate Department of Religions was established for all the other forms of spirituality. State Shinto was funded by the regime, while Sectarian Shinto, the newer Neo-Shinto groups, though regulated and supervised by the government, were on their own for funding and support, as were Buddhism and religions like Christianity, which were considered "non-Japanese."

This separation of State and Sectarian Shinto encouraged a reinterpretation of the Shinto mythology, and made it more acceptable to the critical intelligence of a modern nation. For many, the sun goddess was now simply a noblewoman who had laid the foundations for Japanese culture. The kami were reframed as any entity that produces awe, has superior power, or is especially virtuous. The entire Japanese tradition was rationalized and humanized. The government declared that Shinto was no longer a religion but a sanctification of national ethics and a cult of loyalty to the nation.

The 1890 Imperial summary on education, still regarded by many Japanese as a foundation for ethics, stated:

> Be filial to parents, affectionate to siblings, harmonious as a spouse, as friends true; bear yourselves with moderation and modesty, extend your benevolence to all, pursue learning and cultivate arts, thereby developing intellectual facilities and perfect moral powers. Advance public good and promote common interests, obey laws, and in any national emergency offer yourselves courageously to the State; thereby guarding

and maintaining the prosperity of the Emperor coeval with heaven and earth.[2]

This revolution in values caused organized religiosity to suffer. Disbelief and agnosticism became widespread, particularly among educated and professional classes. A 1920 University of Tokyo study found that 3,000 of its 4,600 students identified as agnostics and 1,500 as atheists, while only one hundred professed to practice Shinto, Buddhism, or Christianity. Simultaneously, there were more than 110,000 government-controlled and financed Shinto shrines, with 16,000 priests who proceeded with their duties while not permitted to conduct religious ceremonies. Most of the general populace continued to perform their traditional forms of reverence at a multitude of local and family shrines. They maintained their mélange of spiritual practices, such as pilgrimages to the State Shinto shrines, while they often also professed and practiced various other spiritualties. Most Japanese continued to believe they were an integral part of a cosmic organism permeated by kami nature.

Japanese Imperialism, WWII, and U.S. Occupation

The Meiji regime was a tiny oligarchy that welcomed Western knowledge and technology while depending upon Shinto and Confucian principles to provide the foundations for national and cultural life. Determined to make Japan the leading imperialistic power in Asia, they annexed Taiwan in 1895, participated in the Chinese Boxer rebellion in 1900, annexed Korea in 1910, and, in the 1930s, invaded Manchuria and then the rest of China. During this period, many Western nations, including the United States at the end of the 19th and the beginning of the 20th centuries, had aggressively imperialistic policies. Such worldwide militaristic values led to WWI, during which Japanese imperialism eventually reached as far as the borders of India and Australia. The U.S. responded, and nearly destroyed Japan to defeat it. Japan's WWII population was half that of the U.S., and Japan lost 2.3 million of its people, 800,000 of them civilians. During the last eighteen months of the war, sixty-seven Japanese cities were bombed; 58 percent of Yokohama was destroyed, along with 51 percent of Tokyo and 40 percent of Nagoya. These losses of life climaxed with those killed by the nuclear bombs at Hiroshima (80,000) and Nagasaki (40,000). The U.S. lost 12,000 civilians during WWII.

From 1945 to 1952, Japan was occupied by the U.S. along with its allies, the only time in its history that Japan was occupied by a foreign power. Occupation troops numbered almost 400,000, mostly Americans. MacArthur commanded the US forces; he and his officers chose to preserve the emperor as a figurehead and to hold him harmless for Japan's aggression; ultimately only a handful of top military and civilian figures were executed. These occupation forces depended on the Japanese government to govern and continue their bureaucracy, but supported a new Constitution, which significantly reflected democratic and New Deal ideals.

The new Constitution gave ultimate power to the people, established a two-house legislature (the Diet) with a strong cabinet and prime minister, a multiparty political system, and a bill of rights. It also granted the first women's suffrage, established a land-reform program that overwhelmed the feudal landholding system, and redistributed ownership so that only 10 percent of agricultural land remained worked by non-owners. Trade unions, workers' rights, and labor standards were established; the education system was reformed with American-style junior and senior high schools, and the Japanese language was simplified to better reflect ordinary speech. Police and local governments were decentralized into districts or prefectures. Marriage provided spouses equal legal rights. Article 9 of the Constitution outlawed belligerency against other nations, renounced war as an instrument of state policy, and banned the maintenance of a standing army. It also stated that Shinto was no longer an instrument of the state and had no connections with government and banned militaristic and ultranationalist teachings.

Once again, the Japanese people had to make revolutionary cultural and spiritual adjustments in response to new realities. For seven years, U.S. military forces could veto almost any government policy they disapproved of and maintained occupying forces throughout most of the country. At the end of the war, millions of Japanese were homeless and starving, and for several years, much of the energy of allied forces was expended in the distribution of food and medical supplies. US experts worked with the Japanese to rebuild their economy and governmental and public systems. While the constitutional changes liberated women, the Japanese, ironically, worked with occupation forces to supply thousands of young Japanese women as prostitutes for the soldiers. These women often volunteered in order to support their struggling parents, but as so-called women of the new Japan, remained a startling contrast to the Constitution's liberation of women.

Many Japanese were traumatized into a lethargic state; the black market, and gangs proliferated, but the reforms of the occupation helped most to regain both their cultural and economic foundations and strength. When the Korean War began, the U.S. and its allies needed Japan to rebuild its armaments industry in order to supply the allied fighting forces in Korea. Former Prime Minister Abe advocated strongly for constitutional revisions that would permit Japan to substantially rearm and militarize.

Neo-Shinto and Neo-Buddhist Groups in Japan

There were thirteen denominational/sect Shinto organizations before WWII; now there are more than 800, free to formulate their own beliefs and ceremonies, which vary significantly, including some oriented toward personal healing, deep breathing, or specializing in mountain ascents— especially of Mount Fuji—to experience ecstatic communion with Japan's great spirits.

Konkokyo

Konkokyo is one of the Sect Shinto denominations. It was initiated by a farmer, Bunjiro Kawate, who survived a serious midlife illness. In 1859, he began to help people with their illnesses and difficulties by mediating between kami and people. Kawate felt many Japanese misunderstood the kami by considering them to be dangerous and threatening. Instead, he argued that all people could merge their hearts with the true nature of the traditional kami, *Tenchi Kane No Kami,* or *Konjin,* kami's essence, and by embracing this essential kami, could participate in becoming *ikigami,* aspects of divinity, themselves. He believed all beings and entities are in profound interrelationship with one another, that kami pervades the world, and that the universe itself is the parent of God. Suffering is caused by people's disregard for these divine relationships among all things. Human lives may be improved by practicing gratitude, mutual helpfulness, and prayer, and, when appropriate, by apologizing. After death, all beings return to kami, but the deceased's spirits remain in this world. Kawate was renamed *Konko Daijin* and became the first Patriarch of the Konkokyo religion. The Konkokyo scriptures, articulated by Kawate, are published in five volumes as *Konkokyo Kyoten*: the first volume are the revelations, the second his memoirs, and *Gorikai I, II, and III*, are teachings conveyed to his followers and lectures by his disciples. Here is an indication of its first two volumes.

Kami's way is to create a glorious world of coexistence and mutual prosperity by all belonging to kami. Kami's presence fills the whole world. People may think they have broken their bonds with kami, but kami never breaks their connection with people. All are kami's children. Ikigami means Kami is born in each of us. You don't need to practice religious austerities or magic; instead, pursue your occupations diligently. Treat everyone with respect because kami regards all people as equal, and do not be greedy or selfish. Often, people forget humility when they make a fortune or become famous, but the more virtue you acquire the humbler you need to become. Be in harmony with the universe, pray with a sincere heart. A heart of love is the heart of kami.

The Meiji regime did not initially accept Konkokyo as a legitimate religion. Though its ritual practices were much like Shrine Shinto, its no-nonsense teachings and intimate process of mediation or spiritual counseling between its clergy, called *mediators,* and its members appeared somewhat threatening to the traditional spiritual and political authorities until after WWII. A later publication, the *Kyoten Gorikai II,* published in 1987, featured Konkokyo mediators' comments on wisdom they had learned, often attributed to Konko Daijin. Here are some illustrations:

Live a happy and harmonious life and pursue your work with gratitude; these will be life's blessings. Think of your everyday work as practicing religious austerities. People are people because of kami, and kami is kami because of people. Don't discriminate against other religions or follow one religion obsessively. In this faith, there are no taboos or impurities. Death is like a deep sleep; so you need not fear it. People need to pay their taxes; taxes are as necessary for civilization as digestion is for the person. Without government, there is disorder. We mediators simply mediate the requests of our members. Open your heart, have a broad mind, and be a person of the world. Prayer gives heart to people. For a heart that feels pity reveals kami.

All religions are good. Think of your everyday work as practicing religious austerities. Live a happy and harmonious life and pursue your work with gratitude; these will be life's blessings. Man is man because of kami, and kami is kami because of man. Prayer is not necessary but gives heart to people. Shinto and Buddhism are both within faith. Don't discriminate against other religions or by following one religion obsessively. Open your heart, have a broad mind, and be a person of the world. In this faith, there are no taboos or impurities. Death is like a deep, deep sleep; do not fear it. People need to pay their taxes; taxes are as necessary for civilization as digestion is for the person; without government, there will be disorder. A heart that feels pity is a kami, but (we mediators) are not ourselves kami, but simply mediate the requests of our members.

I became acquainted with Konkokyo as a group affiliated with the International Association for Religious Freedom (the international ecumenical organization with which my denomination is affiliated). Yoshi Matsuda, a young member of its clergy, was a fellow student during my first seminary year. At present, Konkokyo has about half a million members worldwide, including a few North American and South American congregations.

New Buddhist Denominations

The largest of the 20th-century religions is Soka Gakkai Buddhism, with as many as 12 million members worldwide. Founded in 1930, it is based upon the writings of Nichiren Buddhism, and places the chanting of the *Lotus Sutra* at the center of its devotional practice. Many Soka Gakkai leaders were imprisoned during WWII. After the war, its third president, Daisaku Ikeda, moved Soka Gakkai toward mainstream acceptance, but it is still widely criticized as gnostic, manipulative, and an ego cult for its leaders.

Another modern form of Nichiren Buddhism is Rissho Kosei-Kai (RKK) which is the largest member group in the International Association for Religious Freedom. Rissho Kosei-Kai was founded in 1938 by Myoko Naganuma and Nikkyo Niwano who based their doctrines upon the *Lotus Sutra*. Niwano's son, Nichiko, and daughter, Sama, are now RKK's leaders.

RKK venerates Nichiren as the Great Bodhisattva, believes in the Buddha-nature of all beings, evangelizes on behalf of the *Lotus Sutra,* and invites all its members into *hoza,* intimate group-support sessions. Hoza are groups of laity who meet daily to share their problems and shortcomings, and receive support, advice, and trust from one another. RKK strongly supports interfaith efforts for peace, actions on behalf of UNICEF and the UN, and has developed programs to alleviate world hunger and poverty and to promote environmental sustainability. RKK has about 2 million members, including several North and South American congregations.

Religion in Japan Today

Contemporary religious accounts suggest that most Japanese today are spiritual rather than religious; they don't profess belief in a governing deity or identify themselves as weekly religious practitioners. Nonetheless, they continue to crowd shrines at holidays, leave written prayers at temples and shrines at critical life junctures, and honor family events. Ritual blessings are offered for sports teams, new buildings, even at the "retirement" of long-serving machinery. Most Japanese continue to use and adapt aspects of Shinto and Buddhism when they feel these are necessary or convenient.

As they have for eons, they also adopt foreign traditions that they find attractive. For instance, Western-type weddings are popular among many Japanese with no other Christian associations. As a Unitarian Universalist minister in suburban New Jersey at many Christmas seasons, I heard inquiries about when we'd set up for our Christmas Eve service; then, a young non-Christian Japanese couple arranged for to me officiate at their wedding, in our sanctuary, just hours before that service.

Millions of Japanese use Shinto shrines for weddings and other life-cycle ceremonies, but they usually choose Buddhist priests at death because they perform "better death ceremonies." A 2008 survey of the Japanese found that 39 percent identified themselves as religious, most of them identifying as Buddhists, but 83 percent of Japanese also regularly practiced some Shinto rituals. The government has licensed 180,000 different religious corporations. Practitioners who visit a Shinto shrine enter through the *torii* gate, wash their hands and mouths, remove wraps, clap hands, kneel and bow, leave an offering, pray, bow again, and leave. Worshippers enter the outer sanctuary, but seldom the inner sanctuary, home for revered objects symbolic of the kami being in residence. At home, most Japanese have a *kamidana,* a family altar or "god-shelf" that holds photos of their ancestors, images of patron deities such as Amaterasu or Inari (rice goddess), a sacred mirror, and strips of paper that contain sacred texts. Many worship there daily.

During our 2017 visit, we noticed that the homes we visited usually had both a Buddhist and a Shinto altar, at which they prayed regularly. At the public Shinto shrines, we routinely encountered beautifully dressed families celebrating their children, at ages seven, five, or three. Most Japanese have a visceral relationship with a nearby Shinto shrine, and many Buddhist temples also have many worshippers. We watched part of a Shinto wedding at a shrine, officiated by both a male priest and a female shrine attendant. Also, we saw many processions of Shinto priests, and encountered several Buddhist services in progress.

In Japan, the way of the kami, or deities, has from ancient days often been easily reconciled with Bushido, the way of the warrior. The Samurai code survives as an ethic of demanding self-discipline and a tendency to remain unquestionably obedient to superiors. The Japanese spiritual way is founded upon disciplined intuition. Life is perceived as profoundly social and practical. People are trained to sense the mood in each situation and to respond in tune with understanding their place in that situation and the appropriate behaviors in it. Stoic forbearance is greatly esteemed. Emphasis is placed upon education, diligence, and delay of personal gratification. The work ethic controls many lives—people commonly work ten hours a day, even to exhaustion, and then spend additional hours eating and drinking with fellow employees.

Much of Japanese life is a matter of *face,* i.e., how others perceive and judge your behavior. This engenders considerable loneliness, as people live a primarily "masked me" at work, socially, and even with extended family, as opposed to a "real me," perhaps revealed when they are alone, with intimates, or in anonymous situations. The gap between these two presentations of self is called *kodoku* (lonely). Before WWII, spiritual consciousness enforced social harmony and helped build community, and still dominates many lives;

however, most Japanese have also become consummate consumers and are somewhat more self-centered.

When I returned to Japan in 2017, I again found the people I encountered polite, graceful, and diligent. They are extraordinarily concerned about doing things correctly. For example, there are few trash receptacles because people take their waste home. Most follow the rules, are generous and self-effacing. This cultural emphasis on conformity and cooperation with one's surroundings makes society function with amazing smoothness and facilitates many aspects of contemporary life. We saw no homeless people in the streets, little public intoxication, few signs of poverty, even in rural villages, which are mostly populated by the elderly, and consistently experienced superb public order even amidst dense crowds. Most urban workers commute by bicycle and/or public transit, and walkers usually make way for cyclists. Younger people routinely give their seats to the elderly. People stand in lines and follow directions in public settings with no apparent impatience.

Elements of Japanese Spirituality that I Find Troubling

I believe the integration of religion and nationalism, spirituality and patriotism serve religions and spirituality badly, and makes politics and governments idolatrous. Undoubtedly, people need to integrate their ethical actions with their spirituality and religion, and many of the most powerful and important human actions occur within government and politics. Conflating these realms ideologically, however, serves all of them badly and produces a host of unhealthy consequences for all these vital realms of human activity. When any people mistake themselves as the only true, complete, or superior group, they replace appropriate self-respect with a religion of nationality or ethnic idolatry, and worship something that is not and should not become worthy of reverence or unquestioning allegiance. This tendency to meld national and ethnic identity with spirituality and religious practice continues to make any people vulnerable to national and ethnic pride, which mistakes personal desires or political or bureaucratic priorities for virtue.

As it did during Japan's imperialism, this can lead to monstrous hubris, with suicidal soldiers and robotic allegiance to militarist dictators. Since WWII, Japan has done much to move past its warrior history, but its continued cultural assumptions of a special national or cultural relationship with the divine, and the consequent cultural tendencies toward spirituality and ethical superiority, not only perpetuate its alienation from its Asian neighbors but also limit its own promise of future progress as a nation and as a people. Japan has yet to publicly admit and seek forgiveness for its terrible human-rights violations in Korea, China, and elsewhere during its imperialist period. Also, Japan must change its immigration policies, because there are simply not enough employed Japanese to ensure its future as a nation. I found the Japanese I met extremely hesitant to "dilute" their homeland with immigrants; and while the Constitution makes women equal, male chauvinism continues to prevail. The Japanese, like many other nations and peoples, need to get off their cultural pedestal, shed their sense of cultural superiority, and face up to their continuing errors regarding hierarchy, gender, and ethnicity.

Elements of Konkokyo and Japanese Spirituality I Find Particularly Interesting

In 1967, when I began seminary, I knew little about Japanese culture. This changed abruptly when I met Yoshi Matsuda, a young, neo-Shinto clergyman, a member of Konkokyo, which, along with the UUs and other religious groups, are partners in a small, liberal world ecumenical organization, the International Association for Religious Freedom (IARF). My wife, Madhavi, was adjusting to new circumstances. We had just married, and she and Yoshi were the only resident Asians at Meadville. We three became friends, each learning how to function in new roles. Yoshi was away from his mother and hometown and from Konkokyo headquarters for the first time; suddenly a foreign student immersed in a different religion and culture. Madhavi was newly married in surprising circumstances, and I, an activist, erstwhile political scientist and secular humanist, was beginning seminary and married life. During Christmas break, Yoshi traveled with us to my parents' home in Wichita, Kansas. By the time Yoshi returned to Japan in the summer of 1968, he and I were soul mates. A year later, I applied for and received a research grant for 1969–1970 to study Gandhians in India, and then to spend July 1970 in Japan to interview Konkokyo clergy about their spiritual encounters/counseling methods as mediators between kami and their members. I found Yoshi Matsuda, both in July 1970 and October 2017, to be an outstanding person who exemplified loving gentleness, patient helpfulness, and intuitive insight.

I was a child of WWII, but like millions of young Americans, I remained relatively untouched by it, while Yoshi Matsuda lost his father, a soldier, to the atomic bomb at Hiroshima. It's too easy for Americans today to forget the scale of the fire bombings of Japan that preceded the nuclear detonations at Hiroshima and Nagasaki. Viewing the documentary film, *The Fog of War* graphically reminds viewers of the scale of the devastation.

When I interviewed Konkokyo mediators throughout Japan in 1970, I discovered a group of dedicated professionals who combined traditional Shinto prayers and rituals with contemporary understandings and counseling techniques. Konkokyo mediators listen closely to their members, guide them with practical advice fitted to their personalities and provide them ritual support and spiritual inspiration. They are intent upon remaining attentive to the natural world and the spiritual world, which they perceive as embracing all of humanity. For example, I watched as each of three Konkokyo mediators spoke with a member troubled by alcoholism. In one case, a traditional prayer was offered; in the second, there was a counseling dialogue, and in the third, the elderly mediator, after many excuses from his longtime congregant, grabbed him by the front of his shirt, lifted him off the ground, and said, "You need to change your behavior right now!"

We all realize different words and deeds work for different people and in particular circumstances. Spiritual professionals use what they know about their members, combined with what they feel will aid them in their particular struggles, mediated by their faiths, or as the Japanese would phrase it, guided by the kami in that present moment. One fascinating aspect of Konkokyo mediation is that spouses of mediators regularly take on the mediator's role in their absence. Like so much of spiritual ministry, we try to serve people whenever they reach out.

For most Japanese, *amae* explains their concept of love and dependence. Amae is the presumption of another's love, even their indulgence. Most Japanese aren't trying to become independent of others, but rather to develop a more mature form of dependence upon their family, colleagues, and/or chosen spiritual or secular community group. Both the emphasis on saving face in public and amae within intimacy help the Japanese to be other-centered rather than I-centered. The first person (I or me) is not much used in Japanese, since expressing feelings directly suggests a breakdown in their preferred process of intuitive, nonverbal communication. They often demonstrate closeness by what is not said or spelled out. The intimacy that may develop between a Konkokyo meditator and member, or within a Rissho Kosei Kai hoza group, provides new mediums for appropriate amae or intimacy.

The Transparent Spirituality of the Japanese Aesthetic

In our 2017 visit to Konkokyo headquarters, I again encountered an amazing expression of this intuitive wisdom for communicating intimately in a particular moment and situation. In 1970, I had met with the 4th Patriarch, Rev. Kagamitaro Konko and with his two young adult sons. In 2017, Yoshi had arranged for us to meet with the 5th Patriarch, Rev. Heiki Konko, the older of the two young sons I had met in 1970. When we met in 1970, I had watched his father mediate with congregants at Konkokyo's primary sanctuary, and his headquarters was then a relatively modest traditional wood building. Now, the patriarch was an elderly man with physical limitations, surrounded by a set of gigantic modern denominational buildings. We met in the front entry of his home. He appeared in some physical distress, and I felt we were both beset by the difficulties of reaching across language barriers and the generations that had passed since I was last in Japan. Then, he suddenly got up and left. I assumed that our visit had ended, but he returned shortly, more at ease, with a piece of paper that he presented to us. He explained that it was a copy of a drawing his five-year-old granddaughter had done of his wife and him. Suddenly, we were no longer strangers but fellow grandparents. He had deftly communicated that what was most important about what we shared was beyond ourselves and concerned generations after us. His granddaughter, her parents, and his other son, joined us for photos and brief interchanges. He had gently communicated that what really matters are our intimate connections of love, care, and mutual respect, which his sons also exemplified, and as he, his brother and his father had done nearly fifty years earlier.

The uniquely Japanese aesthetic, with its modest and flexible use of space, is expressed beautifully in their *ikebana* (flower arrangements), bonsai (trained trees and shrubs), and gardens. The Japanese flower arranger endeavors to express sympathy for the life of flowers and plants. A Japanese garden is not intended to become a mass of color or a profusion of blooms, but to convey how an arrangement of shrubbery, trees, and rocks can be beautiful in all life's seasons. It is intended as a meditative feast for the eyes, but even more to feed the visitors' souls, since the beautiful should evoke a realization of the whole of life. The traditional Japanese garden, with its irregular terrain, rock-studded ponds, and waterfalls, becomes the world in miniature. Even the sere garden made only of raked sand and carefully placed stones evokes our unity with creation. We are but waves on life's evolving ocean.

Enamored as a child by Chinese landscape paintings, I've become a great fan of Japanese gardens, bonsai, and woodblock prints. They convey the sense of balance that manages to be harmonious without being symmetrical. They also celebrate the arid, jagged, and even ugly aspects of life, and help us see their beauty. As a child of the Kansas plains, I learned early to appreciate plain, dry landscapes without any obvious extravagance, so it's understandable that I'm drawn to art that celebrates a crippled older person, a strange-looking cat, or an unbalanced scene. My wife, Kathleen, has helped me understand the tough love of an effective gardener, and I perceive this sort of care in Japanese bonsai, gardens, and landscapes.

We can all get involved in nurturing the world around us. During our 2017 tour, we had beautiful views of Mt. Fuji from Lake Tanukiko, and visited the magnificent Kenrokuen Garden in Kanazawa near the Sea of Japan. In Kyoto we strolled around the Golden Pavilion, meditated at the Ryoanji Temple stone and gravel garden, and walked through an extraordinary bamboo forest adjacent to the Okochi Sanso hillside garden that overlooks the city. With Yoshi, we then visited the Korakuen garden at Okayama, with its symbolic rice paddy and vineyard, during one of the two monthly one-hour periods when the resident, red-crowned cranes are allowed to stroll through the garden along with visitors. To me, each of these episodes felt as blessed and holy as people's accounts of the best moments in their chosen spiritual sanctuaries.

Martial Arts and Spirituality

During my forty-year UU ministry, I periodically presented a sermon on a topic proposed by a member of the congregation. In New Jersey, a woman who had taken up martial arts invited me to speak on "the spirituality of the martial arts." She was involved in Kung Fu, but as I studied the various martial arts, all of which are intended primarily to help people defend themselves without unnecessary harm to their attackers, I discovered that there was a 20th-century martial art, intended to be purely defensive, called Aikido, developed by Morihei Ueshiba. In 1988, I participated in an Aikido workshop led by Harvey Konigsberg at the Omega Institute. Aikido actions are almost always circular, revolving around your center of gravity. You don't grapple with your attacker. Instead, you learn to turn "like a door on a hinge," get out of the line of attack and take control of the force directed against you, and use it to lead your opponent where you want him to go. The force of the attacker propels him there. If necessary, you can also use joint-locking techniques, which immobilize the attacker, who stops trying to move to avoid further pain. *Ai* in aikido means harmony. Violent forces disrupt harmony, so Aikido practitioners don't "win fights"; instead, they seek peaceful reconciliation. The *ki* in Aikido are the energies that represent the essence of existence. We are all born with ki, but many adults have lost their ability to access it effectively. Most martial arts focus on gaining or regaining access to ki, but aikido stresses it from the outset. Unfortunately, the mass-media popular view of martial arts is usually aggressive. Aikido takes the harmonious and nonviolent foundation beneath martial arts and makes it a way of "fighting" that's analogous to nonviolent activism, i.e., it's assertive and powerful without becoming violent. At its best, Aikido turns disruptive energy into harmonious energy, the humane assertion of ki.

Summary

In my month in Japan, now two generations ago, I perceived the Japanese as greatly chastened by the decimation of WWII. They combined diligent spirits with graciousness and gentleness. While occasionally just a fascinated tourist, I was granted an intimacy of access to Konkokyo homes and sanctuaries, as well as to their beliefs and lives, that few outsiders are permitted. This helped me work more effectively with the congregations I served. Religious professionals try to help people gain, regain, or retain their access to the holy, which the congregants know or hope for within themselves, among family, friends, and colleagues, and in the world. Ultimately, faith is how one feels and what one does, rather than primarily an ideology or dogma.

In 2007, Kathleen and I joined an IARF group for a spiritual retreat at Tsubaki Shinto Shrine in rural Granite Falls, Washington. Its priest, Junmai Ginjo, is an American Shinto priest of Jewish parentage as well as an Aikido master. The climax of our retreat was a *misogi shuho,* or water purification. We stripped to sacramental undergarments and submerged ourselves in an icy mountain stream, an exhilarating experience. Swift-flowing water is a great setting for an act of purification. As Junmai Ginjo explained: Kami and humans work together to rid them of negativity, receive vitality from Earth and inspiration from Heaven, and engage us in the spiral dance of divine energies. Since there are inevitably errors, we need to remove obstructions and adopt skillful means to return to harmony with our life missions. Doing so, we can continue to make daily progress through four levels of consciousness: to be physically, mentally, and spiritually present, and learn to differentiate and continue to reintegrate while we remain grateful and hopeful, and use our intuitive wisdom.

Japanese culture is a primary example of many centuries of syncretism. The Japanese combine varied religious beliefs and practices in both their individual lives and their national culture. They continue to shape them into coherent entities, which they perceive as unique and particularly Japanese. Like the Chinese, the Japanese people remain believers that humanity, and especially their own people, are cocreators with the divine powers of Earth and the cosmos. This sense of mutual responsibility with the ultimate powers produces high standards in both their personal and national behavior.

Chapter 11
Zoroastrianism

Why Consider Zoroastrians?

Z oroastrianism has influenced other religions far out of proportion to its statistically insignificant number of contemporary followers. Westerners know Zoroastrians as Magi; South Asians call them Parsees, and Iranian Zoroastrians today are Gabor. Scholars have now agreed that relatively advanced civilizations existed in what has been called the "cradles of civilization," including an area that stretches from Turkey, through Syria and Iraq, along the Nile, and farther east through Iran to Pakistan and India, where 5,000 years ago there were farmers and fairly civilized towns, as in the north Chinese plains and eons later in Latin America.

In the middle of the second eon BC, both Iran and India were invaded by militarily superior horsemen from a region that stretched from the Ural River above the Caspian Sea east to the present land of the Chinese Uyghurs across the central Asian steppes. Their speedy chariots and weapons made these horse soldiers capable of conquering more advanced people. Their leaders often then adopted many of the more advanced elements that flourished in the lands they conquered. These invaders shared similar Indo-European languages (Farsi in Persia and Sanskrit in India). Some have attributed the dominance of these "Aryan" invaders to their polytheistic pantheon of nature deities and their sacrifice-based cults attended by a priestly class that cooperated with their warrior-chief rulers. Whether Aryans brought these elements into Iran and India or adopted or adapted them from their already resident peoples from existing practices, in these new lands, is largely surmise as opposed to scientifically confirmed fact.

Central Zoroastrian Beliefs and Practices

Between 1500 and 600 BC, the prophet Zoroaster (in Greek, Zarathustra) lived and significantly changed existing Persian religion. The Zoroastrian scriptures say that Zoroaster lived for thirty years as a normal man; then, after bathing three times in a holy stream, he became the spiritual twig of the religion. A female spirit tempted him with many pleasures and powers, but she was spiritually ugly. Zoroaster withstood her entreaties and died when he was forty-seven.

The Zoroastrian Creator God, *Ahura Mazda,* is all good. Good and evil have distinct sources: *Spenta Mainyu* is progressive mentality, or God's creative energy, while *Angra Mainyu* is destructive mentality, the energy that opposes it. The evil powers, *Druj,* in Western faiths called the Devil or Satan, try to destroy God's good creations. Ahura Mazda is not immanent in the world as a superhuman. His creation is represented on Earth by a host of spirits and angels; through them, the works of God become known to humanity. These spirits help direct humans in their worship and aid them in performing good works. Creation is immanent in the world as a self-creating universe with consciousness as its special attribute. Humans uniquely participate in this consciousness. Truth and order are central; their antitheses are chaos, falsehood, and disorder, which result in conflicts that involve the entire universe. Humanity plays an essential role in this cosmic battle, which continues as long as the Earth. Humanity's good deeds are not only necessary to ensure the happiness of individuals but are crucial to keep cosmic chaos at bay.

Two central principles of the Zoroastrian faith are maintaining life and combating evil. To maintain life, Zoroastrians are urged to marry, have children, work, and when possible possess land and animals. All forms of asceticism are scorned as life-renouncing. Zoroastrians are taught to combat evil in both their family and at work. They are urged to be active citizens, to obey society's laws but also help keep public order, be politically active, and aid human progress.

Zoroastrians believe life is a temporary state in which people are expected to take an active part in the continual battle between truth and falsehood. Before birth, the soul of each person has already been united with a guardian spirit (*fravashi*) that has existed since the Creation. During life, this spirit is an individual's protector. On the fourth day after a person's death, each human soul is reunited with its fravashi. Their life experiences are appropriated for use in the battles between good and evil energies, which continue in the spirit world as they did during our lives.

Zoroastrian Scriptures

The Avesta was the original Zoroastrian scripture proclaimed by Zoroaster, but most of it has been lost; only a few of its hymns, the *Gathas,* survive. An idea of their contents:

> At the beginning of life the holier Mentality said to the opposing Mentality that was more hostile: 'nothing (about us) can agree'....Mazda is the father of the working Good Disposition, which is Justice; Love, who produces good deeds, is his daughter....Mazda blesses all existent things.... A prayer for guidance: Let just men exercise their faculties of choice so that they may develop convictions to distinguish between the benevolent and the evil, to improve their communities, and to hold justice in union with good political power through both words and deeds.[1]

A later version, the Zend-Avesta, contains this passage:

> Mithra, god of the rolling countryside, is Ahura Mazda. I am the One of whom all questions are asked, understand knowledge, am creator of all good things, the healing one, all-knowing one. In its Abodes of the Soul: after death, first there is wind, then one's own conscience, then a not-rejecting of the poor, then good thoughts, words, and deeds, and finally, endless light.[2]

Finally, there are the Pahlavi Texts, a translation of the Avesta into the Middle Iranian or Pahlavi language from the Avestan language, beginning about 250 CE.

In *Birth and Vision of Zarathustra:*

> The good go to the sky heaven because of their deeds
> while demons, fiends, wizards and witches are paralyzed
> below ground in hell. Priests' dispositions: innocence,
> discrimination, authoritativeness, struggling day and night
> with their own fiend, and throughout life remaining steadfast
> and dutiful. The dispositions of the righteous include:
> rewarding doers of good works and punishing criminals
> through established laws for the sake of progress, forcing
> malice away from your thoughts and quickly being repentant
> of your own sins, helping religion move forward, advancing
> despite adversities, remaining obedient to rulers and priests.[3]

In *The Function of the Righteous:*

> The Creator created humans to become determiners of wis-
> dom, promoting understanding and goodness, and the pro-
> gress of Creation....The labor and trouble of the good may
> be more in this world while their reward and recompense
> more certain in their spiritual existence, while the comfort
> and pleasure of the vile may be more in this world, while
> their punishment and pain in the next. (After death, all souls
> cross the Chinvat Bridge on the way to heaven or hell.) The
> Chinvat Bridge becomes a broad bridge for the righteous
> while for the wicked it resembles the edge of a razor....But
> at the end of the world, all men come together....The first
> man and woman were created perfect; however, they devel-
> oped antagonisms in their minds, thus, becoming corrupted
> by demons.[4]

Historic Evolution of Zoroastrianism

In the centuries that followed, the Persians were often fearsome enemies for ancient European empires, and major impediments to European dreams of conquering the Asian East. In 440 BC, the Greek historian Herodotus wrote of the Persian Achaemenid dynasty (648–330 BC) and their Zoroastrian Magi priests who by 550 BC had great influence in Emperor Cyrus's court. At its height during his reign, the Persians ruled an empire that controlled the world from the Balkans and North Africa to Central Asia. Cyrus's rule included the Babylonians, who had conquered the kingdom of Judah and taken a Jewish minority as slaves to Bagdad. These slaves preferred Persian rule to Babylonian because the Persians were much more tolerant of the Jewish religion and other faiths besides Zoroastrianism. In a grab for power directly after Cyrus's death, some Zoroastrian magi supported an imposter as the emperor's son and heir, so when his actual son, Darius, became emperor, he further strengthened the ability for non-Zoroastrian religions to coexist within the empire. Nonetheless, Zoroastrianism continued to gain popular strength in subsequent Persian empires.

Alexander the Great conquered Persia in 33 BC; his forces burned Emperor Xerxes' library, and many of the Zoroastrian sacred texts were destroyed. The Parthian or Ascidian dynasty (224 BC–AD 226) then regained Persian independence. During that period, the god Mithra, with its powers for good, became the most popular manifestation of Ahura Mazda. Mithra was now perceived as a savior. Mithra's "soldiers' religion" became as popular as Christianity in the Roman Empire of the 1st century AD. When the Sassanid dynasty came to power (AD 226–631), the Persians built many new Zoroastrian temples and were increasingly suspicious of Christianity, particularly after Emperor Constantine declared his empire Christian in 313. Zoroastrianism remained the dominant religion of the Persian Empire until the Arabs overthrew the Sassanid dynasty in 631. Zoroastrianism remained the dominant religion in the Persian cradle of Western religion for more than 1,000 years, from before the Babylonian captivity of the Jews until the arrival of the Islamic Empires.

After the Arabian Conquests

After the Arabs conquered Persia in 631, Zoroastrianism began its decline. Initially, there was little active conversion to Islam within the Persian Empire; however, since its Islamic rulers held all non-Islamic religiosity in contempt, those who wanted to get ahead in politics and commerce tended to convert to Islam. Some Persian rural areas remained Zoroastrian strongholds, but sufficient persecution continued so that by the 8th century AD, most remaining Zoroastrians had immigrated to the western Indian state of Gujarat. Later, most Indian Zoroastrians, called Parsees, moved to Bombay (now Mumbai).

The Zoroastrians remaining in Iran today are called Gabor. There are still a few rural enclaves, but they've been thoroughly marginalized by Iran's present Islamic Republic, especially because the preceding Pahlavi dynasty (1920–1970s) had favored Zoroastrians, who flourished by moving from the countryside into Tehran and held many professional and governmental posts. Today, fewer than one in 1,000 Iranians are Zoroastrian.

Historical Impacts of Zoroastrianism on Judaism, Christianity, and Islam

In *Avesta Eschatology*, Lawrence Mills provided a useful perspective on Zoroastrian influences on later theologies.

> Zoroastrian doctrine exerted the most decided influence on the development of Jewish and Christian theologies.... because Jews entered a new intellectual world during their captivity....Persian Jerusalem became more Iranian than Babylonian, with the idea of eternity in the Deity. Exilic Jewish priests were in daily contact with ritualistic Zoroastrians—like their five periods of daily prayer....The later Zoroastrian scriptures emphasize human immortality in the light of accountability, and bodily resurrection....The Jewish doctrine of the later days was an exilic innovation. Zoroastrianism was the first occurrence of the doctrine that virtue is its own reward, and vice its own punishment....The

primary six laws of the Zoroastrian universe all subsequently appear in Judeo-Christian thought: the truth of natural sequences as the rhythm of existence, the loving mind of the Good that guides the righteous, the power of God whose opposite is chaos, the creativity of mind-directed labor and service, peace of mind's satisfactions, and the eternal life which overcomes death.[5]

Influences on Judaism

It is understandable that the Jews returning from the Babylonian exile would rebuild Judaism with some Zoroastrian elements. Their temple had been destroyed, and their elite exiled for generations into a Zoroastrian religious environment. Both the necessary permission and most of the funds that enabled the Jews to rebuild the Temple of Solomon came from a Persian Zoroastrian emperor who had given them the opportunity to return to and "restore" their homeland and its faith there.

In pre-exilic Judaism, Satan, the powers of evil, were still under the service of God, as in *Job*. Post-exilic Jews not only embraced the forces of good but admitted the often apparently more potent forces of evil. Satan became the eternal enemy of God. Still fervent monotheists, post-exilic Jews could now believe there needed to be a Messiah at the end of time. They became imbued with a more elaborate sense of what happens after death, including spirits, angels, and demons. They felt more strongly that time mattered, and that people must speak up and act upon their beliefs, but need to do so with subtlety in the face of usually stronger, non-Jewish political powers. Many post-exilic Jews believed in an eternal battle between good and evil, and like Zoroastrians, that a benevolent God might save even the worst sinners at the world's end.

Influences on Christianity

Christianity was significantly shaped by Zoroastrian ideas, particularly those of the Mithra cult, which in the first centuries of the Christian era became as popular among Roman citizens as Christianity itself. Among the

Roman legions, Mithra became identified with Invictus, the Roman sun god, who was especially worshipped on December 25. Zoroastrian rituals of blood atonement, its belief in a savior at the end of time, the battle between good and evil, guardian angels, a heavenly journey of the soul, a heavenly book of record, a kingdom of God, bodily resurrection, a strong sense of fellowship, a strict moral code and self-discipline, a personal salvation after death for the faithful in a sky heaven, horrible punishment for the wicked in an underground hell, and its central sense of divine justice are among the multitude of Zoroastrian ideas that became parts of the Christian tradition.

Influences on Islam

Persia was the strongest indigenous religious culture the Muslims conquered in which they were still able to eventually convert most of its people to Islam. In Iran, however, Islam became significantly Persian, including many Zoroastrian ideas and some Zoroastrian practices. Islam already had devils, called *jinni,* but the Zoroastrian idea of an eternal battle between forces of good and evil became more dominant. Much of Islamic religious literature, and many of its legal scholars, acclaimed writers, poets, scientists, and artists, were either themselves Persian or spent significant portions of their lives in Persia in the centuries that followed. Numerous Zoroastrian ideas had also already impacted Islam through Judaism and Christianity before Islamic armies conquered Persia, like its five daily prayer times. In the earliest Islamic decades, all Muslims were Sunni Muslims, but in Islam's major schism, Shia Islam developed in Persia (now Iran), and Iran became and has remained the spiritual center for Shia Islam.

Shi'ism began with the assassination of Ali and his son, Hasan, in 661. Ali, the fourth leader of Islam after the death of Muhammad himself, was not only Muhammad's son-in-law but also his blood cousin (unlike the three earlier post-Muhammad Islamic leaders, and all those who followed). For Shia Muslims, their history begins when, Muawiyah, governor of Syria, secured Ali's and Hasan's assassinations, then seized control of Islam from its "rightful bloodline descendants." Ali was married to a Persian princess, and they had a son, Husayn, who became the next Shia Iman after his father's and brother's murders. Husayn refused allegiance to Muawiyah or his descendants and was killed in a battle in 680. Since then, the Shia-Sunni split within Islam has been the primary sectarian division and often the basis for intra-Islamic violence, war, and devastation. Shia history remains bathed with betrayal, bloodshed, and martyrdom. Unlike the Islamic leaders who preceded them, Ali and Hasan ruled from outside of Saudi Arabia. This geographic distance between these two political and spiritual centers of Islam has continued from 661 until today.

In the 20th century, this Sunni-Shia division has been strongly reinforced politically, and its intra-Islamic violence reignited by the present Iranian Shia Islamic Republic's radical theocracy, which supports its Shia militant clients, and by the opposing Wahhabi-Salafist fundamentalist Sunni monarchy in Saudi Arabia and the Gulf States, whose elites often support their jihadist Sunni militant clients. This Saudi-Wahhabi brand of Sunni Islam has, with their oil wealth, dominated the modern Sunni tradition, while Iran's Shia theocracy dominates the Shiites' political agenda. Most militant Islamists, both Shia and Sunni, reflect their mutual sense that Muslims unlike themselves are heretics and feel betrayed by them. The Zoroastrian clear division between good and evil, from gods to regimes to individuals, has nourished this willingness to perpetuate decimation on those who don't share one's definitions of true religion. Zoroastrianism includes angels, archangels and demons, and Satan, who is a fallen angel who tempts humans to sin but is still God's servant and the personification of evil.

Zoroastrianism in India

By the 8th century, most Zoroastrians had moved to India. During the British colonial period, many moved on to Mumbai, where many achieved a Western education and served in the colonial bureaucracy, became professionals, or entrepreneurs. They are called Parsees, and now there are fewer than 200,000 in India among its 1.4 billion people. Many are well-educated professionals and intellectuals, and several of India's major industrial families are Parsee (including Tata, Godrej, and Wadia), so Zoroastrians continue to wield cultural influence out of proportion to their small population. Some Parsees have immigrated out of India and play important global roles, among them orchestra conductor Zubin Mehta.

Parsees revere earth, air, fire, and water, but especially fire and water; they often visit natural locations that feature water, and perceive it as the symbolic source of wisdom, while fire is the primary symbol of spiritual insight. Their places of worship are called fire temples because priests keep a sacred fire constantly burning. Entrance to non-Parsees is prohibited, but Parsees are free to enter whenever they wish. They share the Hindu sense that certain spoken sounds are holy in themselves, like mantras. Devout Parsees offer most of their daily prayers at home altars by lighting a flame there. Fire temples are generally shrines for priests rather than for communal worship. Most Parsees only go to a temple to ask priests to perform a ceremony or special prayers for them in exchange for fees. The priesthood is hereditary; priests marry and have families. There are three ascending levels of priesthood: Ervad, Mobed, and Dastur. As fees are generally insufficient, many priests have additional, non-priestly jobs. Prayers offered by the priests are chanted in ancient Avestan, normally understood mystically rather than linguistically.

In their youth, Parsees of both genders are given a sacred undershirt (*sedreh*) and a ritual cord (*kushti*) that they bind around the waist three times; they always wear them, except when bathing. The teenage occasion of this investiture and binding is the *Navjote* ceremony, which is followed by a large public celebration, much like a Bar/Bat Mitzvah in Judaism. The cord is retied several times a day with accompanying prayers. There is also a binding during the marriage ceremony. An important annual holiday for Parsees is their thanksgiving, or *jashan*. Traditionally, to remain a Parsee in good standing, they must marry another Parsee. The diminishing size of their community has resulted in much cousin intermarriage, which has led to an unusual proportion of genetic ailments, but also produces some startlingly handsome people.

The geographic divisions between rural and urban Zoroastrians, and between the Zoroastrian groups in Iran and India, have produced three Zoroastrian subsects with different calendars. All three calendars, however, have twelve months of thirty days and one month of five days. (Ethiopian Coptic Christians have the same calendar divisions—could this have resulted from ancient caravanning Zoroastrian magi or wise men?) Zoroastrian rituals are month-centered, with special days for the key elements of fire and water, as well as for special spirits, and, at year's end, prayers for dead relatives and friends. Their subsects' calendar divisions have resulted in two different late-summer new year's in India and one, at the spring equinox, in Iran. As with other religions, the various Zoroastrian subsects perceive themselves the true followers of their faith, accept different scriptural elements as legitimate, and have somewhat different rites and prayers, but share much in common.

After death, the Parsee undershirt and cord are placed on the clean body. There are special prayers for the soul's safe passage across the Chinvat Bridge on the third and fourth days after death. The Parsee's reverence for earth, air, fire, and water has led them to an additional dilemma at death: Since they must not pollute any of the four elements, how are they to dispose of corpses, which they believe to be corrupted? Their solution has been the Tower of Silence. They place the bodies of loved ones atop these towers, where the flesh can be eaten by carrion birds, and the bones bleached by sun and wind. This practice has created neighborhood misunderstandings. My Indian mother-in-law's Mumbai flat was downhill from such a tower, and on a few occasions a body part would be dropped on her seaside balcony by a wayward bird.

The Parsees generally got along well during the British colonial period, which made them politically suspect after Indian independence. Such complications are likely for any spiritual minority that keeps its rituals private from outsiders while, within civil society, appearing ready to respond to the priorities of the dominant political forces, which helps some in such communities to become successful and wealthy.

Elements of Zoroastrianism that I Find Troubling

I knew nothing about Zoroastrians until I read Nietzsche's *Thus Spake Zarathustra,* in which the founder of Zoroastrianism stated that people should be faithful to the earth and life but question traditional morality. Nietzsche's iconoclastic individualism lent itself to idiosyncratic isolation and cultural arrogance and was unfortunately abused by many to undermine their traditional moralities, which paved the way in Western societies for various extremisms such as fascism and anarchy.

The Zoroastrians' dualism of good powers and evil powers has allowed practitioners within various spiritual traditions to promptly label their opponents creatures of Satan while considering themselves and their spiritual allies pure and righteous. Likewise, their stories of the spirit world before and after earthly life inspired many religious people to invest far too much of their lives into being "saved from this life." I don't believe that there is a good god and an opposing evil god, or that people or their actions, individual or collective, can be categorized as only good or evil. I find that the Zoroastrian black-and-white version of ethics and morality, and its inextricable linkage with conflicting divine forces has been one of the most pernicious aspects of global religion. This infection of other historic religious traditions continues to lead to immeasurable global harm and dysfunction. Its dichotomy seduces people into believing that since there is a perfect, i.e., only good God, that people should strive to literally be without sin, allowing them to believe that they and their leaders can choose to destroy the evil and preserve the good as they understand them.

I honor the elements of nature, but the Zoroastrian obsession with keeping a few elements "pure" has greatly complicated their followers' lives. I don't think purity rituals serve much more than metaphorical purposes. The Parsees' discouraging intermarriage and prohibiting non-Parsees from their places of worship are likely to increase misunderstanding and hostility between themselves and others. When a religion discourages its members from knowing and understanding outsiders, or discourages non-members from knowing about their religion, it becomes likely that outsiders will distrust them, and through consequent ignorance or misinformation nurture bigotry and disdain, and excuse hate and violence.

Elements of Zoroastrianism that I Find Relevant

In 1969–1970, during my first nine months in India, I had the opportunity to discuss Zoroastrian principles and practices with several outstanding Parsees, to read some of their scriptures, and attend several Parsee celebrations. These individuals were remarkable, and almost universally diligent even when they had inherited wealth. Many expended their energies in volunteer work, the arts, professions, or family businesses. Whenever possible, they were also generous philanthropists. They took life seriously and acted responsibly. They tried to affirm life and resolutely resist evil. Many of the women, and some of

172

the men, were quite liberated; they advocated for intermarried Parsee families to be embraced as Parsees and favored allowing women to become priests, a traditionally male preserve. Parsees are often reformers, but they usually have sought to do so within existing laws and prevailing customs.

Many Zoroastrians are interested in connecting their Parsee beliefs with Hindu teachings, and perceive Zoroastrianism and Hinduism as having common roots. They stress a friendly contract between humans and the spiritual world, in which both parties have continuing work to do to preserve and enhance the wonders of Creation and to resist temptations toward evil, which could easily result in violence, pollution, or chaos. I greatly value the Parsees' enthusiasm for life and their daily efforts to resist life's many temptations toward arrogance, violence, and the violation of other individuals, communities, or of the Earth itself. I agree with the Zoroastrians' insights about needing to remain active participants, both individually and as members of effective communities. Parsees continue to be inspirations toward a more progressive, sustainable, and peaceful world. It's a shame that many in other religious traditions have clung to Zoroastrian ideas about an eternal war of good and evil, the powers of Satan, and a continuation of these battles and divisions even after death, instead of being inspired by the Zoroastrians' enthusiastic embrace of life and their strong sense of humane responsibility and civic activism.

Chapter 12
Judaism

Central Jewish Beliefs and Practices

Judaism set the foundations for the theological tenets of Western religion: focus upon a single God that is active on Earth and in history. The Jewish God, usually named Yahweh (YHWH), is both benevolent and judgmental. Judaism emphasizes the study of sacred scriptures as its basic tool for spiritual growth. Its Ten Commandments became both its central tenets and its primary symbol. They include: worship the one God, do not worship idols or take the Lord's name in vain, keep the Sabbath day sacred, honor your parents, and do not kill, commit adultery, steal, bear false witness against your neighbors, or covet what is theirs. Judaism's basic ethical belief is refusal to do to another what you would not want done to you. The sacred history found in the Torah, along with their historical tales, prophetic books, and wisdom books evolved into the Judaic scriptures. They also became the Christian Old Testament, and many of Judaism's prophets and stories were integrated into the Qur'an.

Jewish ancestry is traced through the mother. Devout Jews light Sabbath candles at the Friday evening meal, and many attend services in their synagogues. The most orthodox Jewish men spend much of their lives studying Torah and develop a working knowledge of the Hebrew language in order to focus on the Torah and the books of rabbinic dialogue and analysis (the Talmud, Mishna, and Gemara). Most Jews, however, learn only enough Hebrew to complete an early adolescent coming-of-age course: bar mitzvah for boys, and bat mitzvah for girls, which enables them to recite basic ritual prayers and occasionally read a portion of the Torah at a synagogue service. The most important Jewish holidays include the autumn High Holy Days, which begin with *Rosh Hashanah* (New Year) and end, on the tenth day, with

Yom Kippur, when many Jews fast and attend services, and during which they seek God's forgiveness and renew commitments to ethical living. The spring Passover celebration is focused on the Seder, a symbolic meal at which the story of the Jews' escape from Egypt, acceptance of the Ten Commandments in the desert, and entrance into the promised land in Israel are celebrated and their covenantal relationship with God is renewed. *Hanukkah* is a celebration of the Maccabean revolt and repurification of the Jerusalem temple from unwelcome Hellenization. Most Jews share a strong sense of ethnic identity, value education highly, and strive to live ethical, successful lives.

The Historic Evolution of Judaism

The sacred histories of religions are often in conflict with their actual histories, and this is true with facets of Jewish history. These differences led Judaism, and other Western religious traditions rooted in Judaism, to struggle with central theological, philosophical, and ethical issues. For example, the first two chapters of the Torah tell dramatically different stories about the creation of humanity. In the first, woman and man are created simultaneously and spiritually equal, while in the second, Yahweh created the first woman out of the first man for his pleasure and benefit, and proclaims that the Earth was created for humanity's benefit. Another scripturally diverse answer is to a geographic question that remains divisive within Judaism: what land did Yahweh promise to the people Israel? Different answers appear in Genesis 12:1–3, 6–7:

Get out of your country into a land I will show you; Canaanites were then in that land, unto thy seed shall I give this land (what is now northern Israel, west of the Sea of Galilee and south of Mt. Tabor).

And 15:18: Unto thy seed I have given this land, from the river of the Egyptians (the Nile) unto the river Euphrates.

The first promises but a small portion of what is now Israel, while the second promises the present nations of Israel, the Palestinian territories, all of Jordan, Lebanon, Syria, and portions of Egypt, Iraq, and Saudi Arabia. Jews have sometimes claimed more than the first, but never controlled even a third of the second, and no Jewish organization has illusions of doing so.

The Torah's sacred history proceeds with the patriarchs Abraham, Isaac, and Jacob. Jacob's sons envied their youngest brother, Joseph, and sold him into Egyptian slavery. His spiritual descendant, Moses, was rescued and raised by an Egyptian princess. As a young adult, Moses killed an Egyptian and then fled Egypt. Years later, Yahweh spoke to Moses from a burning bush, and ordered him to leave his peaceful exile and return to get the enslaved Jews out of Egypt. Moses then led his people through the Sinai wilderness for forty years and received the Ten Commandments from Yahweh. Because Moses often challenged Yahweh, he was excluded from entering the promised land.

Later books tell of generations of battles that resulted in the Jews' gradual conquests of the peoples already resident in what is now Israel. At that time, the Jews were still separate tribes with ruling judges, and remained so until three successive kings: Saul, David, and Solomon (1025–931 BC), ruled Israel. During Solomon's reign, Israel developed into a sophisticated nation and completed the great temple in Jerusalem. After Solomon's death, the kingdom split into the two kingdoms of Israel and Judah. By 586 BC, the Assyrian Empire had conquered the Jews and destroyed their temple, and some Jews were taken into Babylonian captivity. By BCE 530, a new generation of Persians under Cyrus, and later Darius, allowed the Jewish exiles and their descendants to return to Israel, and provided the finances to rebuild the temple. Now Jews ruled again, but only in Judah, and often remained in internal conflict. In AD 70, the Romans sacked Jerusalem and destroyed the temple. There would not be another Jewish ruler in Israel until 1948, when it once again became a Jewish nation.

Jewish Scriptures

The Jewish scriptures are divided into three sections: Torah (teachings, law, and Jewish way), *Nevi'im* (the books of Joshua, Judges, Samuel, and Kings, Isaiah, Jeremiah, Ezekiel, and the latter prophets), and *Ketuvim*, or Writings. The Torah and Prophets were in their present form by the 4th century BC, while the Writings section was questioned until the 1st century. According to Jewish tradition, prophesy ceased about 400 BC, and there could be no new scriptures thereafter. Wisdom stories are likely the oldest; *Job* arose from pre-Jewish sources. The poetic Proverbs, Psalms, and the Song of Solomon were written during David's and Solomon's eras. Jews and Christians arrange and interpret these scriptures differently.

The books of the Torah are Genesis, Exodus, Leviticus, Numbers, and Deuteronomy. Scholars discern four distinct strands in the Torah: J, E, P, and D sources, composed by different groups with distinct views, that continued to be edited, changed, and adapted according to new circumstances through the centuries.

The J source, composed as early as 930 BC, is the Yahwahist. It emphasizes a personal God, YHWH, whose character is known by his actions. J explains morality, rivalries, the necessity of labor, differences among languages, and emphasizes family. It stresses Jews' attempts to break through God's limits, and repeats a recurring pattern of sin, punishment, and mercy. Yahweh is the deliverer of the Jews, who are His particular responsibility, but ultimately, Yahweh will bless all nations. It highlights episodes of particular interest to Jews from Judea.

The E, or Elohist source, emphasizes a more generic and impersonal deity who speaks through prophets and dreams rather than through personal appearances. It emphasizes prophetic leadership, the fear of God, and the covenant with God. It is concerned about Israel's propensity to violate its covenant. There is also an emphasis on the more specifically religious aspects and focuses on the Kingdom of Israel. The E source began eighty years later than J (850 BC), and provides more than one third of Genesis and at least half of Exodus.

The P, or Priestly source, emphasizes a God who is interested in ritual and favors the priests. Yahweh is the Creator, but He is distant and not particularly merciful. P begins generations after E, and includes the first chapter of Genesis, substantial portions of Exodus and Numbers, and practically all of Leviticus. It is filled with genealogies, lists, dates, numbers, and ritual laws, and was probably composed during the Captivity period.

The D, or Deuteronomist source especially addressed the Jewish exiles in Babylon. It emphasizes God's vengeance for disobedience, urged Jews to turn back to God and follow Jewish laws. D passages appear only in Deuteronomy and began in the 6th century BCE. The Torah was declared official by the temple elite in 444 BC

Prophets were prevalent throughout the ancient Near East, but only a few were presented in Jewish scripture. Prophets were intermediaries between God and the people, bringing God's words to the Jews but also bringing people's queries to God and interceding with God on their behalf. While the priesthood was exclusively male, prophets could be female or male (Judges 4, Kings 22, and Joel 2), and were also seers and visionaries. Early Jewish prophets were often king makers or king breakers. The 8th-century prophets, such as Amos, Hosea, and the early books of Isaiah and Micah, were instead critical of Jews' self-righteous religious practices and abuses of social justice. They lived facing Assyrian intimidation, which ended the kingdom of Israel and brought Judah under Assyria's control. Prophecy's third period was during the Babylonian captivity, from Nahum to Jeremiah and Ezekiel. After the Persian king Cyrus came to power and allowed Jewish captives to return, there was a fourth set of prophets who participated in building the Second Temple, from Ezra through the final chapters of Isaiah and Malachi. Daniel is the only possibly apocalyptic book in the Hebrew Bible; however, Jews consider it a Wisdom book, while some Christians consider it Prophetic.

Jewish Presence in Israel

In 8000 BC, centuries before any Jews arrived, the region had established towns and farming villages. About 2000 BC, Semitic peoples, like the Amorites (later the Canaanite ancestors of Palestinians and Israelis), first appeared, and by 1500 BC, Egyptians ruled the region and there were references in documents about marauders called Habiru. According to modern scholars, the Habiru became the original Hebrews—Semitic fighting tribes that welcomed other marginalized peoples who, like them, were unwelcome intruders into Canaan, living as seminomadic groups on the outskirts of Canaanite settlements. These pre-Jewish Habiru weren't the only newcomers interested in taking over Canaan—Philistines arrived from Crete. By King David's time, this land was a quilt of contending tribes and peoples.

Jewish sacred history presents Abraham as a Semite from Ur (Iraq). The Talmud said that Abraham initially worshipped idols and helped build the tower of Babel. Then, Yahweh said He would confound Babel (then one people with a single language), divide them into seventy nations with different languages, and choose Israel to be in charge. Yahweh favored these wandering herders over farmers and townspeople who were then the majority of those living in Israel. The Jews were greatly influenced by the generations they spent in Egypt, for Egyptians held ideas about monotheism and considered themselves their deities' preferred people.

At the time of the first successful Jewish invasions, much of present-day Lebanon, Syria, Jordan, and Israel was known by the Greeks as the land of the Canaanites or Phoenicians, who were sailors and ship builders They exported cypress and papyrus throughout the Mediterranean. Their industrial city, Tyre, was famous for its purple dyes, and Sidon as their center of learning. Canaanites-Phoenicians probably developed the first widely used alphabet and were skilled mathematicians. When Jewish tribes of wandering herders conquered this agricultural "land of milk and honey," it already had a cultural and commercial sophistication superior to that of the Jews, who adopted much from it.

It's likely that the tribes that later became the Jews were already practicing circumcision of males, had become strict monotheists with a personally concerned but judgmental deity, and considered the Ten Commandments their ethical foundation even before they became united as a nation. Few were literate beyond the palaces and temples. The Assyrian conquest of Israel in BCE 586 depopulated Israel by about 80 percent; 40,000 were enslaved into the Babylonian Captivity; most of them were used to build canals in Iraq. The forty-five years of captivity, however, permitted some Jewish exiles to become more literate, and they were greatly influenced by Babylonian and Persian civilizations. When they returned to Judah and rebuilt the temple, they came bearing a significantly different Judaism, changed by elements of the Zoroastrian theology, including their eternal battles between a good God and an evil superhuman figure, and with new emphases on the end of the world, salvation, and an afterlife. Differences between the oral traditions of the Jewish majority left behind and the returning captives with their revised sacred texts heightened internal tensions felt until today.

When the captives returned, the Kingdom of Judah was all that was left of the Promised Land. Power remained in Persian hands, though the Persians usually allowed local leaders and customs to hold sway. The Torah and temple again governed the religious life of the literate elite; however, a connected but different tradition continued to expand among ordinary Jews and their local leaders. Between 334 and 323 BC, Alexander's armies conquered the Middle East. When Alexander died, the region was split among Greek generals. Jews were controlled first by Greeks resident in Egypt (Ptolemaists) and later by Greeks resident in Syria (Seleucids). Many Jews became increasingly attracted to Greek culture. Greek became their language, and Hebrew scriptures were translated into Greek. During the reign of Seleucid ruler Antiochus IV (BC 175–163), the rural masses and their leaders from the Maccabee family felt that Hellenization was destroying Judaism. By BC 161, the Maccabean revolt succeeded, and Judah Maccabee purified the Jerusalem temple. By BC 63, the Roman general Pompey controlled Jerusalem and soon ruled Palestine. King Herod became the appointed Roman ruler between BC 40–4.

Rabbinic Judaism

The rabbinic tradition strengthened after the destruction of the First Temple and two generations of exile. Rabbinic Judaism has been the dominant form for most of the last 2,000 years. The Talmud, its written foundation, comprises 250 million words in 6,000 pages, assembled into thirty large volumes, and is acknowledged as the sequel to the Torah. The Talmud has interpretations of the Torah, Prophets, and Writings; and is divided into the Mishnah and the Gemara. The Mishnah represents about a third of the Talmud, with six orders of laws: agriculture and prayer, Sabbath and festivals, marriage, divorce, and family relationships, civil, criminal, and court proceedings, sacrifices and temple traditions, and ritual uncleanness. The Gemara comprises the remaining two thirds. It often proceeds by questions and answers, with rabbinic commentary on almost every conceivable subject.

Before the First Temple had been destroyed, Jews had already settled far beyond the kingdoms of Israel and Judah. Emigration has continued thereafter throughout Jewish history. For several centuries, there were two competing versions of the Talmud: the Jerusalem Talmud, composed primarily in Tiberius on the Sea of Galilee; and the Babylonian Talmud, which became the Talmud's dominant version, begun among Iraqi Jewish communities before the captivity. While the Jerusalem Talmud contained agricultural laws and reflected the ideas and practices of those left behind in the Holy Land, the Babylonian Talmud had no agricultural laws, but added sacrifices and an emphasis on impurities—significantly impacted by Iranian magi. The Mishnah contains the rules and rituals of the Jewish religion, and the rights and obligations of people in civil society. Here are passages from the Mishnah portions of the Talmud:

> The Holy one gives man his soul....He sustains the whole world and judges every day....He tempers justice with mercy, charity, honesty, and loving kindness, which are tools of human social and moral existence....For the ways of peace, we must support the poor of the Gentiles and clothe their naked as well as the poor of Israel.

The Gemara contains interpretations of dreams, legends, medical writings, astronomical observations, messianic notions, resurrection of the dead, and the Day of Judgment. For many centuries, there was only a single manuscript of the Talmud, but by 450, the Jerusalem Talmud had an officially edited version. Not until 1523, however, did a printed version appear in Venice, and in 1965, El Am finally began to publish an English version of the Talmud.

By BC 150, there was a Greek translation of the Hebrew Scriptures, the Septuagint, composed in Alexandria, Egypt. A Samaritan version of the Torah likely preceded any extant Hebrew Torah or surviving original Septuagint. Aramaic and later Greek became the widely understood languages among Jewish communities; Hebrew was often followed by Aramaic and later Greek paraphrases written in adjoining columns so that congregants could understand. In certain Jewish communities, Samaritan, Syrian, Aramaic, or Greek might be used at services. By the first century AD, the Septuagint became the dominant Old Testament text until the Protestant Reformation.

The most famous Rabbi in the concluding years of the past eon and the first generation of the present one was Rabbi Hillel, often considered the father of rabbinic Judaism. Hillel grew up in Babylon and didn't come to Jerusalem until he was forty. Within a few years he became the head of the Sanhedrin, the temple's highest court, serving from BC 30 to 10 AD. Hillel was probably a student of Essene thought; he became attracted to the Pharisaic movement, and championed Midrash exegesis, which is the Biblical interpretations used to justify the oral law. Rabbi Hillel was committed to the poor and preached social justice and social reform. One of his notable rulings was to protect creditors, which allowed the poor to borrow money, since creditors were guaranteed eventual full payment. Hillel emphasized that Jews should practice the ideals of Maccabean piety. He elevated the life of the mind, arguing that careful study was the primary means available to help people understand God's words, and that people needed to combine their piety with activism in order to make desirable changes in society. Hillel's most famous admonitions include: "What is hateful to you, do not do to your neighbor; that is the whole of the Torah; the rest is commentary; go and learn" and "If I am not for myself, who is for me? And when I am for myself alone, what am I? And if not now, when?"

By BC 63, General Pompey had conquered Jerusalem for the Roman Empire. King Herod was appointed by Rome as Israel's leader and reigned from BC 40 to BC 4. By his time, Jews resided throughout the Roman Empire. In the 1st century AD, most Jews in Israel were illiterate farmers, laborers, or tradespeople, devout within their families and at their synagogues. Among the Jewish elite, there were four distinct groups: Sadducees, Pharisees, Essenes, and Zealots, who together numbered less than 20,000. The Sadducees were the priests and their families; they were focused on the temple and its liturgies and strove to accommodate their foreign rulers. Pharisees were the most important and popular elite contingent (perhaps 6,000); they believed that their interpretations of the oral explanations more adequately explained both the scriptures and appropriate behavior. Rabbi Hillel was a Pharisee. The Essenes were a secretive sect who viewed only Essenes as children of light, and sought isolation from other Jews, whom they considered children of darkness surrounded by evil. The Zealots were those who revolted against foreign rule and sought radical political change.

By 66 AD Jews rebelled against the Romans. In 70 AD Jerusalem fell, the temple was again destroyed, and thousands were killed or scattered. There would not be a Jewish majority in Israel again until 1948. For 1,800 years, Jews represented less than 20 percent of Israel's residents. Persecution of Jews remained widespread until Emperor Hadrian died in 138. By 200, 10 percent of the entire Roman Empire may have been Jewish, with significant communities in Egypt, Iraq, and Syria. By the 2nd century AD, Christianity was becoming a separate religion. The Roman emperor Constantine became Christian, and in 337, Christian conversion to Judaism was outlawed. Thereafter, Jewish congregations were curtailed and sometimes proscribed. Jews emigrated for opportunity, but now also because of violence or expulsion. By the 4th century, Jewish communities had spread across North Africa, Europe, and the Middle East. By 379, there was a Jewish community in India, protected by its Hindu ruler.

Judaism in an Increasingly Islamic World

When Muhammad introduced Islam to the world (570–632), he worked with and learned from Medina's Jewish tribes. Soon after his death, however, most Saudi Arabian Jews had either converted to Islam or had been killed or driven away. Generally, subsequent Islamic rulers tolerated Jews and Christians, requiring them to pay a greater tax than Muslims, and to wear identifying insignia (a yellow sash for Jews, a blue one for Christians).

Though Rabbinic Judaism continued to dominate Jewish life, there were Jewish movements that challenged rabbinic Judaism, like Karaism (from Hebrew *qara,* to read), which repudiated the oral tradition as divine law, and instead considered the Hebrew Bible the sole authentic source of doctrine and practice. In the 8th century in Persia and Babylon, the Ananite subsect developed a code of life independent of the Talmud, considered the Hebrew Bible self-explanatory and its personal interpretation vital, and followed strict rituals and ascetic practices. The Ananites refused to participate in Hanukkah and objected to ritual objects as non-scriptural. They failed to ever become a major Jewish subsect, but Karaites spread throughout the Middle East and Eastern Europe and produced a mass of polemic literature in Hebrew and Aramaic.

Jewish communities eventually existed throughout much of the world. Jews in different cultures did their best to preserve worthy elements of their ancestral heritage while also successfully integrating into their adopted cultures; many played important roles in their nations' histories. In almost every culture, there were, however, also incidents of terrible anti-Semitic violence. In some Islamic countries, Jewish communities had a significant amount of self-government in relation to issues of Jewish life and culture. In many Middle Eastern and North African nations, Judaism has had a long and varied history.

In Islamic Persia (now Iran), Jews, along with Zoroastrians and Christians, were initially given the status of *dhimmis* (protected persons, or People of the Book). They were exempted from military service, paid special taxes, and were given the right to practice their religion and to receive the security and financial welfare provided for all citizens. Mongols invaded Persia, and by 1258 treated all religions equally. One Mongol ruler preferred Jews for administrative positions; he appointed a Jew to be his primary minister. After the monarch was murdered, Persian Jews suffered a period of violence instigated by Islamic clergy. Succeeding regimes returned religious minorities to the dhimmi system, but many Jews were forced to convert to Islam. In 1383, Timor conquered Persia, and killed so many skilled Muslims that he imported skilled Jews to develop his empire's textile industry. The Safavid dynasty (1502–1794) made Shi'a Islam Persia's state religion, excluded religious minorities from public places, and believed Jews were "spreading impurities."

Centuries later (1925–1979), the Pahlavi dynasty prohibited mass conversions and made ritual uncleanness illegal. Iranian Jews moved to cities, took important positions, and gained significant financial wealth and influence, but Reza Shah's Nazi sympathies prompted a decline in tolerance for Jews, and the 1948 creation of Israel provoked further challenges for the 150,000 Iranian Jews. By 1976, the poorer half had immigrated to Israel. For Jews, the reign of Muhammad Reza Pahlavi (1953–79) was the most liberated, successful period in Iranian history. By the 1970s, only a single percent of the Iranian Jewish population were poor; many were wealthy, including scientists, professors, and doctors. Prior to the Islamic Revolution, there were 100,000 Iranian Jews; after 1979 a majority immigrated to the U.S. or to Europe. The new Iranian Republic did provide religious minorities formal equality and freedom to practice their religions and gave each minority religion a seat in Parliament; however, de facto discrimination remains prevalent. There are 85,000 Iranian Jews today. They own many businesses. Iran has eleven functioning synagogues, many with Hebrew schools. In 2007, when non-Iranian Jews urged Iranian Jews to immigrate to Israel, the Iranian Jewish community stated that their nationality was not for sale.

A History of Early European Jewry

In the Roman Empire, Jews were treated fairly if they paid taxes and did not rebel. They could become Roman citizens, and some became wealthy and served in government. After Emperor Constantine became Christian in 313, constraints began to be put upon Jews. When the Goths and Visigoths invaded the empire, they treated Jews like other conquered peoples, and Jews flourished until the Visigoth rulers became Roman Catholics, beginning in 589. By then, Roman Catholic "replacement theology" argued that Christianity had replaced Judaism, that Judaism was inferior and should be restricted, and consequently medieval European Jews often worshipped privately. An economic reality, however, somewhat offset growing prejudices against Jews. Since Christians could not then collect interest and were therefore unlikely to loan money, Jews became important sources for loans which provided them important economic roles in medieval societies, and many moved into Italy, France, Germany, and Spain.

When Muslim invaders conquered Spain in 718, Jews welcomed them. For the next 350 years, Muslim Spain became Judaism's cultural center. Jews came from everywhere to study and to prosper financially. Jewish philosophers, mathematicians, astronomers, poets, and rabbinic scholars created important cultural and scientific works, translated Arabic texts into romance languages, and Greek and Hebrew texts into Arabic. In the 900s, when Rahman III and his son, Al-Hakam II, ruled, Jewish scholarship flourished, and many Jews held high positions. Jews had their own legal system and social services. In 976, the caliphate began to dissolve. In a massacre in Granada in 1066, 4,000 Jews were murdered in a day. In 1090, the Almoravids, a puritanical Moroccan Muslim sect, invaded Spain, and Judaism was again suppressed.

Bahya ben Joseph Ibn Pakuda, Solomon Ibn Gabirol, and Moses Maimonides were considered the most learned medieval Jewish scholars in Europe. Pakuda (1021–58) served as a judge of the rabbinical court. His *Duties of the Heart* was the first attempt to systematize Jewish ethical teachings. Pakuda was an ascetic and a contemplative mystic. His ethics argued that people needed to use both the wisdom of the head and of the heart. His precepts included:

God cannot be grasped by reason, but only felt by the longing soul. Worship is whatever recognizes the benefits of life and does beneficial acts. Jewish law avoids either sensuality or contempt for life. Those with advanced consciousness realize that the soul is eternal, trust in God, and proceed with sincerity of purpose, and humility. They confess their shameful acts, and through changes of heart alter future conduct, and discontinue sinful habits. Religious practice is the exercise of self-control shaping passions in the service of God. The love of God is the goal of all ethical self-discipline. *Duties of the Heart* (1925)

Ibn Gabirol was a younger contemporary of Pakuda. Gabirol served to "Occidentalize" Greco-Arabic philosophy and to restore Neo-Platonism in Europe. In *Fons Vitae,* he argued that all things are composed of form and matter, even God and spirituality. Three of his aphorisms:

"The test of a good man is to be patient with bad news. As long as a word remains unspoken, you are its master. Once your utter it, you are its slave. His five sequential steps in the acquisition of wisdom are "silence, listening, memory, practice, and teaching others."

The most enduring medieval Jewish thinker was Maimonides (1135–1204) who grew up in Cordoba and became a prominent physician and philosopher. Fearing less-tolerant Muslim rulers, he and his family escaped, first to Morocco, briefly to the Holy Land, and finally to Egypt where he became for decades the physician of the Egyptian ruler Saladin. Maimonides's fourteen books of commentary, the Mishnah Torah, became the authoritative Torah for centuries. His *Guide for the Perplexed* sought to harmonize the teachings of Judaism with Aristotle's philosophy; it's the most important Jewish text between ancient and modern times. His near creedal principles of faith are: "God is Creator and guide, the only worthy object of worship, revealed through the prophets, especially Moses who received the Torah from God. God is all-knowing and does reward and punish humans. The Messiah will come, and the dead will be resurrected." Medieval Jewish philosophy revolves around Maimonides.

Maimonides said there were two kinds of beliefs: true beliefs about God, which produce intellectual perfection, and necessary beliefs, which improve social order. For instance, God does not actually get angry (a true belief), but it's a necessary belief that people think God gets angry at them for doing wrong. He ranked levels of philanthropy: best is finding someone a job or providing an interest-free loan so the person can become independent, and the lowest form is giving out of pity. He argued that God created the virtuous, while evil arises where good is absent. We might think that evil predominates, but looking at the universe, good obviously predominates. There are three types of evil: evil caused by nature; evil that people bring upon others; and evil that people bring upon themselves. Those whose merits exceed their iniquities are righteous, while those whose iniquities exceed their merits are wicked, and the most grievous evils are practiced by those who think that everything written in old books is true.

Persecution during the Christian Crusades, Inquisition, and Protestant Reformation

By the 10th century, most of Europe was ruled by Christian monarchs who had made Christianity the state religion. Throughout Western Europe, some Jews were valued professionals and wealthy financiers, while many others were hardworking craftspeople and farmers, but Jewish populations and their worship became more restricted, and violence became a continuous threat and periodic occurrence. Natural catastrophes, plagues, and unexplained deaths were often falsely blamed upon Jews. Jewish culture flourished, but the Jews' relationships with regional religious majorities varied from harsh persecution to cooperative coexistence.

From the 4th to the 6th century, political control of the Holy Land had moved from Roman to Byzantine hands beginning with Emperor Constantine the First, who had made Christianity the state religion and moved his capitol from Rome to Constantinople. In 661, Muawiyah the First was crowned uncontested Caliph of the Islamic world in Jerusalem, and by 691, the Dome of the Rock on the Jewish temple mount was completed as the first great Islamic architectural monument. Islamic control of the Holy Land galvanized Christian Europe into religious mania from the First Crusade in 1096 until the Crusades ended around 1320. As the First Crusade was organized, crusaders and envious locals destroyed Jewish communities along the Rhine and Danube rivers. During the Second and Third Crusades, French Jews especially suffered. In 1290, all English Jews were banished, and Jews could not return to England for 365 years.

In 1120, Pope Calixtus II issued the papal bull *Sicut Judaeis,* or the *Constitution of the Jews,* which was intended to impede anti-Semitism by forbidding Christians from taking Jewish property, harming Jews, disturbing their celebrations or cemeteries, or forcing them to convert. Although this remained the official Roman Catholic position until the 15th century, and many Christians did protect their Jewish neighbors, across Europe and in those parts of the Middle East under Christian control, centuries of Christian Crusades exploded with anti-Jewish violence. After the Crusades ended, persecution continued with Inquisition tribunals, which equated heresy with treason, and sanctified an era of terror formalized by an edict of Pope Lucius III. In 1469, Ferdinand and Isabella began the Spanish Inquisition, and in 1492 forced Jews to choose conversion, exile, or death in Spain and its colonies. Other nations followed. By 1542, Pope Paul II broadened the persecutions of the Inquisition to include Protestants and all non-Christians. Sixteenth-century inquisitions were the most horrific, and the Roman Catholic Church did not officially suppress them until 1834.

The six centuries between 1200 and 1800 reflected distinctly different Jewish histories between Western-Central Europe and Northeastern Europe, while Jewish histories elsewhere differed from either of these.

A Jewish Renaissance in Poland

During the 15th and 16th centuries, Poland and what is now northwest Russia became a center for Jewish culture and scholarship. The Polish empire was tolerant of Jews and sold them a monopoly on the sale and distribution of alcohol, a source of steady capital. Most of the world's Jews came to Poland in the course of those two centuries; most lived in autonomous Jewish communities over which the rabbinate had almost total control. Their leaders collected governmental taxes and kept 30 percent for their patronage. These rabbis became not only spiritual advisors but also judges and legislators. Their perspective was shaped by Bohemian Rabbi Jacob Pollak and his Polish pupil, Shalom Shacna (1500–1558). They practiced *pilpul,* or sharp reasoning. Their spiritual descendant, Moses Isserles, or Rema (1520–1572), drew up a new code of Jewish law. This Jewish renaissance in Poland profoundly influenced European Judaism.

In 1772, Russian Czarina Catherine II instituted the Pale of Settlement, restricting Jews to parts of Poland, the Baltics, and Ukraine. By the late 19th century, its Jewish population reached 4 million. Jewish villages and towns were called *shtetls.* She ended the Jewish control of alcohol production and distribution as well as the rabbis' taxing authority, which impoverished the Jews. Thereafter, many Russian Jews became secular, joined unions, started political parties and joined progressive social movements, developing a Russian consciousness. However, most Jews remained isolated, marginalized, and impoverished, and sporadic violence and prevalent anti-Semitism continued. At the end of the 19th and the beginning of the 20th centuries, several million Jews from the Pale of Settlement immigrated to the U.S.

Jewish Mysticism

There had been earlier messianic and mystical movements within Judaism, but now these ideas swept through eastern European Judaism. Solomon Ibn Gabirol may have originated the term *kabbalah* for organized Jewish mysticism, embodied in a 13th-century text called *The Zohar.* In Poland, under Isaac Luria (1534–1572), kabbalah took a messianic turn, and Luria stands as perhaps the most influential mystic in Jewish history. The Zohar argues that there are four levels of Torah interpretation: direct, allegoric, imaginative comparisons using *Midrash,* and *Sod*—the inner esoteric-metaphysical meanings expressed in kabbalah. For kabbalists, mysticism reveals Judaism's true meaning, while Jews with more rationalistic views considered many kabalistic interpretations heretical or antithetical to Judaism. Kabbalah became an entire mystical spiritual system for Jews. Until the end of the 18th century, it was a part of the mainstream Jewish tradition, particularly in northeastern Europe.

Kabbalah practice divided into three distinct traditions: Zohar-Luria, a more ecstatic group, and a magical practice. The Zohar-Luria branch wished to understand and describe the divine realm and believed themselves superior to Maimonides' rationalism. Abraham Adularia best represented the ecstatic tradition that argued for mystical union with God, while the magic version tried to change the world and the divine realm with acts of white magic. All kabbalah tends toward secrecy, demands guidance from strong leaders and believes wisdom is primarily intuitive. The teachings of Israel ben Eliezer, or the Baal Shem Tov (1692–1760) had a profound effect upon the Jews of Central and Eastern Europe. His followers practiced a fervent Kabbalah Judaism called Hasidism. A Russian, Shneur Zalman (1745–1812) became the Chief Rabbi of the Chabad branch of Hasidic Judaism, which believes that the mind rules over the heart and emotions.

Belief in the eventual coming of an anointed one, a messiah or *moshiach*, is a long-held, fundamental Jewish tenet. The anointed one will simply be a man, but also a descendant of King David, and will become a political leader who gains sovereignty over Israel, gathers Jews from the whole Earth, and restores the temple and its sacrifices and laws. Before his arrival, there will be war and suffering, and after his arrival Israel will become the center of world government, establish Jewish law as the universal law, and all people will peacefully coexist, because everyone will by then have grasped the truth. Jews disagree about whether *Moshiach* will come when he is most needed or when Jews have become most deserving.

Moshiach does not mean savior; the Christian concept of a divine being who will sacrifice himself to save people from the consequences of their own sins is contrary to Judaism. Jesus did not live up to Jewish expectations about an anointed one. A century after Jesus lived, another Jew, Simon Bar Kokhba ("Son of the Star") better fit Jewish messianic expectations. He led brief battles against the Romans, temporarily seized control of Jerusalem, planned to rebuild the temple, and resumed sacrifices on its former site. In the centuries since, there have been many others who claimed, or were considered by some, to be the anointed one. Most famous was Sabbatai Zevi, born in Turkey in 1626. He was arrested by the Ottoman Sultan, and in 1666 was forced to become Islamic. After that, Jewish leaders prohibited Kabbalah study for years. In the 18th century, Jacob Frank gained popularity as the anointed one, but converted to Catholicism.

The European Enlightenment and Western and Central European Jewry

In Western and Central Europe, Judaism was much affected by the Renaissance and Enlightenment, which began in Italy in the 1300s, and spread throughout Western and central Europe by the 1500s. Jews were important participants in the Renaissance; Christian scholars developed interest in learning Hebrew and studied with Jewish scholars. The American pilgrims considered making Hebrew the official language of Massachusetts colony. Jews became involved with book publishing, distribution, and sales, and many Jews participated in scientific, literary, and artistic accomplishments. Though still excluded from some Western European countries, Jews were welcomed in Protestant countries and regions that sought their skills. By 1579, a Jewish community thrived in Holland. In 1655, Jews were readmitted to England, never again to be expelled. In Germany and the Austro-Hungarian Empire, Jews held influential positions between 1550 and 1800.

Spinoza

Seventeenth-century Holland was the cosmopolitan center of Europe, and an elite community of Spanish and Portuguese Jews became prominent there. The most famous was Baruch Spinoza (1632–1679). From a Portuguese Jewish family and heir to a large import-export firm, he became a partner in the firm as a teenager. At eighteen, Spinoza received his father's permission to study Latin with Francis van den Enden, a freethinker and revolutionary republican who mocked traditional values and religion. When Spinoza's father died, Baruch gave away his estate and moved in with his teacher's family. Spinoza became a philosopher for the Dutch republican middle-class democracy movement and for rational-ethical religion based upon his *Ethics, Theological-Political Treatise,* and *On the Improvement of the Understanding.*

Spinoza believed that God, nature, and reality are one, the same entity and power. We must learn the laws of nature, but natural law does not pursue human good, but rather eternal laws of cosmic nature of which humanity is only a tiny proportion. People can be happy by learning to live rational lives but need to make their reasoning, appetites, and environments compatible.

Habits of virtue take a lifetime of experiential learning. We need to understand our desires so that we do not become slaves to them. Piety means doing justice and living with charity with our neighbors which requires altruism. Effective altruism requires altruistic social norms enforced by societies. People need to be trained to live effectively within societies. Reason stimulates people to action; their creative efforts lead to human cooperation; then, humanity can build a kingdom of friendship and unselfishness. Salvation can be achieved by self-disciplined individuals acting in a rational manner cooperatively. Spiritual community becomes a community of rational persons striving cooperatively for truth through loving actions.

The Growth of Liberal and Integrationist Judaism

Spinoza's ideas were part of a growing trend within Western European Judaism that continued through the 19th century. It embraced belief in natural law, universal order, and confidence in human reasoning, advocated a rational and scientific approach to religious, social, political, and economic issues, and promoted a secular view of the world and a sense of progress. The French Revolution bestowed citizenship on French Jews. By the mid-19th century, Germany was unified, and its industrial expansion and educational vigor looked like a land of freedom compared with the oppressive regimes in Eastern Europe. In Germany and the Austro-Hungarian Empire, Jews could leave their ghettos, engage in commerce, learn any trade, and attend public schools and universities, conditions that became a magnet for adventurous Jews throughout Europe. Its intellectual leader was Moses Mendelssohn (1728–1786) who argued that Jewish improvement required both the adoption of German culture and the acquisition of equal rights. He translated the Pentateuch into German. His commentaries featured modern ideas about the philosophy of religion. Young Jews embraced an emancipated Torah enriched by contemporary poetry and science. Secular reading became a Jewish passion, and emancipated Jews lived in a secular and integrated world of business and books. In places like Berlin and Prague, the Reform and Conservative revolts against Orthodox Judaism later took place.

A clear emotional division opened between the ghettoized and often Hasidic Jews of northeastern Europe and the integrated and secular Jews of Western Europe. Yiddish (a combination of Hebrew and German that originated in German ghettos) flourished in Eastern Europe, while Western European Jews increasingly spoke and read in the languages of their nations. Throughout Europe, splits developed between traditional Jewish religionists and Jewish modernists. In Western and Central Europe, the split took three directions, with many Jews assimilating in their surrounding communities, some converted to Christianity or became nonreligious, and others remained traditionally Jewish.

In northeastern Europe, the split was more between religionists and Jewish culturists who wanted to become secular, cultural, and worldly. Some Jewish culturists argued for Jewish national and cultural autonomy within their nations of residence, while others sought a territorial solution within formerly Russian territory or in the Holy Land. In Eastern Europe, religious Jewry divided between the *Misnagdim* and the *Chasidim*. The Misnagdim argued for rational persuasion based on objective sources, which they saw as in opposition to the Chasidim, whose individualities were melded into their leaders who, for them, represented divine manifestations. Chasidim practiced enthusiastic ecstatic worship; Misnagdim believed that ecstasy easily became blindness to moral sensitivity. Many took fresh interest in both Hebrew and Yiddish, and Yiddish saw its European cultural zenith in yeshivas (Orthodox academies). Eastern European Jews perceived themselves to be islands of religious and cultural growth within a sea of non-Jewish ignorance and backwardness (since a greater proportion of Jews than Christians were literate), while Western European Jews increasingly saw themselves as outstanding members of their nations of residence.

Jewish populations affected by Islamic influence are called *Sephardim* (Spanish) Jews, while the Jews of Western and northeastern Europe are called *Ashkenazim* (German). Eons-old Jewish communities in Ethiopia, Yemen, and India do not fit easily into either category. After 1492 and the Inquisition, most Spanish and Portuguese Jews immigrated to southeast Europe, then under Turkish Islamic control. The Jews of North Africa and the Middle East are called *Mizrahim* (Eastern Jews), but are considered Sephardic. Until modern times, Sephardim were generally more integrated into their local non-Jewish cultures than most Ashkenazic Jews because Jews in Islamic lands were generally less segregated and religiously oppressed until after 1948. The beliefs and practices of Sephardic Jews are more like those of Western Jewish Orthodox believers; the Sephardic community has not generally divided into separate denominations. Sephardic thought and culture have been strongly influenced by Arabic and Greek philosophy and science. Their special shared language, Ladino, combines Spanish and Hebrew elements.

Reform Judaism

Reform Judaism was born out of the French Revolution. Rabbi Abraham Geiger proposed that Jewish observance be changed to become more appealing to modern people. His scholarship demonstrated that Jewish life and practice had continually changed throughout its history to meet new needs and circumstances, and he argued this transformation process needed to continue. New congregations were organized which instituted mixed-gender seating, services in German, single-day festivals, and these congregations added cantors and choirs.

The earliest North American Jewish settlers were Sephardic, and the first congregations were Shearith Israel in New York City (1684) and Congregation Mikveh Israel in Philadelphia (1740); both active today as Orthodox congregations. It was in the mid-1800s, however, when millions of German Reform Jews immigrated to the U.S., that Judaism became a dynamic aspect of American life, and Reform Judaism became the dominant Jewish belief and practice system. It was organized by Rabbi Isaac Mayer Wise, who arrived from Bohemia in 1846, and moved to Cincinnati, then on the edge of the American frontier. Rabbi Wise wrote the first American Jewish prayer book (1857), founded the Union of American Hebrew Congregations (1873), began Cincinnati's Hebrew Union College (1875), and organized the Central Conference of American Rabbis (1889). By then, more than 90 percent of American synagogues were Reform.

The Columbus Platform of 1937 held that God is revealed in the beauty and orderliness of nature but also in the vision and striving of the human spirit, and that revelation is continuous. Each generation is obligated to adapt the teachings of the Torah to its own needs. Reform Jews do not have required faith elements, but generally share a belief in God as defined in the Torah and agree that the Torah demonstrates divine inspiration. They emphasize human rationality, argue that each Jew has a stake in reinterpreting the Torah, and believe that living individuals may equal or exceed past prophets. Reform Judaism embraces pluralistic debate, interpretation, and practice, welcomes sincere converts from other faiths or no faith, makes provisions for interfaith families, and has a strong sense of social commitment, embodied in the concept of *tikkun olam* (repairing the world).

Conservative Judaism

The roots of Conservative Judaism arose in 19th-century Germany in reaction to the new Reform congregations. In 1886, Sephardic Rabbis Sabato Morais and H. Pereira Mendes founded the Jewish Theological Seminary (JTS) in New York City. Its prominence dramatically increased when renowned Cambridge Talmudic scholar Solomon Schechter became its president, and the seminary became a magnet for American Jewish scholarship. In 1913, the Conservative movement formed the United Synagogues of Conservative Judaism. Conservative Judaism enjoyed rapid growth in the first half of the 20th century, and became the largest American Jewish denomination by midcentury. It combines some modern elements, like mixed-gender seating, along with traditional Jewish practices, which appealed to first- and second-generation Eastern European immigrants who found Orthodoxy too restrictive and Reform Judaism strange. In the 1950s and '60s, as Americans moved to the suburbs and strove to achieve a comfortable conformity, Conservative Judaism occupied a sweet spot that combined traditional Jewish beliefs and rites along with American mainstream practices.

In 1963, Mordecai Kaplan separated from the Conservative movement to form a distinct denomination, Reconstructionist Judaism. The Reconstructionists wanted to combine historically relevant Jewish traditions with liberal innovations in liturgy and ritual, and to empower progressive social and activist practices. In 1968, they formed the Reconstructionist Rabbinical College. The denomination has remained small.

Neo-Orthodox Judaism

Neo-Orthodox Judaism arose as a reaction to the temptations of the knowledge that arose from the Enlightenment and to modern European freedoms. Rabbi Moses Sofer (1762–1839), who said, "that which is new is biblically prohibited," was particularly important. Rabbi Samson Raphael Hirsch (1808–88) persuaded the Prussian government to allow Neo-Orthodox congregations (1876) to legally split from the Reform congregations that dominated the German Jewish community. Neo-Orthodoxy wanted to embrace all Jews as part of their community, to separate themselves from secular temptations, and to maintain firm rabbinic control in their communities. Modern Neo-Orthodoxy has become passionately evangelical: it tries to bring non-practicing and secular Jews back into regular Jewish participation and, hopefully, active membership in Orthodox communities. A Chabad branch of Hasidic Judaism immigrated its entire community to Brooklyn; then developed a global missionary movement to evangelize "wayward" Jews.

Zionism

Since the Roman destruction of the last ancient Jewish political state in AD 70, there had been Jews who hoped there would again be a State of Israel. Their desire to emigrate there is called the *Aliyah,* or ascent. At the end of the 19th century, systematic efforts to create a Jewish state and to emigrate there became a nationalistic way to bring Judaism into the modern era. In 1882, Baron E. J. de Rothschild began to buy Palestinian land and finance Jewish agricultural settlements and industrial enterprises in Palestine. By 1890, there were thirty Jewish farming communities there. It was, however, the publication of *The Jewish State* in 1897 by Austro-Hungarian journalist and playwright Theodor Herzl, and his subsequent organizational efforts, that created and truly nurtured the Zionist movement. In the second Aliyah, between 1904 and the beginning of WWI, 40,000 Jews immigrated to Ottoman-occupied Palestine, mostly from Russia, where they had faced increasing insecurity. By WWI, half of them had left Palestine. Those who stayed established the first kibbutz and self-defense forces, created Tel Aviv as the first modern all-Jewish Palestinian city, revived the Hebrew language in Palestine, and began Jewish political parties.

During WWI, the British agreed to give Arabia to the Arabs if they would fight the Turks, and so began the Arab revolt. On November 2, 1917, British Foreign Secretary Balfour wrote a letter to Baron Walter Rothschild stating that the British government would support the establishment of Palestine as a national home for the Jews, as long as "nothing shall be done to prejudice the civil or religious rights of the existing non-Jewish Palestinian residents, or that would compromise the rights of Jews living in any other country." By 1923, another 40,000 Jews had emigrated, mostly from Eastern Europe. They built roads and towns and established the General Federation of Labor. By 1929, another 59,000 emigrated, mostly from Poland, where Jews faced growing prejudice and economic turmoil. Largely middle-class, this group started many businesses. As the decade before WWII began, 230,000 more came to stay, most from Germany and Poland. Many were professionals and business leaders who helped establish industries, oil refineries, and the port of Haifa. In 1937, the British proposed a partition between Jewish and Arab areas of Palestine; both groups rejected the idea, and thereafter violence between Jews and Palestinians increased.

WWII and the Holocaust

By 1930, millions of Jews were integrated citizens and active participants in the civic affairs of many European nations. Millions more lived elsewhere. There was also deep anti-Jewish prejudice among the non-Jewish populations throughout Europe, and a global economic depression exacerbated people's ethnic and religious anxieties. Hitler and his Nazi philosophy swept Germany; and then, as the Nazi war machine attacked Poland and other nations, the horrific persecution of the Jews began. The Nazi Holocaust was the most systematic attempt in history to eliminate a religion. In 1930, there were 15 million Jews worldwide: 4 million in the U.S., 3.5 million in Poland, 2.7 million in the Soviet Union, 1 million in Rumania, and nearly a million each in Hungary and in the Palestinian Territory. As Hitler seized control, thousands of Jews emigrated away from nations threatened by Germany, but most Jews remained at home, focused on personal concerns. The death camps remained "secret," even from many who lived near these killing factories.

How to fathom why more was not done to stop the Holocaust? WWII blew up much of the world. There were eventually at least 45 million civilian deaths worldwide, another 15 million deaths in combat, and another 25 million wounded. The Soviet Union lost 24 million, China 20 million, Germany 8 million, Poland 5.6 million, Indonesia 4 million, India 2 million, Vietnam and Cambodia 1.5 million each, Yugoslavia 1 million, and Rumania 750,000. France, Greece, Hungary, Italy, Korea, the U.K., and the U.S., each lost half a million people.

During the Holocaust itself, 11 million people died, 6 million of them Jews; 6 million were Polish citizens, half of them Jewish and the other half Christians. Among non-Jews killed were Roma gypsies, disabled people, LGBTQ individuals, black children of German soldiers, non-Jewish spouses, Christian clergy, and activists who resisted the Nazis. More than 80 percent of the Jews in Poland, the Baltic countries, Germany, Austria, and Slovakia, 50 to 80 percent of the Jews in Greece, the Netherlands, Hungary, White Russia (Belarus), Ukraine, Belgium, Yugoslavia, Romania, and Norway, and 25 to 20 percent of the Jews in France, Bulgaria, and Italy died in the Holocaust.

Israel Becomes a Nation

The horrific events of the Holocaust revolutionized post-WWII Judaism. The world's guilt impacted developments in Palestine as Israel became a nation again, at the same time as much of the globe was transforming itself from a world of European colonies into one of independent nations. During WWII, 100,000 Jews escaped from Europe to Palestine. In 1944, the World Zionist Organization began its "One Million Plan," and made it their top priority to bring all Jews dwelling in Islamic lands to live in Israel. Between the end of WWII and 1948, 250,000 Holocaust survivors immigrated to Palestine. On November 30, 1947, the United Nations approved the partition of Palestine into Jewish and Arab areas. The Jews accepted this, but the Arabs rejected it, and civil war began. On May 14, 1948, the State of Israel declared itself an independent Jewish State. The United Nations accepted it as a member. The surrounding Arab nations invaded Israel, and Israel repulsed their attacks and conquered additional territory. Thereafter, some 850,000 Jews immigrated to Israel from Muslim countries.

The first Arab-Israel war ended in January 1949. In 1967, in a six-day war, Israel defeated the Palestine Liberation Organization (PLO), Egypt, Jordan, and Syria, which were aided by other Islamic nations. In 1973, Egypt, Syria, Jordan, and Iraq lost a third conflict, the "Yom Kippur war." In 1979, Egyptian President Sadat and Israeli Prime Minister Begin signed a peace treaty between their nations. In 1982, Israel fought a war against Lebanon, which had the assistance of Syria and of Hezbollah Palestinians living in Lebanon. In 1993, the PLO's Abbas and Israel's Peres signed the Oslo Accords. In 1994, Jordan and Israel signed a peace treaty. In 1995, an orthodox Jew assassinated Prime Minister Rabin. In 2006, Israel again fought a war with Lebanon. There has been continued strain and aggression between Palestinian residents in Israeli-held territories, most recently with the Hamas regime in the southern Gaza territories, and continued tensions between the PLO-led Palestinian West Bank and Jerusalem territories, particularly in connection with Jewish settlements, which continue to expand.

In 1920, there were 700,000 people in Palestine. Eighty percent were Arab Muslims, most of them land-owning farmers or town dwellers. There were about 76,000 resident Jews, most of whom had entered Palestine after 1880, and about 77,000 Christians, mostly longtime-resident Eastern Orthodox Arab Christians. By 1948, there were 1,900,000 residents in Palestine. Two thirds were Arabs and Muslims, 98 percent born in Palestine. Palestinian prosperity preceded WWI because of modernization and Palestine's integration into the world economy. Today, there are about 8.3 million people in Israel; 75 percent are Jews, and 21 percent are Arabs, both Muslim and Christian. Two thirds of the Jews are *sabras,* born in Israel; the rest are *olim,* first-generation immigrants, 22 percent from Europe and the Americas, the rest from Islamic, African, or Asian nations. Half of Israel's Jews are Ashkenazic, most from Russia and Eastern Europe, while the others are Sephardic. There are 2,600,000 Palestinians in the West Bank territories, another 200,000 in East Jerusalem, and another 1,650,000 in the Gaza Strip—a total of about 5.7 million Palestinians in presently held Israel or Israeli-held territories. Eighty percent of the Palestinians are Sunni Muslims, 9 percent Druze, and 9 percent Arab Christians. Judaism, Christianity, and

Islam all have holy places and centuries of history in this shared Holy Land. That the Israeli government and military sometimes act like a neocolonial regime in a postcolonial world remains a continuing source of hostility.

In 2012, the world's Jews numbered 13,860,000; 6,240,000, about 45 percent of the total, lived in Israel, about 75 percent of Israel's population. 6,800,000 self-identified practicing Jews lived in the United States, and 1,500,000 additional U.S. citizens were of Jewish ancestry or were members of a U.S. Jewish household. American Jews represented about 55 percent of the world's Jews, and about 2 percent of the total U.S. population. France had 600,000 Jews, three fourths of 1 percent of its population, and Canada had 360,000 Jews, about 1 percent of its population. The United Kingdom and Argentina each had more than 200,000 Jews, each about one half of 1 percent of their populations. Russia, Germany, and Brazil each had more than 100,000 Jewish citizens, and a plethora of other nations had thousands of Jewish citizens.

Jewish ideals and values have been and continue to be woven into American culture, including constitutional law, tolerance, progressive values, literacy, and ironic humor. American culture has become more Jewish. One third of American Jews born after 1980 do not identify themselves as religious, 60 percent of American Jews who married since 2000 have a non-Jewish spouse, and a third of them are not raising their children as Jews. Many contemporary Jews identify as culturally Jewish but ignore most traditional Jewish practices. In his article in *Living Judaism* titled "Peoplehood," Rabbi Wayne D. Dosick argues that Judaism is certainly not a race, since Jews are of every race, color, and physical characteristic, but rather that their unique greatness is the interdependence of their religion and their peoplehood, built upon their shared history, languages, literatures, and lands. I would argue that most other world religions could make parallel claims, since they also have sacred places, texts, languages, and histories.

Elements of Judaism that I Find Troubling

The idea of being a special, divinely chosen people diminishes the spirituality of the chosen, because "chosen-ness'" inherently separates its believers from others and often leads them to consider themselves superior. It tends to provoke suspicion, prejudice, and alienation between the chosen and "others." People get along better with others when they interact regularly and treat them as equals. The chosen are likely to minimize contact with outsiders except for obtaining necessities or seizing economic opportunities because the chosen are predisposed to view nonbelievers in their particular faith as corrupting influences.

At North Florida University, my mostly evangelical Christian clergy colleagues doubted that I had been "saved," so I was treated respectfully but as an outsider. When a young Chabad Orthodox Jewish rabbi joined, the Christian evangelicals more readily saw him as their colleague, for he too was evangelical, shared more of their theology, and was only proselytizing "wayward" Jews. He too perceived his sect as chosen, and they worked together to separate themselves and their flocks from the worrisome corruption they felt permeated the university.

Religious nationalism is bad for religion, harmful to spirituality, and divisive for citizens. The Israelis' persistent choices to marginalize and even dispossess their resident Palestinians, whether Islamic or Christian, as well as their continued choices to act as a colonial power over them, betray Judaism's central ethical principles and nurture a political conflict that remains a cancer that threatens their valiant efforts to become a great nation. I can only hope that Jews and non-Jews alike will find ways to heal this open sore on the world's body politic. I admire the multitude of good things Israel's people have done, and I was impressed during my 1974 visit there. I support Israel's continued success, but I believe that diaspora Jews, like those in the United States and Canada, best exemplify what a sustainable human future will be—a flourishing salad bowl of peoples with many ancestral faiths and heritages that combine individually chosen ideals with just and compassionate cooperation in a pluralistic world.

Rituals are only meaningful to me if they aid people's understanding and actions. I doubt that repeating principles in a seldom-understood liturgical language, whether Hebrew, Latin, Arabic, or Sanskrit, adds much value to anyone's spirituality. People should choose the traditions they find valuable and practice them. Life's hard lessons are best taught in everyday language and demonstrated in repeated practical situations. Coming-of-age rituals are important, and almost every culture has them, but what the young learn needs to be of enduring value to those who make those efforts. When these rituals become more like family reunions, I wonder about their spiritual depth. Many Jews, as those in other faiths, seem to limit their congregational participation to primary holidays and their families' adolescents' coming-of-age rites.

Elements of Judaism that I Find Particularly Relevant

In my youth I had little direct contact with Jews. One of the few Jews in my little Kansas town started out as an immigrant metal collector and became a prominent, wealthy citizen. He impressed my father, and I read his autobiography. My maternal grandparents hired a Jewish immigrant couple and then helped them to find work more appropriate to their education and former positions in Europe. When I began my three years at Washington University, a significant portion of its student body, faculty, and surrounding neighborhoods were Jewish. My first girlfriend there was a Jew from Chicago. We attended Sabbath services, and my first Seder was at the home of the director of the St. Louis B'nai B'rith—a Jewish service organization that promotes cordial relations between Jews and non-Jews, as the Anti-Defamation League fights anti-Semitism, and the Hillel Foundation leads Jewish college programs. My closest colleague there was a Jewish graduate student whose mother was a Quaker. We spent many hours together pursuing our academic programs, engaged in progressive activism, and having fun.

The next summer, I wanted to visit Europe; lacking funds, I found a summer job in Germany. I had not studied German, and wondered how I'd get along, but had a fascinating summer loading and unloading trucks. My closest friend there was a fellow American whose parents, both medical professionals, had escaped the Holocaust. After finishing our employment, we traveled in Europe together, and our friendship lasted for many years. We spent time with one another's families and lived together with other Jewish friends of his for two other summers. These close friendships reinforced the literary and spiritual connections I'd made particularly through reading the novels of Saul Bellow and Isaac Bashevis Singer, and being philosophically and spiritually inspired by Spinoza's and Buber's ideas and actions.

In the decades since, I've often felt allied with aspects of the Jewish tradition such as its emphasis on learning and on fully using one's experiential and critical facilities. In my hometown, I'd always felt a bit the outsider, so I identify with the tendency of many Jews who wished to become integrated into their surroundings while finding ways to remain distinct. Their visceral belief that spiritual matters need to become empowered in efforts to provide a strong and happy home and vibrant friendships and associations, while also doing one's part to try to heal a broken and imperfect world, fit my own spiritual understanding. During my forty years of active UU ministry and community activism, and in my friendships, some of my fondest colleagues and closest friends were Jews.

Ten percent or more of many UU congregations have Jewish backgrounds; many still identify as culturally Jewish, though they choose a UU congregation, just as many other UUs who grew up in other traditions perceive themselves to be UU while they continue to treasure aspects of their ancestral traditions. Throughout my ministry, I celebrated the Jewish High Holy Days, Hanukkah, and held a congregational Passover Seder each year with the congregations I served. In the Paramus, New Jersey, congregation, one third were of Jewish ancestry and a half-dozen congregants had grown up in German or Dutch Spinoza societies in Europe. In Paramus, we developed a jubilant Hanukkah pageant in addition to our Christmas pageant, and a Yom Kippur service for that holiest day of the Jewish year.

The Jewish High Holy Days exemplify an invaluable way to face up to one's sins, the continuing need for forgiveness, and how to find appropriate ways to live with our own and the world's errors and imperfections. We do need to confess to the people we have wronged and make amends with them. If they are deceased or have become inaccessible, it's valuable to make comparable amends with others who face comparable situations. I embrace some Jews' radical understanding that God makes mistakes, and that there are times in any life when individuals need to argue with God and forgive Creation—a healthy way to come to terms with those tragedies that we've neither caused nor earned. Pondering the Jews' eons of exile, exclusion, and distrust, I'm challenged to live with the integrity at the heart of the Jewish tradition.

The Passover Seder celebrates a wise understanding of freedom—the liberty to take responsibility for your own life and for the decisions of your chosen institutions and communities, the opposite of anarchistic, libertarian, or laissez faire liberty. Most major life decisions aren't easy. Many of our efforts don't get resolved in our lifetimes, so I agree with the Judaic understanding that we're not just trying to live and be personally happy but are called to help heal this beautiful world, which remains broken, imperfect, and often tragic. Creation is amazing, but it needs our help. It means much now to celebrate the Seder in the home of my daughter and her Jewish husband.

Hanukkah isn't mentioned in the Jewish Bible because it celebrates the post-scriptural victory of the Maccabees in 165 BC and their rededication of the Temple, that they believed had become too Hellenized. Except for a few hundred years in the time of their kings and in modern Israel, most Jews have lived in cultures in which they were a minority. Historically, Jews often were forced to live separately by anti-Jewish laws or bigotry, but some Jewish communities have chosen to live apart from non-Jews, including most Orthodox Jews today. Notably, Jews have often been among the most intellectually advanced, and professionally and economically progressive within their nations. Most Jews in the United States are fully integrated Americans, completely at home here, while millions of Israeli Jews live happy, successful lives in Israel, an officially Jewish nation. American Jews light their Hanukkah lights as Jews assimilated in America, while many Israelis light theirs as patriotic Jews embracing Maccabean ideals.

Hanukkah is representative of a classical struggle for any ideology. When, how much, and in what manner do you change your traditions and practices to fit into current culture and circumstances? Traditionalists and conservatives tend to resist change, while liberals and reformers tend to welcome it

I came to consider the Book of Job as one of the most important books of Jewish scripture. Job is eventually patient with the genuine tragedies, heartaches, failures, and foolishness of life, but impatient with falsehood and injustice. Job's captivity is finally turned because he prays for his often not-helpful friends. Job's example in facing up to life's tragedies and our own and others' inadequacies, while also taking a stand against dishonesty and injustice are central to Judaism. For me, doing so is necessary to live a mature ethical and spiritual life. Many other elements of the Jewish Bible have also become part of my spiritual wealth.

In early 2017 I had the privilege of participating in an adult education program on Jewish mysticism taught by Rabbi Larry Raphael, the recently retired primary rabbi of San Francisco's Temple Sherith Israel The many principles of Jewish mysticism he emphasized spoke deeply to me. He reminded us that all spirituality is metaphoric, and pointed out that Kabbalah had returned to Judaism an understanding that everything is a metaphor for the primary reality that lies within. Questioning is half of any answer, and spiritual people should not reduce everything they encounter to something they already know. Jewish mystics strive to liberate sparks of divinity in every experience, which for Rabbi Raphael is the best way to repair Creation. Mystics realize that God is not *an other* but *being itself.* People's stubborn insistence on their own independence prevents them from realizing the divine. God is a constantly flowing presence available to all honest and persistent seekers in the here and now. We cannot reconcile the sacred and the secular, yet at the pinnacle of the universe, they are reconciled. The search for holiness begins in service but ends in gift and benefit. When we most truly and deeply love, we cannot adequately explain how that love feels, but in being loving, we become a part of God in the continuing act of Creation.

Martin Buber

The 20th-century Jewish humanist-existentialist-mystic philosopher Martin Buber has been a most important influence upon my spiritual understanding. He was born in Vienna in 1878 and died in Jerusalem in 1965. He was raised by a grandfather, Solomon Buber, a rabbinic scholar, and Martin grew up hearing Hasidic stories. He became a professor of philosophy at the University of Frankfurt, and the editor of *Die Welt* (The World), a leading Zionist newspaper. His 1923 essay, *I and Thou,* made him famous. When Hitler came to power, Buber resigned and founded the Office for Jewish Adult Education. In 1938, he immigrated to Jerusalem and became a professor at Hebrew University.

Buber's philosophy as summarized in *Between Man and Man* is founded on mutual relationships between people in communities. Relationships of respect and understanding make us humane, by our treating each other as ends rather than only as means to our own satisfaction. In this realm of the between, people discover their essential being and speak to and act with God. Our purpose is to hallow life by building communities that heal the world and aid the work of Creation. Truth is gradually disclosed through experiencing our responsibilities. We must struggle to reconcile differences, and act politically without allowing our truths to become politicized. Institutions can degenerate into collectivities, create obstacles, and even destroy community, so they need to proceed cooperatively, free for dialogue and action.

We will inevitably live much of our lives in *I-It* relationships, in which people and groups objectify, possess, or manipulate others. Whenever possible, instead, we need to act in *I-You* relations, in which we contact others directly, and actively seek fresh connections. The goal is to evolve into *I-Thou* relationships, in which we interact intimately as friends, companions, and colleagues, consider others as our spiritual equals, and refuse to use bad means to try to achieve good ends. I-Thou relationships help the individual become a genuine person, help the collective become a community, and point to the quest for God.

Buber's God is a verb and a four-letter word. Buber states that we can know three attributes of God: 1) The Thou of ourselves and other people, as Socrates did; 2) in our relationships with the natural world, as Goethe did; and 3) as intuitions of potential spirit, as Jesus did.[1] We should concern ourselves with God only to confirm that the world is meaningful. We imitate our portion of the divine by truly turning to one another with love, joy, and humility, in being a part—but only a part—of the whole. In the end, we are not asked why we weren't Moses, but why we failed to live up to our own potential. Dogmas exclude the possibility of new revelation. The weaknesses of private spiritualities are that they try to eliminate the differences that necessarily endure between ourselves and the cosmic and eternal powers. Prayer and ritual are helpful only when they help us focus on realistic tasks.

Self-defeating psychological forces drive people's distrust. Evil is indecision, our refusals to respond. Our original sin is that of remaining within ourselves. Responsibility without freedom is slavery, and freedom without obligation is abandoning oneself to aimlessness, the essence of evil. We need to try to convert evil into good, to mutually reconcile our differences, and to do this first and foremost within ourselves. We accomplish our worthy aims by facing reality, including its inevitable suffering. We must set limits and demand responsible behavior from ourselves and others, live with as little injustice as possible, and act in love and community.

Buber was a passionate Zionist from his young adulthood until his death but advocated and organized for an Israel that was a binational state in which Jews and Arabs could live together in peace and brotherhood as two peoples able to develop a common homeland into a republic for both. He cofounded the Covenant of Peace organization, which advocated for this binational state, with a political party in Israel for that purpose, and after 1948 urged Israel to participate in a federation of Near East states. Buber enriched the spiritual lives of millions and re-popularized the Hasidic stories. Here is a story I have adapted and used often at the Jewish High Holy Days.

When the students of a famous rabbi asked who best exemplified the Day of Atonement, he urged them to secretly watch a nearby tailor. The tailor took down a big book and said: 'God, these are sins I have committed against other people; I have confessed and made amends to them, or will do so to those in comparable circumstances in the days to come. And these are the sins I have committed against Creation itself. I ask your forgiveness; guide me in making appropriate amends.' The students were awed by his records, his confession, and his pleas for forgiveness. Then, one noticed that the tailor had now taken down a bigger book. The tailor continued: 'God, these are all the sins that life, Creation, you, God, have committed against me in this year; however, this is the Day of Atonement, so as you have forgiven me, so I forgive you. *L'chaim!* To life!

Chapter 13
Christianity

Central Christian Beliefs and Practices

C hristians embrace the Jewish Old Testament as the foundation of their scriptures and in its God, but that God then chose to incarnate himself as his only Son on Earth, Jesus. They believe Jesus preached love of God and neighbor, urged us to consider everyone our neighbors, and demonstrated his teachings with healings and affirmations for all who would accept and live them. Jesus was crucified; Christians believe he then rose from the dead as Christ, and that he will judge everyone at the end of history. God is pervasive in the world as the Holy Spirit, which can influence people's lives through their faith, prayers, and good works. This combination of God, Christ, and Holy Spirit are three beings, yet a single entity, the Trinity.

Most Christians pray, and many participate in a congregation by attending Sunday services. Their scriptures, the Holy Bible, contain both the Old Testament (with the same writings, but arranged differently from the Jewish Bible), and the New Testament, which contains four Gospels (narratives about Jesus' life and teachings) and a series of letters, or epistles, mostly written by Paul, and a few writings by other early Christians. A person becomes a Christian by joining a Christian congregation or church, and usually also by Baptism with water; most people are baptized as infants, some as adults, some with sprinkled drops, others by immersion. The most important sacrament is Holy Communion, a memorial with bread and wine or grape juice, which represent the grace of life and faith, or the body and blood of Jesus Christ. While the most devout read the Bible regularly, the Christian majority depend on their clergy for Christian teachings. The primary Christian holidays are Easter, a spring holiday that celebrates Christ's resurrection, and Christmas, a winter holiday that celebrates Jesus' birth.

Christianity is the most widespread religion, primarily because many Christians are eagerly evangelical; they want to "save souls" by persuading people to adopt their version of Christianity. Christians publish their scriptures and songs—hymns and psalms—in indigenous languages, and often accommodate their worship and customs to fit regional customs and preferences. During colonial eras, people who became Christians were more successful in colonial administrations.

The Historic Evolution and Geographic Dispersion of Early Christianity

Jesus was born and died a Jew in a Jewish world. By BC 63, General Pompey had conquered Jerusalem for the Roman Empire, and King Herod was its ruler (BC 40–4). By Jesus' time, Jews lived throughout the Roman Empire, and were 10 percent of its population. Rabbinic Judaism was dominant, and a clerical elite maintained scriptural and temple sovereignty in Jerusalem. Competing prophets variously heralded rigid traditions or changing formulations, healings or catastrophes, an imminent end of the world or the coming of messiah(s). In the late 1st century AD, the Jewish-Roman historian Flavius Josephus, identified four Jewish elites who numbered in the thousands: Sadducees, Pharisees, Essenes, and Zealots, while the vast majority of Jews remained illiterate, uneducated farmers and workers.

The Sadducees were the priest class, unconcerned with Jesus until he received Roman attention just before his death. The Pharisees were the most important and popular of these elites (6,000 people); they were businessmen and their allies, and steadily gained religious and political power. They believed that their oral explanations clarified the scriptures, and they adopted many Hellenistic ideas such as the immortality of the soul, the resurrection of the body, divine reward or punishment in the afterlife, frugal living, careful diet, and they were often pacifists. In the Gospels, the priest Nicodemus, who came secretly to warn Jesus and later publicly defended him, was a Pharisee. The Apostle Paul remained a Pharisee. Rabbi Hillel was a Pharisee. The Essenes were a secretive Jewish sect that flourished from the 2nd century

BC until the end of the 1st century AD. They were mostly ascetics who saw themselves as children of light and all others as children of darkness surrounded by pervasive evil. They participated in baptisms, celebrated a holy meal of bread and wine, and believed in the confession of sins and in spiritual survival in the afterlife. John the Baptist had Essene leanings. Essenes awaited two Messiahs: a priest and a king, whom they expected would defeat their enemies and establish them as the true Second Covenant. The Zealots were the Jewish patriots who resisted Roman domination. The Jewish-Roman war (67–70) destroyed any Jewish state for the next 2,000 years. All the Zealots, Essenes, and Sadducees were eliminated during the Roman-Jewish War. Only remnants of the Pharisees survived after 70 AD.

Jesus

Jesus was one of the Jewish commoners. The Gospels say that he was born during Herod's reign, and grew up in a simple home with siblings, an older father, who was a carpenter, and a younger mother. Jesus became a carpenter. It appears he could read Hebrew, but probably spoke mostly Aramaic; there's no evidence that he knew Greek. When Jesus was about thirty years old, he was baptized by John the Baptist; only then did he become a teacher and healer for his final three years, during which he wandered with a small group of followers across the Jewish hinterland. On his last visit to Jerusalem, after he and his closest followers had celebrated the Passover meal, Jesus threw money changers out of the temple and said he could rebuild the temple in three days. He was then accused of treason by the Roman governors and the Jewish elite, who organized a mob that denounced him, and he was condemned to be executed by crucifixion, a punishment common under Roman law.

Jerusalem's population had recently doubled as new workers arrived to expand the temple and create a center of Jewish commerce on the temple grounds. When Jesus told these temple rebuilders that he could do their job in three days and disrupted the merchants' buying and selling, it wasn't hard to gather a mob against this little-known prophet. After his death, Jesus' followers began to teach that Jesus was the Messiah, had gone to heaven, and would return to save those who believed. Jesus' own objective was likely the reform of Judaism rather than the creation of a new religion. During his ministry, and for a century after, his followers were primarily Jews.

The Gospels portray Jesus as a kind and generous man who welcomed everyone into his fellowship, whether they were Samaritans, Roman soldiers, tax collectors, or prostitutes. It's unlikely that many of his followers were either Pharisees, who considered themselves morally separate and superior, or Essenes, who struggled to remain separate from a sinful world. For Jesus was a man who healed on the Sabbath, consumed what and when he chose, and enjoyed life with everyone who treated him with respect. He fit few of the typical characteristics of a Jewish prophet or leader, even fewer of the Jew's expected Messiah's. Even to his closest followers, Jesus was a confusing and challenging figure: he wasn't the political savior that Zealots sought, was certainly not an advocate for temple hierarchy or wealth and was neither priest nor king. He taught some Pharisaic doctrines, but also challenged and mocked the Pharisees. In some ways, he taught and lived like an Essene, and was almost certainly influenced by them, but remained embedded in the world, and never advocated that people should live in separation or renunciation. Jesus likely did not foresee the world's imminent end, and clearly believed that everyone could have immediate and ceaseless access to God. His Kingdom of God had no special privileges, only additional responsibilities: forgive and you will be forgiven; be forgiven your debts to the extent that you forgive the debts owed you, and love is its own reward, for we are rewarded by doing what is worthy as compassionate persons. Jesus was a master storyteller. His parables and stories bring the Gospels alive along with those choice admonitions that millions perceive as virtuous but that are so challenging to put into practice, such as loving your enemies or giving away your wealth. His parables allow people to transition from an actual place to an ultimately real place, at least in their hopes.

Some wonder whether Jesus actually lived the life ascribed to him, but since we have independent references from both a Jewish-Roman historian, Flavius Josephus and a prominent Roman Senator and historian, Tacitus, I see no reason to doubt that Jesus was a historical figure, or that the Gospels reflect the outlines of his life and ministry. Josephus's *Antiquities* (AD 93) state that Jesus was called the Messiah, was a wise teacher, and was crucified by Pilate. Josephus also refers to Jesus' brother, James, and to the death of

John the Baptist. Tacitus's *Annals* (AD 116) refer to Jesus being called Christ, his execution by Pilate, and the existence of early Christians in Rome.

The Early Disciples

In the Gospel of Mark, 3:14, twelve of Jesus' closest followers during his ministry are named Simon Peter, brothers James and John, Andrew, Philip, Bartholomew, Matthew, Thomas, another James, Thaddeus, Simon the Canaanite, and Judas Iscariot. None of them wrote any of the Gospels. They became the Apostles. Judas, who may have been a disappointed Zealot, betrayed Jesus, and since they wanted twelve, to parallel the twelve Jewish tribes, the others then appointed Matthias to replace Judas. We now have strong evidence that Mary Magdalene was likely Jesus' closest confidante, a financial benefactor, and quite possibly his most important disciple. In the Gospels, she discovers the empty tomb, first sees the risen Christ, and first proclaims to the doubting male disciples that Jesus had risen. There is evidence that she then became a leading spokesperson for an evolving Christianity, while many of the Apostles remained practically invisible.

As Christianity began to grow, it initially did so among Hellenized Jews and among Gentiles (non-Jews) who attended Jewish services, attracted to their monotheism and high ethical standards. Roman law then exempted Jews from worshipping the imperial gods, but these Gentile participants were publicly required to idolize the Roman gods and emperors. Christianity's earliest controversy was whether non-Jewish converts needed first to become Jews, by being circumcised and following Jewish dietary laws. Since Hellenists disliked circumcision, and were disinclined to change their eating habits, conversion remained unpopular. For Jews, Jesus had failed Jewish expectations for a Messiah, and Christian teachings presented a challenging mixture of Pharisaic and Essene ideas along with parables that undercut both. As Christians increasingly emphasized Jesus as the Christ, only Son of God, God on Earth, and considered Christ comparable to God—all ideas challenging both to Judaism and Hellenists, both groups began to challenge Christians, who increasingly extricated themselves ideologically from both their Jewish roots and their pagan contexts.

If Jesus wrote anything, it hasn't survived. Scholars have convincingly demonstrated that none of the New Testament authors were with Jesus during his living ministry. Initially, Christian teachings were repeated orally; then, as Christianity spread, were transcribed and compiled into "Sayings Gospels," which are now considered to be the earliest Christian scriptures. In 1945, papyrus codices were discovered in sealed jars buried near Luxor, Egypt. The Nag Hammadi library of Gnostic Christian texts are representative of these early scriptures. The most famous of them being the Gospel of Thomas. In their book, *The Five Gospels*, a group of 200 Biblical scholars came to consensus about what Jesus most likely said and intended as they examined, phrase by phrase, the scriptural gospels and the "sayings" gospels of Thomas and of Mary. These earliest surviving Christian scriptures, along with the best current scholarship, assert that many of the parables and some of the most life-affirming, inclusive, and hopeful admonitions are likely the closest to Jesus' spoken words.

In *Beyond Belief: The Secret Gospel of Thomas,* Elaine Pagels examines the Gospel of Thomas, which proclaims that the divine light is shared by all; that we are all made in the image of God. Each of you is part of that same stream from which I, Jesus, came and did my best to embody, but I am not your Master, God is our master. The Kingdom of God is here and now, in you and all things. You are the children of the living Father. People either discover the light within that illuminates the whole universe or live in darkness within and without. When we awaken spiritually, we experience God and are involved in the Kingdom here and now. If you bring forth your best, it will save you. Commit yourself to what you know is worthy of hope and love.

The Gospel of Mary makes clear that there were significant disagreements among the earliest disciples about Jesus' beliefs and teachings. The gospel rejects that Jesus' suffering and death are the path to eternal life, arguing instead that as Christians discover their true selves, their souls can be set free from the powers of matter (ignorance, desire, the foolish wisdoms of flesh and wrath, and the fear of death). It asserts that people need to use their minds, and are fully one with the natural world. Magdalene's Gospel criticizes oppressive power, offers faith in a hopeful spiritual progress available to all, and encourages her colleagues to model egalitarian practices and to preach hope and inclusion instead of death and despair.

Paul

The earliest of the official Christian texts were almost certainly some of Apostle Paul's Epistles (letters) in the New Testament. Paul (AD 5–67) grew up in Tarsus, Turkey, a large Mediterranean trading city and home to a renowned Hellenistic university. Paul was a Hellenized, Greek-speaking Jewish Pharisee and a Roman citizen from a well-established family. He became a devoted Jew and enthusiastically persecuted the "Jesus Jews." Then, on his way to Damascus to bring some of them to judgment, he was struck down by a vision in which the resurrected Christ appeared in a great light. Paul was struck blind; then, he heard Christ commission him as an apostle to spread faith in Christ and to teach his doctrines to the Hellenistic world. Three days later, in Damascus, the Christian Ananias healed Paul's sight and baptized him. Over the next twenty years, Paul converted many to Christianity; he became a master organizer, gathered funds, and established and strengthened congregations. After three years of evangelizing in Turkey, he journeyed to Jerusalem to provide funds he had gathered from his new congregations because Jerusalem's Christians were being attacked by more orthodox Jews, and Jerusalem faced a famine (AD 45). He wanted to convince them that the Gentiles he was converting should not be required to be circumcised or forced to follow all the Jewish laws in order to be accepted as Christians. Later, Paul spent time in Antioch, Syria, Philippi, Thessalonica, Berea, Athens, Corinth, and Ephesus. Finally, he was arrested in Jerusalem, imprisoned for two years, then sent to Rome to stand trial, and was executed.

Jesus is the heart and soul of Christianity, but Paul did the most to transform Christianity into a separate and popular religion. He was an Apostle for the risen Christ, not for the human Jesus, and announced that the risen Christ had set divine-human relations on a new course. In Philippians 3: 2-3: "He is a Jew who is a Jew inwardly; the real circumcision is a matter of the heart, spiritual not literal. We are the true circumcisions who worship God in spirit." The risen Christ had opened God's covenant with Abraham to anyone freely motivated by love and gratitude, but Paul also remained a Pharisee, and argued against self-indulgence. God's covenant was a corporate, moral existence in the church of Christ. Individuals are only valued by their membership and responsible participation within these Christian congregations.

Of the New Testament's twenty-seven books, fourteen are attributed to Paul, and seven Epistles have scholarly consensus as his writings: Romans, 1st and 2nd Corinthians, Galatians, Philippians, 1st Thessalonians, and Philemon. Others have been written or completed by followers, but probably reflect Paul's beliefs. The book of Acts is about Paul's travels. His influence on Christianity is profound and pervasive. He was a dedicated Christian supersalesman. "To the Jews, I became as a Jew, in order to win Jews; to those under law I became as one under the law—though not being myself under the law—that I might win those under the law….I have become all things to all men, that I might by all means save some." (1st Corinthians 9:19-22)

As an educated Pharisee, Hellenized Roman citizen, and man of the world, Paul appealed to the growing population of Hellenized, educated, ambitious bourgeois people in the Roman Empire, whether ancestrally Jews or pagans. Like them, he wanted to pick and choose among Jewish, Roman, and Greek concepts and practices. His views combined a general resurrection of the dead along with the Greek belief that immortality depended upon bodily survival.

Paul's ideas evolved. At first, he clung to Jewish laws, but before his death, he argued that Jewish laws might be impediments to salvation. Since he wanted to persuade everyone, his epistles are a minefield of sometimes contradictory and conflicting doctrines and practices—people are saved by faith alone, but also need to be responsible members of their Christian communities, bound by rules and prohibitions. In Galatians 3:28: "There is neither Jew nor Gentile, neither slave or free, nor male and female, all one in Christ Jesus." Yet, he believed women should remain subordinate to men. Pagans who failed to accept Christ remained beyond salvation. People are responsible, yet God had caused everything before they were born.

The Gospels

The New Testament was written over generations by people without direct experience of the religion's founder or his ministry. It is accurate to understand the four scriptural Gospels not only as different stories of Jesus' life and meaning but also as a debate among competing Christian schools of thought. The synoptic Gospels: Matthew, Mark, and Luke have many parallels. All three called Jesus a Son of God, were concerned with the relationship between rich and poor, and with whether foreigners were to be considered "of their people." They all considered Jesus a son of God because he was an ordinary person who attained no extraordinary position during his life.

The earliest gospel was the Gospel of Mark (after AD 70) and was based on an earlier document. Mark wrote in Greek for Gentile Christian converts. His chronology begins with John the Baptist's baptism of the thirty-year-old Jesus, which made Him God's son, and ends three years later with Jesus' death and His encounter with three women disciples: Mary, mother of James, Mary Magdalene, and Salome. In its later versions, Jesus appears only to Mary Magdalene who tells the other disciples; then the risen Christ appears and tells them to "go into all the world proclaiming the good news to the whole Creation. The one who believes and is baptized will be saved; but the one who does not believe will be condemned." (Mark: 16:14-17). It portrays Jesus as a heroic man of action, an exorcist, healer, and miracle worker. He is the son of God but keeps his identity secret by speaking in parables. Mark's Messiah is a servant, suffering on behalf of others. The coming of the Holy Spirit marks him as Messiah.

The New Testament begins with the Gospel of Matthew, composed in Greek by AD 110. For Matthew, Jesus was the Son of God from birth through resurrection and returned to fulfill the Old Testament prophesies. Matthew's community was composed of Syrian Jewish-Christians who tried to strictly abide by Jewish laws, yet its membership became increasingly Gentile. Matthew's vision was a church in which Jews and Gentiles would flourish together. His Gospel alternates five sections of Jesus' history with five sections of Jesus' teachings, like the five books of the Torah. The Sermon on the Mount climaxes the first set. The second shares three miracles and two disciple stories, to teach about mission and suffering. The third presents parables on the sovereignty of God, and Jesus urges his followers to teach the Kingdom of God on Earth. The fourth reveals that since Jesus will be killed, his disciples must take responsibility. Peter declares Jesus the Christ, the Son of the living God, and Jesus responds that on this bedrock the Christian church will be built (16:13-19). In the fifth history, Jesus says that this generation will not pass away before all these prophecies are fulfilled (24:29-34). Having risen from the dead, he tells his disciples that he has been given "all authority in heaven and Earth," and gives them the Great Commission: "Go and make disciples of all nations, baptizing them in the name of the Father, Son, and Holy Spirit, and teaching them to obey his teachings since he will be with them to the very end" (28: 18-20).

The Gospel of Luke and the Acts of the Apostles make up a two-volume work, a fourth of the New Testament (AD 110). It provides an outline for the Church's liturgical calendar and continued being substantially revised for another century. A religious and political history of Jesus and his successors divides time into three ages: the time of the Law and the Prophets—from Genesis to John the Baptist; Jesus' time; and the period of the Church, from the risen Christ to his second coming. Jesus Christ was the greatest savior because he fulfilled the Old Testament Messiah prophesies. The Holy Spirit is uniquely important, a celebration of Spirit's enabling power lived through shared inclusive fellowship. Christianity's future is in Gentile hands.

The Gospel of John, fourth of the canonical Gospels, was published in the 2nd century, the last except for the Book of Revelation. John crafts a stirring defense of his dogmatic positions. John 20:31: "These are written so you may believe Jesus is the Christ, the Son of God, and that by believing you may have life in his name." John isn't interested in Christians being accepted by Jews; he criticizes the synoptic Gospels, and systematically tried to discredit the Gospel of Thomas, whom he satirized as "doubting Thomas," quite unlike the Church's Apostle Thomas who evangelized in Syria and India. John's Gospel begins with a hymn to the logos, the Stoic word for "reason," because Christ supersedes earlier figures. For John, his Gospel superseded earlier testaments. He emphasized *parakletos:* helper, advocate, and comforter; he perceived the Holy Spirit as Christ's earthly alter ego, so the Holy Spirit needs to pervade His Church.

The Early Christian Church

The 1st century AD in Christian history is called the apostolic period when Christianity was still largely a Jewish phenomenon. The post-apostolic period ran from 100–380, when Christianity became clearly distinct from

Judaism. Christians were tolerated in some places and suppressed elsewhere. Separate Christian communities became different in belief and practice, and congregations developed a hierarchical organization. The Christian population grew by 40 percent each decade. This phenomenal growth can be ascribed to its relatively high moral-ethical foundations and devout personal practices, and its promise of a physical afterlife with potential salvation for anyone. It combined strengths of Judaism without its separateness or alien elements for the Hellenized world.

Christian debates then were about who Jesus was and was not, how Christians should act, and who was in charge. Initially, all baptized Christians were considered priests—the foundation, an eon-plus later, for the Protestant belief in the "priesthood of all believers." Urban Christian communities began to have bishops whose responsibility was to organize and oversee their area's congregations. Smaller, rural congregations developed leaders who rarely became priests, instead volunteering in person-to-person activities, with prominent women leading some services. By the time of the First Epistle to Timothy, however, women were to remain quiet during worship, and never to instruct men or assume authority over them. The Epistle to the Ephesians ordered women to submit to their husbands, and Christianity fell into a dominant paternalism. Initially, the Jerusalem congregation was preeminent, but by the 2nd century, Rome, Alexandria, and Antioch had grown more important.

Christianity spread first to Asia Minor, North Africa, and Arabia, then into East Africa, southeast Europe, and India. In AD 301, Armenia became the first to declare Christianity its official religion and national Church. There followed an explosion of scripture writing, theological debate, and spiritual experimentation with Alexandria, Egypt, as its center. Desert hermits mimicked Jesus' time in the wilderness, and evolved into communities of monks and nuns in search of spiritual elevation. North Africa was where most early doctrinal and theological fathers of the Christian Church originated.

Tertullian (AD 155–240) grew up in Carthage, became a lawyer in Rome, and is called the Father of Latin Christianity. He named doctrines such as the Trinity, identified the developing scriptures as the Old and New Testaments, and announced Christianity as the true religion, relegating other widely practiced spiritualities as superstitions. Origen (AD 184–254), an

Egyptian who spent most of his life in Alexandria producing a "corrected" Old Testament and gathering books that became the New Testament, was preeminent because he organized what became the official Christian scriptures and was the most important early Christian theologian. For Origen, God was not Yahweh but the First Principle, and Christ, the Logos, was subordinate to Him. He considered matter temporary, perceived souls as preexisting, and believed in universal salvation. These doctrines later became heresies, so despite his central role in Christian dogma and practice, Origen was never sainted and by the 6th century his non-orthodox views had become anathema. For Origen, Jesus was in essence only a most instructive example, and his death an act of self-sacrifice for the greater good.

Arius (AD 256–336) was born in Libya of Berber ancestry, trained at Antioch, and became a priest in Alexandria. He emphasized the Father's divinity over the Son. His opposition to Trinitarian Christology made him the primary enemy at the First Council of Nicaea, organized by Emperor Constantine in AD 325. Arius clearly emphasized the supremacy and uniqueness of God the Father. He believed that Christ possessed neither the eternity nor the true divinity of the Father. Christ was simply the most perfect of God's children. Arianism became a principal heresy yet continued to have many advocates from the eastern Middle East to Arian missionaries among Germanic tribes. Athanasius (AD 296–373) was an Egyptian Coptic Christian and the twentieth Bishop of Alexandria. His *Life of Saint Anthony* became the model monastic biography. Athanasius led the ideological battle against the Arians and became the hero of the First Council of Nicaea. He is seen as the pillar of the Church by Roman Catholics and honored as the Father of Orthodoxy by Eastern Christianity. His creed became the basis for the Nicene Creed, which for centuries was the basic Christian dogma. In AD 367, Athanasius introduced the present Old and New Testaments, and is venerated by all major Christian branches.

The Roman Empire Embraces Christianity

For nearly 300 years, Christianity grew as an illegal sect that rejected Roman gods and rules and promoted self-mastery as the means to freedom and spiritual renewal. In AD 250, when Emperor Decius required every Roman citizen to worship the Imperial cult, Christian citizens were confronted with an impossible situation: those who refused were subject to the death penalty. By AD 285, the Roman Empire had become vast, 50 million subjects in a territory that extended from Britain to Armenia. Emperor Diocletian divided the Empire into a western state with its capital in Rome, and an eastern state with its capital in Constantinople. Then, when Emperor Constantine made Christianity a respected imperial institution, Christian doctrine, instead of emphasizing freedom, began to emphasize the bondage of original sin. Emperor Constantine the First was introduced to Christianity by his mother Helena. In AD 312, at the Battle of Milvian Bridge, Constantine commanded his troops to adorn their shields with a Christian symbol; after winning the battle, Constantine was able to claim control in the West. In 313, he issued the Edict of Milan, legalizing Christian worship. Thereafter, he supported the Church financially, built Christian sanctuaries, granted tax exemptions to the clergy, returned confiscated Church property, and promoted Christians to high office.

By 330, he had built his new capital in Constantinople, with many churches and no pagan temples, and sent his mother to Jerusalem to decide upon the official resurrection site. Helena changed its location from east of Jerusalem to within the city walls, where a temple to Venus had previously stood, and changed or confirmed other Christian sites in the Holy Land. Constantine changed the date of Jesus' birth from its scriptural springtime to the winter equinox, a popular pagan festival for the "indomitable Sun," and changed Easter so it would no longer coincide with Passover. Before Constantine, Christians were baptized upon joining a congregation. Constantine added baptism near the time of death, which fit with a pagan belief that baptism washed away sins. The weekly Sabbath was changed to Sunday. Cremation had been the usual death ritual, but Constantine's own interment made burial the new Christian rite.

Constantine laid the foundation for the doctrine of *symphonia:* that religious and political leaders should work in harmony to realize God's Will on Earth. Constantine participated in the Council of Nicaea, believing that he was "bishop for those outside the Church." This ideal found concrete expression in the Byzantine Empire and endured. The Church is called upon to pray for those in power; orthodoxy is both a personal and a public faith, and Christians are challenged to be good citizens, committed to public service, philanthropy, and lay political involvement. At the Council of Nicaea (AD 325), the leaders voted against Arian doctrines. Until then, Christian controversies had been matters of open and diverse debate. Afterward, Church councils determined dogma; they also disciplined and expelled people and ordered the murder of heretics as enemies of Church and state. This council produced the Nicene Creed, still widely used.

We believe in one God, maker of Heaven and Earth. In one Lord Jesus Christ, the only begotten Son of God, being of one substance with the Father, by whom all things are made; who for us, and for our salvation, came down from Heaven and was incarnate by the Holy Spirit of the Virgin Mary, and was made man, was crucified, suffered, and was buried, then rose again and ascended into Heaven. Thence He shall come again, with glory, to judge the quick and the dead; whose kingdom shall have no end. And in the Holy Spirit, who together with the Father and Son is worshipped, and who spoke from the prophets. In One, Holy, Catholic and Apostolic Church, we acknowledge one baptism for the forgiveness of sins, the resurrection of the dead, and the age to come.

Between AD 382 and 404, Jerome composed the Latin Bible, the Vulgate, which was the standard Latin Bible and Roman Catholic text for centuries and became the first published book in the West in 1456. Early Christian missionaries favored by Arian emperors had spread Arian doctrines among the Germanic tribes and elsewhere on the outskirts of the empire. During the 5th century, the school of Edessa under Nestorius, Patriarch of Constantinople, argued that Christ's divine nature and Jesus' human nature were distinct persons. Consequently, Mary could not properly be called the mother of Christ, but since Mary as the mother of God had become extremely popular, this became a new divisive issue. At the Council of Ephesus in AD 431, the Nestorians were rejected, and a major schism erupted. The Nestorian churches separated, and to avoid persecution, many Nestorians fled to the Persian Empire, where some already resided, and the Persian Christian Church became independent. In 451, at the Council of Chalcedon, it was determined that Christ's divine and human natures were separate but part of a single entity. Many rejected this, which resulted in the creation of a separate union of churches including the Syrian-Palestinian, Armenian, and Egyptian Christians that became Oriental Orthodoxy.

The Rome and Constantinople halves of the Roman Empire flourished equally until the reign of Theodosius I (AD 379–95). Then they began to decline, because of Germanic incursions in the west, and territorial overreach given their available resources in the east. Theodosius's Christian zeal upset the still-prevalent pagans, as well as many Christians who did not believe in the Nicene Creed. By AD 476, Germanic armies had triumphed in the west.

Augustine

Augustine (AD 354–430) was the most important European Christian thinker in this period. Born in North Africa, he moved to Carthage, continued his studies, and found a mistress with whom he had a son. After his mother forced him to abandon his mistress, Augustine moved to Rome, and then to Milan to teach rhetoric. In Milan, Paul's Epistle to the Romans and Ambrose's preaching finally resolved Augustine's philosophical doubts about Christianity, and he was baptized. He returned to North Africa with his son and friends, who lived together as a monastic community. He became Bishop of Hippo, and later died as Vandals besieged the city.

Augustine's theology combined Christian orthodoxy and Neoplatonic philosophy, as found in *The City of God*. From the Neoplatonists, Augustine argued that God was the ineffable One, the Good from which the soul developed but remained incorporeal as part of God. He believed in predestination and that evil is the corruption of a creature's goodness. Before the Fall, humans were free to not sin, while after the Fall, people were free only to sin—original sin is inherited. Only through Christ's grace can people be restored to the freedom not to sin, and this will be the only liberty that people will have in Heaven. Human freedom is simply the will to respond to God's irresistible grace. Augustine also argued that the powers of the Church and the sacraments remained valid even when those serving them were imperfect or even corrupt.

Augustine's "Just War" doctrine has had enduring influence. He argued that there are four justifications for a nation to ethically engage in a war: 1) *Just authority*, based on a legitimate political and legal process; 2) *Just cause,* appropriate responses to substantial wrongs committed; 3) *Right intention,* the actions taken not only right the wrongs committed but are also proportional to the wrongs; and 4) *Last resort,* when every other means has been sincerely attempted. Augustine also set appropriate limits to how a war may be carried out: 1) *Proportionality* – the use of only the force necessary to pursue the just cause and intention; 2) *Discrimination* – nonmilitary people should never become targets, and careful discrimination between combatants and noncombatants; and 3) *Responsibility* – a country is not responsible for war's unexpected side effects when its actions have clear intentions for good consequences, minimize bad effects, and the benefits of the war outweigh the damage inevitably done.

Post-Roman Empire and Early Medieval Christianity

Between AD 400 and 800, pagan tribes gradually destroyed the Roman Empire, while Asian warriors and then Islamic forces threatened the Byzantine Empire. A feudal economic and political system evolved in which people survived on lands controlled by local nobles who collected taxes and enforced their rule with hired knights. In the 5th century, Saint Patrick began Ireland's Christian conversion; Augustine of Canterbury played a comparable role in England. In 496, the Frankish King Clovis I converted to Christianity, which spread to German lands by the 700s. As the Empire collapsed, the Church's power and landholdings grew. Pope Stephen claimed Italy from Rome to Ravenna, which remained under papal rule until the 19th century.

Between 800 and 1299, the Roman Catholic Church not only became spiritually central but also dominated European economic, social, and sometimes political power. In 787, Charlemagne issued his *Charter of Modern Thought;* he sponsored the Carolingian Renaissance, which organized clerical schools and spread literacy among the clergy and court officials. Latin became Europe's language. More parish priests were able to read their Vulgate Bibles. The soul of medieval Christianity was within the monastic movement; only there could men who lacked noble status hope to become literate and perhaps powerful. In AD 529, Benedict started the first monastery. A Benedictine monk became a missionary to England; Ireland already had a stricter Celtic monastic rule. By the 9th century, the Benedictines became the standard of monasticism throughout Europe. As many departed from its simplicity and self-sufficiency, one group separated itself in 1098 and became the Cistercians (now Trappists), whose goal was to return to farming, self-sufficiency, and austerity. By 1150, they had established 500 abbeys, and became the primary European force for technological diffusion. They initiated lay brothers (*conversi*) who practiced chastity and obedience, but usually remained illiterate and more worldly, which softened monasticism but also created a spiritual serfdom.

In the 12th century, there developed two mendicant orders, the Dominicans and the Franciscans, whose monks did not isolate themselves but worked among the people. Dominic (1170–1221) was an aristocratic Spaniard. He established a preaching order whose monks were well-educated and made their livelihoods through the popularity of their preaching. They became teachers, added teaching nuns, produced great scholars such as Albertus Magnus and his disciple, Thomas Aquinas. While many became fervent missionaries, Dominicans also often led the suppression of unorthodox teachings and participated in inquisitions against heretics.

Aquinas

Thomas Aquinas (1224–74) was the most important Christian philosopher and theologian of the European Middle Ages. An aristocratic Sicilian, he attended the University of Naples where he was attracted to Aristotelian philosophy. He became a Dominican monk and a professor at the University of Paris, a protégé of Albertus Magnus. Aristotle's ideas were the great intellectual challenge of these centuries. Aquinas became the "dean of the Scholastics"; he integrated Church dogmas with Aristotelian wisdom. Pope John XXII made Aquinas a saint (1323), and Pius V declared him the Universal Doctor of the Church (1567). Aquinas's one-sentence argument was that God's grace does not destroy nature but perfects it, and that revelation does not diminish the achievements of human reason but simply completes them. People can know many things, but to have the truths of faith, they require divine revelation. Nature does not instinctively incline us to virtue, so we need reason, practice, and faith in order to discover and persevere in virtue.

Aquinas's theological virtues are faith, hope, and charity, and his four cardinal virtues are prudence, temperance, justice, and fortitude. Non-Christians could display virtue, but Christian faith was required to practice charity. God governs creation through eternal law. The laws of nature are discovered through reason; the foundation of natural law is that good must be practiced and evil avoided. Human laws are natural laws applied by societies through their governance. Divine law is the law specially revealed in Christian scripture and put into practice by the Roman Catholic Church. Political leaders must be controlled by maintaining laws that live up to the Church's doctrines and ethics. Sin is the abrogation of reason or revelation and is evil. War needs to be a last resort, and practiced only within limits.

God is united, but best described by the Trinity: The Father generated the Son or Word, and this eternal generation produces the Holy Spirit or Love of God. Christ restores our divine nature by removing sin. The goal of human existence is union with God. After resurrection, body and soul are reunited with God, and thus enjoy both spiritual and physical blessings. Hope of resurrection provides the motivation to sacrifice earthly passions and pleasures for heavenly union. Heretics will be excommunicated, but should also be executed by cooperative governments, which became the justification for inquisitions. In his *Summa Theologiae,* Aquinas wrote that by his crucifixion, Christ gave God more than was required to compensate for the past and future sins of the whole human race. Punishment is a morally good response to sin; like medicine, it restores harmony between the wronged and the wrongdoer. It is possible to substitute for another's sin if the offender joins his will to those undergoing punishment, which is the foundation for the Roman Catholic view of penance as self-inflicted pain in equal measure to the pleasures of sin. Mortal sins include idolatry, murder, theft, adultery, and slander committed knowingly and willfully. If a person confesses and repents, God forgives him, but if he dies before doing so, he is lost to God and Heaven forever.

Francis of Assisi

Francis (1182–1226) was the carefree son of a wealthy merchant in Assisi, Italy. Captured in a regional war, Francis became seriously ill in prison. Returned to Assisi, he vowed a life of poverty, renounced his wealth, preached the nearness of God's kingdom, and began to attract rich and well-born followers. In 1210, Pope Innocent III established the Franciscan Order of Friars Minor directly under papal supervision. In 1212, he initiated Franciscan nuns, the Poor Clares, named for Francis's spiritual companion. In 1220, Francis made an unsuccessful trip to the Holy Land to convert Muslims. Scholarship was not initially encouraged among Franciscans; nonetheless, by 1254 they had a seminary, and the order eventually nurtured great scholars such as Bonaventure, Duns Scotus, and William of Occam. Social service and mission, however, remained the Franciscans' central commitments.

Except for Jesus himself, Francis of Assisi has remained without peer in Christianity as a symbol of Jesus' gentle love and effective empathy, because Francis recognized that humans can be joyful and sustainable creatures within God's natural kingdom. His song *Canticle of the Sun* recognizes the sun as a central symbol of Creation's energies, embraces the whole Earth, and invites all to be of understanding heart, forgive others, do their parts, bless life, and live with eagerness and humility. One of Francis's prayers has become a world favorite:

> Creator, make us instruments of thy peace. Where there is hatred, let us sow love; where there is doubt, faith; where there is despair, hope; where there is darkness, light, and where there is sadness, joy. Grant that we may not so much seek to be consoled, as to console, to be understood as to understand, to be loved, as to love; for it is in giving that receive; it is in pardoning that we are pardoned, and it is dying to outgrown ways that we are reborn to the life of the spirit.

Eastern Christianity during the Medieval Centuries

After AD 330, Rome and Constantinople were Christian rivals. African and Asian Christian communities were increasingly different from either Rome or Constantinople—linguistically, culturally, and spiritually. After 431, the North African Coptic Christians, Armenian Christians, and Syriac Christians separated themselves. For Eastern Christians, Christ was one incarnate nature, with divine and human natures united. They thought Western Christianity was making Jesus' mother, Mary, too prominent. Syriac Christians were welcomed in the Persian Empire and later protected by the Prophet Muhammad. By the 7th century, Eastern Christian Churches not only included Egyptian, Armenian, and Syriac Churches but also Eritrean, Ethiopian, and Indian Churches, spreading even into Central Asia and China.

Roman popes were jealous of Constantinople's successes. They began to argue that only their formulations were dogma, and that Rome should be in charge of all Christians. By the 7th century, they had ceased communicating. After the baptism of Vladimir of Kiev (AD 989), Byzantine Christianity spread beyond southeastern Europe into what became Belorussia, Russia, and Ukraine. The final division between Roman and Byzantine Christians came in 1054, when pope and patriarch excommunicated each other. This schism has never healed; they remain separate, with distinct rites, practices, and leadership.

Byzantines believed that all bishops equally inherited Peter's legacy, that the Holy Spirit arose only from God, and they favored painted icons. Roman Catholics claimed Peter for Rome alone, believed the Holy Spirit flowed through Christ, and favored statues. Eastern monasticism took two forms, Greek and Syrian, and a strong mystical stream flows throughout Eastern Orthodoxy, while in Roman Catholicism mysticism has usually been suspect. Byzantines used local languages, permitted local and regional control, and allowed priests to marry and have families.

In 1453, Constantinople fell to the Islamic Ottoman Empire. For the next four centuries, Eastern Christendom was under Islamic control. The Ottomans granted Christians the right to practice, but they could neither build new churches nor evangelize. It's a credit to the strength of their faiths that millions of Byzantine Christians maintained their communities through these centuries even as primary Christian sites became mosques. Ottoman domination produced a static Orthodoxy, which nurtured incidents of violence climaxed by genocides in Assyria, Greece, and Armenia. The 1915–17 Armenian genocide killed 1.5 million Armenians and displaced millions more. Ottoman domination nurtured corruption, extending even to people buying clerical positions. During this period, Russian Orthodoxy became the largest and strongest portion of Eastern Orthodox Christianity.

Roman Catholicism During the Dark Ages

Monarchs had taken to appointing bishops themselves, often in exchange for bribes or promises (simony); other rulers kept bishoprics empty while they collected the Church's taxes. In 1075, Pope Gregory VII declared that all monarchs were under the pope's control and that only the pope could appoint bishops. By 1122, throughout Western Europe, serfdom and increased taxes had caused liberty and well-being to plummet. Local forces gained power in a feudal system in which most remained poor and dependent on local nobility and clerics.

For the first 1,000 years of Roman Christianity, the primary emphasis had been upon the saving nature of Jesus Christ and the accessibility of paradise through Christianity. Christian art displayed three levels of their understanding about paradise in their churches: God's Heaven was on the ceilings; the walls were earthly paradises where a pastoral Christ and departed saints presided; and the floors represented humanity's earthly paradise. Communion was enacted as a celebrative feast of life, not only with bread and wine but with the bloodless bounty of harvests: olive oil, honey, vegetables, and fruits. This first millennium generally represented and celebrated a grace-filled Earth and an even more peaceful and pastoral Heaven available to the many through God's grace and Christ's life and teachings.

In the 9th century, as Charlemagne reduced the Saxons to serfs, a whole new Christianity became prevalent and then dominant, with a bloody Christ on the cross as its primary symbol. The entrances to Gothic cathedrals vividly depicted an end of the world where Christ judged the multitude suffering in hell while a fortunate minority ascended to Heaven. Previously, wars had been widely condemned as un-Christian, and scholars marshalled many necessary conditions to justify violence. Now, the changed emphasis was sacrificial atonement for the abundance of sin.

Christian Crusades

In AD 1095, Pope Urban II initiated the first crusade. "Whoever goes on the journey to free the church of God in Jerusalem can substitute the journey for all penance for sin." In 1098, Anselm of Canterbury provided the new doctrine of atonement. The burden of sin was overwhelming, not only one's own misdeeds but also the enormous burden of humanity's original sins. Anselm painted a depressing verbal picture of irredeemable sin. What, he asked, could humanity possibly offer in gratitude that would be of sufficient value to repay Christ's sacrifice on the cross? "Man absolutely cannot give himself more fully to God than when he commits himself to death for God's honor." To kill or to be killed for God was now the fastest way to paradise. Communion, the central sacrament of Christianity, evolved from being a celebration of the good in life and the grace of Heaven into a reenactment, by symbolically eating his flesh and drinking his blood, of Christ's sacrifice on the cross. The focus was no longer on life and grace but on death and sacrifice. Paradise could no longer be partly in the present with the kingdom of God on Earth and hope of Heaven. Sin made hell the likely outcome for most, with Heaven only in the hereafter and only for a preselected minority who would become the saved. The redemption of this world was now replaced by inevitable global destruction. The Dark Ages transformed Christianity into a legacy of exploitation of the Earth and justifications for violence and militarism that Christianity still struggles with today. (For these insights, we owe Rita Brock and Rebecca Parker a great debt for their books, *Saving Paradise: How Christianity Traded Love of This World for Crucifixion and Empire,* and *Proverbs to Ashes: Redemptive Suffering and the Search for What Saves Us.* Also see Matthew Boulton's "Cross Purposes," in the *Harvard Divinity Bulletin*).

The Roman Catholic Crusades were focused on establishing the dogmas of Roman Catholicism as the only legitimate form of Christianity, and on seizing European control of the lucrative Middle Eastern trade routes. The first crusade captured Antioch and Jerusalem, but also destroyed many European Jewish communities. The second crusade, fifty years later, recruited 200,000 European soldiers but failed to take Damascus. After Saladin seized Jerusalem again in 1187, the Third Crusade, famed for Richard the Lion-hearted of England and other monarchs, seized only Cyprus and Acre. The Byzantine Christian patriarch, facing Islamic attack, asked Pope Innocent III for financial aid to hire mercenaries; instead, in 1202, Innocent, who promoted recruitment to the Fourth Crusade "to conquer Egypt," instead sacked Constantinople, the Byzantine Christian capital, and thereby fatally weakened the Byzantine Empire and Eastern Christianity. Byzantine churches were converted into Roman Catholic churches, Byzantine Christian treasures were taken to Europe. European power was reestablished in Jerusalem for a century, but the primary victims of the Fourth Crusade were the Byzantine and Eastern Orthodox Christians.

Later in the 13th century, Roman Catholic Teutonic Knights, endorsed by the pope, tried to conquer Orthodox Russia, but were defeated at the Battle of the Ice (1242). Sweden also carried out several crusades against Orthodox Christians. In southern France in the early 1200s, there was a crusade against the Cathars, Christians who believed that Jesus had been adopted by God as his son. The Cathars treated women as equals and opposed oaths. The Church also tried to root out the Waldensians, a sect begun in France by Peter Waldo, who argued for the priesthood of all believers and that each congregation should control itself. Waldo denied the existence of purgatory, saw popes as the anti-Christ, and believed the rich should share their wealth. Waldensians spread into Italy and became precursors of the Protestant Reformation. As Islamic forces weakened in Spain and Eastern Europe, there were crusades there, often against non-Roman Catholic Christian communities and Jews, instead of the retreating Islamic forces.

Other Influencing Factors During the Middle Ages

During this time, there were also growing mystical strands within the monotheistic religions. Mysticism emphasizes individual, disciplined spiritual search inside the individual mind and spirit, perceives God, or the holy, as ineffable, and urges the individual mystic to seek spiritual fulfillment through imagination, gratitude, and encounters with nature and other people. An extensive mystical movement had developed within Islam. Mysticism spread to some Jews and to Eastern Orthodox Christianity. Roman Catholic Christianity was the last of the monotheistic religions to generate strong mystical medieval strands, with 14th-century figures such as Hildegard of Bingen (1098–1179), Gertrude the Great (1256–1302), Mechthild of Magdeburg (1208–82), and Meister Eckhart (1260–1327). Eckhart wrote that God flows into the very essence of all things. Mystics were often ecstatics who taught or healed commoners. Because they questioned Roman

Catholic doctrines and practices, mystics were distrusted and occasionally excommunicated by the church hierarchy.

From 1309 to 1417, Europe experienced a proliferation of competing popes controlled by competing monarchs. A Czech priest, Jan Hus (1369–1415), charged the church with corruption, urged priests to face the congregation during communion and share the communion wine with all congregants, and urged democracy in the church. His execution engendered the brutal Hussite Wars, which lasted from 1419 to 1436. In England, John Wycliffe (1330–1384) had written of the Church's corruptions, advocated for the supremacy of the Bible, and for a direct relationship between men and God without interference from priests or bishops.

This chaos of conflicting popes and monarchs was finally resolved with the Council of Constance, which deposed three popes and elected Pope Martin V, whose tenure lasted from 1417 to 1431. He managed agreements, rebuilt churches, and tightened the church's organizational structures. In 1420, Pope Martin V invited Christians to unite in a crusade against followers of Wycliffe, Hus, and other heretics, and organized papal wars against Italian regions. Since canon law prohibited interest, Martin approved annuities, which allowed interest to be paid. Slavery was then widespread in Europe, Africa, and Asia; Pope Martin denounced enslavement of European Christians but authorized an African slave trade.

Beginning in 1347, Europe began to suffer horribly from plagues, which killed one third of Italy's 10 million people and eventually killed as many as 200 million people in 14th-century Europe. Plagues challenged the clergy's claims that faith could help believers avoid human disasters. Simultaneously, an influx of immigrants fleeing Islamic attacks and oppression brought Byzantine Christian ideas, the superior scientific and technical knowledge of Islamic scholars, and Aristotle's emphasis on evidence-based knowledge and inductive reasoning to Europe, and nurtured a renaissance of classical Greek knowledge, scientific observation and experimentation, and artistic creativity. Gutenberg's invention of metal moveable type (1438), and the Latin Bible he published in 1456, gave the power of scriptural knowledge to anyone who could read, which diluted the Church's earlier near-monopoly on knowledge. Exemplary of this intellectual ferment was Desiderius Erasmus, a Dutch humanist and Roman Catholic scholar who pointed out many errors in the Vulgate Bible. For instance, earlier Bibles made no mention of a doctrine of the Trinity. Erasmus believed new knowledge would deepen spirituality and argued for human freedom; his works were banned. These cultural disruptions and intellectual changes made a reformation of Christianity almost inevitable. The church's sale of indulgences had begun during the Crusades and proliferated thereafter. People could buy forgiveness not only of their own sins but also for the sins of deceased relatives and friends waiting in purgatory.

The Protestant Reformation

The Protestant Reformation began with Martin Luther's 95 theses (1512), which attacked the practice of indulgences as unchristian. Luther (1483–1546) was a German peasant who became an Augustinian monk and a theology professor at Wittenberg University. He was sent to Rome in 1511 and was affronted by the wealth, corruption, and politics of the papacy. His foundational theological argument was justification by grace alone through faith in Jesus Christ. People cannot earn forgiveness by their good works but only through their faith. God freely forgives our sins. Christ's atonement is based on God's love, not upon human merit. Ethical actions without Christian faith contribute nothing to one's state of righteousness. Luther believed in the sacredness of all vocations and in the priesthood of all believers. He urged secular leaders to reform the church, blessed only two sacraments: baptism and communion, published a German Bible, composed hymns, and urged civil authorities to establish public schools. Peasant revolts had begun on his behalf (1520), but by 1525, Luther was so dismayed at the mass of commoners with hopes for human goodness and social progress that he announced that princes received their powers from God and urged them to "put down the rebels as they would mad dogs," to end these peasant wars.

Lutheran churches formed in Germany, Denmark, Sweden, and Norway, and spread throughout Europe. In Switzerland, Ulrich Zwingli (1484–1531) led Zurich into a different Protestantism. His "67 Articles" (1523) granted clerics the power to marry, limited them to the Bible, removed all images from churches, and banned clerical robes. He argued that Christ made only a symbolic presence at communion. His morality, civic unity, rationalism, and humanism spread throughout Switzerland, and his ideas evolved into the Puritan and Reformed traditions.

In Geneva, John Calvin established a Protestant theocracy. His *Institutes of the Christian Religion* (1536) became a model for Protestants in the Netherlands, West Germany, France, and Scotland. He stressed God's sovereignty, human sinfulness, and discipline. Jesus' crucifixion was "penal substitution," to satisfy God's wrath. Christ takes the punishments of all saved persons who are the elect, those chosen before birth for salvation by God while the vast majority of humanity are destined to eternal damnation from before birth. Those predestined for salvation will inevitably receive grace and Heaven's benefits on Earth, which made success and prosperity signs of God's blessing. Calvin's emphasis on vocations as a righteous way of changing the world helped Calvinists control societies and remains the foundation of the current "Protestant ethic." His logical philosophy appealed to many, and led by John Knox, Calvin's civic theocracy roused nationalism in Scotland, where the Calvinists became Presbyterians, inspired Calvinistic nationalists in Holland, and engendered religious wars between French Roman Catholics and Calvinistic Huguenots. Calvinism began to become the dominant expression of Protestantism.

The English Reformation began because King Henry VIII wanted a new consort and found it expedient to replace papal authority with his own supremacy. His associate, Thomas Cranmer, implemented this separation from Rome, introduced an English-language Bible (1538), and dissolved the monasteries and seized their assets, which gave great estates and wealth to the Crown and nobility. This Anglican faith, an Erasmus-influenced combination of Roman Catholic rites and worship with Lutheran and Calvinistic ideas, became a traditional liturgy combined with a humanistic and rational philosophy that permitted biblical criticism.

These early forms of Protestantism (Lutheran, Reform, Calvinist, and Anglican) came to be called the magisterial reformation because they combined allegiance to certain theological teachers and their secular rulers. Other, smaller, forms of early Protestantism were called radical reformers because their communities formed outside of state sanction and advocated more extreme doctrinal changes.

Anabaptists were colleagues of Zwingli who found no reference to infant baptism in the Bible, and thus argued that only adult baptism should be allowed. They favored a clear separation between Church and state, supported congregational polity, and believed that their members should separate themselves from participation in war and government as much as possible. They evolved into the Mennonites, Hutterites, and Amish, who emphasized the rights of individual conscience and pacifism, and separated themselves from civic politics and aspects of modernity. Many Anabaptists were killed.

Another group was the Unitarians. In his *Errors about the Trinity,* Michael Servetus (1511–1553), an early Spanish Unitarian, declared the unity of God and the humanity of Jesus. He was burned at the stake by John Calvin. Italians Laelius and Faustus Socinus fostered these Unitarian ideas and spread them into Poland where Socianism became, for a generation, a mass movement, until it was suppressed in 1660; thereafter, some of its members escaped to the Netherlands. The Polish Socinians published the *Racovian Catechism* (1660), which became popular throughout Europe as an easily read early Protestant pamphlet. It holds that the only true God is the Father, and that Jesus is only "God" because of his bestowed authority to act for God and that The Holy Spirit was simply the power of God. In Transylvania, now the Hungarian-speaking western section of Romania, Francis David established the Unitarian faith, where it survives today. Theophilus Lindsey founded the First Unitarian Church in London (1774), and Unitarian doctrines became popular among several of America's founding figures (Jefferson, Franklin, John Adams, and John Quincy Adams). It was, however, the magisterial reformation traditionalists, working with their rulers, who attained the most success in numbers, wealth, and territory.

The Roman Catholic Counter-Reformation

Protestantism became popular in most of Northern Europe except for Ireland and territories under the control of the Holy Roman Empire. In 1527–28, Rome was sacked, largely by German Protestants, and Roman Catholicism suffered significant losses in membership, territory, and wealth. At the Roman Catholic Council of Trent (1545–63), every dogma questioned by Protestants was reconfirmed as elements of the true faith. Roman Catholic tradition and scripture were declared equally valid in judging faith and morals; this remained Roman Catholic orthodoxy until Pope John XXIII convened the Second Vatican Council in 1962–65. Popes after the Trent Council required a signed Trinitarian creed to validate any individual's questioned confession. Some worked for moral reforms within the Church. Pope St. Pius V (1566–72) supported Catholic education to improve popular piety, increased alms for the poor, supported hospitals and missionaries. St. Teresa of Avila established branches of Carmelite nuns to help lead these efforts. Ignatius Loyola founded the Jesuit Order (1534), and Jesuits became the new leaders in education and missionary efforts.

The Roman Catholic hierarchy also resorted to force, fighting wars against German Lutherans, Dutch Huguenots, and English Anglicans. The inquisitions condemned individuals, who were tortured, often killed at celebratory public executions, and their property confiscated. The Spanish Inquisition killed hundreds of thousands. To combat Protestantism, Pope Paul III created the Holy Office of Inquisition in 1542. Their inquisitions did not completely end until the 20th century, and the Church still bans heretical writings. Worldwide, Roman Catholic colonies either forced indigenous peoples' conversions or enabled their genocides. This inspired a few similar policies among some magisterial Protestant colonists, who also gave their clergy significant power in their colonies. By the 17th century, 35 percent of Northern Europe had returned to Roman Catholicism.

The Effects of the Enlightenment on Christianity

By the 17 century, European civilization was increasingly dependent on a much larger group of middle-class businesspeople, craftsmen, and professionals. Millions were reading the Bible and perceived themselves to have spiritual dignity and individual rights. René Descartes (1596–1650) embraced intellect alone and sought to refute Michel Montaigne's (1533–92) skepticism about anything being certain. Descartes felt that God could be known only through introspection, yet he craved a kind of mathematical certainty. In *Pensées* ("Thoughts," 1669), Blaise Pascal wrote that in this new world, belief in God had become a personal choice. Isaac Newton (1642–1727) wanted to rid Christianity of mystery and posited a watchmaker

God who simply unfolds the laws of physics that Newton and others were discovering. Newton's God was sovereign in all, yet essentially passive, and Newton felt that the only relevant commandments were to love God and neighbor. In *Critique of Pure Reason* (1781), Immanuel Kant held that people were extricating themselves from reliance on external authorities, and that the way to God and spiritual fulfillment was through moral conscience; he believed, however, that God was necessary for virtue to be rewarded with happiness. The focus of religion had begun to shift from God to people as reason and science became the standards.

People maintained that political and economic sovereignty should be shared with the masses through democracy and enterprise. Democratic revolutions in the United States and France spread slowly worldwide. The personal God of Christianity and Judaism helped give rise to a more pervasive sense of human worth and individual dignity, which provided foundations for individualism, mass literacy, democracy, capitalistic enterprise, and individual rights.

Among its proponents, this growing worship of individuality could, however, also degenerate into idolatry, heartless exploitation, and violence against those who stood in their way. Native peoples were slaughtered; Africans were brought to new countries and enslaved; women and children were denied most human rights. The French Revolution collapsed into mass executions and anarchistic violence. Jefferson wrote beautifully about inalienable rights while keeping slaves and impregnating enslaved women. Capitalism nurtured larger middle classes but also created mass urban poverty and exploitation.

Deists such as Tindal, Voltaire, Lessing, Paine, and Jefferson held that God was the Creator but does not guide or intervene in nature or human affairs. Reason alone is sufficient to deduce all that is necessary to know about God's nature and purpose. The practice of virtue, grasped through reason, is the best foundation for spiritual practice. Scotsman David Hume (1711–76) led empiricism to its logical conclusion; he turned a cold eye upon religion and mystery, and maintained that people needed no intellectual tools except their own senses and the wonders of rationalism, technology, and science. Many emphasized the appalling crimes committed by adherents of religion, and saw reason and science as capable of overcoming centuries of superstition and bigotry, but these new bourgeois elites often joined with old elites to exploit the masses within their own populations and throughout "their" colonial worlds.

Some Calvinist reformers evolved into Puritan and Pilgrim, as well as Presbyterian and Reformed denominations. In 1649, under Cromwell, Puritans came to dominate England and held sway in the northeast of colonial United States from 1620 until the end of the 1700s. They objected to Church ornaments and ritual, avoided ecclesiastical authority, rejected Christmas as too joyful and pagan a holiday, and tried to create religious utopias among their elects. Persecuted in Europe, the Puritans now in charge in New England drove other dissenters away.

The First Protestant Awakening

In the decade of the 1730s, particularly in England and the United States, there occurred the First Great Christian Awakening because for many, the existing Christian groups felt stale and unresponsive. This first awakening was characterized by revivals: special events at which people were exhorted to renew their faith with fiery preaching, which extolled a deep sense of guilt and an overwhelming need for redemption by Christ Jesus. This awakening produced Pietism in Germany, evangelical renewal among German and Dutch Reformed, spread among slave populations, and gave rise to the Methodist, Friends (Quakers), and Baptist denominations.

Baptists believe baptism is only for those mature enough to make a conscious and personal commitment to Jesus Christ as Lord and savior. The local congregation is firmly in charge, and the gathered church members are joined by God into a communion of life and service under Lord Christ. They hold firmly to the New Testament and—until recently—to separation of church and state. Though they have strong local ministers and lay leaders, Baptists have joined into voluntary unions and conventions. In the United States, Baptists are the largest Protestant denomination, but like other Protestant denominations, are subdivided into many separate groups: northern and southern, white, ethnic, and black, conservative and moderate, rich and poor. Strongly evangelical, they baptize by full immersion, and embrace and empower everyday people. Former President Jimmy Carter is an active, liberal Baptist, while the more conservative Southern Baptist Convention is the largest U.S. Baptist group.

The Quakers, or Society of Friends, reject compulsory church attendance and military service, make no distinction between clergy and laity, treat genders equally, and reject oaths, creeds, and even the necessity of sacraments. They consider their own mystical experiences more authoritative than scripture itself, particularly through spiritual silence and group sharing of inner wisdom. Friends in colonial United States had an influence on American ethics far out of proportion to their modest numbers. I am attracted by the Quakers' community activism and brave nonviolence. I've often worked closely with Quakers in their disarmament and civil-rights efforts, and did extensive training with their successful nonviolent programs among prison inmates, who were taught the efficacy of collaborative dialogue in conflict resolution.

Methodism began in England with brothers John (1703–91) and Charles Wesley, who held that they were practicing the method of life given in the Bible. They opposed rationalism, deism, and religious indifference, and engaged in preaching in fields and factories to reach the common people with new hymns, emotional preaching, and working-class examples. They organized twelve-person Bible classes whose attendees prayed together weekly and whose leaders visited each individual weekly. They formed districts and conferences, appointed bishops, and held annual meetings with members and ministers from area churches. They combined Anglican liturgy with Puritan personal behavior, embraced free will, good works, and a new birth in love of God and living a religious life through worship, festival, and personal behavior. They never unified, but the United Methodist Church is the largest U.S. Methodist group, with a mix of small-town conservative and urban, often liberal congregations. They are mainstream Protestants. My adolescence was spent in a Methodist Scout troop, and its leader was one of my primary male mentors.

The Second Protestant Awakening

The Second Great Awakening, during the first thirty years of the 19th century, focused on the unchurched and sought to establish in them a deep sense of personal salvation. Puritan New England became divided into the more liberal, rationalistic Unitarians and the more conservative Congregational traditions. This awakening helped Universalism to flourish. It began in England, and preached a loving God who would save all humanity; Universalists believed there was no hell, and embraced everyone as children of God with inherent goodness. In the 19th century, a sizable portion of the American urban intelligentsia became Unitarians, while a flood of working-class folk embraced Universalism's enthusiastic Christian affirmations of no hell and universal salvation, and they built many frontier churches. The first major American philosophical-spiritual movement was Transcendentalism, which held for individual direct spiritual experience, believed that non-Christian traditions contained necessary wisdom, and were entranced by the new European critical biblical scholarship. Many Transcendentalists were Unitarians, while many Universalist women activists began to actualize the Transcendentalists' transformational social dreams; they opposed slavery, war, the destruction of nature, and oppression of the poor, and were in favor of the ordination and empowerment of women. Many Europeans and Americans became empiricists who believed in a social contract and tried to pursue the common good by testing their spiritual truths against worldly wisdom.

The Second Awakening also gave rise to new American religious denominations. Mary Baker Eddy founded the Christian Scientists in Boston; she claimed that she had discovered Jesus' methods for divine healing, which she summarized in *Science and Health with Key to the Scriptures.* In 1830, Joseph Smith began the Latter-Day Saints (LDS) with his *Book of Mormon,* which described God's activities among ancient Native Americans who he explained had descended from the lost tribes of Israel. The LDS failed to cooperate with governmental entities, partly because of their belief in polygamy, particularly popular among their leaders. There was violence, and Smith was murdered. In 1847, his successor, Brigham Young, led 147 remaining Mormons across the frontier to what became Salt Lake City, Utah. Young was a great organizer; people poured into his new communities, and by the time of his death, there were 357 Mormon communities in Utah and farther west.

The LDS Church believes that the Trinity is three separate Gods, and that people do not inherit original sin but instead earn it through their lives and receive personal punishments and rewards. The Book of Mormon is a new revelation, and equal for them in importance to the Bible. They evolved an effective denominational organizational system. Local congregations, stakes, are joined into a district. Globally, top leadership is a male hierarchy council of seventy, with twelve apostles, a president and two counselors. Mormons urge all their young males (and, recently, some young women) to become missionaries for two years. The Mormons organized a thorough internal welfare system in which members pay 10 percent of their income to their stake but are helped by their stake if they lose their jobs or face financial difficulties. Mormons have secret rites for members, are family oriented, and friendly to outsiders. Until 1890, their belief in plural marriage kept Utah from becoming a state; then, a Mormon president had a new revelation and revoked polygamy. Mormons had deemed people of color inferior and ineligible for membership, but in the 1970s, as they began to missionize extensively in the developing world, their president had a new revelation and accepted people of color as full-fledged Saints. The LDS has become a large, global religious movement, and is one of the fastest-growing denominations, both in the U.S. and worldwide.

The Third Protestant Awakening

The third Great Awakening began in the mid-19th century and continues today. It is anti-intellectual and anti-elite but is strongly pro-capitalistic, free enterprise, politically and socially conservative, theologically traditional with a male dominant ideology. It combines a strongly evangelical Christianity based upon rejection of selected aspects of modernity, especially disdaining scholarly criticism of the Bible, scientific theories that they perceive to be in conflict with Bible teachings, ecumenical efforts, and progressive social views. These fundamentalist Christians believe in Biblical inerrancy (that each word of the Bible is literally true). They organize as independent congregations united in loose federations of churches, including Churches of God, Holiness churches, Church of Christ, 7th Day Adventists, and later, Jehovah's Witnesses, and then Pentecostal movements like the Assemblies of

God. Generally, these churches have been and are strongly regional, patriotic, chauvinistic, and militant.

Two wealthy Los Angeles businessmen, Lyman and Milton Stewart, distributed 3 million copies of twelve booklets (1910–1915) expanding the "five fundamentals" of the conservative Presbyterians: 1) inerrancy of scripture; 2) the virgin birth and deity of Jesus Christ; 3) Christ was the substitute in atonement for the sins of believers; 4) the physical resurrection of Jesus and the saved; and 5) Christ's miracles. As fundamentalism evolved, it added justification by faith, a literal heaven and hell, premillennialism: that Christ would return to rule the earth from Jerusalem for a thousand years before which the world would have degenerated rapidly into war and chaos, and that the Bible is free of any error. Fundamentalists ask strangers if they have been saved, or are born-again, and generally believe that all non-fundamentalist Christians are not real Christians. Worldwide fundamentalism has split existing Protestant denominations and undermined many congregations. Fundamentalists distrust government bureaucracies and internationalism, while often supporting repressive governmental policies and wars against other groups, and oppose liberal social, political, and economic policies.

However, since the 1970s, they have become strongly Republican and generally oppose: affirmative action on behalf of people of color, increased immigration by people of color, a woman's right to birth control or an abortion. Fundamentalist evangelicals became a primary America political power when they elected Donald Trump as President of the U.S. They now dominate many state legislatures and play a central role in the Republican Party, so that a rural and suburban minority controls the politics in many southern and central US states. Evangelicals now face a quandary whether fundamentalism is more about a narrow sectarian, self-justifying nationalism or instead the equal application of Christian principles to everyone.

We need to distinguish between facts and fictions in American religious history. Most colonists probably did not attend church. American history is riddled with crypto-faiths, indifference, and spiritual paranoia. As Stephen Prothero says in *American Jesus: How the Son of God Became a National Icon*: Americans have constantly remolded and reimagined Jesus to fit their needs, re-casting Jesus in their own image. Princeton professor Kevin Kruse points out that it was not until the 1950s that Americans added "under God" to the pledge of allegiance, "in God we trust" to postage stamps and paper money, or made it the nation's motto. This movement began as a business effort to identify business and corporate interests with a Christian America, and climaxed with President Trump's election, perhaps the most un-Christian President in American history.

Fundamentalist Evangelical doctrines also stimulated a charismatic movement within Roman Catholicism. Especially in Latin America, millions of former Roman Catholics have either abandoned Roman Catholicism for evangelical Protestant churches or become charismatic Catholics, with exuberant worship and many evangelical personal practices. In Africa, many former Roman Catholics and mainline Protestants have joined evangelical, conservative Christianity churches. Many present U.S. mega-churches (thousands of members) are ethnically inclusive and youth-oriented with television ministries and an enthusiastic embrace of 21st century electronic media. Almost all are still dominated by patriarchal, authoritarian leadership with fundamentalist outlooks. Millions of unchurched contemporaries share a partly fundamentalist belief system: fearing hell and an imminent end of the world, which is used to justify focusing upon selfish short-term happiness, perceiving prosperity as 'proof' that they are among the elect who will be saved, or 'raptured' suddenly into heaven.

Christian Thought in the 20th and 21st Centuries

Starting in the late 19th century and continuing to the present, liberal Christianity has diversified to a remarkable extent and increasingly emphasized the Social Gospel in which Christian principles are actualized through political programs and economic policies. This movement was inspired by Walter Rauschenbusch and a host of women and men reformers who helped to create progressive policies and programs which lifted millions out of oppression and poverty and helped to nurture a more just and tolerant world. In contract, many conservative Christians rejected much of modernity, retreated into Biblical literalism, pessimism about earthly life, and clung to eschatological hopes for heavenly rewards for their true believers. Meanwhile, the middle-of-the-road Christian majority continues to meld Christianity's teachings into their modernized lifestyles, rejecting either secularism or fundamentalism.

Of the world's seven-plus billion people, about 2.5 billion are Christian, still by far the largest religious group. Over half the Christians, or about 1.25 billion, are Roman Catholics, 800 million are Protestants, 300 million are Eastern Orthodox, another 100 million are Oriental Orthodox and Church of the East, and at least 50 million are Fundamentalist Evangelicals. In the United States, about 51 million are Roman Catholic, 34 million are Baptist, 14 million are non-denominational Christians, 14 million are Lutherans, 9 million are Methodists, 6 million are Presbyterians, 4 million are Pentecostal, 3 million are Episcopal, 3 million are Latter Day Saints, and 2.5 million are Church of Christ, and another 10 million at least are members of a plethora of other smaller denominations. Christian populations in the U.S. are regionally distinct: Southern Baptists dominate the Southeast, Roman Catholics the Northeast and Southwest, Methodists the Midwest, and LDS the West.

Congregational participation is higher in the United States than other developed nations. Generally, however, church attendance has plummeted in Europe and is in decline in the United States. Rev. John Dickerson, a leading evangelical minister, wrote that while 25 percent of Americans may be counted as members of evangelical churches, only 7 percent are actually committed members, and a majority of young adult evangelicals are quitting church. A generation ago, Latin America was dominated by Roman Catholicism; today evangelical fundamentalism and charismatic and liberation Catholicism are exploding in popularity there. Many Asian "missionary" Christians are still in standard Protestant denominations, but evangelical fundamentalism and Mormonism are spreading there too. About 45 percent of the world's Pentecostals reside in sub-Saharan Africa. Russia has evolved from being violently anti-Christian to Putin developing an alliance like that of the czars with the Russian Orthodox Church; Russians are half of the world's Eastern Orthodox. Middle East and North African Christianity dwindled from 25 percent of the population in 1900 to less than 5 percent today. Many have immigrated to the U.S. and other more democratic, tolerant places—7 million Armenians live outside of Armenia. Eight million of the 10 million remaining Christians in the Middle East and North Africa are Egyptian or Ethiopian Coptic Christians.

Elements of Christianity that I Find Troubling

I don't believe that Jesus was, or intended to be, the only child of God, or is necessary for all peoples' salvation, or that he died so God would forgive us our sins. Why would God find it necessary to sacrifice God in human form so people could be forgiven sins that God made them capable of and likely to commit? I revere Jesus as a prophet of love and shared humanity who realized that every person has the divine immanent within us, and that our central human task is to actualize those elements of virtuous energy and power in our lives as we are able to realize them. It is tragic that Christianity has so thoroughly and often submerged this human and humane Jesus, an excellent model of compassionate empathy and human love, under the domination of a judgmental and self-contradictory Christ. I identify with the Gospel of Matthew's sermon on the mount, not with the narrower judgments of Paul, the Gospel of John, or the horrific fantasies in the Book of Revelations. Christianity has repeatedly lost its way in efforts to grasp ecclesiastical or political power, whether against heretics, in religious wars, or when fundamentalists defy knowledge, scientific findings, and our shared humanity with ignorance and bigotry.

Until the Crusades, Christians appeared to see Jesus more as savior than as condemning judge, and believed that God was asking people to live with love and justice instead of excusing violence and violation as shortcuts to absolving them of their transgressions. Today Islamic crusaders often call Christians today crusaders, tempting them to act similarly, instead of helping humanity to live sustainably in peace together. I do not worship a god crucified, but I do revere Jesus as a man of empathy and love. Living in despair about this life is a prolonged suicide. Faith rests upon hope and love, not upon desperation and destruction.

Christians who condemn all who fail their narrow tests for being saved in Christ are for me unchristian and anti-spiritual. Faithful people attempting to force others into their faith become sacrilegious and destroy their own spiritualities. For every human individual and all nations have both sacred and imperfect elements, are worthy and broken, sinful and saved. We need each other, and can find peace, fulfillment, and sustainability only in a shared human future. We must become global citizens and embrace a worldwide spirituality or condemn humanity's future.

Elements of Christianity that I Find Most Relevant

I grew up in a Christian and largely Protestant town, played the piano and organ at two Protestant churches, received my doctorate at a seminary, and served for forty years as a Unitarian Universalist minister. Nevertheless, my personal relationship with Christianity began and has remained more as a student of Christianity rather than as an advocate for Christianity. This era has provided magnificent opportunities for appreciative and critical consideration of religions in general and Christianity in particular. Biblical archaeology and anthropology, along with philosophy and traditional spiritual academic disciplines have allowed people today to know much more about the evolution of religions' actual histories and to better distinguish between myths and facts in religions. My birth family's skepticism and lack of regular church attendance made us part of an already growing plurality of Americans who perceived themselves to be spiritual, but not religious. I read through the Bible twice in junior high and high school. A good deal seemed trivial, some nonsensical, but other stories and passages became enduring inspirations. Christian mentors, teachers and peers enhanced my faith in Jesus as a loving and compassionate man, while my parents continued to reinforce my skepticism about Christianity as the only true faith or as the complete answer to my spiritual aspirations.

Soon after beginning college, I joined the Unitarian Universalist Church where an older sister was the coordinator for the children's programs. For the first time, I felt that I could in good conscience become a member of a religious community. The following year, I taught the "Church across the Street" curriculum about other denominations to the congregation's junior high students. We would spend one week learning about a denomination, then attend one of its worship services, and then spend the following Sunday talking about our experience there. Our visits included the Catholic cathedral, a Jewish temple, and a fundamentalist African American congregation, and a tent revival. During my final undergraduate year, I took a world religions course and wrote a paper comparing positions on war and peace that included interviews with the Catholic bishop, a rabbi, several Wichita ministers, and some hesitant Chinese Buddhists and Taoists in San Francisco.

In college, I readily identified myself as a civil rights and disarmament activist, as a humanist, a philosophical naturalist, and existentialist, but was not comfortable calling myself a Christian. I was looking for the historical not the mythical Jesus. I could agree with Gandhi who had called himself a Sermon on the Mount Christian (Gospel of Matthew 5-7). I could believe in that Jesus, and Christians involved in the civil rights, peace, and anti-poverty movements were among my visceral inspirations.

During graduate school, my spiritual practices included involvement with a YMCA tutoring project in an African American suburb and in peace activism. The campus YMCA Director became a spiritual guide. After proposing to my Hindu-Jain fiancée, I failed my doctoral exams and was discouraged from completing a political science doctorate, and needed to decide whether to: be drafted to fight in Vietnam, go to work as a federal employee, or attend a Unitarian Universalist seminary. I took the civil service exams, worked as an Immigration officer at O'Hare airport in Chicago; then, got married, and became a student at the Unitarian Universalist's Meadville Seminary and the University of Chicago.

Suddenly I was awash in the Christian scholarship, in dialogue with scholarly, activist Christians, and was also soon student-ministering with UUs trying to place themselves in relation to Christianity. In the UU congregations that I served over the next forty years, I helped them celebrate Christmas and Easter with joy and satisfaction. The birth of each child is a holy occasion, and every child can potentially help to save the world. People become powerful and are able to empower others through their relationships of community and love. We all deserve both the everyday miracles of nourishment and growth represented in the communion of bread and the mysteries of transcendence, insight and creativity represented by communion grapes. We need not forsake any useful and constructive aspect of our human heritage. Like the author of John's Gospel, I see God's spirit on earth to be the Holy Spirit, and believe every human, at their best is able to nurture aspects of that Holy Spirit.

Roman Catholic Thinkers Who've Inspired Me

I admire Roman Catholicism for its attention to philosophy and among some to mysticism. I agree with its willingness to recognize that Creation is both transcendent and immanent and that the soul is the seedbed of ultimate meaning. Like many Catholics, I try to shape my faith into practical service and to persevere with courage through life's tragedies.

Five Roman Catholics and a recent Catholic movement have been particularly important. My adult life has been bracketed by two amazing popes, John XXIII (1958–63) and Pope Francis. John helped celebrate a post-colonial world, faced problems of modern labor, and promoted better living conditions to make peace possible. Vatican II lived after him and revolutionized millions of Roman Catholics, including many Roman Catholic clerics and laity I worked with in community efforts. Now, we are blessed with Pope Francis, the first pope from the global south. He has taken our global ecological and income inequality crises seriously and is pushing Roman Catholicism into the 21st century. May he continue to liberate their Church.

I love the evolutionary theology of French Jesuit priest and paleontologist Pierre Teilhard de Chardin. I urge you to read *The Phenomenon of Man* and *The Divine Milieu*. He recognized how evolution could be connected with humanity's search for spiritual understanding. He had few illusions about life's tragedies, and understood that both science and civilization could be abused. He turned evolutionary history into a sacred drama moving selectively and sometimes constructively, toward greater complexity and greater consciousness. He perceived the divine as a vector and believed that humanity was moving into a new stage of psychic evolution, *the reflective step.* For him, this was the key to understanding the divine: penetrate, intellectually unify, and harness the energies that surround it. The conflicts of the future will be between the acceptance and rejection of progress. The evolutionary ahead plus the spiritual upward are bound to further the human forward. Humanity needs to move beyond nationalism and individualism to globalism and cooperative interdependence. He perceived the collaborative processes of scientific research to be a good model for the future. We must shake off our ancient prejudices and build the Earth. Individuals need to: be dedicated to truth, willing to resist evil, strive for good, and practice self-transcending love. In doing so, humanity will increasingly evolve centripetally, with intercommunication and socialization on a planetary scale, manifesting *agape* and harmony with the divine. Humanity needs to evolve from arrogant autonomy into loving *ex-centration*, adoring the world and life by doing justice for a global humanity and to sustain our planet.

I celebrate Mother Theresa. This Albanian turned Indian citizen trained in Ireland and spent most of her life in India, teaching for a generation in an elite school, but who then began working with the poorest of the poor at her Calcutta Home for the Dying, her gentle hospice in the worst of circumstances. I spent a day volunteering there and caught a fleeting glimpse of her. She organized a new order of nuns, the Sisters of Charity, with accompanying brothers and laypeople. Her Sisters of Charity have become a world-wide source of blessed service in poverty areas. After her death, the world discovered that she had lived her life wracked with doubt, facing dark nights of the soul, and questioned the foundations of her Christian faith. Since each of us is a struggling, striving individual ourselves, this inspired me further. "It is not how much we do, but how much love we put into the doing, a lifelong sharing of love with others."

Karen Armstrong is British, a former Roman Catholic nun, and an important spiritual writer who argues we should no longer accept the image of God as a divine tyrant imposing an alien law on his unwilling servants. She rejects traditional religions' pessimistic anthropologies and pervasive personal guilt, replacing them with rationality and decency, so that feelings do not degenerate into indulgence, aggression, or neurotic egotism. Faith needs to be tested by critical thinking. She advocates a mystical spirituality based upon the grace found in many world traditions and invites us to practice lives of compassion. We need to feel with others and then learn how not to inflict upon them the things that damage. We need to grow beyond the imprisonments of egotism and self-interest, to overcome aggressiveness, and emphasize empathy and collaboration. I particularly recommend her *Battle for God*, which spells out the dangers of fundamentalism in Judaism, Christianity, and Islam.

Liberation theology began among radical Latin American Roman Catholic priests who combined Marxist social analysis and Social Gospel activism with their Roman Catholic faith. It was developed by Gustavo Gutierrez in his *A Theology of Liberation: History, Politics, and Salvation*. A Peruvian Dominican Roman Catholic priest, he is now a professor at Notre Dame University who argues that Christians should act in loving solidarity with the poor and protest against injustice and oppression practiced by societies against them. Radical societal structural changes will be needed. Christians need to confront the realities of social sinfulness, breaking the institutional spiral of violence, and embracing Jesus' way of revolt against injustice and exclusion both personally and in their societies. Liberationists had been isolated by the Catholic hierarchy until Pope Francis.

Variations of Liberation theology have been adopted by many Christians throughout Latin America, Africa, Asia, and by many feminists and African Americans. I learned more about Liberation theology during my semester of teaching with Archbishop Desmond Tutu, the leader of the Anglican Community in South Africa, who had been a leader in overcoming apartheid and was the co-leader of their Truth and Reconciliation process.

Modern Protestant Christians and Movements Important to My Jesusian Faith

In seminary, I studied the quest for the historical Jesus and critical Biblical scholarship. Albert Schweitzer's *The Quest for the Historical Jesus* found no resurrection and argued that it was not Jesus' death that was significant, but instead that Jesus' greatness lay in his *reverence for life* ethics and belief that people needed to become servants to those most in need. A contemporary stage of Schweitzer's quest is represented by the Jesus Seminar, which seeks to identify 'authentic' Christian teachings using critical Biblical scholarship. The third stage combines social science with the Gospels by people like Harvey Cox, who place Jesus within his community contexts while highlighting Jesus' enduring messages. As a Harvard Fellow, I attended Cox's course on Jesus, and found it a revelation. Religion is a continuing drama between cultures and faith. To become real, religion needs to live within our worlds of work, power, and social arrangements. Cox's Jesus enables people to live with the earth and to base their spiritual practices upon endeavoring to do justice with love to all people, thereby participating in a continuing spiritual revolution. Cox's

Christianity is an intimate, personal worship based upon loving common sense and nonviolent social ethics.

I studied Paul Tillich's seminal three-volume *Systematic Theology* with his primary disciple, Professor Schroeder. Tillich was born a German Lutheran but opposed Hitler and became an American existentialist Christian. He argued that myth is the door to all aspects of culture—that depriving people of myth would silence all experiences of the holy, depriving religion of its language. We need to combine the scientifically objective realities and the mythical, to objectify the transcendent through the mediums of intuition combined with fulfilling conceptions of reality. I find Tillich's Christian existentialism useful. Our spiritualties reflect the totality of our human experience. Our imagination produces seeds of growth and bubbles of transcendence. Our imaginative sharing helps save us from absurdity.

Two other Protestant figures of special significance were the Niebuhr brothers. In 1987, I studied H. Richard Niebuhr at Harvard. He admitted the relativity of all historical religions but believed that Christian faith could enable people to avoid a tribal perspective. Faith allows people to rely on something beyond finite hopes. Revelation is beyond scientific proof; so, it requires personal existential decisions of trust and loyalty. Sin for Richard Niebuhr is both: disloyalty–failure to worship the true God, and idolatry—giving loyalty to things less than God.

His older brother, Reinhold Niebuhr, practiced the Christian ethics he taught for many years at Union Seminary. He supported labor unions in Detroit, was active in New York's Liberal Party and with Americans for Democratic Action, and for years was the editor of *Christianity in Crisis*. Though he remained a strong proponent of putting your faith into practical political organization and action, he also made people confront the inevitability of human egotism. No individual, group, or institution could claim to be free of destructive egotism, but it was much more difficult to maintain a moral society than it was to become a substantially ethical person. He was especially concerned with the sins of good people in social contexts. I strongly agreed with his last book, *Man's Nature and His Communities*, in which he argued that consistent self-seeking is self-defeating, while self-giving is bound to contribute to self-realization. It is a person's communities which provide them with the security to love, and it is within these communities that love can be practiced. He still advocated for the saving grace of faith in God and Jesus because they can move us beyond selfish egotism and idolatry but admitted that the common grace of doing justice and living with love within communities is where people are forced to deal with their residual self-interest. Common grace shows itself in parental affection, self-forgetfulness in crisis, deeds of responsible citizenship, and acts of creation. By itself, common grace can produce sufficient discrimination and discipline to guard against parochial loyalties. Goodness armed with power tends to become corrupted and even pure love without power will be destroyed. I particularly like two of Niebuhr's aphorisms.

> Nothing worth doing is completed in our lifetime; therefore, we must be saved by hope. Nothing true, beautiful, or good makes complete sense in any immediate context of history; therefore, we are saved by faith. Nothing we do, however virtuous, can be accomplished alone; therefore, we are saved by love. No virtuous act is quite so virtuous from the standpoint of our friend or foe as from our own; therefore, we are saved by the final form of love which is forgiveness.[1]

And his serenity prayer: "God, grant me the grace to accept with serenity the things that cannot be changed, the courage to change what should be changed, and the wisdom to distinguish the one from the other." The 12-step program's version makes it personal: "what I cannot and can change." He would argue that society may help you change what you can't individually change, and that there are societal injustices that should be changed; he would not have been satisfied with only what you can change as an isolated individual.

Dr. Martin Luther King Jr. serves as an excellent example of a Christian activist. He was devoted to liberal Christians' search for truth but refused to abandon the lights of reason. King was concerned that many liberal Christians had become too optimistic about human nature. For reason, devoid of the purifying powers of faith, can never free itself from distortions and rationalizations. Religious experience is an enduring acquaintance with the divine. It is humanity's primary path to transcendence. Spiritual experience and practice are open to all types of human intelligence and socioeconomic circumstances. Dr. King worked on behalf of African American civil rights but also opposed unjust wars, and worked diligently for peace and to overcome the economic injustice and poverty that dehumanize so many ethnic groups.

I admire Protestants' determined focus on the centrality of the individual conscience-soul, the importance of interpreting the Golden Rule inclusively, and interpreting scripture critically, testing it against your own experiences and the best standards of current scholarship. I believe that a faith without works is dead, that peoples' living faiths are what they do in society with other people, and that we learn our living faiths through our lives' experiences. People are saved by grace, by the grace of Creation, the innumerable graces of nature and human society, and the blessings of their intimates and communities. Most of grace is common grace: nature and human beings, but for me, transcendence is real, and universally accessible. As Roman Catholic writer, Richard Rodriguez, said in one of Bill Moyer's interviews (*On Faith and Reason*, PBS): "Reason has a sister....intuition is to trust the transcendental, to trust the essential mystery of life ... for example, love is not reasonable. Love defies reason." President Jimmy Carter embodies a model Protestant Christian in his willingly to put his faith into effective practice in the world and with his continued spiritual growth in retirement.

Process Theologies

Process theology fits well with my probabilistic and evolutionary thinking. It builds beyond: the empiricism and social contract ideas of the 18th century, moral imperatives, Transcendentalism, Social Gospel, and evolutionary ideas of 19th century, and the pragmatism, humanism, existentialism, ecumenicalism, and liberation movements of the 20th century. Alfred North Whitehead in *Process and Reality,* held that there was no necessary division between what is scientifically observable and what is deeply felt and experienced aesthetically. Religious experiences are emotionally and aesthetically felt, then rationalized, and finally moralized. Religion is both what is most permanent about the nature of things, and the art and theory of our internal lives. He wrote that the world is dynamic, organic, and social. The world is a creative, interdependent process of dynamic entities giving and receiving from one another. Reality is a society of societies, growing together into an ever more complex unity.

My favorite process theologian, Henry Nelson Wieman, spent much of his career at the University of Chicago, and became a Unitarian. His books include *The Source of Human Good* and *Man's Ultimate Commitment*. The knowledge of God is derived from our experiences in the natural world. God is the source of human good—those processes that endure, despite frustrations and even destructive conflicts to enhance the qualitative meaning of our lives. Whatever obstructs creativity, or undermines healthy communities, including some religious practices, is evil. God is the creative event. People tend to become committed to certain created events, thereby becoming idolatrous. An idea is real only when it interacts. We gain understanding through processes of assimilation and accommodation.

Jesusian

As a Jesusian, I believe that Jesus was saying that all people are children of God, unique elements of a sacred and evolving Creation. Jesus' non-violent activism, his embrace of the poor, oppressed, the stranger and abandoned are inspiring. I agree with Jesus that love is the heart and soul of spirituality. We need to love both what is most worthy about life (the love of God or Creation), and to do practical good for real people. Because humans inevitably remain egotistical, we need communities and governments in order to actualize our moral principles and ethical ideals. In many situations, being fair and working for justice are the best that we can do with most people most of the time. Love is the ideal, but it takes empathy, patience, courage, and perseverance which challenge all of us in our actions.

God appears to me to be neither all powerful nor all good from a human perspective. I find God to be the unfolding process of Creation, including the evolution of human communities and civilizations. With Unitarian Theodore Parker, I believe that the arc of the universe is long but that it bends toward justice, and I agree with Christian scripture and with Dr. Martin Luther King that on Earth God's work must truly be our own. If we want Earth to be sustainable and humanity to live in peace and to do justice with mercy and love, then, we must make significant sacrifices on behalf of the common good and for humanity's global future in our blessed lives. Christianity is about embracing life and this world, celebrating the immanence of God and the spiritually eternal in each person. The Earth and the heavens are not enemy camps but one reality. My Jesus was a living person practicing love, realizing that life and the Earth are sacred, knowing that we were born ok the first time. We need to learn how to reframe our angry energies and savage, vengeful feelings into progressive policies and helpful service. This will be to live in grace and love embodying the Holy Spirit.

Chapter 14
Islam

Central Islamic Beliefs and Practices

To become a Muslim, you must commit yourself to five requirements. The first is to declare that there is no God but God (Allah), and Muhammad is his messenger. The second is to pray five times a day facing Mecca, on awaking, at noon, midafternoon, sunset, and before sleeping, beginning each prayer with the Qur'an's opening verses: "In the name of God, the merciful and compassionate, praise be to God, Lord of the worlds, merciful and compassionate one, Master of the day of doom. Thee alone do we serve, to thee alone we cry for help. Guide us on the straight path, path of them thou have blessed, not to those with whom thou art angry, nor to those who go astray." The third is to give 2.5%, or one fortieth, of your wealth annually to the poor and needy. The fourth is to abstain from food and drink from sunrise to sunset for the month of Ramadan, and the fifth is to make a pilgrimage (the Haj) to Mecca at least once in your life (finances, health, and family obligations permitting).

Legend says that Allah told Muhammad to have Muslims pray 50 times daily, but Muhammad then met Moses who convinced him that people could not manage 50 prayers daily; so, Muhammad returned to Allah, and they negotiated until agreeing upon five daily prayers. Initially, Muhammad had Muslims facing Jerusalem, but later changed the direction of prayer toward Mecca. The 2.5 percent annual wealth tax was a substantial act for economic justice. Ramadan reinforced an annual period of prayer, fasting, and peace which Meccans were already doing. The Haj confirmed Mecca's centrality and peoples' spiritual equality.

Muslims believe that every people received their own messenger(s) from God. Jesus was the last messenger sent to the Israelites, but Jews have consistently strayed from the path of surrender, and Christians have lost their way in the maze of Western cultures. Each messenger spoke their people's language and followed their customs, yet the core faith taught by all was to surrender to the will of the Power that is greater than you. Doing so, you find peace and freedom; then, you must continue doing what is right and beneficial for others. Muhammad brought the *Qur'an*, which Muslims believe is the perfect and final message from God, and it is their duty to spread its truths. Allah is more loving than a mother with her children. The oppressed and exploited will receive mercy and justice in death. Allah does not favor any particular individual, ethnic group, or country because He created all humans as spiritual equals. Allah is the ultimate cause of whatever happens; however, people may earn his favor, but only through virtue and piety. At the Day of Judgment, each will be judged by what he has done, or failed to do that he should have done. Gratitude toward Allah is the heart of worship; faith resides firmly in each person's heart and is proved by his deeds.

An infidel (*kafir*) is one who is ungrateful. Believers should commit no excess, remain anxious to please God, yet mindful that whatever people accomplish can never be compared to Allah's blessings. There have been four historic stages of faith and evolving stages of scripture: the monotheism of Abraham, then Moses' Ten Commandments, followed by Jesus' Golden Rule, and finally the Qur'an with its practical explanations for how to love our neighbors and worship the one God. Some things are forbidden, many are indifferent, and some are obligatory. Primary obligations include: submission to Allah, gratitude for his multitude of blessings, and their believers' lifelong struggles not to forget (*ghaflah*) their relationship with God. Daily prayers remind them of that divine relationship. They must continue renewing their faith through whole-hearted giving to others and faithful actions within their religious community.

God is one, but He has numerous angels who are His instruments and communicators. Earlier scriptures were corrupted, while every word of the Qur'an is, for many Muslims, literally Allah's word and work, and remains unquestionable. The Qur'an mentioned twenty-six prophets, but much of their teachings have been forgotten or misunderstood, and there will be no true prophets after Muhammad. At the end of history, life on Earth will end, the dead will be brought back to life, and everyone will be held accountable for their deeds and sent to heaven or hell for eternity.

People are invested with intelligence, individual dignity, and the liberty to choose good or evil, and are thereby responsible for their actions, yet Allah determines the destiny of all things and has pre-ordained their outcomes. This same dilemma confronts many Muslims, Jews, and Christians alike.

Islam's Historic Evolution

By 8000 BC, the Arabian marshes already contained hunter-gatherers from Africa and nomadic shepherds from the eastern Mediterranean. By 5000 BC, peoples had settled its coasts and oases and were cultivating crops and raising cattle. As civilizations arose in Egypt, Mesopotamia, Ethiopia, Iran, and India, trade routes developed crossing the Arabian Peninsula. By the 2nd century BC, wealth flowed through Arabia because of these caravans and because of the production and sale of frankincense and myrrh in which Arabia had a monopoly. Made from tree bark and grown in Yemen, their fragrant resins were burned for everything from sanctifying religious ceremonies to masking stench.

By AD 117, the Roman Empire controlled the Arabian Peninsula. As its traditional religions waned, Judaism and Christianity found many proselytes. The subsequent Byzantine Empire kept the Bedouins under control until 600, by cooperating with Ghassanids, a Syrian people who had arrived in the Arabian Peninsula in the 2nd century AD. From 244–249, a Ghassanid Roman Emperor, Philip the Arab, considered himself the first Christian Emperor and negotiated peace with the Persian Empire. The Arabian fragrance monopoly was costing Christians a fortune; so, they began condemning their use, and the Arabian trade never regained its former importance.

Mecca is forty miles inland from Jeddah, Saudi Arabia's present capital. By the 1st century BC, Romans already identified Mecca as a place of religious pilgrimage. For Meccans had responded to the continuous warfare among Arabian tribes by making their city not only a trade route hub and center for the spice trade, but also an annual place of pilgrimage, with its famous well (Zamzam), and temple (the Kaaba) that contained a gigantic black granite cube that held a small meteorite or volcanic fragments, and had been objects of Arabic veneration for centuries before Muhammad. This monument and object(s) later became the central focus of Muslims' primary pilgrimage, the *hajj*. Pre-Islamic pilgrims entered peacefully to drink from the Zamzam well, circle around the Kaaba, settle disputes, negotiate alliances and marriages, trade and spend money. Objects of worship then included gods, goddesses, and jinn (demons). Allah was among them, already considered creator, provider, and determiner of destiny, but believed to be inaccessible to human intervention compared with other deities. By Muhammad's birth, his Koresh tribe dominated Mecca, with help from Ghassanids and Persians. Muhammad was born (AD 571) into this city of caravans, trade, tribal spirituality, and negotiation.

Muhammad

His father died before Muhammad's birth; his mother died when he was six; then, his paternal grandfather parented Muhammad for two years. Thereafter, young Muhammad was controlled by a paternal uncle, who treated him badly. Nevertheless, Muhammad became gentle and trustworthy, ready to help others, and disgusted by Arabians' fighting and immorality. As a young man, he was hired by a wealthy widow, Khadija, who owned a flourishing caravan business, and he traveled with caravans for a few years, seeing Damascus and Jerusalem. Khadija, impressed by his prudence and integrity, proposed marriage to Muhammad, and they married in 595. Khadija was fifteen years older, educated, successful, and powerful. Muhammad was illiterate, poor, with little chance of advancement without her support. Their marriage allowed Muhammad to spend much of his time in religious meditation in a nearby mountain cave where Muhammad joined Arabian contemplatives (*hanifs*) who worshipped Allah exclusively.

The next fifteen years were comfortable and financially secure for Muhammad under Khadija's protection and support. However, they must have been difficult for her. She had two sons and a daughter from previous marriages, and her marriage with Muhammad grew criticism from her social circle. Khadija managed both her business and their family because Muhammad was preoccupied with his spiritual practices. He did not have his first revelation until fifteen years after their marriage. Illiterate and untrained, his initial response to this revelation was to believe that he was possessed by a demon or was crazy, and he attempted suicide, but Khadijah stood by him. At 42, he preached his first public sermon, but attracted few followers. In 619, after 24 years of marriage, Khadijah died.

Muhammad then asked his most powerful follower, Abu Bakr, for Bakr's six-year-old daughter, Aisha's hand in marriage. Muhammad temporarily acknowledged the three most worshipped Meccan goddesses, Allat, Mant, and al-Uzza, (who represented birth, marriage, and death) as deities, but then recanted his announcement; these became Islam's "Satanic" verses. In 620, Muhammad reported being carried to Jerusalem and Paradise and meeting other prophets causing more Meccans to convert to Islam.

Representatives from three Jewish tribes from Medina, a town of 12,000 people, 280 miles north came to invite Muhammad to rule Medina. Facing danger in Mecca, Muhammad and his followers escaped to Medina in 622. This date (the *Hijra*) begins the Islamic calendar and heralds Muhammad's metamorphosis from a lonely, attacked prophet to a political and military leader. He consummated his marriage with Aisha, now age nine. In 624, he united Medina, and carried out his first forbidden raid against a Meccan caravan. Mecca retaliated, but Muhammad's forces won the battle and Muhammad ordered those captured killed or sold for ransom. Then, he broke his own treaty by besieging a Medina Jewish tribe whom he exiled. In 625, Meccans won a battle against Medina and wounded Muhammad so he exiled a second Medina Jewish tribe, and had most of the third Jewish tribe murdered.

In 628, Muhammad met pagan Meccans and concluded a ten-year truce. In his later years, Muhammad made several additional marriages to secure tribal alliances. In 630, Muslims conquered Mecca; Muhammad rode to the Kaaba and recited verses from the Qur'an while his men destroyed whatever they considered idolatrous. This was the first of many non-Muslim worship places to be forcibly converted into mosques. Muslims conquered the Bedouins, capturing their huge wealth, and now ruled Arabia, and Muhammad sent his warriors to force conversions among the remaining non-Muslim Arabian tribes. In 631, he attacked Tabuk, his first Christian conquest, forcing them to pay a non-Muslim tax and to submit to Islamic rule. He made his farewell pilgrimage to Mecca in 632. As the conquests of

Christian and Zoroastrian territories began, Muhammad's spent his last days in Medina with Aisha, now nineteen.

Muhammad was a remarkable man. Without formal education, he began what has become the world's second largest religion. An illiterate, he dictated the Qur'an which has become the most recited and the most often memorized book in the world. Untrained as a politician or warrior, he ruled Medina and ultimately Mecca, carried out military engagements, and negotiated treaties. By imposing Islam upon Meccans while maintaining its status as a successful pilgrimage destination, he persuaded the Meccan majority. His marriages served him well. He provided comfort for millions, destruction or despair for thousands, and the Arabian Peninsula had finally been united by an Arabian.

The Qur'an

The Qur'an is divided into 114 chapters, or *Surahs*, organized, after its opening prayer, from longest, surah #2, "Heifer," with 286 verses, to the shortest, #114, "Mankind," with six verses. The opening prayer sets the tone: it states that there is only one merciful and compassionate God who is angry when people go astray. The faithful who follow a straight path are those whom God has already blessed. Although all believers are equal in his kingdom, leadership, rank, and degree are joined with greater and lesser degrees of responsibility in life, which depend upon true knowledge and insight. People should be God's steadfast servants, patiently enduring hardship, using kind words and practicing charity with the less fortunate, love each other, fear God and worship in solitude, controlling their anger—for a scholar's ink is greater than a martyr's blood.

The Qur'an is 80 percent the length of the New Testament. Millions of Muslims memorize elements of or all of the Qur'an in Arabic. Though translated into most of the world's languages, only Arabic is considered sacred (like Sanskrit, Hebrew, or Latin for other religions). Muslims believe the Qur'an should be recited and understood in Arabic. That is a challenge in the Islamic world today, since 90 percent of the world's Muslims do not understand Arabic. It is neither their native nor mastered language, while millions more remain functionally or literally illiterate in any language. So, for most Muslims, it is more the sound and rhythm of the recitation that is valued, rather than a careful analysis of its ideas. Most Muslims presently remain dependent upon their religious or legal scholars, and/or their political leaders to determine for them what the Qur'an means, and also how Muslims should live, since many find the Qur'an's Arabic text beyond their understanding.

When Muhammad was forty, sitting alone in a mountain cave, a voice spoke saying: *"La ilaha illallah"* (There is no God but God) and that Muhammad had been appointed, like earlier prophets including Adam, Abraham, Noah, Moses, David, Jesus, and others, to receive the words of Allah and to share them. For the rest of his life, Muhammad continued to receive messages. He came to believe they came from Allah through angel Gabriel. He could neither read nor write; so, he recited them to followers who sometimes wrote them down, but in no systematic fashion until years after his death. During twenty-three years of revelations his circumstances changed dramatically. At first, he was a lonely spiritual seeker without followers. Only in Muhammad's last twelve years did he did have a sizable following and during most of those years, he lived in Medina, consumed by ruling a town, military battles, and Arabian negotiations.

The Qur'an is an unusual mixture of statements, some seemingly contradictory. They detail religious messages about God, prophets, angels, afterlife and spiritual practices involving scripture, prayer, alms, fasting and pilgrimage, but also address issues of family life (marriage, divorce, women's rights, multiple wives, and property rights), as well as rules of war, statements of peace, forgiveness, and gentleness. The Qur'an portrays both an Allah that embraces all followers of the Book (Jews, Christians, and Muslims), who is merciful, forgiving, and understanding, but also an Allah that judges harshly, and supports violence and martyrdom. Here are a few tolerant and compassionate Qur'an passages:

> 57:20: The life of the world is a sport and pastime. 5:48: To everyone (Allah) has given a law and way. 2:257: Let there be no compulsion in religion. 2:190: A righteous war must either be defensive or to right a wrong. Do not attack first; God hates an aggressor.

And the following are Qur'an passages illustrating the harsh Allah that supports violence and martyrdom:

2:191: Slay them where you find them until there is no more interpreting, and religion is for Allah. 4:95: Allah has given preference to those who fight with their wealth and their lives above those who sit at home. They will receive a huge reward. 8:60: Whatever you spend for the cause of Allah will be repaid to you, and you shall not be wronged. 9:5: Fight and slay the pagans, but if they repent and establish regular prayers and charity then open the way for them, because Allah is forgiving.

The Qur'an ranks the battle against evil within your own heart above battles against others. The great jihad is the battle within one's self. Punishment is appropriate for wanton wrongdoers but should only be equal to the injury inflicted. In a war, agreements are to be honored, treachery avoided, civilians spared. In economics, Muhammad has no objection to profits, competition, or entrepreneurial ventures, but acquisitiveness and competition should be balanced by fair play and compassion. The collection of interest is outlawed; so, lenders needed to become partners in any venture. Men can have up to four wives, but each must have separate quarters and be treated with equal esteem. Men have certain rights over women (wives and daughters should not make friends with those unacceptable to their father or husband, and remain chaste). But women also have rights—revolutionary ones for Arabia in AD 632: outlawing infanticide, making marriage the sole locus of the sex act, requiring a woman's consent for her marriage, allowing women to initiate divorce as a last resort, and to keep their property and inheritance after divorcing.

Muhammad did not hide his personal limitations and resisted any effort to inflate himself beyond his humanity. He said Allah had not sent him to work wonders. That his only miracle was bringing the Qur'an, presented himself only as a preacher of God's words, a bringer of God's message to mankind. He said if people wanted to see miracles they only had to look around to see God's amazing handiwork in nature and His incredible orders and ingenuity in the world.

A significant portion of the Qur'an builds upon stories from the Old Testament and the New Testament that Muhammad had heard. He recited Adam as the first prophet. The idea of original sin was rejected. Eve was not blamed for Adam's mistakes, and people were not sinful because of their ancestors' misdeeds. Muhammad anointed Abraham as the head of the scriptural tribes, the original monotheist, first Muslim, and believed that Abraham had sanctified Mecca's Kaaba. Muhammad traced Arabs' ancestry through Ishmael, son of Abraham and his servant, Hagar, banished after Abraham's wife Sarah conceived her own son, Isaac. He said Isaac's descendants had become the Jews, while Ishmael's descendants had become the Muslims and perceived Abraham's willingness to sacrifice Isaac to be exemplary of religious faithfulness. Many Muslims annually sacrifice a scapegoat, as Yahweh allowed Abraham to do in Isaac's place.

Mary is generally considered the most revered woman in the Qur'an. Muslims accept the virgin birth of Jesus. The Qur'an says: Your Lord says it is easy for Me. God simply commanded "Be" and Jesus was. The infant Jesus defends his mother: I am a servant of God. He has given me scripture and has made me a prophet. Jesus made prayer and charity his duty, claimed to be a sign of God and a messenger to the Israelites. But Muhammad believed that the Jews had strayed from the spirit of truth and placed their trust in legalism, burying their sense of mercy. He felt Jesus preached a return to truth, rejecting all that men had falsely added. Jesus' good news was that love and mercy would overcome hate and anger. God granted Jesus the ability to perform miracles. While Jews thought that they had crucified Jesus, God had instead removed Jesus to a place with Him, to return at the end of days. Jesus' followers had tried to maintain his teachings but were corrupted by Greek and Roman influences so that only a little of his truth survived. Strange doctrines: like Jesus being a man-god, God dying, saint worship and God being made up of three parts while accepted by Christians, were considered corruptions of Jesus' teachings by Muslims.

Huston Smith pointed out that the apparent incoherence of the Qur'an has its cause in the incommensurable disproportion of the Spirit (the uncreated Qur'an) by the limited resources available in language (the spoken or written Qur'an), just as God's power and ingenuity are gigantic in proportion to the best and wisest of human endeavors and understandings. The Qur'an has 192 references to God's compassion and mercy as compared with seventeen references to God's wrath and vengeance. Smith proposes that we substitute the term commitment for surrender, to better understand that the devout Muslim's intention is not to give up but rather to strive so that nothing worthwhile in ourselves is withheld. Smith argues that the Qur'an embraces individuality because it urges believers to commit themselves to fully recognizing their unique potentialities through their commitments to God's will.

The Islamic Community: The Ummah

In *Religions of the East,* Joseph Kitagawa wrote about the gradual reshaping of the Bedouin consciousness through its Islamization. The organizational form that arose was the *Ummah,* the community of the faithful. Initially, Muhammad's doctrines were antagonistic to Bedouin traditions: attacking their tribalism, individualistic freedom, disinterest in regular worship, and tendency to murder their leaders. But Muhammad evolved into a political leader seeking alliances and built his Islamic community upon the foundation of a reformed social solidarity among Arab peoples. Family and tribe are central to Bedouins. Muhammad produced four daughters and two sons; but his sons died young, so, it was first his fathers-in-law and then his sons-in-law that inherited Islamic leadership. During his political evolution he gradually refocused Islam on ethnicity by eliminating Jewish and Christian elements and substituting ideas and practices he identified as Arabian. Ummah identifies an ethnic, linguistic, or religious group of people who are the objects of a divine plan for salvation. He argued that each people had an ummah, and Islam was the Arabian one, but as he began to control non-Arabian territory, his ideas of ummah changed to embrace anyone who surrendered to Allah and Muhammad, for all converts were now included in Allah's community.

This Arabization of Islam has remained a source of conflict, producing an enduring sense of ethnic hierarchy and has complicated Islamic subdivisions. Fully 87 percent of Muslims now are not Arabs. Yet, Arabians continue to identify Arabia not only as the homeland of Islamic history and the geographic focus of its mandated pilgrimage and worship, but believe that Arabians are the "truest and best" Muslims, often calling non-Arab Muslims *mawali*, clients, and have sometimes charged them the 20 percent non-Muslim land tax. The emergence of Saudi Islamic fundamentalism in the 19th century and its global influence because of Saudi and Gulf State oil wealth in the 20th and 21st centuries have compounded this sense of special privilege. In their organizational, legal and theological systems, if not always in their politics, Islam has retained an implicit hierarchy with Saudi Arabians on top, other Arabs next and non-Arab Muslims below, complicated by realities of particular times, places and the prejudices of various Islamic groups.

Since the Islamic community implied a definite political system from its beginnings, it has always been more difficult to separate the spiritual and religious elements of Islam from its social, political and economic traditions and practices. As Kitagawa argued, its mosque has always also been its public forum—sometimes its military drill ground as well as its place of worship. Islam's prayer leaders sometimes became its military commanders, as Muhammad had been. Islam's egalitarian foundations tempted any mosque leader, self-described expert, tribal leader, or military commander to begin proclaiming Islamic truths for all Muslims, while condemning other's actions, and justifying their own deviations from the Qur'an. By the time of Muhammad's death, the dream of the Islamic community was to become the spiritual unity of all of humanity. This universal conversion has yet to be historically realized, but remains a prevalent dream envisaged by many Muslims, as an analogous dream still inspires millions of Christians.

Putting the Qur'an and the Hadith into Written Forms

While Muhammad was alive, no attempt was made to record either his life or his words. It took Islam's leaders generations to put the Qur'an into written form and collect Muhammad's other sayings and deeds from those who were alive during his lifetime. Muhammad's words and actions, separate from his Qur'anic recitations, were compiled as the Hadith. Compiling the Qur'an and Hadith was a long, complicated process because most Arabians were illiterate, while many of his literate followers were pagan Meccan elite or converts from Judaism or Christianity, and likely influenced by those ancestral traditions and political conflicts. The assembly process was called the *Sunna,* the ancestral usage of the prophet and his followers. The Hadith contains many pre-Islamic Meccan and Arabian traditions along with Muhammad's and his followers' innovations, developing over the first two centuries after Muhammad's death. A century later, the Sunna-Hadith was declared judge over the Qur'an, rather than the Qur'an governing the Sunna-Hadith. In 886, Ahmad Ghulam Halil declared Sunna "the foundation of Islam; whoever deviates from it in any religious matter is an unbeliever." Nonetheless, doubts about who is a "true Muslim" continue to linger.

For devout Muslims, the Qur'an comes directly from Allah; its messages and admonitions of the Hadith are considered close to sacred; so, the actual history of this collection process provides challenges to the faithful, since published scriptures are without exception done significantly later and possibly quite differently from the original prophets' recitations. Muhammad made this clear when speaking about Jewish and Christian prophets and their traditions, but then exempted himself and his own recitations, as did his followers later.

Islamic History after Muhammad

Within fifteen years, his followers had conquered all the centers of the ancient Near Eastern civilizations including the Persian and Byzantine empires and had a territory as vast the Roman Empire. Within a hundred years, they were challenging the Tang dynasty in China and their power stretched 5,000 miles west to Spain. It was the only time that an empire based upon a single faith, bound by its laws and devoted to its principles, ruled so much of the Earth. It uprooted Persian Zoroastrians, Buddhism in Central Asia, and eventually challenged Hinduism in the Indus valley. It established Arabic as a world language and became the primary repository of knowledge for centuries.

Arabian society had been based upon intertribal conflict. Now, Muslim leaders re-directed their fighting energies outward so as not to tear their Islamic empire apart. Jihad promised both earthly and heavenly rewards since soldiers could keep 80 percent of captured booty and were declared martyrs with special access to heaven when killed in battle. But why were these small Muslim armies so successful? Scotland's St. Andrew's Professor, Hugh Kennedy, responds with a three-part explanation. For the first hundred years, Muslim armies exploited the presence of plagues and continuing Persian and Byzantine Empire battles with each other. For the next 50 years, Muslims used their empire's new strength, while in later centuries, Islamic conquests were carried out mostly by non-Arabs: Mongols, Turks, and Mughals, who allowed them to surrender and pay a 20 percent land tax, but continue to live much as before, unless they rebelled; then, their cities were destroyed and populations killed or enslaved.

Fred Donner, in *Muhammad and the Believers: At the Origins of Islam*, explained that Islam evolved from an ecumenical, syncretic, pietistic, and millenarian cult into a more dogmatic and exclusivist faith. For its first several generations, other religions regarded Islam as an open-minded and not especially threatening faith. In 660, Jerusalem's first Muslim governor was a Jew. The term "Muslim" came into common usage only in the 8th century; before then, believers appeared to be a community that embraced many faiths. Over time, Islamic internal doctrinal and dynastic divisions created a strong sense that orthodoxy needed to be enforced, that resulted in Islam hardening its boundaries against other religions.

Kitagawa divides Islamic history into four periods. An initial 400 years of phenomenal expansion with the absorption of many non-Arab peoples into the Muslim community, and the infusion of many Persian and Greek influences into Islamic thought. Then, in the 11th–14th centuries, when Crusades caused significant losses of Islamic political prestige and territory, including Mongol and Tartar invasions and temporary European Christian intrusions, there developed significant elaborations of Islamic philosophical and spiritual concepts and practices, and impressive scientific and medical progress. In the 15th–18th centuries, non-Arab, multiracial Muslim empires ruled military dynasties: the Turkish Ottomans, Shi'ite Persians, and Indian Mughal empires. Finally, from the 18th century to the 1920s, Western dominance caused Muslim empires to disintegrate. There were many Islamic religious modernists and political progressives and many Western methods and technologies were adopted, but there was also significant ideological resistance to European civilization. I suggest a fifth period is now occurring composed of nationalism, modernization, and secularization, which are opposed by fundamentalism, oil money, and pervasive Islamic sectarian tribal conflict.

In 733, at the battle of Tours, Charles Martel stopped Islam's European advance, or much of Europe might have become Islamic. Its conquests elsewhere meant that Islam was enriched by Greek-Roman civilizations in the west and by Persian civilization to the northeast. These varied peoples converted to Islam, but in turn their more advanced cultures enriched Islam. Jews and Christians were usually allowed to continue their lives and worship as long as they paid the non-Muslim 20 percent tax on their production (as compared with the 2.5 percent Muslim converts' tax to be used for the Muslim poor). Many of these non-Islamic peoples converted in order to survive or to flourish with the victors, while others undoubtedly had a spiritual change of heart as they converted. Muslim practices did often also culturally advance these cultures from Persia to Spain by increasing women's rights, nurturing a more tolerant view of religious and cultural diversity, or more openness to technological and cultural innovations. For hundreds of years, Islamic populations became among the more advanced civilizations wherever they settled.

Islamic Law, or Shari'a

The Muslim community takes its political, legal, and cultural responsibilities as seriously as its religious responsibilities. Unlike the Western separation of law and religion, or church and state, Islam perceived their legal systems as the practical applications of their religion. Muslims perceive three sources for their laws: The Qur'an, the Sunna-Hadith, and *fiqh*, (intelligent understanding), which includes consensus among legal scholars (judicial precedents), analogical deductions, and independent judgments. Four schools of *Sharia* law developed within Islam: *Hanafi, Maliki, Shafi,* and *Hanbali.* The Hanafi school is the most influential, with considerable personal reasoning, and is prevalent in India and its western neighbors. Maliki thought rests on consensus and is prevalent in Africa. Shafi belief depends on consensus and analogical reasoning, and is practiced in the Middle East, India, and Indonesia. Hanbali remained insignificant until the 18th century when Wahhabis revived it in Saudi Arabia where it has since dominated.

Every Sunni Muslim is expected to belong to one of these four legal schools. Until the 19th century, the Ummah continued to expand the Sharia as eternal and universal for every act of life.

Sunni Islamic History

Abu Bakr, father of Aisha, was Muhammad's first successor (632–634), and Umar, whose daughter, Hafsah, married Muhammad, was the second (634–644). The two were prominent Meccans, early converts, and Muhammad's close companions. Umar was a brilliant leader. From North Africa to Persia, he pushed the Byzantine Empire out of areas it had held since Alexander the Great, and established control over military and provincial administrations. Uthman (644–656) was the third successor. He married Muhammad's daughter Ruqayyah. Uthman established the Qur'an's first standard text by 650. These three ruled from Medina. Ali (656–661), who was Muhammad's cousin and married to Muhammad's daughter Fatima. His son, Hasan, briefly served after him; both ruled from Iraq.

The Syrian governor, Muawiyah (661–680) became the sixth caliph. He shifted the ruling hierarchy from Muhammad's in-laws to an "elected" leadership, became the first Umayyad caliph, and was followed by fourteen more who ruled from Damascus, Syria (661–750). The next effective caliph, Abd al Malik (692–705), established the principle of *jama'a*, that the only adequate basis for Islamic solidarity was Arab customs and legal traditions. After AD 750, two separate Islamic dynasties ruled for the next 300 years: the Umayyads, now headquartered in Cordoba, Spain (756–1031), with eight emirs and eleven caliphs, and thirty-seven Abbasid caliphs who ruled in Baghdad, Iraq (750–1258). During those Abbasid caliphates, Turkish soldiers became powerful regional rulers in Egypt and India. Seventeen additional Abbasid caliphs ruled from Cairo (1261–1517); in parts of North Africa, there were fourteen Fatimid Dynasty Ismaili Shia caliphs (909–1171), and twelve Almohad caliphs (1145–1266). So from 750 to 1266 Islamic politics experienced incredible diversity instead of unity.

Shia Muslims

Shia Muslims are the major Islamic sectarian minority, representing as many as 15 percent of all Muslims today. Their revolt arose out of a dispute about the appropriate successor after Muhammad. They believe that he had chosen Ali, who was not only his son-in-law but also his blood cousin. They mourn the assassinations of Ali and his sons Hasan and Husayn and consider them to be the true post-Muhammad Islamic leaders. They reject the first three caliphs, and Muawiya, who engineered Ali's and Hussein's deaths, and reject the Sunni's subsequent process of selecting caliphs as temporal rulers. Instead, Shia Muslims believe in their leaders (imams) because they are Muhammad's "blood descendants," but are also divinely ordained leaders and the final interpreters of Islamic spirituality and law on Earth. As Shia lost political battles, the Shias emphasized that their imams were invested with a special spiritual knowledge that gave them the right to interpret religious, mystical, and legal knowledge to the community. The most learned are known as ayatollahs (literally, "sign of God"). Shia rejects the four Sunni schools of law and many other policies and practices of the Sunni majority. Husayn and his family's deaths are commemorated annually on *Ashura,* a day of somber ritual marked among some Shiites by self-flagellation. Often oppressed by Sunni Muslims, Shiites have a strong sense of persecution and a tendency to perceive themselves as martyrs. Theirs is a piety of protest; they hold that it is sometimes necessary to fight tyranny, even to the point of dying a martyr's death. The elevation of their imams and their tendencies toward individual interpretations of Sharia by their semi-divine leaders are the primary distinctions between Shia and Sunni Muslims.

Shia has become subdivided into subsects with different theologies and leaderships. The largest group is called Twelver Shiism, because they accept the first twelve Shia imams beginning with Ali and believe that the twelfth imam disappeared in the 9th century and will return to lead all Muslims. The second largest is the Ismaili, who recognizes only the first seven imams. They arose in 9th-century Yemen and spread rapidly throughout much of the Islamic world, often pursuing military and territorial power. In 930, a group of them raided Mecca and removed the Black Stone from the Kaaba for twenty years. The Ismaili was and is today perceived to be a great threat by many Sunni Muslims, and yet has had significance influences upon Islam. The Ismailis are themselves divided; the most notorious subset called the Assassins, who developed south of the Caspian Sea, used hashish to "taste paradise," and often practiced covert murder of first Muslim and later Christian leaders whom they considered enemies of their state. They survive today as the Nizari, whose present leader is the nonviolent Agha Khan. The Zaydi Shiites are found in Yemen; they reject both the hidden imam and the imams' infallibility.

Other sects have rites and Islamic credentials that are doubted even by other Shiites, including the Syrian Alawites, also resident in Lebanon, who consider the pillars of Islam as symbolic rather than applied, and celebrate some Christian holidays. Some Turkish Kurds are Alevi Shiites, and the Druze community differs even more from other Shiite groups. Some of the more radical Shia communities elevate Ali and his descendants to a position of respect above Muhammad himself, and give them semidivine status as avatars. (Karen Armstrong, *A History of God: The 4,000-Year Quest of Judaism, Christianity and Islam,* 163.) The Druze sometimes identify themselves as Unitarians, so I have an Israeli Druze tile representation of Jesus on my bedroom wall.

The Islamic Golden Age

From 800 to 1200, Islamic lands expanded worldwide. Their capitols were centers of culture, and their wealth, technology, science, medicine, and philosophy were far more advanced than most of Europe's. Logic played an important role in Islamic philosophy; it favored inductive reasoning. Muslims recognized atomism early as foundational to physical reality and made many useful astronomical observations. An evolutionary theory developed by Al-Jahiz (776–869) asserted that environmental factors influenced organisms to develop new characteristics to ensure survival by transforming them into new species. In the 13th century, Nasir al-Din Tusi explained how elements evolved from minerals into plants, then animals, and then humans. He averred that hereditary variability was an important evolutionary factor, and explained that some animals developed fighting characteristics while others focused on means of flight; that ants and bees developed complex communities to protect and cooperate among themselves, and that some apes had probably evolved into humans. In 1025, Al-Haytham proposed aspects close to standard scientific methodology: observation, problem, hypothesis, experimental testing, results analysis, conclusions, and publication. Avicenna's *The Canon of Medicine* (11th century) is almost modern, with experiments, clinical trials, and human drug testing.

Collecting the Hadith and codification of the Sharia law formed the chief activities of Muslim religious scholars during the first four centuries after Muhammad. Islamic scholars Al-Farabi, Avicenna, Averroes, and al-Ghazali challenged and improved upon aspects of Aristotle's ideas. They developed theories of freewill and human reason, testing them against their faith in God's unity and control. The most important religious thinker was Abu Hamid ibn Muhammad al-Ghazzali (1058–1111), considered a "renewer of the faith" that appears only once a century. Ghazzali, a Persian, became an advisor to the Seljuq sultans in Isfahan, Persia, and then a professor in Baghdad. In 1095, he underwent a spiritual crisis, then abandoned his career, disposed of his wealth, and adopted an ascetic lifestyle because he wanted to confront the spiritual experience directly and grasp the Qur'an's "ordinary meanings." He was instrumental in helping systematize Sufism (Islamic mysticism) and brought it into mainstream Islam. He believed that all causal events and interactions are not material connections but rather the immediate and present Will of God. He vehemently rejected elements of Aristotle and Plato that had until then been foundations of Islamic thought, and he synthesized the varied Islamic philosophical-theological schools. He favored the Sufis' mystical state of prophecy, attained through disciplined spiritual practices (see his spiritual autobiography *Deliverance from Error*), believed God to be a constant flow of divine life throughout reality, and held that although our lives are essentially predetermined by God, people are nonetheless responsible for their actions. His *Revival of the Religious Sciences* contains sections on worship, norms of daily life, ways to perdition and to salvation. It became the most recited Islamic text after the Qur'an and Hadith. Al-Ghazzali did much to integrate Sufism with Sharia and strengthened Sunni Islam against Ismaili Shiites. His disciple, Ahmad ibn Rush (1126–1198), influenced Maimonides's Judaism, as al-Ghazzali's thought had influenced Aquinas's Christianity.

The Mongol Disruption

The 1200s began with the Islamic world still strong and vibrant. The Crusaders had been defeated, and Muslims had retaken Jerusalem in 1187. The threat of the Ismaili Fatimid had been stopped, and there was a powerful Islamic Empire in Persia; however, Mongols under Genghis Khan invaded from the Asian steppes. Their military practice was to offer peace if attacked peoples admitted defeat without a fight, but if the Mongols met with resistance, they killed or enslaved everyone. Genghis Khan's third successor put his brother, Hulagu Khan, a grandson of Genghis, in charge. Hulagu wished to destroy the Muslim world. Baghdad had been its center since 762; its libraries and intellectual community were unrivaled in the world. In 1258, the Mongols destroyed Bagdad, then proceeded westward to conquer Syria and Palestine. Though they failed to destroy Islam, the Mongols left deep and enduring political, economic, and military scars across the Muslim world. The political institutions that had held Islam together had practically been eliminated, and Mongols ruled these Muslim realms for more than the next hundred years. Over decades, they converted to Islam and became absorbed into Persian/Turkish cultures, but their depredations had produced such weakness among Muslim institutions that it undermined the Muslims' confidence. Mongols' policies of tolerance, even sponsoring a diversity of spiritual practices if these religions did not try to threaten Mongol political or military control, cast grave doubt on any Islamic pretensions of universal spiritual mastery.

The Ottoman was the final Muslim empire. There were thirty-three Ottoman caliphs, who usually ruled from Turkey (1362–1924). Overall, international Islamic caliphates lasted 1,291 years. Since 1924, there has been no internationally accepted Islamic leader. Abu Bakr al-Baghdadi, the leader of ISIL (the Islamic State in Iraq and the Levant), briefly claimed a caliphate in some Syrian and Iraqi territories, while the head of Boko Haram, Abu-Bakr Shekau, claimed a caliphate in a few conflict zones in sub-Saharan Africa.

Sufis

Throughout the history of Islam there has been a perennial spiritual split between the Muslim majority, fixed upon an all-powerful and fate-determining deity, and generally content with fixed doctrines decided by their leaders, and a significant Muslim minority (Sufis) who focused upon the immanent Allah within, and believe that God must be encountered directly by the individual in order to be wisely expressed in daily life. They consider Muhammad the first Sufi. Small groups practiced this personal spiritual path almost from its beginnings; they often wore woolen robes (*suf* means wool); thus, Islamic mystics become known as Sufis. Be intent upon loving the pitcher less and the water more—focus not upon dogmas, standard prayers or recitations, but upon encountering God directly. Huston Smith suggests three primary Sufi routes to the divine: love, ecstasy, and intuition. Rabi, an 8th-century female saint, represents the love path; she sang that God's love was at the core of the universe, and that love was never more obvious than when the object of love appeared to be absent. The ecstatic route (standing outside of oneself), holds that it is possible for individuals to have experiences like Muhammad's night journey—trancelike, infused grace—and wanted these encounters to be applied in everyday life. This ecstatic mysticism is visual and visionary, and medieval Persian poets such as Rumi embodied it (Qur'an 5:59: "God loves them, and they love him, but Allah loves his creatures more than they love him.") The third route is an intuitive path that uses the feelings of love and ecstatic experiences to reinterpret Qur'anic recitations and Hadithic admonitions; it uses the mind to perceive truths with the eye of the heart to enable recognition of the myriad objects that God dons as he continues to create reality, and thus allows divine light to shine through. Ghazzali exemplified this path.

Historically, Sufism's evolution can be placed into three periods: classical (7th–10th centuries), medieval (11th–14th), and the popular period of greatest influence from (15th–18th). In the classical period, most Sufis were isolated individuals remembered primarily as symbols. Such concepts as *faqr* (pious poverty) and *tawakkul* (total trust of and surrender to God), and ritual practices like *dhikr* (continual repetition of the divine name) and *sama* (singing, playing instruments, dancing, and recitation of poetry and prayers) were widely practiced. The most recognized classical Sufi is the Persian Husayn ibn Mansur al-Hallaj, remembered as a joyful martyr and model mystic lover. During the medieval period, theorists consolidated and synthesized Sufi teaching and practice. Ali Hujwiri focused on the struggle with the lower self, while the Hululi focused on the incarnation of Spirit. Sufi Orders were established. Ghazzali systematized Sufism in the east, and Spanish mystic Mohi-ud-din Ibn-e-Arabi, familiar with Christian as well as Islamic categories, systematized Sufism in the west. Arabi also described God in ways that both fascinated and angered many Muslims.

The most enduring advocates of medieval Sufism were its poets, most prominently Rumi (1207–1273), Sa'di (1290), and Hafiz (1390), all based in Shiraz, Persia. The most famous, Jalal-ad-Rumi, was born in Afghanistan; when he was thirteen, his family escaped to Turkey where his father became a professor. Previously Roman Anatolia, this region gave Rumi his name, "of Rome." Rumi's father spoke of union with God in startlingly sensual terms, and shared secret Sufi doctrines with Rumi. After his father's death, Rumi, now in his twenties, took over his father's role. Like most Sufis, he married and had a family. His life seemed that of a normal religious scholar until he met Shams of Tabri. Shams asked Rumi who was greater, Muhammad or the most celebrated Sufi, and Rumi replied that Muhammad was greater because while the Sufi had taken a gulp of the divine and stopped, Muhammad had continued to evolve and to digest the divine until his death. Shams disappeared for years so that Rumi could discover his own leadership. Rumi's most famous writing was his *Mathnawi*, six volumes of poetry written during the last twelve years of his life. It includes ecstatic poetry, theory, folklore, and jokes.

In *Mysticism: A Study in Nature and Development of Spiritual Consciousness*, Christian mystic Evelyn Underhill outlined five traditional stages of mysticism. The following are some of Rumi's writings about these five stages, as included in Coleman Barks' *The Essential Rumi*.

Awakening: The soul is here for its own joy....Fierce attention, clear discernment, helpful teachers, simple strength, honesty with oneself, all help to clear the ego and dig under our false premises toward one-pointedness....Stop trying to turn a profit from every human exchange....two types of people are on the spiritual path, blindly religious people and those who obey out of love.

The blindly religious people have ulterior motives, conform, and memorize. And those who obey out of love disappear into whatever draws them to God. Where ever I go: mosque, synagogue, church, I see one altar.…When you fail to respond to human warmth and love, your non-responding breeds violence and coldness.

Purgation: No one is grown up when caught in lust and greed. Mankind's fighting is totally futile.… Beliefs, desires and comforting habits so often imprison reason. Four birds keep you from loving: the rooster of lust, the peacock of wanting, the crow of ownership, and the duck of urgency. A true person is calm and deliberate. Keep your intelligence white-hot and your grief glistening, so your life will stay fresh.… Find the thorns in ourselves and pull them out, making a more peaceful world.

Illumination: Because a child does not understand a chain of reasoning, should adults give up being rational? If people do not feel the presence of love within the universe that does not mean that love is not there.

Dark nights of the soul: Illumination is not a permanent state; we remain imperfect and separated from our transcendent moments.… Existence gives you hope from one source, then satisfaction from another. Get completely empty, then tears come and stubbornness dissolves.…Open your hands if you want to be held.…Act generously.…First comes knowledge, then doing the job, much later, perhaps after you're dead, something grows from what you've done.…Progress comes through continued slow movement. The universe came into being gradually.

Union: I am so small. How can this great love be inside me? Your eyes are small, but see enormous things.…Tragic knowledge, grief, life as gradual subtraction happen, and you need to learn from them, but the remaining essentials are love, laughter, and companionship.…A wall alone is useless, but put three or four together and they support a roof and keep you dry and safe. You may be happy going alone, but with others you will get farther and go faster. Love is not possible without a beloved.

Popular Sufism evolved into orders with shared communities and charismatic leaders. The leaders of the orders were called *shaikhs,* distinguished by their self-discipline and charisma. Often from wealthy or respected families, they had usually enjoyed youthful worldly experiences; then, through a divine vision or unusual human encounter, became Sufis, and eventually were given credentials and chosen as the successors of an acknowledged master. Primary international orders that developed included Qadiriyya, Suhrawardiyya, and Naqshbandiyya, as well as regional orders like the Egyptian Badawiyya. Each had distinct loyalties, but generally minimized conflict through interdependence.

Sufi Islam became the dominant form of Islam in the Ottoman and Mughal empires; they probably represented 80 percent of the Muslim populations. After the Safavid ruled the Persia territories, their Shia Islam consistently attacked Sufis because they sometimes prayed to Muhammad or revered saints, often did not cooperate with political leadership, and tended toward Sunni Islam. In Mughal and Ottoman lands, some Sufi orders threatened both political leadership and religious orthodoxy. Qadiriyya and Rifa'iyya orders gained international prominence, while Badawiyya and Shadhiliyaa intensified Islam in northeast Africa, and Chishtiyya and Suhrawardiyya dominated India.

Sufis believe that humans may grow through four stages in their spiritual quest for union with God: actions that reflect our animal natures; individual spiritual practices like piety and prayer; growing beyond individuality to positively affect others through earnestness, ecstasy, and love, until they reach absorption into the divine. In absorption, the devotee moves beyond ego but neither ceases to exist nor mistakes herself for God. Silent meditation is often more profound than speech. Devotees strive to develop a riverlike generosity, sunlike affection, and earthlike hospitality, striving to practice love, tolerance, understanding, and respect.

Kitagawa's third stage of Islamic history and Smith's third stage of Sufi development coincided in the 15th to 18th centuries, which experienced the development of three multiracial Muslim empires ruled by military dynasties. There was no unity in the Ummah (the Islamic community) because the rule of an Arab caliphate under the Ottoman Turks had little influence beyond its own boundaries. Persian territories were ruled by Shiite

Muslim Safavid, and Mughal emperors ruled the Indian subcontinent. They fought each other and often warred internally. Their regimes built enduring political-legal bureaucracies, but usually remained largely unconcerned with spiritual orthodoxy; instead, they practiced spiritual and cultural pluralism that entailed interfaith dialogue and multicultural learning. The Indian subcontinent was unique among Muslim-ruled nations because most of its Hindu majority never converted to Islam. The subcontinent's Islam became permeated with Hindu and Buddhist ideas and practices. In Asian areas where Islamization was only beginning, such as Indonesia and the rest of Southeast Asia, Sufi shaikhs often arrived along with Muslim traders, and their charisma and public ceremonies attracted more attention and support than later orthodox Muslim leaders, so South- and East-Asian Islam became more open and inclusive from their beginnings.

The Indian Muslim Renaissance

Shortly before AD 1000, the Asian-Turkish slave armies of the Mamluk Sultanate conquered Afghanistan, and later what is now Pakistan and the fertile lands of the Indian Punjab. The Delphi Sultanate became the powerful state in North India and continued through five successive Turkish-Afghan dynasties. Its ruler from 1236–40 was a woman, Razia Sultana, the only Muslim woman to rule in South Asia until the 20th century. She established schools and research centers, included non-Islamic philosophers in their libraries, believed that the spirit of religion was more important than its dogmas or rules, and pointed out that Muhammad himself had spoken out against overburdening non-Muslims. By 1310, Muslims had captured the Pandyan southern Hindu capital and controlled most of the Indian peninsula, though their power in the south remained weak. Firuz Shah Tughlaq (1351–88) abolished torture, and built forty mosques, thirty colleges, a hundred hospitals, and 200 towns surrounding Delhi. At the end of the 14th century, Tamerlane sacked Delhi. Babar (1483–1530), a descendant of Timur and Genghis Khan, expanded the Mughal Empire. These rulers supported religious tolerance and religious intermixing so long as they could maintain political control. The Hindu bhakti movement and Hindu scholars like Ramanuja and Ramananda flourished, as did Kabir, and Guru Nanak, the founder of the Sikhism.

Akbar, the greatest of the Mughals, ruled from 1556 to 1605. He listened to Persian poets and Shia teachings, visited Sufi retreats, married a Hindu princess, was influenced by Hindu scholars and Jain ascetics, and questioned Sunni orthodoxies. He conquered what is now Northern India and controlled more south Asian territory than the British ever did. He involved Hindu leadership in ruling his empire and organized a well-run administration that provided extensive tolerance for religious diversity and cultural creativity. Akbar remained illiterate, but developed a great library, organized philosophical and ecumenical spiritual discussions, and had his courtiers read to him from India's literary diversity. He published a syncretistic spiritual document, the *Din-i Ilahi*, intended to include the best aspects of various religions. Like the Sufis, he encouraged each person to purify himself through yearning for God, discouraged lust, sensuality, slander, and pride, and encouraged piety, prudence, abstinence, and kindness. He forbade animal slaughter, condoned celibacy, and abolished the tax against Hindu pilgrims. From Zoroastrianism, he took reverence for fire and the sun, and welcomed Christian missionaries into his ecumenical discussions. Akbar received more public support than all other Islamic emperors combined.

Mughal syncretism led to a tremendous cultural flowering. Indian music, dance, art, and literature flourished. Scholars from different faiths and ethnic communities gathered to discuss ideas and practices; these reached the common people and enriched their faiths and heritages. Akbar ordered that the Hindu scriptures, the Atharva Veda, Ramayana, and Mahabharata, be translated into Arabic and Persian. Sufi spiritual ideas were deepened by other religions, and Sufi practices strongly influenced all the religions in the Indian subcontinent. This spiritual renaissance didn't deny the worth of personal pieties, but it concentrated instead on qualities that benefited others as well, such as kindness, companionship, and compassion. Personal piety needed to be continually tested for sincerity, while qualities that help others are consistently respected by people and acceptable to and rewarded by God.

The Impact of European Colonial Rule on Islam

In 1498, Spaniard Vasco de Gama returned from India with a boatload of spices and other valuables that earned investors a 3,000 percent profit that began four and half centuries of Western incursion and conquest. Aurangzeb had further expanded Mughal territorial control, but soon after his death in 1707, Mughal power diminished rapidly, and British control steadily increased. Aurangzeb had been a cruel ruler and a narrow religious bigot—the first religiously conservative Mughal ruler. He was particularly intolerant of the Sufis who had long dominated Islamic spirituality in south Asia, so when Western colonial scholars began to study Islam, they usually focused on early Islam. Sufi orders often resisted European colonialists; so, colonial policies actively discouraged Sufi organizations, particularly the original *mujahidin* (holy warriors), a group of North Indian Sufi religious activists. During the 19th century, militant anti-colonial Sufism characterized Islamic groups from the Russian steppe to Indonesia. By the 20th century, primarily because of colonial suppression, no Sufi community had either the political or spiritual power it had earlier enjoyed.

European nations increasingly seized control, and with military support, extracted raw materials, imposed high taxes, curtailed indigenous manufacturing, and superimposed their own preferences. They usually allowed traditional conservative political and religious hierarchies to continue so long as they cooperated politically, but often ended existing systems of social cooperation and democratic government. For centuries, India had economically and socially been a village society, with cooperative land use and forms of village democracy; the British replaced these with private landownership and a parasitic relationship between rajahs and colonial administrators. Local reformers were usually marginalized or imprisoned. Colonial policy was "to divide and conquer." National colonial powers often fought among themselves, so territories changed borders and powerbrokers arbitrarily. Globally, peoples and territories were forced into geographic entities that arbitrarily mixed conflicting religious, ethnic, and tribal groups.

This decay and destruction of Islamic empires coincided with considerable modernization and the imposition of Western values by colonial commands. Some Islamic colonial peoples became educated and modernized; for them, individuality, rational processes, and democracy became popular. Muhammad Abduh in Egypt said that reason was the key to faith in God in Islam. Muhammad Iqbal in India held that Islam is a doctrine of self-assertion that teaches man to attain worldly power and attempt the conquest of both self and non-self.[1] Others became militantly anticolonial, and clung to their ancient, unrealized dream of global Islamic unity. Most Muslims remained illiterate and depended upon Islamic direction from local clerics and tribal leaders who were generally negative toward European values but cooperated with colonial rulers as long as their clerical control was not threatened. Then, as the 20th century began, Jamal ad-Din al Afghani transformed the theocratic ideal of Pan-Islamic unity into independent Islamic nationalisms.

When WWI began, the Ottoman Empire was heavily in debt to European governments. Young Turks had displaced the last powerful Sultan, which effectively ended the Ottoman Empire, and Turkey allied with Germany against Britain and France. After the war, Britain and France divided the Middle East: Britain took control of Iraq, Kuwait, and Jordan, while France controlled Syria, Lebanon, and southern Turkey. Zionists lobbied the British government for the creation of a Jewish State in Palestine. The British government promised Arabian Sharif Hussein's control of the Arabian Peninsula if the Arabs would fight the Turks. Their flag of "Arab revolt" later served as a model for the flags of several Middle Eastern nations. The League of Nations drew up a map with European colonial mandates over Middle East countries. Many of the boundaries still stand; most were drawn without regard for the wishes of the people of these nations, and in ways that failed to consolidate their ethnic, geographic, or religious cultures; sometimes they even conspicuously divided peoples against one another. Indigenous rulers Hussain in Arabia, Faisal in Iraq and Syria, and Abdullah in Jordan were enthroned, but the British and French held the real authority.

There was an exception: A Turkish army officer, Mustafa Kemal Ataturk, seized control of Turkey from the Allied forces, created the Republic of Turkey, and served as its president from 1924 until his death in 1938. He successfully transformed this former seat of the Ottoman Empire into a modern and secular nation-state. Under his leadership, thousands of schools were built, primary education became free and mandatory, women were given equal civil rights, and the peasants' tax burden was reduced.

Middle Eastern and North African Islam Today

Today, there are 1.6 billion Muslims in the world. Forty-three per cent live in four Asian nations: Indonesia, Pakistan, India, and Bangla Desh; they are not Arabs. Four hundred twenty-three million live in the Middle East and North Africa and are Arabs. In addition, there are 90 million Persians (50 million in Iran, 9 million in Afghanistan, 6 million in Tajikistan); 85 million are Turkish (75 million in Turkey, 6 million in Europe, and 3 million in North Africa). The next two largest Muslim ethnic groups are 50 million Pashtuns and the 30 million Kurds; both are ancient peoples without their own countries who have been marginalized by the rest of the world.

The Pashtuns (31 million in Afghanistan, 14 million in Pakistan) ruled the Indian Sultanate and much of Afghanistan for centuries and then became a semi-independent people caught between British and Russian colonial ambitions. Pashtuns have continued to dominate Afghanistan in the modern era: forming most governments until 1973, then became the heart of the mujahedeen fighting the Russians, and later constituted most of the Taliban soldiers and leadership at war with Western nations. Afghanistan's recent leaders, Hamid Karzai, and Muhammad Ashraf Ghani, are Pashtuns. In Pakistan, Pashtuns are the second largest ethnic group; both Nobel Peace Prize laureate Malala Yousafzai and her attackers are Pashtuns. Almost all Pashtuns are Sunni of the Hanafi legal school. Some Sufi songs and dances are part of Pashtun society. Pashtuns are divided among themselves into 400 competing patriarchal tribal groups. Some can read or recite the Qur'an in Arabic, but most don't understand Arabic, so they remain vulnerable to radical teachers and leaders. Many now want to separate themselves from the Taliban and seek to understand the Qur'an for themselves. Non-Pashtuns perceive Pashtuns as fiercely independent, persistent warriors.

The 30 million Kurds in Turkey represent 23 percent of its population, 18 percent of Iraq's, 10 percent of Iran's, and 9 percent of Syria's. Kurds form majorities in a contiguous geographic region that includes southeastern Turkey, northern Iraq, northwestern Iran, and northeastern Syria. Half of all Kurds live in Turkey, another 24 percent in Iran, 18 percent in Iraq, and 4 percent in Syria. Others have emigrated to Germany or elsewhere in the West. They form coherent political and cultural forces in modern Turkey and Iraq, and potent, geographically concentrated minorities in Iran and Syria. While most Kurds are Sunni Muslims who belong to the Shafi'i legal school, they remain the most religiously diverse Muslim ethnic group in Western Asia. They often take great liberties with spiritual practices, so other Muslims sometimes doubt whether Kurds are Muslims at all. Many participate in mystical practices and are in Sufi orders, or continue to be affected by Zoroastrian ideas. A million Iranian Kurds are Yarsan, a syncretic religion that explicitly rejects class, caste, and rank, that set them apart even from other Iranian Kurds. Turkey has many Alevi, a Shia group that helped establish the Safavid Dynasty. In Iraq, there are some 500,000 Kurdish Yazidis who believe in the periodic reincarnation of seven holy beings that help God to renew the world. Some are Shia. Kurds remain a coherent, often militant, people who oppose Sunni extremism and Arab domination.

Islamic Counter-Reformation: Saudi Wahhabism, Iranian Theocracy, and Violent Jihadists

The post-colonial Islamic world has nurtured a large majority of Muslims who wish to live peacefully and tolerantly in a multicultural and multireligious world that allows their families fair opportunities to live, prosper, and practice their chosen forms of Islam. There have, however, also arisen three major varieties of reactionary, fundamentalist, coercive Islamic regimes that seek to dominate the Islamic world and who attack any form of Islam different from them: Saudi Wahhabis, Iranian theocracy, and violent jihadists. Conservative tendencies have been a deep stream throughout Islamic history; however, there had never been a militant, religiously conservative or reactionary wave until the 20th century. From AD 850 through 1350, there were occasional reactionary Sunni scholars such as Ahmad ibn Hanbal (died 855), Taqi ad-Din Ibn Taymiyyah (1328), and Ibn al-Qayyim (1350) who called themselves *salaf* ("early generations") and rejected all innovation or the introduction of anything that they perceived as unlike the earliest Muslims. They rejected not only Shia and Sufi Muslims as idolaters but also considered most other Sunni Muslims as false because they revered saints or kept amulets. Salafists were unpopular because they attacked other Muslims.

Ibn Taymiyyah (1263–1328) is the best-known Salafist. A professor of the Hanbali school of Sharia in Damascus, he opposed innovations, rejected Muslims' efforts to develop an evolving consensus based on new circumstances, and opposed speculative theology or any allegorical or symbolic spiritual interpretation. He asserted that believers shouldn't try to understand the Qur'an but simply submit to its mysteries and leave all to Allah. He regarded an Islamic state as necessary to implement Islamic law and to impose the disciplines needed to keep Muslims on the true path. Jailed for his verbal attacks against other Muslims, he spent much of his life in prison, and until the modern era his ideas were accepted by few Muslims.

Wahhabi Islam

In the 1700s, a new Salafi doctrine, Wahhabi Islam, was created by Abd al-Wahhab. Born in the Saudi Najd, he studied in Basra, Iraq, and then returned to the Najd. He claimed that all Muslims were infidels if they failed to convert to his doctrines. In 1744, Muhammad ibn Saud, ruler of a Najd town, vowed to protect Wahhab, and Wahhab pledged support of Saud and his descendants. Wahhab advised Saud to stop taxing local harvests and assured him that Allah would compensate him with conquest booty and increased receipts from sharia-appropriate taxes. They declared jihad upon other Najd tribes. Muhammad bin Saud's son, Abdul-Aziz bin Muhammad, used a convert-or-die approach to expand his domain. By the 19th century, they had conquered Mecca and Medina. In 1802, Saud-Wahhabi forces attacked Karbala, Iraq, killed most of its people, and enslaved the rest. In 1803, they massacred the male population of a Saudi city and enslaved its women and children. As Saud domination expanded into areas with Shia and pluralistic populations, Wahhabis enforced compulsory conversion or eradication of non-Wahhabi Muslims.

In 1818, the Ottoman Empire defeated al Saud, leveled his capital, and exiled its leaders. For the rest of the 19th century, the Saud-Wahhabi domain was protected only by its isolation, backwardness, and lack of resources, and there was a strong aversion in Wahhabi territories to mixing with any non-Wahhabi Muslims. Then, in the early 20th century, a fifth-generation descendant, Abdul-Aziz Ibn Saud, began to conquer the Arabian Peninsula again and founded Saudi Arabia after WWI. His reign saw 40,000 public executions. Wahhabis began to seek fellow Salafists elsewhere in the Muslim world, and found them, particularly among the Hadith in India, and Islamic revivalists in Arab states who shared the permissibility of "purification" of Islamic idolaters. In the 1920s, an anthology of Wahhabi treatises that became popular throughout the Muslim world praised Ibn Saud as the savior of Islam's holy cities and a practitioner of authentic Islamic rule. In 1926, Ibn Saud convened a Muslim congress that involved most Muslim associations and governments. In 1939, oil was discovered, and by 1946, Saudi Arabia was pumping millions of gallons and was a rich regime.

By the 1950s, another major movement in the Islamic world was secular nationalism, personified by Egyptian President Gamal Abdul Nasser. The Saud-Wahhabi regime saw this movement as a threat because of its secularism, its military leaders without royal or tribal credentials, and its populist, socialist, and democratic pretensions. At a 1962 conference, ways to combat both secularism and socialism were discussed. The World Muslim League was established and opened offices globally to oppose inimical trends among Muslims and to reject harmful "Western ways." Wahhabis made common cause with Salafists and Islamic revivalist Muslim Brotherhoods everywhere. With petro-billions, they began a massive campaign to fund thousands of schools (nursery schools, madrassas, and seminaries), mosques, and Islamic centers, print and disseminate religious literature, train future Islamic scholars in Wahhabi Islam doctrines, and send them throughout the world to run these new Islamic establishments.

When regimes clamped down on the Islamist Arab Muslim Brotherhood in Egypt, Iraq, and Syria, many fled to Saudi Arabia. Thereafter, the Muslim Brotherhood's transnational revival movement greatly impacted Wahhabi ideas because Brotherhood refugees staffed much of Saudi Arabia's new educational system. They inculcated anticolonialism and aggressive individuals acting independently rather than as followers of a monarch. The Brotherhood's educational and research leadership effectively took control of Saudi intellectual life, and the world's future Islamic leadership absorbed not only Wahhabi beliefs but also Brotherhood militant activism.

When the 1973 oil crisis quadrupled the price of oil, Saudi Arabia became a dominant international power. In any four days in 1974, Saudi Arabia now earned more than its annual profits before the embargo. In 1975, Saudi Arabia spent $3 billion to spread Wahhabi Islam globally, more than the combined propaganda budgets of the U.S. and the U.S.S.R. By 2007, it had spent more than $100 billion on these efforts: built more than 1,500 mosques, 210 Islamic centers, and most of the schools in the entire Islamic world. It also created research institutions and theological seminaries, published books, funded thousands of scholarships, research grants, and countless media efforts. In the last fifty years, 90 percent of all Islamic expenditures have been funded by the Saud regime. The Wahhabi-Saud allegiance has transformed the Islamic world and has now endured for more than two and a half centuries. The Saudi minister of religion is always a Wahhabi descendant, while the Saud dynasty still rules Saudi Arabia and dominates much of Islam today.

Iranian Theocracy

Iran is home to one of the world's oldest civilizations; its history of urban settlements dates to at least 4000 BC. The Achaemenid Empire of Cyrus the Great (500–330 BC) spread from Persepolis to span three continents from North Africa to Central Asia, and vast Persian empires continued for nearly 1,000 years. The Islamic conquest of Persia (633–656) ended the Sasanian Dynasty, but Islamization progressed gradually, and rather than replace the existing Persian culture, was largely absorbed by it. By 1501, Iran was reunified as an independent state by the Safavid dynasty, which established Shi'a Islam as the official state religion. The 19th and early 20th centuries saw the destruction of Persian power by Russian and British intrusions. The discovery of oil in 1908 intensified British interest, and Allied forces seized control during WWI. The Pahlavi dynasty, under Reza Shah (1925–41), modernized Iran with dramatic reforms that alienated much of the population. During WWII, the Allies again seized Iran. After the war, Mohammad-Reza Pahlavi took charge. In 1951, when the democratically elected Prime Minister Mohammed Mosaddeq planned to nationalize Iran's oilfields, America's CIA and Britain's M16 supported a military coup. The Shah then ruled autocratically, further modernized, and created the largest Middle Eastern military. While his rule produced a wealthy middle class, it failed to significantly improve the economic prospects of most Iranians, and further alienated the conservative clergy by exiling critic Ayatollah Khomeini.

Demonstrations against the Shah began in January 1978; the Iranian Islamic revolution culminated in the approval of a new theocratic constitution, and in December 1979, Ayatollah Khomeini became Supreme Leader. His revolution was populist, nationalist, and Shi'a Islamic. Its constitution is based upon the concept of *velayat-e faqih,* the idea that people require "guardianship" in the form of rule or supervision by leading Islamic clergy rather than by the state. Iran's rapidly expanding capitalist economy was replaced by populist Islamic economic and cultural policies. Much of Iran's industry was nationalized; laws and schools were Islamized, and Western influences were banned. The Iranian Islamic revolution created fear and distrust in the non-Islamic world, and considerable enthusiasm and interest within the Islamic world because the world again had a powerful, Islamic theocratic nation-state.

Twelver Shiism is pervasive in Iran, Iraq, Lebanon, and Bahrain. For centuries, they had withdrawn from politics, but in the 20th century, activist Twelver groups in Iran and Lebanon flourished. Since 1979, the Shia branch of Islam has again had a powerful political and spiritual leader. To consolidate power, Khomeini suppressed secularists, leftists, and more traditional Muslims, and executed opponents and many Iranian Kurds. His success in the 1980s Iran-Iraq war strengthened his power and made him a hero to millions of Muslims.

After Khomeini's death, Ali Khamenei became supreme leader. During his eight years, Iran became a clerical oligarchy. Succeeding him was the pragmatic conservative Ali-Akbar Rafsanjani, a reformer determined to rebuild Iran's economy, cut military expenditures, promote birth control, and normalize relationships with Saudi Arabia and others. In 2005, Mahmoud Ahmadinejad was elected president. During his eight years, Iraq was invaded by the U.S. and its allies, and Iran's security forces became more independent from other political leaders. After Ahmadinejad's reelection in 2009, there were widespread protests, and Khamenei issued a fatwa that forbade the production, stockpiling, or use of nuclear weapons. Hassan Rouhani became president in June 2013 and ended the West's Iranian oil embargo until America's withdrawal from the Joint Comprehensive Plan of Action (JCPOA), or "Iran nuclear deal," in May 2018.

Iranian oil wealth and advanced security forces make Iran the godfather of Shia populations throughout the Islamic world. Iran is the most powerful foreign influence on Iraq and has trained thousands of Shia Iraqi militiamen; it also provides support for Shia forces in Syria, Lebanon, and Yemen. Iran largely created Hezbollah, which has successfully driven back Israel, and is now the most effective military force supporting Assad's Syrian regime. Hezbollah continues to play a central role in Lebanese politics. Iran has the largest national Shia population today: 90 percent are Shia, but there are also Shia majorities in Azerbaijan (75 percent), Bahrain (75 percent), and Iraq (65 percent), and sizable minorities in Yemen (46 percent), Lebanon (46 percent), Kuwait (30 percent), Pakistan (20 percent), Turkey (20 percent), the United Arab Emirates (16 percent), Syria (15 percent), and Afghanistan (15 percent). Most Shia groups, however, also have their own long-range agendas.

A Pew Research Center study (8/9/2012) of thirty-nine countries in which a significant proportion of the population identifies as Islamic, focused on Islamic beliefs and tolerances. In thirty-two of these countries, more than 50 percent of Muslims believed that there was only a single correct way to be Muslim. In the countries of Eastern Europe and the former Soviet Union, more than 80 percent held this view. Sufis are widely accepted as Muslims in South Asia, but their orthodoxy is often questioned in other Muslim nations. In Indonesia, the largest Muslim country, 56 percent identify as "just Muslim," while another 26 percent identified as just Sunni. Among Sunni, there are also regional differences in acceptance of Shias as Muslims; 75 percent of Iraqi and Lebanese Sunni Muslims agree, while in the Palestinian territories, Jordan, and the North African nations, less than half of Sunni Muslims consider Shias to be Muslim.

Violent Jihad

In 1964, an Egyptian radical author and Muslim Brotherhood activist, Sayyid Qutb, wrote *Milestones,* a manifesto that became a theoretical justification for violent jihad. He asserted that holy war (a term that did not appear in the Qur'an) should be waged not only defensively to protect Muslim lands but also offensively against "enemies of Islam," and claimed that any Muslim leader who failed to apply Sharia should be declared an infidel and removed from power. Qutb basically advocated anarchy: A truly Islamic polity would need no rulers. True Muslims would need no judges or police to practice divine law. He argued for systematic violence by a revolutionary vanguard, first verbally and then by destroying existing structures. This perverted reasoning has been used ever since to justify the slaughter of hundreds of thousands of Muslims by anarchic Muslim jihadists, first in Afghanistan and then throughout the world, and to date, also killing 11,000 or more non-Muslims.

In December 1979, Abdullah Yusuf Azzam, a Muslim Brotherhood cleric with ties to Saudi religious institutions, issued a fatwa—an individual obligation for all Muslims—to combat the Soviet invasion of Afghanistan. By the time of the Soviet withdrawal, more than 50,000 non-Afghan Muslim volunteers had fought in Afghanistan, half of them from Saudi Arabia. Saudi Arabia and the other Gulf States financed these campaigns with petro-billions, and the U.S. supported the effort. These seasoned warriors then returned to their home countries radicalized; they now believed that the regimes in their home nations did not represent the Islamic political ideal; they angrily rejected Western domination of international politics, and remained, at least theoretically, ready to participate in any effort to revive Islamic world domination.

Saudi power has eroded somewhat since 1979, but millions of Muslims today basically know only the Wahhabi version of Islam. Its propaganda machine still publishes such ideas as: Muslims should always oppose and hate infidels; democracy is responsible for all horrible wars; Shia and many Sunni are infidels. Yet, Saudi Arabia itself remains a human mosaic. Most of its eastern oil region is Shiite, the south peninsula is Yemeni, and the north is Syriac; only the Najd plateau is home to the House of Saud. Two thirds of Saudi workers are foreigners with temporary visas, mostly Asian Muslims who also constitute two thirds of the workforces of Kuwait, Qatar, and the UAE.

Scholar Mehrdad Izady estimates that native Wahhabi Muslims account for only about one-half of 1 percent of all Muslims, with some 5 million in the Persian Gulf region, and 4 million in the Najd (Saudi Arabia has 23 million people). Most of the rest live in Qatar or the Emirates (some 40 percent of their populations are Wahhabi). Even among professed Wahhabis, there is a spectrum of religious and ethical practices and beliefs. Unlike Saudi Arabia, Qatar has liberalized: it allows women to drive and travel independently and permits non-Muslims to consume alcohol and pork. Qatar has no religious police to enforce public morality, and its clerical class lacks significant power. The powerful Al-Jazeera global media empire is headquartered there.

Saudi Arabia and the predominant Shia power, Iran, are increasingly investing their resources, energy, and national power in support of reactionary Muslim regimes of their predominant sect, and funding terrorists allied with their aims and ideologies. There is an arms race between the Gulf States and their clients and Iran and its clients. In his key publication, the erstwhile leader of the ISIS insurgency in Syria and Iraq, Abu Bakr al-Baghdadi, held that "jihad is violence, crudeness, terrorism, deterrence, and massacre." ISIS circulated Saudi Arabian Wahhabi religious textbooks in its schools; its videos show Wahhabi texts plastered on their missionary vans. Al-Qaeda offered martyrdom during combat; in addition, ISIS and Boko Haram offer booty and slave women. They are simply criminal enterprises that destroy their region's cultures, rob them of their histories and resources, enslave their women, and turn their captive children into suicide bombers who murder fellow Muslims. They have no more legitimate claim to being practicing Muslims than an American racist mass murderer or a Jewish Israeli terrorist has to representing their faiths.

Violence and anarchist nihilism became the goals for ISIS and Boko Haram. While Saudi Arabia and other Gulf States, and Iran and Pakistan have been the primary creators of these violent jihadist genies, they are also now real threats to these authoritarian governments. For the Taliban, Hamas, Hezbollah, Muslim Brotherhood, and Boko Haram, who idealize a global Islamic order, authoritarian militancy has been married to conservative social sensibilities and hostility toward globalization. As old orders collapse and new regimes stumble, jihadists have turned terror into an end in itself. The number of volunteer violent jihadists remains a tiny portion of the world's 1.6 billion Muslims. A 2015 U.N. study proposes that 100,000 have joined violent jihadist groups globally. Tragically, this combination of 7th-century savagery and 21st-century media manipulation continues to seduce many

Muslim youth into seeking glory and honor in a world where neither seems likely in their home environments.

The Islamic Majority: Multicultural, Tolerant, Individualistic, and Modern

By the late 19th and early 20th centuries, millions of Muslims had begun to gain a modern education and become productive members of increasingly modern societies. Two outstanding examples were Muhammad Abduh in Egypt and Muhammad Iqbal in India. Muhammad Abduh (1849–1905) studied at a mosque and at al-Azhar University where he was a student of Pan-Islamist Jamal al-Din al-Afghani. Abduh's career included a professorship of logic, theology, and ethics, editor of an official state newspaper, exile to Ottoman Lebanon where he helped establish an Islamic education system, becoming an anti-British activist in Paris, then a return to Egypt to become a judge and the Grand Mufti (Egypt's highest religious position) for his last seventeen years. Abduh believed that Muslims could not rely on clerical interpretations and should use their own reason to keep up with a transforming world. He urged people to detach from their ancestors' world, and he disapproved of any slavish imitation of tradition. He felt Allah's greatest gifts to humanity were independence of thought and opinion and freedom of the will. Using them, humanity could find happiness. He perceived Allah as educating humanity from its childhood through its youth, and now evolving into adulthood. He sought to abolish racial discrimination and religious compulsion, favored equal gender rights and the end of polygamy, worked diligently to promote harmony among all of Islam's branches, and advocated friendship and cooperation among religions.

Born in Punjab, India, Muhammad Iqbal (1877–1938) became a lawyer, philosopher, politician, and poet. He is widely regarded as the inspiration for Pakistan becoming a separate nation, and as a central figure in Urdu literature. His birthday is celebrated as a Pakistani public holiday, and in India he is still honored as a poet and philosopher, and his *The Reconstruction of Religious Thought in Islam* continues to be an important Muslim text. Iqbal held that space, time, and matter are interpretations placed upon the free creative energy of God. He advocated translation of the Qur'an into local languages so that every Muslim could read and understand it. He viewed the Ataturk Turkish state as a better model than Arabian imperialism, believed that only a democratic republic was consistent with the Islam's spirit, and believed that democracy was necessary to liberate the powers of the contemporary world. He praised Sufis for having shaped and directed the evolution of Islamic religious experience, and he believed that ultimate reality becomes embodied in rationally directed and socially responsible human lives. Prayer is humanity's response to the universe's silence, and a way to discover our own worth as a dynamic element within reality. He exhorted Islamic reform to break free of its fear of innovation and evolution, trusted that humanity could grow beyond naïve faith and careworn ideologies into discovery of Allah's creative unfoldment.

In 1969, Zakir Husain died in office after serving as India's first Muslim president. I met members of a liberal religious Muslim group he had sponsored called the Islam in the Modern Age Society. It was composed of leading Indian and global Muslims who advocated lives rooted in traditional Islamic faith and practice but informed by scientific spirit and equipped with the intellectual and material resources of the modern age. They encouraged Muslims to become integral members of their national societies and the modern world, urged liberal interpretation of Islamic principles, and harmonious relations among members of different religions through the study of other faiths, dialogue, and cooperation.

Today's Islamic Population

The worldwide Islamic population today is exceedingly diverse. Of the 1.6 billion Muslims, 1 billion (62 percent) live in South and East Asia. Another 322 million (20 percent) live in the Middle East (Egypt 80 million), Turkey and Iran, (75 each), Algeria, Sudan, and Iraq (each with 30-plus), while Saudi Arabia has 25 million. Another 15 percent, 243 million, live in sub-Saharan Africa (Nigeria, 76 million, Ethiopia 29 million, Tanzania, 13 million, and Senegal, 12 million-plus). Europe has 44 million Muslims, Russia 16 million. The six former Soviet Islamic-majority Asian republics (Uzbekistan, Azerbaijan, Tajikistan, Kirghizstan, Kazakhstan, and Turkmenistan) collectively have 54 million. France has 5 million, 8 percent of its population; Germany has 4 million (5 percent), and the U.K. has 4 million. The total Islamic population throughout the Americas is 5 million, about one-half of 1 percent of the world's Muslims.

In the United States, Islam comprises the fifth largest religion with 2.8 million; 78 percent of U.S. citizens identify as Christian, 15 percent as unaffiliated, 1.8 percent as Jewish, 1.2 percent as Buddhist, and 0.9 percent as Muslims. Forty-five percent of U.S. Muslims have arrived since 1990, and 70 percent have become citizens. Thirty-four percent emigrated from South Asia, 26 percent from Arab-speaking countries, 25 percent from Africa, and 15 percent from elsewhere. Among U.S. Islamic converts, 64 percent are African American and 27 percent Caucasian. Among U.S. Muslims, 50 percent identify as Sunni, 16 percent as Shia, and 22 percent do not have a sectarian affiliation. Statistically, American Muslims are significantly more devout, more educated, and wealthier than average Americans. Except for Jewish women, Muslim women are the most educated group in the United States. Six thousand Muslims now serve in the U.S. military. While Muslims are less than 1 percent of the U.S. population, 10 percent of our physicians are Muslims—many serving in rural or poverty areas.

African American Muslims often have separate mosques located in inner-city poverty areas, while immigrant Muslims tend to have their mosques or centers in upscale suburbs or wealthier urban areas. Many immigrant Muslims perceive African American Muslims to be a cult and not true Muslims because their founder, Wallace Fard, claimed divine status, and his successor, Elijah Muhammad, considered himself a prophet—both forbidden doctrines for traditional Muslims. His son and successor, W. Deem Muhammad, shifted his movement back toward the Muslim mainstream; however, Louis Farrakhan then further divided their movement and renewed claims and traditions that separate his group from most Muslims.

Elements of Islam that I Find Troubling

Given Muhammad's life, I am mystified as to why women are so widely repressed in many Islamic societies. Muhammad's success would have been impossible without Khadija's guidance and support through twenty-four years of marriage. In every conceivable way, she was a liberated woman upon whom he was dependent. Only at forty-eight was Muhammad on his own, and his wives remained his soulmates until his death. The Qur'an's pronouncements were revolutionary for 7th-century culture in providing women considerable independence and rights that were new for Arabia. Given the strong masculinity of Muslim men, and Islam's absolute principle of human equality, how can so many Islamic men fear the empowerment of Muslim women? Are they unable to control their lust, or doubt their female relatives' full humanity?

Muhammad's violent military actions and political manipulations, followed by an Islamic history so filled with political conflict and doctrinal division, continues to make it difficult for many Muslims to distinguish between political power and spiritual wisdom. Many also still seem to resist modernity itself—trying to seize its advantages while remaining unable to change the outworn elements of Islam's 7th-century tribalism. In centuries past, many Islamic leaders were more tolerant than predominantly Christian regimes, but that is not true now. Most predominantly Muslim nations are now 90 percent or more Muslim. Many are increasingly intolerant of even their own Islamic minorities, which completely betrays Islamic principles.

Daunting educational and economic problems still face Muslim-majority nations: 40 percent of the Muslim world is illiterate, a percentage representing half of the ten nations that constitute 75 percent of global illiteracy. More than 50 percent of Muslim women are illiterate, and 25 percent of all Muslim children received no education. The fifty-seven Muslim-majority nations host fewer than 600 universities for their 1.6 billion people, while India alone has 8,400 universities, and the U.S. 5,758. In a Chinese ranking of world universities, not one Muslim-majority institution was among the top 500. Mohamed Charfi, former minister of education in Tunisia, concludes that Muslims need to embark upon major educational and societal reforms if they wish to see Islam flourish in the twenty-first century. The combined annual GNP of the fifty-seven Muslim countries is less than $2 trillion; the GNP of Germany alone is $2.1 trillion, India, $3 trillion, and the U.S., $10.4 trillion. Muslims represent 22 percent of the world's population yet produce less than 5 percent of its GDP. The average growth rate in per capita income for Islamic countries is less than one half of 1 percent per annum. More than 25 percent of Muslim young adults are unemployed. Islamic surveys found that most Arab youth hoped to migrate away from any Islamic nation.

In the 21st century, Islam needs a major spiritual reformation, along with more personal freedom and political and economic opportunities for their people, particularly their women. They need to stop being misled, bought, or sacrificed by a tiny nest of so-called Muslims who worship idols from a long-gone past. The vast majority must actively practice courage and ingenuity in order to curb un-Islamic perversions of their faith that betray humanity.

I see two conflicting strands within Islam. One has gone against the Prophet Muhammad's explicit wishes and turned him into an always-to-be-revered demigod whose every supposed deed and idiosyncrasy must be repeated forever. This militantly fundamentalist strand regards even fellow Muslims with different beliefs as infidels. This is madness for any faith or ideology. The other, much more predominant, strand within Islam advocates and practices a simple, democratic spiritual practice of faith in one God and in historic prophets. This vast Islamic majority remains open to individuality, new knowledge, and progressive societies. It represents most ordinary Muslims, as well as most Muslim prophets, scholars, legal experts, and clergy, and every significant Islamic contribution to world history.

Elements of Islam that I Find Most Relevant

My introduction to Islam was my father's recitations from *The Arabian Nights* and *The Rubaiyat of Omar Khayyam*. *Arabian Nights* conveyed that everything is the work of Allah, and that everyone is at the mercy of circumstances. As Sinbad says, from what destiny writes, there is neither refuge nor flight. Many of Khayyam's quatrains are familiar: #51: "The moving finger writes and having writ, moves on: nor all piety or wit can lure it back to cancel half a line"; #66: "I sent my soul a letter of the afterlife. My soul answered I myself am heaven and hell."

My study of Islam began with an undergraduate course in world religions. Islam's apparent simplicity, straightforwardness, and equality in belief and practice impressed me. Islam received human faces as I rode across the country with an Iraqi engineering student, hitched a ride in Europe with Lebanon's minister of education, and became a close friend with an Iranian graduate student. I was moved by Malcom X's published epiphany against racism after his Hajj to Mecca and Medina, when he realized that Islamic believers came in all races and cultures, and that during the Hajj, at least, they embraced one another as brothers.

My first exposure to Islam's collective power was at a London airport in 1969. It was the noontime obligatory prayer, and on the floor in a hallway, fifty Muslims from all over the world prayed together. Ten days later, I spent a week in Egypt and was submerged into an Islamic culture with its plaintive calls to prayer, people stopping on the street to pray together, and with my first visits to mosques and Islamic shrines. During months in India, I visited primary monuments from India's Mogul centuries, including the Taj Mahal, mosques, palaces, and Kashmir's Mughal gardens. In 1974, I spent a week in Iran, where I was awed by the gorgeous Islamic architecture in Isfahan, Shiraz, and Teheran, and later spent a week in Indonesia.

Through IARF activism, I became acquainted with progressive Muslims from several countries. There was at least one Islamic participant in most of the Unitarian Universalist congregations I served, and I usually celebrated at least one Muslim holiday annually. In Jacksonville, Florida, I taught Muslim students in my college courses and cooperated with the local Iman in social justice and disarmament activities. That congregation developed a close relationship with a group of Turkish Muslims, and shared meals and dialogue at meetings.

A healthy, brave, and progressive Islamic reformation is already flourishing, but too often it gets lost in the violence and fear of the militant minority. The reformation must take place in those predominantly Islamic countries that are becoming spiritually tolerant, politically progressive, and inclusive, and perhaps even more so in countries that welcome significant Muslim minorities. Here are some examples of progressive Islamic writing.

Tariq Ramadan, Professor of Islamic studies at Oxford University said the codification of its spiritual and ethical teachings in legal and theological systems requires both intellectual and emotional modesty, since there has always been a diversity of accepted readings. Each Muslim needs to remain openminded, critical, and incisive. Muslims need to use both their intellectual and their mystical-intuitive faculties.

Muslim writers abound who articulate elements of this Islamic reformation. In *The Satanic Verses,* Salman Rushdie presented a serious dialogue about the nature and temptations of evil. Rushdie reflects true Islamic principles in arguing that to be spiritual, Muslims must overcome their shortsighted, selfish, angry, violent selves and be reborn to values that embrace humanity and remain empathetic, peaceful, and loving. In 2007, a Secular Muslim Summit called on Islamic governments to reject Sharia law, fatwa courts, clerical rule, or state-sanctioned religion in all its forms, to oppose all penalties for blasphemy, and embrace and practice the U.N. Declaration of Human Rights. In 2015, a full-page ad appeared in *the New York Times,* sponsored by the American Islamic Forum for Democracy, portrayed Islam as a religion that stood for justice and coexistence, and condemned jihadism, Islamism, or a solely Islamic state. It stated that a Muslim's duty is to actively promote human rights, and that Muslims must publicly reject any oppression or abuse committed in Islam's name.

Dr. Reza Aslan (*Harvard Divinity Bulletin,* Autumn 2005) wrote that an Islamic reformation is essential to resolve Islam's long war within. Salam al-Marayani, Director of the Muslim Public Affairs Council, said Muslims can no longer afford to be bystanders but need to be involved in constructive intervention. In *Heaven on Earth: A Journey through Shari'a Law,* Sadakat Kadri wrote that the last forty years of literalist interpretation, especially in Saudi Arabia, Iran, Pakistan, and Sudan, runs counter to a thousand years of Islamic transformation and universality. Historically, Islamic law has not been opposed to change; rather, it has been defined by change, bending toward moderation and malleability. Turkish Islamic scholar Fethullah Gulen leads a liberal Muslim movement that until recently included 300 private schools in Turkey and 1,000 globally, and several universities, while his London Centre for Social Studies addresses migration, social cohesion, and human rights. Gulen advocates for religious cooperation.

The Islamic majority includes a plurality of quietists who try to live the principles of Islam in ways that are peaceful, harmonious, and tolerant. There are also millions of progressive and liberal activists, scholars, and clerics who are devout Muslims, but wish to integrate Islamic and modern principles to empower their fellow Muslims and build a better world. In addition, there are millions of scientific, secular individuals who identify as Muslims but question and doubt some Islamic principles and practices. For most of this vast Muslim majority, jihad translates as the inner struggle against evil within themselves. They realize that there is no reference to holy war in the Qur'an, and that Islam prohibits Muslims from harming civilians, opposes the destruction of natural or agricultural property, and perceives violence only as a last resort and then as a means of self-defense. They believe that human rights and democratic politics are compatible with Islam and essential for its future success. A growing plurality strongly advocates for absolute human equality.

Millions of Islamic women are standing up to demand their rights to an education, a profession, a real choice in whom they love and marry, and for the spiritual and social equality that Islam offers them, including Malala Yousafzai, the youngest recipient of a Nobel Peace Prize. Mona Eltanawy, an Egyptian journalist, wrote that Islam's real enemies are misogyny and patriarchy. All Abrahamic faiths have elements that try to control women and their sexuality. Gender equality is the key. The social-sexual revolution will ultimately save Egypt. Irshad Manji, a Canadian TV host and author of *The Trouble with Islam Today: A Muslim's Call for Reform in Her Faith,* implores Muslims to reclaim their *ijtihad* tradition of independent reasoning to update their religious practices in light of contemporary circumstances, and renounce their religious bigotry and repression of women. Perhaps the most threatened Islamic woman is Ayaan Hirsi Ali, author of *Heretic: Why Islam Needs a Reformation Now,* who states that Islam needs a major renovation; it must keep much of the original, but reject any literal interpretation of Qur'an, Hadith, or Sharia, and reject Muhammad's semidivine status.

Amr Khaled is a popular Egyptian Muslim preacher who sells millions of electronic sermons. He has a huge global Web following, and fills stadiums to tell emotional stories about the Prophet Muhammad with simple morals and practical lessons. He professes that Muslim minorities should fully integrate into their countries of residence: we cannot just come, take, and not participate, and no Islamic renaissance is possible without coexistence. God could have created all humanity as a single religion.

One of my Muslim college students asserted that consensual governance was an important Islamic principle. He referenced the Compact of Medina, signed by the Muslims, Jews, Christians, and polytheist Arabs, which granted the Prophet Muhammad the right to rule but also protected the rights of all of Medina's residents. The student contended that this was democratic, tolerant, and compassionate, and stressed principles of equality, consensual, governance, and pluralism. He had recently returned from Malaysia, which has a two-thirds Muslim majority that treats its citizens (Buddhists, Hindus, Sikhs, and Christians) equally and represents a modern pluralistic and tolerant democracy.

Islam has a strong foundation of useful spiritual principles that include: 1) commitment to a God of all people, manifest in the laws of nature and the realities of life; 2) a recognition that people are diverse, have many able prophets, and our diversity of faiths must be respected and practiced with mutual cooperation; 3) that service to others and the sharing of our resources with others, particularly with those most in need, is central to human purpose; and 4) human beings are strengthened through regular, daily spiritual practices with their siblings in faith and through acts of self-sacrifice and self-discipline that remind them of both of their godly nature and of humanity's substantial spiritual capacities.

Like the Sufis, I believe each person needs to practice spirituality through her own experiences of love, ecstasy, and intuitive union to nurture humanity's future.

Islam does need a major systematic spiritual reformation to restore its best historical elements while it learns to remain faithful to the unfolding of God's Creation within the rights, resolutions, and progress of the 21st century. Non-Muslims like myself need to support these Muslim forces for Islamic reformation, peaceful cooperation, and mutual growth in wisdom. Let us join with them in philanthropy and activist service to a needy world and in shared spiritual experiences, exemplified by American Shia Islamic activist Eboo Patel's nationwide organizational efforts for interfaith youth and young-adult community service projects.

Chapter 15
Sikhism

Central Beliefs and Practices

Sikhs pursue salvation through union with God; they realize this union through a loving God who dwells within their own being and in all people. Separation from God causes suffering. The Sikh faith demands lives of courage, activism, and involvement, practiced through their families and temples (*gurdwaras*), as well community and civic institutions. It requires personal responsibility for one's actions and service to others. It affirms life, commends diligent work, and urges its practitioners to stay prepared to sacrifice for good causes. It celebrates the body and spirit, individual and community, a disciplined sensuality, and a modest, service-oriented materialism. They believe that Sikhism illuminates the incredible scope of God's nature and revelations within the human heart and soul. It presents one universal deity for everyone, asserts that all people are equal, and particularly emphasizes that women are equals to men. Sikhs stress honesty, truthful actions, empathy, humility, kindness, compassion, and love.

The *three pillars* of Sikhism are: meditate upon, recite, and celebrate God's name; earn an honest living; and share with others, particularly the unfortunate. Its *five virtues* are: live truthfully—act fairly, honestly, and by doing justice; contentment—freedom from envy, greed, and jealousy; compassion—overlook others' imperfections and mistakes—not only feel empathy but follow those feelings with effective help; humility and benevolence; and strive to become filled with the love of God. The *five thieves* of Sikhism are: lust, anger, greed, pride, and attachment to possessions—particularly treating any person as your possession.

For Sikhs, God is without form or gender, all-pervading, but outside of space or time. God is beyond intellectual comprehension, yet knowable through our inner eyes and hearts. Sikhs make spiritual progress by deep meditation on union with God, who is without fear or hate. People grow by staying open to new knowledge, but progress spiritually by the experience of understanding through actions with others in their communities. People need to be effective without becoming bullies, remain humble while working hard, and modest while being good and fair. People should make the most of their lives.

While worldly attractions may yield temporary satisfaction, such *maya* (duality) leads people into tragedy, as they are robbed by the five thieves. We escape illusion primarily by focusing on other people and larger communities. We are born into and live in dramatically different circumstances, but God's grace permits us to overcome the temptations of maya, the tragedies of karma, and the barriers of reincarnation. The soul's destination is not a heaven or hell but spiritual union with God, which is accomplished by meditation on God's kindness, celebrating God's grace and gifts, avoiding temptation, and living lives of service. Human life is an opportunity to reunite with God and truth. As this wisdom pervades their lives, people grasp that it is the essence of all religions.

Service is crucial. It includes physical service—doing for others; mental service—learning and teaching; and material service—providing resources to people in need. Sikhs strive to balance work, worship, and service while defending the rights of everyone. Sharing is emphasized, and Sikhs are encouraged to practice hopeful resilience. People should make every effort to restore peace and understanding, but also need to protect the moral order and defend justice, so when peaceful negotiations fail, it may become necessary as a last resort to use violence to restore justice and a moral order.

The central symbol of Sikh devotion is their holy scripture, the *Guru Granth Sahib*. Sikh worship is clearly focused upon their holy book, and Sikh worship practices are almost totally detailed practices to appropriately recite from the Guru Granth Sahib and to honor it. To sing the glories of God is the most effective way to join in communion with God, so worship is important. Sikh worship is focused at home and in the gurdwara, literally the doorway to God. Most Sikhs recite specific passages from their scripture, the Guru

Granth Sahib, from memory immediately after they have woken and bathed. Morning and evening prayers may take about two hours. The first prayer, *Japji Sahib,* is founder Guru Nanak's recitation that reminds practitioners to approach God through melodic recitation, and thus purge negative thoughts. Next is Guru Gobind Singh's *Jaap Sahib,* which teaches that there is nothing outside of God's presence—God is the cause of both peace and conflict, creation and destruction. Devout Sikhs are advised to finish the morning prayers with private meditation on the name of God.

Families often read or chant scriptural passages together, and usually attend gurdwara worship services together. There, worship consists largely of recitations from scripture and repetition of scriptural religious songs. Gurdwaras are open to everyone, regardless of religion, race, or circumstance. Upon entering, worshipers touch the ground with their foreheads as a sign of reverence before the Guru Granth Sahib. Often, their liturgical songs include some 18th-century lyrics that recall past Sikh sufferings and glories and invoke grace upon humanity. Each gurdwara includes a community kitchen, the *Langar,* where volunteers prepare regular community meals for all who wish to attend. I joined in these meals both in Bergen County, New Jersey, and in West Sacramento, California.

Though Guru Nanak discouraged religious ceremonies and rituals, Sikhs ceremonies have developed. After a child's birth, the Guru Granth Sahib is opened at a random point and the child is named using the first letter on the upper left-hand corner of the left-hand page. Sikhs join officially in marriage as adults, without regard to descent or status, in the presence of the Guru Granth Sahib, which the couple circles four times. A married couple is considered a single soul in two bodies. While Sikhs are permitted to divorce in civil court, it is not religiously encouraged. Most Sikhs are cremated at death with special ceremonial prayers. Sikhs have no priests, but employ salaried people to sing hymns, perform Gurdwara services, and perform marriages. Any Sikh is free to read from Guru Granth Sahib, and many become a *granthi*—a ceremonial reader who also looks after the Guru Granth Sahib. Sikhs eat only meat from animals slaughtered in a certain way, so meat is rarely served at gurdwara meals.

Most Sikh festivals celebrate the lives of the ten historic gurus—on their birthdays—or commemorate the martyrdom of those murdered. The most sacred holidays are Guru Nanak's birthday (November 14), and *Vaisakhi,* celebrated from late March through early April, which includes processional singing and carrying the Guru Granth Sahib. April 13 is especially celebrated because the tenth Guru, Gobind Singh, inaugurated the Khalsa and the Guru Granth Sahib on that date in 1699. Other Sikh holidays include *Bandi Chhor Divas,* the autumn festival that celebrates the release of Guru Hargobind from imprisonment (often celebrated at the same time as the Hindu *Diwali*); *Maghi,* a winter festival when children's births are celebrated in memory of forty Sikh martyrs; *Hola Mohalla* (close to the Hindu *Holi*), and includes displays of martial skills in simulated battles. Since 2011, March 14, the birthday of the seventh Guru, Har Rai, has been celebrated as the Sikh's Environment Day, when Sikhs participate in local environmental efforts as a tribute to Guru Har Rai's love for nature and for animals.

Historic Evolution

By the 10th century AD, Islamic armies had invaded the northwestern Indian subcontinent and gradually established regimes in Afghanistan, Pakistan, and northwest and north-central India. This region's fertile heart is the Punjab (region of five rivers), where farmers have flourished for eons. In the 12th century, the Hindu poet Jayadevan stated that religious austerities were of little worth compared to the repetition of God's name (a common Islamic and Hindu practice). Kabir (1440–1518) declared that the love of God alone was sufficient to free people from class and race and to end reincarnation. He scorned idol worship, asceticism, and pilgrimages, advocated a life of sincerity and morality, and urged people to become absorbed in the love of God so their souls could melt into the Absolute. Kabir's teachings were a mixture of Hindu and Islamic doctrines; he used the local language and urged everyone to find a guru to lead them into correct lives. He still has many followers today. During a 1977 assembly that I led in Udaipur, Kabir devotees shared their ecstatic singing.

Guru Nanak

Guru Nanak (1469–1539) founded Sikhism. His parents were Hindu merchants of the Kshatriya (warrior) caste. A pious child, Nanak questioned some Hindu practices and found aspects of Islam attractive. He married, had two children, took a government position under the local Muslim ruler, and worked dutifully. He spent his free time singing hymns to God, accompanied by his Muslim musician friend Mardana. At thirty-one, Nanak went to the river for his morning bath and prayer and disappeared for three days. When he reappeared, he said he had been taken to God's court and given a cup of nectar (*amrit*). Sikhism's holy city, Amritsar, is named for this divine syrup, which represents the adoration of God's name. Nanak was instructed to rejoice in the repetition of God's name and to teach others to do so. He said that there is neither Hindu nor Muslim, so he would follow God's path.

Thereafter, Nanak spent much of his life traveling through the Indian subcontinent to sing God's praises, usually accompanied by Mardana. They might even have reached Mecca and Turkey. Devotees called him Guru Nanak, dispeller of ignorance and bringer of enlightenment. His gentle presence and mixture of Islamic and Hindu doctrines and practices did not threaten either Hindu priests or Muslim rulers. Nanak's ideas seemed a reasonable combination of these two faiths whose respective communities were increasingly in violent conflict. For Nanak urged his followers to overcome pride with humility and anger with courageous nonviolence. He said that a good person avoids quarrelsome topics, does not bully others, and forsakes evil company.

During my second visit to India, I received a copy of *Guru Nanak – The Apostle of Love* by M. S. Surma from a Sikh member of the Bombay city council with whom I enjoyed several conversations. Surma holds that it was Guru Nanak who first conceived of India as a nation and viewed invasions as attacks upon the nation. Truthfulness rids us of fear and hate. Kindliness was as close to understanding God as humans could grasp. Neither the Vedas nor the Qur'an alone is sufficient. He urged people to celebrate their bodies as God's vessels. He admonished the wealthy to become trustees rather than owners, by helping the needy. Knowledge without relevant experience produces cobwebs in which learned people often get entangled. Gurus cannot

307

intercede with God or promise enlightenment, but they can teach people to answer for their actions. Nanak began Sikh congregations as the worship of equals (*sangat*). He instituted Sikh's communal kitchens as effective actualizations of this universal spiritual equality. He believed that women should have equal status with men, called women humanity's conscience, and urged their participation in all religious and social functions.

Nanak urged five daily prayers like a devout Muslim, but said: Let truth be your first prayer, honest living second, good actions third, good intentions fourth, and praises of God your fifth prayer. He welcomed yoga disciplines while remaining fully engaged in ordinary life

Nanak urged people to follow the teachings of whichever religion they belonged to in its true spirit. "Since every religion accepts God as Creator, every person is equal in God's eyes."[1] In June 1539, Guru Nanak announced that his death was approaching; he chose a former merchant and farmer named Lehna to succeed him and said that Lehna should be called Guru Angad. Surma believes that Nanak was the first religious leader to choose his successor during his lifetime. Guru Nanak died on September 7, 1539, at age seventy.

Subsequent Leaders of the Sikh Religion

Nine subsequent gurus led the Sikh religion until the death in 1708 of the tenth, Guru Gobind Singh. The second, Guru Angad (1539–1552) institutionalized the Sikh religion, standardized its worship script, and opened many schools. The third, Guru Amar Das (1552–1574) established religious missions for both sexes, and preached against the practice of *purdah*, women dressing in all-enveloping clothes to hide their bodies from men or strangers, common among Muslims, and against *sati*, the burning alive of a Hindu widow after the death of her husband, then practiced by some Hindus. Instead, he urged everyone to dress modestly and urged widows to remarry. He persuaded Emperor Akbar to remove the tax that non-Muslims were charged when they crossed major rivers. The fourth guru was Guru Ram Das (1574–1581) who developed a Sikh marriage code, created the Sikhs' holy city of Amritsar, and strongly protested superstitions, the caste system, or any need for pilgrimages. These first four Sikh gurus were peaceful mystics. The third, Guru Amar Das, spoke for all: "If anyone treats you ill, bear it. If you bear it three times, God himself will fight for you the fourth time."[2]

The fifth guru was Guru Arjan (1581–1606). He had the Guru Granth Sahib compiled and installed it as the official Sikh scripture (1604). Under his leadership, the Amritsar Golden Temple was completed. He also built a house for lepers. The Mughal Emperor Jahangir ordered him tortured and executed; thus Arjan became the Sikhs' first martyred guru. His son, the sixth guru, Guru Har Gobind (1606–1644), instituted an army of Sikh warrior-saints and waged war against the Emperors Jahangir and Shah Jahan. Under his leadership, Sikhs became a political and military power that threatened Muslim political domination throughout northwest India, and their unequal struggle continued until the time of the tenth guru. The seventh, Guru Har Rai (1644–1661), was persecuted by Emperor Aurangzeb, but died of natural causes at thirty-one. The eighth, Guru Har Krishan (1661–1664), died of smallpox at age eight. The ninth, Guru Tegh Bahadur (1665–1675), expanded Sikhism into the northern and eastern boundaries of the Indian subcontinent, but was executed by Emperor Aurangzeb.

In 1699, the tenth Guru, Guru Gobind Singh (1675-1708), founded the Khalsa, a special initiation for some Sikhs of both sexes who are prepared to commit themselves unreservedly to the faith. Khalsa initiates, the Pure, abstain from alcohol, meat, and tobacco, and wear the five Ks (all begin with the letter K in Punjabi): They don't cut their hair, keep it groomed—symbolized by a comb—maintain cleanliness and health, carry a sword or small dagger to defend themselves and protect the weak, but never in anger, wear a steel bracelet, which represents an unbreakable bond with God, and a special undergarment, always ready for action. All male initiates are named Singh (lion-hearted), and all female initiates are named Kaur (princess). Most Sikhs instead remain *Nanakpanthis*—they practice various degrees of quietism and are dubious about war-making. Guru Gobind Singh proclaimed that there would be no subsequent Sikh gurus. Thereafter, the Guru Granth Sahib became the eternal guru. Guru Gobind Singh was assassinated by Pashtuns working for the Mughal governor.

Guru Granth Sahib

Every historic faith has its revered scriptures, but the Guru Granth Sahib plays a uniquely central role in Sikhism because it is treated as their living monarch and the literal embodiment of God. This scripture is central to every Sikh gurdwara: it rests upon a throne during the day, and in a royal bed at night. Whenever it's moved, five specially clothed barefoot devotees move with it, sprinkling water or flower petals ahead, and instruments are played to announce its presence. No one sits higher than the scripture. The book itself is dressed for each season. In its presence all devotees must cover their heads and remove their shoes, and participants clean themselves before entering its presence. During its recitations, no food, drink, or small talk is permitted. Readers cover their mouths. The only ritual practices comparable in another religion is perhaps how devout Jews treat the Torah scrolls: housed in a special cabinet, paraded through the sanctuary, touched reverently, read with special objects, and kissed lovingly.

The Guru Granth Sahib has 1,430 pages. During Guru Nanak's life, many of his nearly 1,000 hymns were collected and sent to Sikh communities for their morning and evening prayers. The 974 hymns eventually included in the Guru Granth Sahib were said to have been composed by Nanak. His successor, Guru Angad, led systematic efforts to collect Guru Nanak's songs, but also wrote fifty of his own. Guru Amar Das contributed almost as many hymns as Nanak himself, including verses by several non-Sikhs. Many distinguish Sikhs from other religious people. Guru Ram Das contributed additional hymns and continued to winnow "pretender" verses. Guru Arjan established the first official compilation of the Guru Granth Sahib, which also contained songs and sayings by fifteen earlier non-Sikh seers, including thirteen Hindus and two Muslims such as Kabir, Jayadevan, Ramananda, and Fariduddin Ganjshakar. Guru Tegh Bahadur added substantially to the Sikh's sacred songs, and the tenth Guru, Guru Gobind Singh, organized the Guru Granth Sahib essentially into its current form.

The Guru Granth Sahib is organized as a set of Indian musical ragas, but begins with an initial non-raga section which includes major morning and evening prayers, beginning with the *Ek Onkar*—the All Pervading Being; the following nine words are the Sikhs' mantra or *Mul Mantar*: universal principle, creator, sustainer, doer, devoid of fear and of enmity, beyond time, yet existing in its self, but expressing itself through Guru, and rests on mercy. The bulk of the text is in thirty-one ragas, usually connected with emotions or moods and often also with particular times of day or night. Each division is arranged in the chronical order of its quoted non-Sikh seers or Sikh Gurus. There are also 22 traditional ballads, some with a particular tune, others sung in any tune. The end is the *Mundavanee,* or closing seal, which says in part: "the dark ocean-world of our lives is crossed by grasping the feet of God."

The Guru Granth Sahib is written in Gurmukhi script, invented by Guru Angad. It includes Punjabi, Sanskrit, Persian languages and regional dialects, some no longer used; it is often written without spaces or breaks, sometimes without verbs or pronouns. Gurmukhi is now the official written language in Punjab State. Since Sikhism's founders were communicating sacred verses often to illiterate followers, they needed easily learned verses taught them in daily prayers composed over the course of two centuries. Few can comprehend most of its 1,430 pages. As with other religions' that use ancient scriptural languages, many Sikhs recite passages without being able to intellectually analyze their meanings. For its believers, however, all of the Guru Granth Sahib was inspired by God, and is therefore sacred and hopefully intuitively grasped by its practitioners. Sikhs perceive their scripture to be unique because it is both inclusive and contains direct inspiration. However, applying contemporary analytical, scholarly tools to its interpretation remains challenging.

Many of Guru Gobind Singh's compositions were not included in the Guru Granth Sahib, but collected as the Dasam Granth Sahib, a secondary text, which, unlike the Guru Granth Sahib, was not considered part of the eternal Guru itself. The Dasam Granth Sahib contains Hindu mythology and secular stories from many sources. It has five versions whose authenticities remain debated among Sikhs, but several are often included in Sikhs' daily prayers.

Until the late 19th century, there were only handwritten copies of the Guru Granth Sahib. The first printed copy was published in 1864. Max Arthur Macauliffe translated elements of it into English in his six-volume work, *The Sikh Religion: Its Gurus, Sacred Writings and Authors,* which the Sikh community judged as fairly accurate. In 1962, an eight-volume translation in English and Punjabi was published by a Sikh committee, and in the 21st century, the *Khalsa Consensus Translation* has become popular through Sikh websites. Many Sikhs consider it the most accurate translation of the Guru Granth Sahib. Sikhs do not have to learn Gurmukhi (the writing system developed by the Sikhs in India for their sacred literature), and most non-Indian Sikhs don't know it. In gurdwaras outside of India, English translations are often used, but are treated less reverently. Gurmukhi is recommended to fully experience the Guru Granth Sahib. As with recitations of the Qur'an or the singing of Hindu prayers, it is often the rhythm and melody as much as the meaning that convey and inculcate the believers' experience.

The Sikh Empire

After the assassination of Gobind Singh, Sikh leaders focused on military conquest and political leadership. Singh Bahadur largely abolished absentee landlords, and empowered local farmers to become the proprietors of the lands they farmed. Sikh forces ended Muslim rule in the Punjab, and the most powerful Sikh chieftains ruled Lahore; they paid an annual fee to Afghanistan's Muslim rulers to keep them from invading. Through the rest of the 18th century, Sikh leaders dominated the region, but also continued to fight each other. By 1801, however, Ranjit Singh had united them into a Sikh Empire that extended from Afghanistan's Khyber Pass in the west to Tibet in the northeast. Lahore became the administrative capital, and Amritsar was both the Sikhs' spiritual center and the empire's commercial hub. Ranjit Singh created or rebuilt many fortifications, restored Shah Jahan's famous Shalimar gardens, and provided his subjects peace and prosperity that endured until his death in 1839.

The Sikh Empire was unusual in that it allowed non-Sikhs to practice their religions freely and included non-Sikhs in positions of authority. Only 17 percent of the empire's population was Sikh; 70 percent were Muslim, and 13 percent were Hindu. Ranjit Singh gave Amritsar's famed buildings their present iconic form, with walls of white marble and a gold-covered roof. He prohibited the slaughter of cows, and funded renovations to Hindu temples. His empire was also tolerant of Muslims but disallowed their public calls to prayer. After centuries under Islamic rulers, however, Muslims felt subjected, and many still considered Sikhs as infidels.

Dissolution of the Sikh Empire, and Recruitment of Sikh Soldiers for the British Empire

After the death of Ranjit Singh, internal divisions quickly weakened the Sikh Empire. British colonial military forces had by then seized control of much of the Indian subcontinent except for Afghanistan and the Sikh Empire. The British East India Company took advantage of Sikh disunion to launch the Anglo-Sikh wars. At the battle of Ferozeshah in 1845, British forces inflicted extensive destruction, but the Sikhs won by targeting British officers. This was perhaps the greatest global defeat of any British colonial force. Nonetheless, by 1849, the Sikh Empire had been broken into princely states, and the Punjab had a British governor.

Some Sikhs felt superior to Hindus and Muslims, since most Sikhs were successful farmers or soldiers, while Hindus and Muslims were often poorer, and less well-trained or educated. Though Sikh teachings officially reject caste divisions, many Sikh landowners shared prejudices against lower Hindu castes, particularly untouchables, or Dalits. After the Indian Mutiny of 1857–58, existing religious and cultural divisions among Sikhs, Hindus, and Muslims were compounded by mutual religious savagery.

The British were so impressed by the Sikhs' fighting abilities that they rapidly integrated Sikhs into their colonial military and police forces. Until the end of WWII, many Sikhs served not only in the Indian subcontinent but throughout the British colonies. As Sikh soldiers and policemen fought or policed worldwide, often moving their families with them, the Sikh diaspora began. Sikh military forces became legendary in defending the disputed boundaries of Britain's colonial empire. In 1897, a handful of Sikh soldiers held off an attack by 10,000 Afghanis in which all twenty-one Sikhs fought to the death. Thousands more fought in Europe during WWI. They were called the Black Lions because they used swords and carried their Guru Granth Sahibs as well as their modern weapons into battle. In the Allied invasions during WWII, Sikhs were outstanding, particularly in Italy and in Malaysia, where they constituted 60 percent of the British military, and they repelled the Japanese from Burma. Sikhs emigrated to the U.K., Africa, the Middle East, Singapore, Malaysia, Australia, Canada, and the U.S.

Sikh Militancy for Independence and a Sikh State

By 1869, a peaceful Sikh crusade for Punjabi independence occurred, led by Baba Ram Singh Namdhari, whose followers were called Alkalis. They protested the slaughter of cows, advocated for widows to be allowed to remarry, wore homespun garments (as opposed to using imported English cloth or cloth made in English-owned factories), and were devoted to meditation. Their techniques of nonviolent noncooperation, rejection of all British institutions, efforts at self-sufficiency and native forms of democracy, crafts, and cooperative work were later incorporated into the Indian Independence movement led by Mahatma Gandhi.

Immigration to North America had begun in the 19th century and led to significant Sikh communities in British Columbia and Ontario. Sikh farmers immigrated to California, many settling north of Sacramento. In San Francisco, Sohan Singh Bhakna organized the Ghadar Party, which was committed to ending British rule in India through armed revolt and the establishment of an Indian Republic that would guarantee the liberty and equality of all its citizens. They started branches in U.S. cities and in Canada, Shanghai, Hong Kong, the Philippines, Thailand, and Panama, and some members trained in armed rebellion. The Ghadar Movement spread to the Punjab, where the British imprisoned or hanged thousands as terrorists.

When WWI ended, 80,000 Sikh soldiers returned to India, which was already in turmoil. In 1922, a throng of peaceful Sikh families crowded into a constrained area in Amritsar. A British general ordered its sole exit blocked and told his soldiers to kill as many as possible. Three hundred died, and most of the survivors were wounded. This galvanized the Indian independence movement; the Sikhs became fervent proponents of Gandhian *satyagraha* and supported the Indian National Congress and their movement for Indian independence. Some Sikhs, however, continued to struggle internally against those Sikhs who still supported the colonial regime and remained in control of Sikh holy sites and organizational bureaucracy. The Gurdwara Reform Movement initiated a successful revolt in response. Thousands of Sikhs practiced satyagraha, and Gandhi urged activists to come from all over India to study the Sikhs' exemplary nonviolent activism. When India gained independence, Sikhs represented less than 1.5 percent of its population, yet a majority of those the British hanged or imprisoned were Sikhs, and more than 20,000 Sikhs joined the Indian National Army directly after independence.

In 1948, when British colonial India was divided into India and Pakistan (called the partition), the Punjab region was split between India and Pakistan. In the west, millions of Hindus and Sikhs left home, property, and possessions to flee east into India, and millions of Muslims left everything to flee west into the new nation of Pakistan. (A similar division happened in the east, where Bengal was divided into the Indian state of West Bengal and into eastern Pakistan, which later became Bangladesh). There was horrific violence: more than a million people were killed, and millions more were injured during the violence and displacement. Most Sikhs believed they would then be given their own state of Punjab within an independent India. It was not until after the 1965 Indo-Pakistan war, however, that India created a Sikh-majority state, because the prevailing view in India's sovereign nation was multireligious and multiethnic, so Punjab State remained under national control.

Dr. Vir Singh Bhatti, founder of the Khalistan movement, organized Sikhs to separate into their own nation. The movement grew strongest in the Punjab in the 1970s and '80s, with extensive support from Sikhs who lived elsewhere. In the early 1980s, under Jarnail Singh Bhindranwale, a group of armed militants took control of Amritsar's Golden Temple, and in June 1984, the Indian government sent an army, led by a Sikh general, which seized control of the Amritsar sites for the Indian nation. This made most Sikhs feel that their holiest site had been desecrated. In revenge, on October 31, 1984, Indian Prime Minister Indira Gandhi was assassinated by two of her Sikh bodyguards. Violent anti-Sikh riots and many deaths followed. My family was impacted by the consequent militancy: We had stayed in Montreal with Indian friends for several days. Then, in June 1985, our friend's wife and children headed to Bombay on Air India Flight 182. A terrorist bomb set by Canadian Sikh militants destroyed the aircraft. Some Sikh militancy is still alive today, and many Sikhs continue to dream of a Sikh nation, but most realize that fulfillment of their dream is improbable, and they have integrated into mainstream Indian life and that of the other countries where they hold citizenship.

Sikhism Today

Both Pakistan and India have provinces called Punjab. Pakistan's Punjab province is that country's second largest province in area, contains most of Pakistan's large cities, and is by far the most populous, with 91 million of Pakistan's 180 million people. India's Punjab State is only the sixteenth largest Indian state in population, with 28 million people, and the twentieth largest in area. Historically, Pakistani territories had been central to Sikh history, including Guru Nanak's birthplace in Punjab province and Peshawar in northwest Pakistan. Today, there are only 20,000 Pakistani Sikhs. Three hundred-fifty thousand Sikhs live in the U.S. now. Nikki Haley, former US ambassador to the United Nations, grew up as a Sikh before she converted to evangelical Christianity. Sikh groups have held parades in San Francisco, Los Angeles, and New York.

Today, Sikhism is firmly rooted in India, but there are Sikh immigrants in many countries, and a sprinkling of Sikhs in a few Muslim-majority nations, particularly Malaysia. Of the 25 million Sikhs in the world, 21 million are Indian citizens, the majority in the state of Punjab, where they represent 60 percent of its population. Sikhs are the fourth largest religion in India and the fifth largest in the world. Though they represent only 2 percent of India's population, Sikhs have a significant place in the history of modern India. Almost every Indian council of ministers has had Sikh representatives. India has had a former Sikh Prime Minister, Dr. Manmohan Singh, and a former president, Giani Zail Singh. Sikhs represent a sizeable portion of the Indian armed forces and police, including the only living Indian five-star general, Arjan Singh. Sikhs play significant roles among Indian athletes; for example, the only Indian Olympic gold medalist, Abhinav Bindra. Many Sikhs are successful entrepreneurs, and Sikh farmers have been among the pioneers of India's green revolution.

Elements of Sikhism that I Find Troubling

Given the Sikhs' history, tendencies toward sectarian nationalism and militarism are understandable, but they contradict Sikhism's basic principles and undermine the virtues embodied in its spiritual practices. It's good that

316

the Sikhs in India's Punjab have a distinctively Sikh Indian state, but I believe that particularly there, Sikhs need to remain true to their spiritual ideals by practicing inclusive and equitable governance. Terrorism, sectarian militancy, and continued efforts to establish a separate Sikh nation are incompatible with Sikhism's foundational beliefs and a productive future evolution of the faith. For the foreseeable future, humanity will require dedicated military and law-enforcement practitioners, and the continuing service of Sikhs in these forces throughout the world are justifiably valued. I hope that, as the Khalsa continues into the 21st century, Sikhs will reconsider what it means to serve their faith without reservation by concentrating upon nonviolent methods that emphasize sacrifice and service beyond the boundaries of their communities.

The Sikhs' worship of their scripture, the Guru Granth Sahib, is understandable metaphorically, but not literally. I respect it as a symbol of their devotion to mystical union with divinity through recited-chanted song, but since so much of its language is indecipherable for most Sikhs, the Guru Granth Sahib doesn't lend itself to ready analysis or easy application to the challenges and opportunities in their lives.

Elements of Sikhism that I Find Particularly Relevant

My personal experiences with Sikhism have been excellent. I was blessed with a wonderful Sikh family who were members of the UU congregation in Bloomington, Indiana. Paul and Darshi Singh and their two sons were active in the congregation and the university. They were effective civic activists; they were helpful to my Hindu-Jain wife and me during our years there. Paul was neither bearded nor turbaned, but he and Darshi wore the bracelet and honored their Sikh heritage. In New Jersey, a Sikh family lived across the street from the parsonage and next door to the congregation I served. Kulwant and Avtar Singh became friends with Madhavi and me. Our children played together. Kulwant was a leader among the Sikhs of Bergen County. For several years before the local Sikhs built their own gurdwara, they used the Paramus UU congregation's facilities for their meetings. I attended several of their worships and events. I also visited with Kulwant, and we discussed many things. The women in these two Sikh families were strong and thoughtful, simultaneously traditional and comfortably modern.

In Sacramento, I initiated a series of antiviolence ecumenical meetings that brought together more than a half dozen diverse religious communities. The Sikh community of West Sacramento was an enthusiastic participant. Their primary leader was Wadhawa Singh Gill, and his community had 500 voting members. They hosted a meeting of that ecumenical group, and the other congregations were impressed by the efficiency of their community kitchen. Some of their members had been in America for more than a century and had successful agricultural operations north of Sacramento. In San Francisco, I have had the good fortune to work and celebrate with several outstanding Bay Area Sikh leaders in ecumenical meetings.

I'm enthusiastic about many of Sikhism's spiritual principles and practices. I agree with my Sikh colleagues that true religion is not based upon ceremony or temple attendance so much as upon inner experience. That it is more realistic to live in the world as families and communities that nurture our ability to keep our heads above life's tensions and divisions. Spiritual discipline calls for us to take personal responsibility, to rise above selfish desires and dedicate ourselves to serving the larger community and the human future. I too strive to connect with the divine, both within myself and in others. I too seek a courageous, involved, activist life practiced through family and congregation, but equally in the wider world. I too celebrate body and spirit, individual and community, a disciplined sensuality, and a modest, service-oriented materialism.

Together, we stress humanity's spiritual equality and the personal responsibility of individuals. The diligence, resourcefulness, and courage of Sikhs are inspiring. Their characterization of human frailties as "thieves" is intriguing, since lust, anger, greed, attachment to possessions, and pride can so easily steal away our better efforts. Their five virtues make sense to me. I feel blessed to have had Sikhs in my life who have exemplified many of these desirable spiritual qualities. As Guru Nanak said, "Knowledge without relevant experiences can be cobwebs in which learned people often get entangled." And as my friend Kulwant Singh said, "Ask for nothing. Work for everything. Share what you have. Turn no one away."

**Floating Eagle Feather and UU Children, Vancouver,
British Columbia, Canada.**

Section III

Chapter 16
Liberal Religions in an Increasingly Secular World

Shared Liberal Religious Assumptions

Liberal religions arose in response to the challenges that secular thought and modern life present to religious traditions and organizations and the spiritual beliefs and practices of individuals. All liberal religions embrace education, human rights, democracy, science, and technology. Growing out of classical liberalism, they consciously attempt to create, nurture, and strengthen the truths and values they discover and affirm in historic religions and in the spiritual imagination and insights of individuals and communities.

For liberal religionists, truth is always in process; to use theological phrases, revelation is not sealed, but will continue to be discovered and better understood. Liberal religionists' faiths are built on foundations of mutual consent among congregations of free individuals to nurture a fairer and more loving world. Since they enthusiastically believe that people must continue to consciously create and sustain good through chosen organizations and just uses of power, they question whether any single individual or group can ever fully grasp what is or will be beneficial. Recognizing the tragic dimensions of nature and life, liberal religionists no longer assume that progress is inevitable or even always likely, but they do remain hopeful, and embrace lives of responsibility, trust, and celebration. Contrast these faith elements with their perception that traditional, and especially fundamentalist, religions and spiritualities often appear obsessed with evil, guilt, and sin. Liberal religionists dismiss theologies that assume predestination, eternal punishment, or endless despair for much of humanity. Liberal religionists do not believe it wise to spend our lives awaiting justice in a heavenly afterlife. They also disagree with the claims of secular skeptics who embrace a cosmos governed by accidental absurdities, or by the cynics' near-certain dead end of isolated, existentialist despair.

Classical Liberalism

Classical liberalism began in the 17th century with political and economic disputes between King Charles and the English Parliament, climaxed by a civil war in 1640. The consequent *Agreement of the People* advocated popular sovereignty, increased suffrage, religious tolerance, and equality before the law. John Locke is recognized as a father of classical liberalism. He maintained that government rightfully acquires consent from the governed, and that consent continues to be necessary for a government to remain legitimate. There must be a separation between the government and religion because people have a natural liberty of conscience that needs to be protected from any governmental authority. Locke was concerned that individuals left to their selfish desires are often overcome by instincts for survival and power, so humanity needs to escape these dangers by forming collective sovereign authorities capable of negotiating among competing interests within a social contract, and transfer some of their individual rights to governments, while governments need to remain responsive to people's legitimate needs and protect their lives, liberty, and property.

Locke believed that people are not born innately sinful or virtuous, but gain understanding and virtue through a lifelong process of experiential learning. A broad education was necessary for individuals to function effectively as democratic citizens. He embraced economic systems based on competition, free trade, free enterprise, and the sanctity of property. The founders of the United States divided government powers into executive, legislative, and judicial functions to help to ensure due process, the rule of law, and the protection of individual rights. In practice, classical liberalism almost always meant freedom and political power *only* for white male landowners. Few classic liberals thought uneducated people or those without property were capable of prudently wielding political or economic power. Classical liberalism's reverence for property became a useful way to withhold the full privileges of liberalism from most Americans, French, and British until well into the 19th century, and for women and people of color well into the 20th. For much of the rest of the world, liberalism did not become a reality until the late 20th century, or has yet to be fulfilled in the 21st. Its definition of property gradually evolved from owning land to controlling any form of personal property or financial assets.

In 1776, economist Adam Smith published *The Wealth of Nations,* a "bible" for classical liberal economics. He believed that without conscious cooperative planning, an "invisible hand" would direct businesses and individuals toward their collective benefit while they sought their selfish wealth and power. Smith eventually realized, however, that governments needed to intervene so that free enterprise worked effectively, just as Locke understood that individual rights needed to be constrained by governmental powers.

For the new free-enterprise entrepreneurs and the professional and educated classes, Smith's arguments against government interference, and that self-interest and dynamic capitalism could by themselves create public benefit provided powerful justification for maximizing their political and cultural influence, so although individual rights and social power broadened, it continued to exclude most people in every society. In addition, corporations claimed to have the rights of individual persons, without the constraints, responsibilities, and potential negative consequences that individuals faced. This "corporation as person" conceit gave financial "haves" an additional way to protect themselves from the full responsibilities of liberalism while they benefitted from it disproportionately.

Classical Liberal Religion

In most religions and spiritual practices, there are liberal aspects, individuals, and movements. Many historic religions began as relatively liberal responses to their ancestral faiths when parts of them no longer seemed to fit people's evolving beliefs or needs. Historic faiths then either reacted by adapting so as to incorporate the desired changes, or evolved from ancestral faiths (Jainism and Buddhism out of Hinduism, Christianity out of Judaism, Islam out of Judaism and Christianity, Sikhism out of Islam and Hinduism) into new faiths that met new needs. Spiritual mystics as well as revolutionary individuals in each religious tradition are often considered threatening by their conservative colleagues or hierarchical leaders.

During the 18th, 19th, and 20th centuries, emerging religious movements became so different from their ancestral roots that other adherents of those religions no longer considered them members of their faith. For instance, most Reform Jews continued to identify as Jewish, and were not excluded by most other Jews, while Ethical Culturists consciously differentiated themselves from Judaism, though most Ethical Culturists were of Jewish ancestry. Most Quakers remained identifiably Christian, while by the late 1960s, the Unitarian Universalist majority no longer identified as Christians. The original Baha'i communities were Shiite Muslims, but nearly all other Muslims rejected the Baha'i faith as heresy. South and East Asian traditions were generally more embracing of even their most innovative or reformist practitioners—sometimes even comfortably syncretistic—so their liberal movements were less likely to be viewed as having either abandoned their faiths or deserving of exclusion from them. A sampling of liberal religions illustrates these distinctions.

Unitarians and Universalists

Among the earliest movements in the radical Christian Protestant Reformation, Unitarians have existed for over 400 years. Universalists arose first in 17th-century England. Early Unitarians and Universalists were clearly Christian and liberal, with a benevolent Creator, a human Jesus who embraced humanity, and a clear preference for using reason to integrate their faiths into a changing world. Eighteenth-century English and colonial American Unitarians embraced biblical scholarship and challenged orthodoxies. Their Universalist siblings emphasized a loving God and a Jesus who embraced everyone in His spiritual kingdom. The Transcendentalist philosophy broadened both traditions to include non-Christian religions, to approach nature mystically, and to reinforce their determined march toward universal individual liberation and civic efforts to engender social justice. By 1867, they had ordained the first women ministers and included a few members of color. For part of the 19th century, a significant portion of the North American intelligentsia was Unitarian, and the Universalists' cosmic embrace attracted many American frontier families, though most adherents of both traditions remained educated, white, and with at least middle-class financial resources or aspirations.

Since the end of the 19th century, an increasing portion of Unitarians and Universalists evolved faiths that focused on this world and this life, and viewed religion primarily as a quest for right relationships and for activism on behalf of an equitable society. UUs accept themselves as constituents of the natural world and strive to be informed by scientific knowledge. In the first half of the 20th century, more of their independent congregations became philosophically humanistic while maintaining mainline Protestant worship forms and rituals. In 1961, the year that the two denominations officially united and I first became a member, most UUs saw themselves and were perceived by others as more a legitimate way to be religious without required dogmas or rituals than as an "organized" religion. UUs could have the comfort of acting fairly Protestant at Sunday services while they remained rational and broadly tolerant; they didn't really need to believe or practice anything except to be good people and nurture a just social order—an attractive alternative for many modern Americans. Today, while more than a million Americans identify themselves as UUs, there are fewer than 250,000 adult members in some 1,000 congregations, most with fewer than 200 members. With no creed, UUs pledge to live up to their seven principles and six traditions:

Seven Principles: The inherent worth and dignity of every person; justice, equality, and compassion in human relations; acceptance of one another and encouragement to spiritual growth in our congregations; a free and responsible search for truth and meaning; the right of conscience, and the use of the democratic process in our congregations and in society; the goal of world community with peace, liberty, and justice for all; respect for the interdependent web of existence we are a part of.

Six Traditions: Direct experience of the transcendent mystery and wonder, affirmed in all cultures, that moves us to renewal of the spirit and openness to the forces that create and uphold life; words and deeds of prophetic women and men that challenge us to confront powers and structures of evil with justice, compassion, and the transformational power of love; wisdom from the world's religions that inspires us in our ethical and spiritual life; Jewish and Christian teachings, which call us to respond to God's love by loving our neighbors as ourselves; Humanist teachings, which counsel us to heed the guidance of reason and the results of science, and warn us against idolatries of the mind and spirit; spiritual teachings of Earth-centered traditions that celebrate the sacred circle of life and instruct us to live in harmony with the rhythms of nature.

Ethical Culture

Felix Adler (1851–1933) was the son of Samuel Adler, the rabbi of Reform Temple Emanuel in New York City. During his studies, Felix was influenced by Immanuel Kant's belief that the existence of deity and immortality could not be proved, therefore, that morality needed to be established independently of theology. Felix shared his views with his father's congregation, but when they rejected them, he found a teaching position at Cornell University. In 1877, he returned to initiate the New York Society for Ethical Culture. By 1886, similar societies had been established in Philadelphia, Chicago, and St. Louis.

Their principles: Morality is independent of theology; new moral problems have arisen in modern industrial society that the world's religions have not adequately dealt with; the duty to engage in philanthropy so as to advance morality; the belief that self-reform should go in lockstep with social reform; the establishment of republican rather than monarchical governance of Ethical societies; the agreement that educating the young is a culture's most important aim.

Felix Adler advocated deeds instead of creeds and concentrated on ethics and morality instead of ritual or dogma. Ethical Culturists initiated low-cost housing, nursing facilities, and schools, but they resisted religious organization and rarely tried to convert others, though they established regular meetings and life-cycle ceremonies. After a generation of successes, the Ethical Culture movement stagnated until after WWII. Then, in 1946, new Ethical Societies were formed in Teaneck, New Jersey, and Washington, D.C. By 1968, there were thirty societies with a total membership of about 6,000; their suburban congregations developed significantly to provide an alternative religious-education environment for their children. I've led services in the Teaneck and D.C. Ethical Societies, and in 1971 served as summer director for the capitol legislative office, which then served UUs, Ethical Societies, and the

American Humanist Union on national political issues. In 2003, Ethical Culturists agreed: We relate to others in ways that bring out their best and the best in ourselves. By 'best' we refer to unique talents and abilities that affirm and nurture life. 'Spirit' refers to a person's unique personality and to the love, hope, and empathy that exists in human beings. As we elicit the best in others, we encourage their ethical development, their perhaps as-yet untapped but inexhaustible worth.

Humanist Manifestos, Religious Humanism, and the American Humanist Association

In 1933, the first Humanist Manifesto was signed by thirty-four Americans, mostly Unitarians. The most prominent signatory was philosopher John Dewey. It stated that religions throughout the world must come to terms with new conditions created by a vastly increased knowledge and experience. In every human activity, the vital movement is now in the direction of a transparent and explicit humanism. It rejected superstition, demanded the exercise of reason in matters of faith, and declared that our larger understanding of the universe, scientific achievements, and deeper appreciation for the kinship of all people requires a new statement of religions' means and purposes. It advocated taking responsibility for making a better world in which people intelligently and voluntarily cooperated for the common good. It affirmed life rather than denying it, sought to elicit life's possibilities rather than fleeing them, and strove to establish conditions for a satisfactory life, not for the few, but for all.

In 1973, Humanist Manifesto II was published with a wider range of participants: Unitarian Universalists, Ethical Culturists, American Humanist Association members, and many unassociated secular humanists. It admitted that Humanist Manifesto I had been "far too optimistic," but was still dismissive of either a deity that answered prayers, or a salvation-religiosity, but it recognized the wide variety of existing humanisms, asserted that "views that merely reject theism... or are mere negation... are not humanism," and recognized that any philosophy or ideology could become dogmatic. This new manifesto refused to reject humanists who chose to remain in a traditional religion while also embracing a humanist ethic. It continued to rest its hopes on reason, critical intelligence, and scientific methods, but understood that these had to be used in contexts that also cultivated emotions and love, the arts, and religions. Mindful that movements claiming to be human-centered and antitraditional had caused immense 20th-century suffering (racism, classism, ethnic chauvinism, communism, fascism), this document was both humbler and more careful.

There are humanists in all religious traditions, but most attempts to organize religious humanism have occurred in UU, Ethical Culture, and a few avowedly humanistic Jewish congregations, all of which wanted to maintain their historic denominational ties. There are many religious humanists in more mainline denominations (Quaker, Episcopal, UCC, Reform and Reconstructionist Jews, et al.) that hold a variety of theologies and spiritual practices while asserting humanistic ideas and ethical practices.

The American Humanist Association (AHA) was founded in 1941 by Rev. Curtis Reese, a UU minister. It began *The Humanist* magazine, and its headquarters are now in Washington, D.C. In the late 1960s, it secured a religious tax exemption in support of its Celebrant Program, which allowed certified humanist celebrants to legally officiate at weddings and enjoy the rights of clergy. In 1991, it jettisoned its religious tax exemption and resumed an exclusively educational status, but still certifies members to serve as ministers, and is again recognized as a not-for-profit tax-exempt organization. Its goals are to advance secular humanism without theism or other supernatural beliefs, while affirming people's responsibility to lead lives of ethical fulfillment that aspire to the greater good for humanity.

The International Humanist and Ethical Union (IHEU) was formed in 1952. Headquartered in London, it comprises 117 member organizations in thirty-eight countries. It holds an international congress every three years, promotes human rights and humanist values, and aspires to achieve global separation of church and state. In 2014, it agreed upon freedom of personal beliefs while arguing that this respect for freedom did not imply any duty to respect beliefs they disagreed with and announced that satire, ridicule, or even condemnation were vital forms of critical discourse. They asserted that the principles of democracy, human rights, the rule of law, and secularism provide the firmest foundation for the development of open societies.

The Baha'i Religion

The Baha'i religion arose out of Iranian Twelver Shiite Islam, which believes that the Twelfth Iman is still alive and will return at the end of time. In the early 19th century, a subset of Twelver Shia began to expect his imminent arrival. In 1844, a young man from Shiraz, Iran, Mirza Ali Muhammad, declared himself the Bab, or gate to the hidden Imam. After, he appeared to have declared himself the Hidden Imam, his followers began to be persecuted. After two Babis tried to assassinate the Shah, the Bab was executed, and many Babis were killed or exiled. One exile, Mirza Husayn Ali, whom the Bab had renamed Baha'u'llah, the Glory of God, became the new leader of the Baha'is. In 1863, Baha'u'llah announced that he was "He Whom God Shall Manifest," and was banished to Ottoman Turkey where he spent the rest of his life under house arrest. Though not formally educated, Baha'u'llah wrote much of what became the Baha'i scriptures. Baha'is believe that Baha'u'llah was the divinely inspired founder of their universal religion, a mirror wherein the nature of the unknowable God is faithfully reflected.

After his death in 1892, Baha'u'llah's son, Abdu'l-Baha, became their leader. He transformed Baha'i from a Middle Eastern outgrowth of Shia Islam into an international liberal religious movement that made converts not only in the Middle East but in the United States, Europe, and elsewhere. Abdu'l-Baha organized Baha'i World Centre in Haifa, Israel. By his death in 1921, there were 100,000 Baha'is; most were a persecuted Iranian minority, but there were growing groups in India and the U.S. Then, Abdu'l-Baha's oldest grandson, Shoghi Effendi Rabbani, became leader. Educated at Beirut's American University and at Oxford, Rabbani organized Baha'i scriptures, identified the U.S. as the cradle for Baha'i growth, and organized its global movement under a hierarchical leadership in Haifa. One of his goals was to construct a beautiful Baha'i center on every inhabited continent. Since Rabbani's death in 1957, Baha'is have governed themselves through a nine-member Universal House of Justice elected by national assemblies for five-year terms.

Baha'i Beliefs and Practices

Unity is the watchword for Baha'is—unity of God, religion, and humanity. God, the creator, periodically reveals his will through divine messengers. God is personal, all-powerful and all-loving, yet too awesome to be fully comprehended. Both God and the universe are eternal. The Trinity doctrine is contradictory to God's realities. Humans have a rational soul that provides them the capacity to recognize God's centrality and to form a special relationship with God that is earned through recognition, obedience, community service, regular prayer, and spiritual practice. After death, souls pass into the next world where their spiritual development in the physical world becomes a basis for judgment and advancement. Heaven and hell are states of nearness to or distance from God that describe relationships in this world and the next, rather than being physical spaces for everlasting reward or punishment.

Baha'is honor and accept the diversity of cultures as worthy of appreciation and acceptance and endow all historic religions with some validity; however, since they understand religious history to have been a progressive unfolding of revelations from Adam through Baha'u'llah, they believe that Baha'u'llah has fulfilled all previous faiths' messianic expectations, and do not expect another manifestation of God to appear within the next 1,000 years, so The Bab and Baha'u'llah are the appropriate guides for modern humanity.

While Baha'i teachings emphasize ethical and social issues, the writings of the Bab and Baha'u'llah, Abdu'l-Baha, and Shoghi Effendi, which the Baha'i consider divine revelations, or scriptures, have strong mystical qualities. Baha'u'llah's most holy book, *Kitab-i-Aqdas*, contains Baha'is' laws, but his books, *The Book of Certitude, Gems of Divine Mysteries, Seven Valleys,* and *Four Valleys* are all mystic texts. *Hidden Words* contains 153 short spiritual truths. Baha'u'llah said that if people remained selfish, immature, and greedy, even their best schemes would not work. Satisfactory solutions require a change of heart and mind that only a thoughtful and practical religiosity can produce. Abdu'l-Baha said that religion and science are two wings upon which man's intelligence can soar and on which the human soul makes progress. Progress needs both wings; without the wing of science, religion falls into superstition and without the wing of religion, science falls into materialism. When religion is freed from superstitions, dogmas, and outworn traditions, a cleansing force that will wash away wars and disagreements and unite mankind in the power of the love of God.

The first Bahai meeting I attended was in 1968. The unification of humanity is the paramount issue in both religion and politics. The equality of men and women is the two wings on which humankind is able to soar. They advocate for universal education, abolition of the extremities of wealth or poverty, respect for work performed in the spirit of service, and for the progressive establishment of justice, religion, and universal peace as the supreme goals of all humankind. Beginning with their founders, Baha'is have advocated for world government and supported international entities.

The Baha'i calendar consists of nineteen months. Their New Year corresponds to the traditional Persian New Year, called *Nowruz,* on March 21, ending with a required nineteen-day fasting period. Their services are primarily scripture readings, and they eat, consult, and socialize afterward. There are eleven annual holy days. The five-pointed star, the *haykal* (Arabic for temple) and two five-pointed stars interspersed with a calligraphic *Baha* are favorite symbols. Baha'is recite daily obligatory prayers and study their scriptures. Alcohol and drugs are prohibited except by medical prescription. Sexual intercourse is permitted only between husband and wife; premarital, extramarital, and homosexual intercourse are forbidden because traditional marriage is society's foundation. Baha'is praise interracial marriage. Backbiting, gossip, gambling, and fanaticism are forbidden. To perform useful work and service to humanity are, in the sight of God, forms of worship equal in value to prayer or group worship. Baha'is are admonished to abstain from partisan politics and military service. However, since 1983, they have been urged to seek compatible ways to become involved in the social and economic developments affecting their communities of residence.

My Experiences and Reflections on Baha'i

My first Baha'i meeting was in the late 1960s. Most Baha'i gatherings are in people's homes. Jacksonville, Florida, had a modest center; some locales rent spaces. There are now seven global Baha'i Houses of Worship. I have visited those in Wilmette, Illinois, Haifa, Israel, New Delhi (a gorgeous concrete and marble lotus), and Kampala, Uganda. I have found Baha'is to be positive, enthusiastic, hopeful people, who are evangelical about the Baha'i faith and determined to embrace humanity and treat people fairly.

Baha'is welcome everyone, meet in small groups, and largely remain local and informal in organization. One becomes a Baha'i by attending home meetings, joining, and, in some countries, also signing a card that pledges agreement with Baha'i scriptures; beyond that, there are no ongoing participation requirements or commitments. Any group of nine adults may become a local assembly. While Baha'i has no clergy; the international headquarters staff appoints counselors and assistants to work with volunteers at national and local levels. Active members are urged to continually recruit new participants, and activists are encouraged to become *Pioneers,* who move to new geographic locations where they try to interest new people in the Baha'i faith—I've met several in my travels.

Baha'i membership statistics supposedly reflect a growth comparable to the Mormons'. While Baha'is are persecuted and excluded in Islamic countries, the Baha'i still view membership as growing there. According to *The World Almanac,* there are 3.6 million in Asia, including 2.2 million in India, and 350,000 in Iran, 1.8 million in Africa, almost a million in South America, and 150,000 in the U.S. Though I studied religion in India repeatedly during a twenty-year period, I met few Baha'is there. Their houses of worship and historic sites in Acre and Haifa were practically empty, so while I don't doubt Baha'is' global enthusiasm, I do doubt their international statistics.

I find most Baha'i principles constructive and compatible with my own values. Their fervent embrace of diversity and their striving for unity in diversity, their quest for global understanding, balance of science and spirituality, warm local communities, and international responsibility are credible elements of a 21st-century faith. Baha'is seem to have managed better at keeping spirituality in their religion, and their spiritual practices embedded within their ethical activism, than have many Unitarian Universalists, Humanists, and Ethical Culturists. I understand their conscientious objection to military service and their abstention from partisan politics; however, these positions often make Baha'is ineffective because they're unwilling to take sides in any conflict. While they wish to treat women as social equals, their governing House of Justice is limited to men. They seek world peace, but in

334

my experience, they've been unwilling to become involved in disarmament or peace activism as "too divisive or political."

Brahmo and Arya Samaj Movements

Two movements that began in 19th-century India and extended into the 20th century presented liberal alternatives to traditional Hinduism, which had not had a major reform movement since the 15th century. In 1828, Ram Mohan Roy founded the *Brahmo Samaj* in Calcutta. He interpreted the Upanishads as advocating a monotheistic God, created weekly services that included readings from the Upanishads, hymn singing, and sermons based on a Christian model but grounded in Hinduism. He opposed child marriage, infanticide, the burning of widows, and polygamy. In the mid-19th century, Debendranath Tagore assumed Brahmo Samaj leadership. He deemphasized Christian elements, rejected the veneration of images, reincarnation, and avatars, and emphasized the need for social reform, ethical actions, and a scientific education. In 1865, Keshab Chandra Sen challenged Tagore's leadership and the Samaj divided. Sen, while emphasizing the singing of Hindu *kirtans*, was also devoted to Christ and added a more Christian tone to his subsect's services. In India, I worked with the Brahmo Samaj through the IARF. It continues social services, and their historic leadership in the state of West Bengal was impressive. While the Brahmo Samaj remained primarily a Bengali elite movement, a third subgroup, the *Arya Samaj*, attracted grassroots support, mostly in Punjab and Uttar Pradesh provinces. It championed non-idolatrous monotheism and social reforms, but accepted reincarnation and the Vedas. It retained more traditional Hindu worship elements than the Brahmo Samaj, but also rejected the adoration of images, avatars, and yogic meditation—all mainstream Hindu elements that most Hindus are unwilling to forgo.

The Ramakrishna Mission

Ramakrishna (1834–1886) was a mystical Hindu sage. An illiterate devotee of the goddess Kali, he attracted disciples from all levels of Hindu society and impressed Westerners as a spiritual inspiration because he not only embraced a variety of Hindu spiritual disciplines but practiced elements of Christianity and Islam, and concluded that all religions were true. He embraced image worship in order to use form to reach the formless. While focused on Hinduism's traditional God-realization, Ramakrishna supported social services. As he said: "If you want to swim in the sea of Brahman, you must make many ineffectual attempts before you can successfully swim there….the mind when unrestrained luxuriates in idle thoughts, but when vanity and egotism drop away, Divinity manifests itself."[1]

Ramakrishna's foremost disciple was Swami Vivekananda, who founded Vedanta Societies in the United States and Europe, also organized the Ramakrishna Mission in India. Its monks and nuns combined yogic meditation with social service and reform movements, and it became the primary exponent of Vedanta Hinduism worldwide. They established hospitals, orphanages, schools, and lending libraries in India, and their Calcutta center, Gold Park, is a beautiful and moving spiritual complex. I've attended Vedanta Societies in several locations, most recently in Carmichael, California. Attendance at Vedanta Centers and events have introduced thousands of Westerners to Hindu wisdom, particularly the Upanishads. Focused on spiritual liberation, they recognize human differences and point to disciplines that anyone can use to realize their intrinsic divinity, while they also help people face their own limitations and the world's complexity. I cherish Vedanta's recognition that each person is different, so you and I must find our own unique ways to wisdom and grace.

Hinduism and Buddhism Transplanted to the U.S.

Hindu teachers, groups, and spiritual practices have deeply impacted millions of Americans and other Westerners. These influences began with the Transcendentalists and were then much enhanced by the Vedanta Societies in the early 20th century. In the 19th and early 20th centuries, the Theosophical Society, which radically mixed Victorian iconoclastic mysticism with Hindu philosophy, attracted thousands of Europeans and several million Indians. The first resident Indian yoga master in the U.S. was Paramahansa Yogananda, who taught traditional yoga but combined it with his Church of All Religions, which resembled Christian fellowships in structure. A plethora of gurus, seers, and movements followed, which included a spectrum of groups: the bhakti Krishna Consciousness movement with its aggressive and mercenary missionaries; the child guru, Maharaj-ji; Yogi Bhajan's kundalini yoga, which shifted toward a type of Sikhism; the Maharishi Mahesh Yogi, whose Transcendental Meditation provided millions of Americans with a formulistic mantra and a simple meditation practice.

During my forty-year UU ministry, I served many congregants who had had powerful Hindu and Buddhist spiritual experiences, and I interacted with a variety of Hindu and Buddhist organizations. In Bloomington, Indiana, there was an urban ashram with Hindu and Buddhist roots but young American leadership that involved more than a hundred residents and a thriving vegetarian restaurant. In New Jersey, it was primarily individual Jain, Hindu, and Buddhist masters and seminars at the Omega Institute in Rhinebeck, New York. In New Jersey and Sacramento, California, my contacts with Sikhs were more substantial, and in Florida, one Jacksonville congregant's primary spiritual practice was with a Hindu yoga master at his rural retreat. An American Buddhist monk lived in a room of the Jacksonville UU Church, where he translated Chinese Buddhist texts while leading a small meditation group that included several members of the congregation.

According to a survey conducted in April 2015 by the U.S. National Institute of Health, approximately 21 million U.S. adults and almost 2 million children now practice yoga. Nearly 18 million adults and 1 million children practice meditation. Both yoga and meditation are spreading rapidly across all age groups and ethnicities. Millions more practice some form of Tai Chi or Qigong. *Vipassana* is the Pali term for discernment or insight. Vipassana meditators make a distinction between bare, or dry, insights gained without regular, disciplined meditative practice and Vipassana meditation. They focus their practice on three characteristics of Buddhist understanding: impermanence, suffering, and no-self, discerning one's own mental and physical faculties as they really are, which they believe purifies the mind by eliminating mental conflict.

My seventy-five-year-old niece, Rebecca Reagan, has dedicated a considerable portion of her nonvocational life to the *Ba Shin* tradition of Vipassana meditation. Its founder and formative leader was Sayagyi U Ba Khin. The son of Indian Hindu parents, he grew up in Burma, became an accountant, and then learned Vipassana from Burmese Buddhist masters. His Ba Shin tradition now has Indian, American, and European teachers and a hundred centers worldwide. Since the mid-1970s, my niece has sat for two hours daily, and now hosts a small online group from her home. She describes her practice and its effects on her life as follows:

> I learned to detach from my pain, to observe the changes, and slowly quiet the mind's chattering. Gradually, I gained some equanimity. It's challenging to learn to face what is, and not what you want life to be. I have made longtime friends through the practice and feel that this practice was my destiny. It is important, for me, that the religious doctrinal aspects of the practice are inclusive. I am happy also being active in a local UU congregation while remaining dedicated to my daily Vipassana practice. It has given me the ability to become both a freer spirit and a more adequately disciplined and responsible person, but I still have plenty of work to do, including still being too self-preoccupied.

Elements of Liberal Religions that I Find Troubling

My primary concern about liberal religions is the tendency of many of their followers to become so obsessed with individualism that they become closet anarchists and adopt libertarian leanings that make them unwilling or unable to work well together. Many become so dedicated to secularism that they can't accept, express, share, or celebrate their own emotional religious feelings or spiritual practices effectively, which limits their own fulfillment and life satisfaction, and starves their social effectiveness. For me, worship of the individual is self-idolatry and neurotic egotism.

The Relevance of Liberal Religions for Me

This book is essentially about my belief that essential principles of liberal religions may be applied to all global religious and spiritual practices, and that by doing so, those practices would become more useful to people, and help them gain greater spiritual depth.

Chapter 17
Contemporary Indigenous, Neopagan, and Feminist Spiritualities

Indigenous People Today

There are more than 500 million people whose primary spiritual faiths and religious practices are identified as indigenous. Also, by the late 20th century, as many as 2 million non-indigenous people, primarily in Europe and North America, were demonstrating interest in the traditions of indigenous peoples. My brother, for example, attended Plains Indian sweat lodges. Most indigenous religionists today, however, are descendants of the ancient dwellers in those geographic locations; they live in small groups organized as tribes or clans, and primarily work as hunter-gatherers in isolated locations or as subsistence farmers on marginal agricultural lands. They've survived by remaining isolated and/or by adopting useful elements from more dominant cultures. Many have a veneer adapted from a major historic religion, but their predominant religious beliefs and spiritual practices remain indigenous.

Africa has the largest indigenous population, which represents 25 percent of its residents; in India 15 percent, and in Latin America 13 percent overall and 40 percent of the population in its rural areas. Indigenous people endure in every nation. In countries such as China and Japan, many modern citizens believe in and conscientiously practice elements of their archaic faiths, and indigenous practices and beliefs are probably more widespread in other nations than is generally acknowledged.

Indigenous religions vary widely, but tend to share certain elements: Polytheism, the worship of gods, goddesses, and spirits that represent aspects of nature and human life; animism: endowing living things or inanimate objects with spirits and powers that humans may, through connections, knowledge, sacrifices, or rituals, access and use for good or evil. Some objects or practices become particularly sacred while others become forbidden or taboo. Most have spiritual specialists credited with the ability to access the spirit world, heal and/or threaten others, divine the future, or manipulate natural forces with magic, fetishism (using the powers inherent in objects), shamanism (conjuring spirits through bewitchment or exorcism), and magic (aversive, e.g., transferring guilt to a scapegoat, or productive, e.g., rain dances or sacrifices).

Neopaganism

In every UU congregation I served, there was a small group of members who identified their primary spiritual orientation as Pagan or Neopagan. The Jacksonville congregation had a flourishing group of twenty participants in its UU Pagan Circle. One individual there was descended from generations of Polish pagan family roots. Most neopagans, however, become fascinated with a particular archaic spirituality, such as the Egyptians, Norse, Celtic, or Mayan, read about it on their own, and begin to practice some of its rituals and traditions. Others adopt a pagan label and develop an individual or small group practice modeled generally on elements of ancient Western European spiritualities. There are many male neopagans; in my Florida congregation, there was a professional military man who was openly pagan, but neopaganism is predominantly a female and exuberantly feminist movement, and appears attractive to individuals who feel like outcasts from their dominant cultures.

After WWII, ethnic spiritual movements strengthened in Central and Eastern Europe as democracy and religious freedom grew and Communism weakened. These people sought to limit membership to those within their ethnic group and tried to reconstruct the beliefs and traditions of their pre-Christian ancestors. These Reconstructionists emphasize the centrality of their ethnic group in archaic Europe, support authoritarian political stances, resist immigration, and oppose multiculturalism in their nations. Many are attracted to the occult. Such groups have much strengthened in post-Soviet

Eastern Europe, with white power and other allied groups reflecting similar tendencies, often based on flimsier ethnic evidence.

Most other neopagans are eclectic in their beliefs and practices. Most are found in the United Kingdom, other predominantly Caucasian areas of the British Commonwealth, and in the U.S. Wiccan and Druid interests and practices grew in 20th-century Britain, where they held periodic festivals at Stonehenge and other ancient memorial sites. The 1960s and 1970s featured a resurgence of pagan traditions in Britain and the United States. Also, a greater public awareness of paganism was created with the 1979 publications of Starhawk's *The Spiral Dance: A Rebirth of the Ancient Religion of the Great Goddess,* and sociologist Margot Adler's *Drawing Down the Moon: Witches, Druids, Goddess-Worshippers, and Other Pagans in America.* In the 1980s, there were large public festivals, and many variations of neopaganism developed, often heavily influenced by counterculture and new-age ideas, along with communal and back-to-the-land movements. American groups are usually enthusiastically eclectic and welcoming, in contrast to earlier traditional British circles that often-emphasized secrecy and initiatory lineage.

Adler, a UU herself, found that many neopagans had had personal spiritual experiences that involved the presence of spirits, and shared a strong desire to participate in or organize rituals. Most were avid readers who have active imaginations. There are about 1 million neopagans in the United States today. Ninety percent are Caucasian, and 9 percent are Native American. Most have college degrees, a middle-class or higher income, are attracted to folktales and magic, are spiritually drawn to nature, and are often ecologically concerned. Neopagans reject Christian orthodoxies and enjoy contrasting their exuberance, joy, fun, and humor with their views or experience of Judeo-Christianity as solemn and strict.

Most neopagans venerate multiple goddesses and gods who embody forces of nature, aspects of culture, or psychological traits. Some believe these deities are real and can be communicated with, while others view them as Jungian archetypes or other mental constructs that exist in our psyches and meet our need for meaning and order. They acknowledge the faults of their deities. Many neopagans seek to incorporate female aspects of the divine into their worship and their lives, to reinvest aspects of the natural world with spirit, to revere the Earth, and to see everything as interconnected.

They understand ancient peoples to have accumulated wisdom that most moderns have lost, and passionately seek to rediscover this wisdom through reverence and ritual. In 1995, the UU Association added to our UU statement of its traditions, led by neopagans, feminists, and environmental activists: "Spiritual teachings of Earth-centered traditions that celebrate the sacred circle of life and instruct us to live in harmony with the rhythms of nature."

Neopagan Sects

Wiccans are the largest group of eclectic neopagans, encompassing varied forms of modern witchcraft. Wiccans are duo-theistic; they venerate a Goddess and a horned God engaged in a yearly cycle of waxing and waning power. The God is perpetually born out of the Goddess, and the Goddess progresses through maiden, Earth Mother, and crone forms in the course of the year and every human life. The primary times of festival and ritual are seasonal holidays. Wiccans believe in a variety of ancient mythologies and magic, and believe in reincarnation and karma. They seek wisdom, and experience deity, in ordinary life events. Englishman Gerald Gardner initiated the New Forest coven (1939); since then, many forms of Wicca have developed. Most Wiccans perceive themselves as "white" (good-positive) witches/warlocks who live in harmony with nature and other people, and perform helpful and healing acts and rituals, as opposed to "black" magic— trying to harm others.

The second largest pagan group is the Neo-Druids. Druids were the priest caste among ancient Celts. An Order of Druids was founded in 1781, with aspects of freemasonry, and by 1905, rituals were practiced at Stonehenge. An American Order of Druids was founded in 1912, and additional Druid groups were founded beginning in the 1960s. Heathenry groups, usually derived from Norse mythology, also attracted followers. Heathens are polytheistic realists; some believe their deities are genuine entities, others view them as Jungian archetypes. Several Pagan groups are centered on LGBTQ activism: the Minoan Brotherhood, Radical Faeries, and the Adonis group; and two lesbian groups, the Dianic Wicca, and the Minoan Sisterhood.

The connections between New Age spiritualities and neopaganism are many, as are their sources of disagreement and mutual criticism. Thousands of Americans and Europeans have tried elements from both modern trends. New Agers usually focus on an improved future, while neopagans look back to a pre-Christian past. New Age movements typically present universalistic messages that tend to view all religions and spiritualities as fundamentally similar, while neopagans stress the significant differences they perceive between their polytheistic-animistic faiths and the strict monotheisms of the religions of the Book. New Age movements generally show little interest in magic and witchcraft, which conversely are central interests for neopagans. It's not unusual for members of each group to use the other's name as an insult, and to distance themselves from each other. New Agers often think neopagans are too materialistic and are caught in archaic myths and rituals, while neopagans consider New Agers too esoteric and engaging in experimental techniques unrelated to cultural history or everyday realities.

Rituals are central for most neopagans, both in their individual or family practices and in their group and public festivals. Though various neopagan groups have different rituals connected with their ancestral or chosen archaic roots, they all generally strive for altered states of consciousness and hope to shift their mindsets beyond ordinary life. They use visualization, chanting, song, dance, meditation, and drumming to increase the likelihood of religious ecstasy. Neopagans are exceptional among Western religious groups in that they intentionally seek ecstasy, joy, abandon, fun, humor, and even silliness as valid parts of their spiritual experience. Individual and family practices focus on offerings at a home altar accompanied by prayers, song, candles, and incense. Animal sacrifices were common in archaic paganism but are extremely rare among neopagans.

Neopagan Festivals

Neopagan festivals are based on an annual agricultural calendar and on Wiccan combinations and adaptations from European archaic practices. A modern invention called the Wheel of the Year largely adopted Anglo-Saxon and Celtic motifs and names. The American Asatru movement, a branch of the Heathens, added Days of Remembrance that honor heroes of Germanic history and even the Viking Leif Ericson, iconic leader of perhaps the earliest European settlement in North America. This annual cycle honors the perpetual round of growth and retreat, of the Sun's death and rebirth, and is understood to reflect the life cycles of both nature and humans. No ancient community is known to have celebrated all eight of these holidays or sabbats, which include: Yule, Imbolc, Ostara, Beltane, Lithe, Lammas, Mabon, and Samhain.

Yule is the winter solstice, a midwinter time of feasting and gift giving, wreaths, evergreen trees, and the use of holly, ivy, and mistletoe. Imbolc, which falls on the first of February, celebrates the first spring equinox, a time for spring cleaning, purification, and pledges. Ostara, the vernal equinox, is the point when the days begin to grow longer than the nights, a time for fertility and the rebirth of vegetation, and is celebrated by egg decorating. Beltane is the first day of summer. a time for flowers and maypole dancing that celebrates the crowning of the May Queen. Lithe is the midsummer festival, when the sun shines longest—a good time to sail the seas when they're gentle and navigable. Lammas is the first of three Wiccan harvest festivals, celebrated by baking bread, a festival of the harvest's first fruits. Mabon is the autumn equinox, a time for thanksgiving, a recognition of the need to share our bounty with all as the trials of winter draw near. Samhain is a time to honor those who have died, a festival of darkness in which the departed spirits are invited to be among the celebrants.

Most indigenous peoples and most neopagans honor the directions and seasons; many UU congregations honor the primary seasons by "calling the directions" at a Sunday service. The example below is Rev. Joan Goodwin's "To the four directions" from the UUA's *Singing the Living Tradition,* #446:

> Spirit of the East, of air, morning, and springtime: Be with us as the sun rises, in times of beginning, of planting. Inspire us with the fresh breath of courage as we go forth into new adventures. Spirit of the South, of fire, noontime, and summer: Be with us through the heat of the day and help us to be ever growing. Warm us with strength and energy for the work that awaits us. Spirit of the West, of water, evening, and autumn: Be with us as the sun sets and help us to enjoy a rich harvest. Flow through us with a cooling, healing quietness and bring us peace. Spirit of the North, of earth, nighttime,

and winter: Be with us in the darkness, the time of gestation. Ground us in the wisdom of the changing seasons as we celebrate the spiraling journey of our lives.[1]

The Goddess Movement

The Goddess movement is central to many eclectic neopagan movements. It emphasizes a monotheistic Goddess who is given predominance. Goddess spirituality revolves around the sacredness of the female form and aspects of women's lives traditionally neglected in patriarchal history. Goddess worshippers emphasize *her-story,* focus on women's roles, and assert that a relatively peaceful and harmonious period of European prehistory preceded traditional Western history. This Earth Mother era was matriarchal, egalitarian, nonviolent, and focused on the Goddess, but was overthrown by violent patriarchal invaders who worshipped sky gods, believed in power by violation, and cemented their rule through Christianity.

Elements of Indigenous, Neopagan, and Goddess Movements that I Find Problematic

I find various images of the divine useful, but I don't literally believe in them as beings or worship them as sacrosanct idols. I view many natural beings and objects as reflecting spiritual power and aspects of spirit, but don't credit everything as radiating spiritual potency. I seek awe and wonder in what I encounter and believe that things we don't yet understand might appear magical, but I don't usually credit people or situations with magical powers. I respect what I find worthy in indigenous traditions and honor the ways they've produced outstanding individuals and cooperative communities among their practitioners, but I don't systematically practice any surviving indigenous faith. I honor the seasons and aspects of nature, and delight in many neopagans' willingness to find joy, enthusiasm, and humor in their faiths, but I don't believe or practice any current neopagan religion. I perceive Creation to be beyond gender, and celebrate feminine virtues as often superior to male excesses, but I reject attempts to denigrate maleness or femaleness as surely as I wouldn't elevate one race or ethnicity above others.

Elements of Indigenous, Neopagan, and Feminist Spiritualities that I Find Most Relevant

My introduction to indigenous populations was with the Native Americans who had lived in Kansas, as well as the Cherokee and Creek tribes who were the earliest settlers on what later became my family's Georgia farm. By the 20th century, most of the Plains tribes had been driven north or been moved to Oklahoma reservations, to which the Cherokee and Creek peoples were exiled, the terminus of their 1839 Trail of Tears. My personal evidence was the arrowheads I found in Kansas and Georgia. Our summer Scout camp attempted to imitate "Indian" male maturation rituals, which in the third year culminated with finding a ten-plus-pound rock on which you carved your initials. The rock was then hidden five miles away, and with a rudimentary map, I and other would-be "warriors" had to find our rocks and carry them around for the rest of the day. Campers who succeeded were given "Indian" names. The ordeal was meaningful for me. As a young teen, I read John Collier's *The Indians of the Americas*. A sociologist, Collier had been the Commissioner of Indian Affairs under F.D.R. He wrote that American Indian spirituality had expressed reverence for human personalities and the web of life on Earth since the Stone Age and deserved to become a sacred fire in all of us. He helped me understand that the Cherokees and Creeks were as or more civilized than many of the early Europeans settlers, and that aspects of Plains Indian life were as ethical and more ecologically advanced than those of many early white settlers that displaced them.

As an adult, I've read about various contemporary indigenous groups worldwide, and had opportunities for brief visits with indigenous peoples on several continents. My most extended contact was with the Khasi, in the northeast corner of India. They are a modernized people, some of whom have become Unitarian-Universalists. I've had moving spiritual experiences in a number of these settings: an overnight death celebration in the Khasi Hills; a visit with my Jain mother-in-law to a New Mexico Navaho reservation; standing on a hill on Isla Taquile in Lake Titicaca; at an indigenous-controlled jungle lodge in Bolivia's Madidi National Park; a kava ceremony in Fiji; and an Australian walkabout with an aboriginal woman in Kakadu National Park. These contacts have given me a strong sense of those I came to know as having deep wisdom about their native places, strong cooperative and empathetic people skills, and a radiant sense of the sacredness of the natural world and the human family. They have adapted as needed to the modern world but strive to preserve the beauty of their native places and the deep humanity, joy, and insights of their peoples.

My one weekly indigenous-inspired spiritual practice is to don my Blackfoot elkhorn necklace and shake my Lake Titicaca rain gourd as I go around our apartment as part of my Monday morning prayers. This act pays respect to the objects from our personal histories and travels that bless our home which include indigenous objects from six continents. In nature, I often feel awed and at one with the cosmos, and predictably become embraced by a sense of time and space beyond the ordinary.

My primary neopagan experiences have been with neopagan members of the UU congregations I served, particularly during my decade in Jacksonville with that congregation's exuberant and active neopagan group. I find myself moved periodically to use Goodwin's call to the directions, but I don't routinely practice any neopagan rites.

Inspirations I Draw from Feminism and Feminist Spirituality

My own understanding of and support for feminism began in my adolescence when my mother, then in her fifties, went back to school to get a junior college degree. Later, I worked with liberated and militant women in civil rights and disarmament efforts. In graduate school, I helped to start a St. Louis chapter of Students for a Democratic Society (SDS), and women were my primary allies in trying to preserve the egalitarian, democratic, and noncommunist nature of that chapter, in the face of backward attempts by a few other men who believed they knew what needed to be done and wanted to take charge.

In Bloomington, Indiana, from 1971 to 1977, the campus and town buzzed with women's liberation actions that played a central role in my experiences there. Congregation and community were filled with capable, highly educated women, usually un- or underemployed, and seldom sufficiently respected or compensated for their employment. Within months of my arrival, the congregation's women's alliance announced that they would no longer take responsibility for the church kitchen during social events. The congregation became filled with intimate women's groups; many women and men were experimenting with new relationships and sexual experiences. Almost all of us were challenged to change our assumptions and expectations, given the changing consciousness of the women around us. Women of all ages spoke up, demanded leadership roles, and stridently argued for a more liberated culture. In my years there, I helped women who wanted an abortion (then illegal in Indiana) travel to neighboring states where they could safely receive one. I sent those who wanted to have their babies to a Catholic-led service for women unable to raise their babies alone, and the Catholic priest sent women who wanted an abortion to me. Then, in 1973, the U.S. Supreme Court struck down state laws that restricted a woman's right to an abortion during the first trimester of a pregnancy, and granted legislators only limited regulatory rights in the second trimester. In the years since, women's efforts for liberation, equal treatment, and respect have massively impacted the efforts of other civil rights activists, and stimulated greater awareness about global income inequality.

In 1973, Catholic theologian Mary Daly published *Beyond God the Father: Toward a Philosophy of Women's Liberation*. She wrote that Jesus had treated women and men equally, and that Christians needed to do likewise. She announced that God should not be personified at all, that *God is a verb, an embodiment of be-ing*. Every woman can and should uncover the mysteries of her own history. Daly herself began to use the term "Goddess" instead of "God." By 1979, Gloria Steinem had started *MS* magazine and was becoming the Susan B. Anthony of her generation, uniting women in a sisterhood around common needs. Feminism's successes fired a backlash throughout the 1980s and early '90s. Steinem continually reminded Americans that while women had won the right to be educated, run for office, and do "men's jobs," most Americans still hadn't even embraced the idea, much less the policies and actions, that men should do an equitable portion of so-called women's work: childrearing, homemaking, teaching children, and caring for the frail and sick.

In 1982, Harvard psychologist Carol Gilligan published *In A Different Voice: Psychological Theory and Women's Development*, which became a feminist

as important, and which extend therapeutic practices not only beyond ego boundaries but even beyond the limitations of time and space.

Some Higher Conscious practitioners believe there were ancient continents—now lost—with advanced cultures with technologies still unrevealed. This ancient age of spiritual wisdom was replaced in human history by the Age of Pisces, during which technology advanced but' spirituality declined. Now, a new age has dawned, the Age of Aquarius, which will gradually universalize love, joy, peace, abundance, and harmony. There is no consensus about when this New Age began. Perhaps it was in the 1960s, or in 1987 with the Harmonic Convergence (the world's first synchronized global peace meditation), and it might require centuries more to come to full fruition. Meanwhile, individuals should live with ecological prudence and advance their own consciousness, furthering the world's spiritual evolution with global concern for all.

The Evolution and Expansion of Higher-Consciousness Spiritualities

Higher-Consciousness spirituality developed in the 1960s and '70s, reached its peak popularity in the 1980s, and continues to spread and develop. Useful academic references include: James R. Lewis and J. Gordon Melton, *Perspectives on the New Age;* Michael York, *The Emerging Network: A Sociology of the New Age and Neo-Pagan Movements; New Age Religion in Western Culture;* Wouter Hanegraaff, *Esoterism in the Mirror of Secular Thought;* and, Paul Heelas, *The New Age Movement: Religion, Culture, and Society in the Age of Postmodernity.* Also see *Spiritual Life: A Journal of Contemporary Spirituality.*

Susan Brown points out in Lewis and Melton's book that the movement began with the baby boomers, but then grew widely in Western, English-speaking cultures and beyond, partly in response to disappointment felt by many former activists who had failed to change the world, and decided instead to concentrate on transforming themselves. Michael York, a sociologist of religion, suggests Higher-Consciousness spirituality can be divided into three trends: social groups that seek to bring about social change; spiritual groups that seek contact with spiritual entities, especially through channeling; and a spiritual camp that represents a middle path focused on individual development.

Its historical roots reach back to 18th-century seekers such as Emanuel Swedenborg, who tried to unite science and religion, predicted a coming new era, and claimed an ability to communicate with angels, demons, and spirits. A 19th-century proponent, Helena Blavatsky, practiced occult rituals and claimed that her Theosophical Society conveyed the essence of all world religions. A historic progenitor in the early 20th century was New Thought, a Christian-oriented healing movement in the U.S. Carl Jung urged people to develop their shadow sides, tap into humanity's collective unconscious, and prepare for the Age of Aquarius. Edgar Cayce was a seminal influence with his Association for Research and Enlightenment, which focused on his and others' channeling experiences.

In the 1960s, counterculture and hippie movements emerged; they strove to build new paradigms, rejected traditional religions and values, and sought to replace them with communities of individual growth and communal harmony. Zen Centers, Transcendental Meditation, and Soka Gakkai became popular, along with communes and ashrams. New Age workshop centers, such as the Esalen Institute in Big Sur, California, and the Omega Institute in Woodstock, New York, became testing grounds that offered workshops on organizational development, humanistic psychology, and the growth of human potential. Some of the early organizations and scholarship began in the United Kingdom, such as Scotland's Findhorn, founded in 1962, which eventually became an organic-ecological commune.

The 1970s in the U.S. saw the flourishing of Higher-Consciousness ideas, leaders, and programs. Werner Erhard introduced *EST*, a training course that emotionally drained and challenged thousands of participants. Psychologist-turned-Hindu mystic Baba Ram Dass led an exuberant group of advocates that attracted many helping professionals and secular spiritual searchers. Helen Schucman's *A Course in Miracles* (1972) billed itself as a correction to Christianity, based on the premise of original innocence rather than original sin. Marianne Williamson, whose book, *A Return to Love* (1992), transformed *A Course in Miracles* into a New Age scripture and Williamson into a Higher-Consciousness priestess. She focused on ego formation, and promoted religion without rules, and salvation without significant sacrifices. Love conquers all; focus on feelings, and happiness and prosperity will follow. The center of Higher-Consciousness spirituality is the Esalen Institute, established in 1962 on land owned by Michael Murphy, as an alternative to traditional psychiatry, academia, and traditional religions that organized a broad spectrum of workshops "free of dogmas." The first lecturer was Alan Watts; the initial seminar was on human potential. Abraham Maslow became an important Esalen figure, but it was gestalt therapist Fritz Perls whose five-year stay came to characterize Esalen. Encounter-group leader Will Schultz became its resident leader. Murphy has been featured in *Look, The New York Times, The New Yorker,* and *Life* magazine, ran programs year-round, and held conferences in the U.S. and Europe.

Today, Esalen still offers a variety of workshops, from spiritual awareness to wilderness experience and Tai Chi. In 1980, Esalen began Soviet-American exchange programs that included Boris Yeltsin's first U.S. trip. After Gorbachev withdrew from Soviet leadership, he became Esalen's "state of the world" forum chairman. Other exchanges included Chinese, Jews, Christians, and Muslims together who promoted mutual understanding. Workshops and longer programs are pricey. In 2014, Esalen's total revenue was $16 million. Historian Christopher Lasch criticized Esalen as easy spirituality, saying that its techniques encourage narcissism, self-obsession, and spiritual materialism, but Esalen continues as the iconic New Age center.

Michael Murphy remains a preeminent figure in the movement. Esalen's research arm has published a shelf full of books, many with Murphy as lead author. His International Integral Transformative Practice (ITP) provides nationwide programs for aficionados of Higher-Consciousness spirituality. One 2017 program was entitled "New Paradigm Populism: Creating a Path Toward a Spiritual Civilization." It featured "insights from quantum physics, the power of shared purpose and the indomitable will of the heart needed to be fair to our fellow humans. Murphy's 1971 novel, *Golf in the Kingdom,* remains a bestselling golf book, and spawned a nonprofit that explores the transformational potential of sport. The movie version turns golf into a mystic spiritual search that evokes "signals of the damned" (golf carts and Hiroshima) and transcendence—like walking a golf course, "a perspective free from any attachments." His 1992 *The Future of the Body: Explorations into the Further Evolution of Human Nature* provides a cross-cultural collection of extraordinary human functioning including healings, clairvoyance, and feats of superhuman strength.

During the 1980s, there were thousands of New Age shops full of incense, candles, books, tapes, and magazines, and an explosion of New Age masters who led workshops, training courses, healing centers, and provided opportunities for personal transformation. The largest mass New Age event was the Harmonic Convergence in Sedona, Arizona, in August 1987, organized by Jose Arguelles. Participants envisioned a direct physical and spiritual connection with the forces of the universe. The Convergence is considered exemplary of the new paradigm's mass rituals. New Age was significantly transforming itself into Higher-Consciousness spirituality. Finding themselves in an "ocean of oneness," whose energies they saw expressed in varicolored auras that surrounded them and others, participants celebrated the interrelationships and interconnections among all things. They rejected the dualisms of religions of the Book and scorned scientific and secular reductionism in favor of the Gaia hypothesis, ecological concerns, and celebrations of the transformational spiritual evolutions of people like themselves. They sought to recover the sacred wisdom of ancient peoples without falling prey to their ignorance or savagery; to reject society's hypocrisies while reluctant to lose any of its advantages. The physical world was only a meaningful illusion to be used for spiritual growth so that individual souls could move on to higher consciousness.

Scholar Paul Heelas proposed that New Age spiritual practitioners comprised three populations: those dedicated to its ideals who often made their living as New Age professionals—selling books or periodicals, leading workshops, or providing personal healings and counseling; serious part-timers employed in unrelated fields who spent significant recreational time involved in New Age activities; and casual part-timers who got involved occasionally. This fit the 1980s "enterprise culture" perfectly: it was consumer-based, with leaders who marketed their techniques as useful products, even as commodities. Some said their programs guaranteed creativity, success, wealth, or power. Corporations found New Age methods useful tools to increase employee productivity and efficiency. Today, high-tech businesses help personnel practice mindfulness to reduce stress and enhance job performance.

Eckhart Tolle, born in Germany and now a Canadian citizen, has sold millions of copies of *The Power of Now* and *A New Earth: Awakening to Your Life's Purpose*. Tolle believes that the spirituality of traditional religions has become obscured and part of our cultural insanity. Consciousness transcends our ego-based sensitivities; we should not identify with our memories, thoughts, or past emotional pains, and should realize that awareness is separate from ordinary thoughts. This is a prerequisite for personal happiness and to end violent world conflicts. People need a witnessing consciousness, to learn from their mistakes, and must concentrate on actions rather than results or conclusions. Accept the reality of each situation and change what you can. Sin is a lack of love, a mistake to be corrected rather than an evil to be punished. Rationality and science have become our masters. Our destiny is to reconnect with the divine reality of the moment, find portals through which love can enter, and access the infinitely creative womb of existence, all without craving love.

Wayne Dyer became a public television staple. His self-help books and electronic offerings have sold in the millions. His can-do strategies, as well as several of his catchphrases—"avoid your erroneous zones," "escape the traps of negative thinking," and "take control of your life"—have become pervasive. Dyer grew up in foster homes and learned that his destiny was in his own hands. Once a professor of education, he found that he could be more successful as a New Age guru. His philosophical beliefs included sovereign individualism, a higher power, and an eternal human soul: "Your life is a parenthesis in eternity."

Oprah Winfrey has become a media spiritual guide for millions of Americans. Her blessing of a book often guarantees its financial success. *The Oprah Winfrey Show* became the most highly rated in TV history. Now a billionaire with her own media empire, she was raised in the Black Protestant tradition, but doesn't attend church regularly now. She loves what the Black church offers culturally, particularly for addicted people, but seeks a more inclusive spiritual world. Without trying to define God, she wants to help others remain open to the mystical and to mysteries. Her own daily spiritual practices include six hours' sleep, morning silence to center her soul, continuing expressions of gratitude, a gratitude journal, striving to live in the moment, and kneeling to pray before sleeping. Her religious efforts are:

To connect the dots of every heart's yearning for something greater than ourselves, to build a universe of interfaith connectedness where people can see that other people in different parts of the world are very much like them. We each wish to know the power of the divine and to become connected with what is holy and eternal during our lives.[1]

Higher-Consciousness Spirituality Today

By the beginning of the 21st century, there were perhaps a million Higher-Consciousness professionals and possibly 10 million serious part-timers. Higher-Consciousness spiritual participants have been and continue to be mostly white, upper middle-class, and college educated. Higher-Consciousness spirituality is essentially spirituality for the privileged, with costly workshops and isolated retreat centers.

One large branch of the Higher-Consciousness spiritual tree is the healer complex: Addiction counselors, therapists, advisors, and consultants. Some embrace most of the prevalent beliefs, techniques, and accoutrements of Higher-Consciousness; others are either traditional healers with Higher-Consciousness clients, or trained therapists who use some Higher-Consciousness ideas. Most are less interested in proving that life exists after death or in experimentally verifying experiences for consistency than in celebrating their clients' anecdotes of feeling better after extraordinary personal spiritual experiences. For instance, past-life regression is sometimes sought to learn how clients healed from injuries during previous incarnations to better face current physical or emotional challenges. Healers involved with esoteric systems often integrate traditional religious healing models with contemporary technologies; they perform healings not only in person and by touch, but also by letter, phone, email, text, tweet, and Zoom. Their healing may involve acupuncture, herbal medicine, massage, homeopathy, chiropractic, or biofeedback. Millions listen to new age music, world music, or participate in drumming circles, ecstatic dancing, or chanting as spiritual experiences.

The human potential movement unites transpersonal therapists, counselors, advisors, and consultants who try to empower the healthy aspects of individuals who feel that they have been alienated or suppressed. Human potential practitioners take religious and mystical experiences seriously and believe that spirituality can help people achieve equilibrium and fulfillment. They embrace holistic health models, which assert that people become whole by integrating with the wisdom of the natural world and the spiritual powers of the universe. Most are open to the possibility that there are benevolent powers—beyond our ordinary experience or scientific documentation—that are able and willing to help to heal and strengthen people. They all emphasize positive thinking and lifelong development.

The late Frances E. Vaughan, a transpersonal psychologist, addressed Higher-Consciousness spirituality in her book *Awakening Intuition* (1970). She also served as president of both the Association for Transpersonal Psychology and the Association for Humanistic Psychology and was a Fellow of the American Psychological Association. For Vaughan, intuition means trusting one's self. Artistic expression, mystical religious experience, serendipitous scientific breakthroughs, and inventions are all intuitive. Intuition can't be meaningfully interpreted outside of experiences, but also uses sleep, dreams, and reveries. Intuition can't substitute for careful research or data gathering and should never become a substitute for discrimination but can reveal alternatives to us. Experience yourself as the context of your life instead of identifying with those contexts. You have feelings, but you are not the feelings. Sit quietly, notice your body, feelings, thoughts, and images, and consider what you don't need to do about them. Doing this regularly helps to access intuition, but it continues to require effort.

In her book, Vaughan makes a categorical statement that I find unacceptable. "Intuition is true by definition. If a seemingly intuitive insight turns out to be wrong, then it did not spring from intuition, but from self-deception or wishful thinking."[2] This sort of argument becomes a default response to failures or disappointments for every type of perfectionistic ideologue or theorist. When anything does not work as planned, then it cannot be intuition (or whatever is crucial within a perfectionistic faith) that's wrong, but the faulty interpretations or actions of imperfect individuals. Such an assumption is a critical weakness for any ideology, whether religious, scientism, authoritarianism, or higher consciousness.

As a generally well-educated population, Higher-Consciousness advocates crave rational and scientific justifications for their beliefs and practices. While many scientists and academicians dismiss psychic research as pseudoscience, many do combine strong personal spiritualities with illustrious scientific careers and connect their science with their spiritual beliefs. A favorite example is Fritjof Capra's *The Tao of Physics*.

Since new age people believe they are responsible for all the events in their lives, they face a quandary in how or whether they should be responsible for others. Perhaps others need to "learn their own lessons." The question is: How can one get involved in helping others without interrupting one's own learning and growth? However, almost all of them are involved with others and care about them and about the general welfare of humanity, as demonstrated by their various social-action endeavors. Their division about helping others while achieving higher consciousness is likely exacerbated by their relative societal privilege and their considerable discretionary income. Thus the movement is often considered narcissistic or lacking social consciousness by those outside of it.

While traditional religions have usually focused on strengthening their communities and asking practitioners to make sacrifices on behalf of others and the community in order to spiritually progress, Higher-Consciousness practitioners focus on personal responsibility, individual growth, and self-fulfillment.

An entire branch of Higher-Consciousness spirituality focuses on social change, however, and their ideas have a long historic arc. By 1782, the Great Seal of the United States proclaimed a "new order of ages"; two centuries later, Soviet Premier Mikhail Gorbachev proclaimed, "All mankind is entering a new age." Nineteenth and 20th-century Christian socialism, liberalism, and progressivism all declared that educated people had the responsibility not only to succeed personally but also to lift humanity. International organizations share principles prevalent in Higher-Consciousness spirituality. Like internationalists, Higher-Consciousness practitioners emphasize nonviolence, diversity, and sharing available wealth and abundance instead of personally maximizing possession and consumption. Both argue that changes need to become more sustainable, feminist-oriented, and compassionate, and must strive toward global unity and to build community.

Higher-Consciousness community activists are usually reformers rather than revolutionaries, and hope to share their systems' benefits more broadly. They revere democracy, love networking, and enthusiastically use the Web and other electronic means to spread their ideas. They generally believe, however, that they only need to persuade an enlightened minority and prefer to work within informal structures with horizontal networks rather than to strengthen hierarchical institutions. They prefer to spend their discretionary energies on encouraging other spiritually developed individuals to practice lives of community service.

Representative books that focus on community building among Higher-Consciousness practitioners include: Charles A. Reich, *The Greening of America*; Marilyn Ferguson, *The Aquarian Conspiracy: Personal and Social*; Alvin and Heidi Toffler, *Future Shock* and *The Third Wave*; and Corrine McLaughlin and Gordon Davidson, *Spiritual Politics: Changing the World from the Inside Out*. Representative organizations include European Green movements, U.S. groups such as the New World Alliance, Planetary Citizens, or Self-Determination. Relevant journals, include: *New Realities, The Leading Edge Bulletin, New Age Journal, New Options Newsletter, Utne Reader,* and *Lion's Roar*. The Naropa Institute in Boulder, Colorado, the Wrekin Trust in Worcester, U.K., and Hollyhock Farm in Vancouver, Canada, are examples of multifaceted Higher-Consciousness activist institutions. Ken Wilbur exemplifies the continued evolution of this activist consciousness.

Resistance from Other Religious Organizations

Higher-Consciousness spiritualities have drawn strong negative reactions from many traditional religionists, indigenous religious leaders, and neopagans. Evangelical Christians generally see their ideas as false spiritualities and part of a larger cultural conspiracy that draws participants away from true faiths and directs them toward profane or even diabolical principles and practices. They call it "supermarket spirituality," or "improvisational millennialism leading people into mass hysteria." In 2003, the Southern Baptist Convention said New Age spirituality was contrary to Christianity, and the Roman Catholic Church stated that New Age practices did not conform with prayer to God's presence and misled its practitioners. Indigenous spiritual leaders accuse New Age practitioners of trying to steal their spiritual beliefs and practices, and name them "plastic medicine men."

Though neopagans and Higher-Consciousness practitioners share some practices and beliefs, many neopagans consider them "airy-fairy," not sufficiently Earth-centered, obsessed with the future, and not properly reverential of the ancient past. Left-wing political critics argue that personal growth has little impact on needed political changes. Right-wing political critics think new agers are seduced by diabolical plots in favor of world government that undermine time-tested values. Academic critics perceive their spirituality as too narcissistic, libertarian, even anarchistic, and believe that their obsession about requiring consensus in group decisions has often rendered them collectively ineffective.

Insights from the Experiences of My Spiritual Colleagues Ted Scott and Neal Vahle

From 2010 until 2020, I had the privilege of participating in a monthly spiritual group with two remarkable men, Ted Scott and Neal Vahle, both of whom have had much deeper involvement than I with Higher-Consciousness movements.

Ted Scott

Ted Scott, son and grandson of Presbyterian ministers, was raised in upstate New York and Pennsylvania. He attended Wooster College in Ohio, went on to Princeton Seminary, and graduated in 1965. He married his college sweetheart, and served Presbyterian congregations in New Jersey. Ted attended a sensitivity group with Presbyterian ministerial colleagues at which they interacted at a deeper, more authentic level than he'd ever experienced, which made him want to help people experience similar sharing and connection.

After he'd researched educational options, Ted decided to pursue advanced training in organizational development, enrolled in graduate school at New York University, and pursued doctoral coursework, worked in organization development and change management for Bankers Trust, and was then became an independent consultant for many years, specializing in leadership, teams, change, and transition management.

"When I began full-time work on Wall Street, I left the church and for the next twenty years became a very secular person. My religion was the Human Potential Movement." In the summers, he attended the National Training Labs in Maine. His first marriage ended, and he later met his present wife at a Maine Lab session. She was a successful business consultant and part of the Human Potential Movement. Through the 1970s and '80s, they worked in the corporate world, sometimes separately and sometimes together. In 1990, they moved to California. Ted had realized that while corporations were willing to pay well for programs that often substantially helped individuals, his interventions less frequently changed the deepest habits of management practice or how corporations did their business. As a business consultant, Ted became restless and felt drawn again to a more open spirituality.

This led him to reconnect with the Presbyterian Church and to ministry. During the 1990s, he worked exclusively for nonprofits, helping them find and replace executive directors and strengthen their managements and boards. At seventy-eight, Ted Scott is now mostly retired. After forty years of marriage and being an active parental figure to his wife's children, he's now a devoted grandparent. In California he also became curious about other spiritual traditions. He attended Spirit Rock (Insight Meditation) Center as well as other Buddhist centers. In the 1990s, he began to attend the Tiburon Presbyterian Church, and has served as a Parish Associate there for seventeen years. He has led occasional services, provided courses and retreats, and supported other leaders. In 2005, he discovered Spiritual Direction training. Spiritual Directors are transpersonal counselors who work with individual clients, specifically on their spiritual growth. Ted explains: "It is focusing with individuals on their overall meaning and purposes, concentrating together on critical issues that lift or depress their spirits." In 2009, he began to attend the San Rafael Meditation School, which concentrates on helping students develop their capacity to meditate, become more deeply intuitive and aware, and acquire spiritual self-management techniques. Using these tools and capacities has become important for Ted. In his own words, he describes his current thoughts about spirituality:

> I have become more aware of my own space, of how to stay
> focused and centered and present in the moment. I try more

to manage myself in relation to chosen ethical stances and responsible relationships and to connect more with Creation, with nature, society, the Light within us all—more open to co-creation that is happening all around me continuously. I have become steadily more aware of how challenging and humbling it is to live a spiritual life. Remaining spiritually open requires us to live a more porous existence, because we are trying to connect with that which is greater and more enduring than ourselves. Being spiritual is often much more fulfilling, joyful, loving, and abundant, but also more demanding than living in an often unconscious, reactive way or according to other people's standards. I am often good at getting to the transcendent in others, but often less good at perceiving the God within-the immanent within myself. The Meditation School has helped me get better at feeling the light around my heart and resting in that light. There is negative and positive in our 'everyday' world, and in the spiritual world. The world is not fundamentally evil, but there is evil. Mischief is always present. We need to guard against it in the world, others, within ourselves. Is your grouchy self really you? We need to get back to our spiritual being, to become grounded again in these deeper realities.

Every human being has spiritual experiences, but most seem to make little use of them. Their spiritual lives remain serendipitous and unfocused or remain mostly unrealized fantasy happenings as opposed to systematic and progressive engagement between their ethical, social, and intimate lives with their own and others' spiritual depths. To do that, people need to regularly engage in meditation and/or deep prayer, using images, breath, and sensations to experience the transcendent and the immanent, the light, flow, essence, wind at a cellular level throughout our bodies-minds-spirits. Experience is absolutely the key, but we need to test every experience pragmatically, empirically, and check out whether an experience leads us to our best, most ethical and embracing selves. We also need to remain open to new, different, even contrary experiences in order to spiritually advance and progress.

I care what happens to human beings when they are connected to a larger consciousness or Presence within themselves and between themselves. This consciousness needs to rest within the best human rational standards of justice, compassion, and love. I don't want, for myself or others, a selfish, self-centered, frightened, closed-off life. I want openness, whether that it is toward another person, a spiritual practice, or a passage of scripture, verse, or prayer. Many Christian categories are less important, but the spiritual dynamics to which they refer remain vital. We do go on after death. You and I are spiritual beings and that goes on.

I have become open to spiritual guides, usually as energy and presence. These guides are prepared to help, but I need to ask them the right questions, then interpret their responses and decide how to apply them in my life or in the lives of others. My spiritual experiences have consistently been of intuitive knowing, healing awareness, as well as group experiences. Meditation helps to understand what we are taking-in and what we need to acknowledge. I feel more deeply sane. In spirituality, I do not perceive hard, but rather dotted lines. Categories are inevitably inadequate. The experiences always exceed the categories.

Neal Vahle

Neal Vahle (1932–2020), was born and raised in Tracy, Minnesota. He became an enthusiastic and successful athlete, especially as a baseball pitcher. A devout Catholic, he served as an altar boy, played the organ for the choir, and believed that only by regular confession and Holy Communion could people enter heaven. He graduated in social studies from Minnesota's St. John's University, then spent his two-year military career in postwar Germany as a pitcher for the army baseball team. After he'd completed an MA in European Intellectual History at the Catholic University in Washington, D.C., Neal married, worked a series of jobs until he'd earned his Ph.D. in American history from Georgetown University, and then began to teach night classes as an adjunct professor at George Mason University.

For the next twenty-five years, Neal was employed by Evron Kirkpatrick, first as editor of the magazine *World Affairs* at Heldref Publications, but by the time he left Heldref, he was managing ninety employees and the publication of forty-three journals. Kirkpatrick was happy to let Neal build the business and manage its magazines. Neal's Roman Catholicism became increasingly liberal: he integrated his growing family into an African American parish and participated in organizations the bishop had banned. Finally, Neal left Catholicism over the issues of birth control and abortion.

Until 1982, Neal was focused on his "rational, analytical mind, which fit with my Catholicism." When someone talked about learning *intuitively,* Neal presumed they had "dreamed it up." His attitude changed after he attended a workshop with depth psychologist Ira Progoff. One exercise was a dialogue process with various parts of one's life. Thereafter, he used this approach to make decisions. Neal was struggling in his marriage, and they attended Life Spring programs. This encounter work made Neal aware of his dark side: his fears, tendency to see himself as a victim, and need to blame others for his problems or grief. He also practiced Alexander Everett's "rainbow meditation" to enter the inner peace of intuitive knowing. Neal divorced, and attended Unity and New Thought Churches in D.C. from 1983 to 1990.

Neal's life changed dramatically when he brought *New Realities* magazine to Heldref. He became deeply involved in the literature of self-help, personal growth, transpersonal psychology, and non-religious spirituality. Harvard psychologist Herbert Benson taught him his Relaxation Response; he attended workshops at Esalen five times a year, wrote profiles of their leaders for *New Realities,* and worked with Ken Wilbur's *Revision* at Heldref. In 1990, Jeanne Kirkpatrick, who had taken over Heldref Publishing, fired Neal. At fifty-seven, Neal moved to the West Coast, wrote a book on Ernest Holmes, the founder of Religious Science, and became the editor of the *Noetic Sciences* magazine. As a result of his growing interest in the New Thought movement, he wrote a biography of Myrtle Fillmore, cofounder of the Unity religion, which arose from the New Thought Christian movement. The Fillmores believed that the divine existed within people as an indwelling presence. Jesus was a highly evolved human being. Myrtle felt that the spirit of God was pouring out to me, and I rejoice in expressing it. Then, the Unity School principal asked Neal to write the Unity Movement's history, and from 2000–2005, he edited *Unity Magazine* from his San Francisco office.

Neal maintained his strong support for rationality, valued academic credentials, and sought independent support for his and others' spiritual experiences. Simultaneously, he was a passionate advocate for intuition, and believed that most educational institutions, even most religious communities failed to teach people how to become effectively intuitive. He felt that intuition was as important a skillset as rational, analytical reasoning. His intuitive wisdom usually appeared through words and phrases. His process was to address a problem through his inner-knowledge techniques, to ask for an intuitive yes or no, and then to receive a verbal response. Affirmations about our true-good selves and our degree of connection with divine perfection were central to his spiritual practices, and he used them to counter his tendency to obsess about negatives or get caught up in past anger. Neal's spirituality was based on his affirmations and his efforts to stay in the present moment and outwit his demonic self. He had a strong sense of both a true-good self and a demonic self, and Neal felt that he could be easily led astray by his demonic self. "I notice my irritation, anger, or frustration, work at bringing myself back to the present moment, to become grounded again, to re-find my true self."

Sports were central to Neal's life and were his primary ecstatic spiritual experiences during his youth and young adulthood. In middle age he quarterbacked a weekly touch football game, and later in life, tennis became his primary sport. He wrote several sports books. Sports and physical exercise routines remained pivotal to his spiritual development. To apply his approach to life to his tennis game, he stayed focused on the here and now, didn't overanalyze, persisted, and relied on cooperation. "In each tennis match, I sense some perfection."

Neal remained fascinated by, and periodically became involved with, more questioned aspects of spirituality, such as extrasensory perception (ESP). Never motivated to develop his own ESP abilities, he nonetheless perceived

ESP as real, and felt it provided useful skills. He also explored clairvoyance—seeing realities invisible to our eyes; telepathy—reading another's thoughts; precognition—prediction of future events; and prescience—impressions about another person's past, present, or future. Neal has gone to sessions with therapists who help their clients process *past life regressions,* i.e., the use of hypnosis to recover memories of past lives or incarnations by asking questions to elicit memories of past lives. This helped Neal reduce his fear of death and become accepting of reincarnation.

I believe that Neal's working spirituality was a 21st-century Higher-Consciousness version of Norman Vincent Peale's Christianity, as expounded in *The Power of Positive Thinking.* For a generation, Neal was active at Glide Memorial Methodist Church—a progressive megachurch in San Francisco's challenged Tenderloin neighborhood, led for decades by Reverend Cecil Williams. With its hundred-person Gospel choir, and eighty social-service programs that serve over a million meals and provide services for thousands of San Francisco's homeless, Glide is one of the Bay Area's best-known congregations. It has now separated itself from Methodism, and is a social services giant with an Afrocentric choir and a progressive philosophy and agenda.

The core of Neal's daily spiritual practice came from George Leonard's and Michael Murphy's *The Life We Are Given: A Long-term Program for Realizing the Potential of Body, Mind, Heart, and Soul.* Neal participated every Saturday for years for two hours with a group of people who cooperated in Leonard and Murphy's Integral Transformative Practice sessions. Thereafter, Neal continued these *kata* practices on his own, which began with a half hour of body moves followed by ten minutes of meditation, and then affirmations that begin with: "My entire being is balanced, vital and healthy." Then, each practitioner makes up a second affirmation appropriate for that day in his or her life. Neal explained that he needed these practices because "for many years I woke up every morning very depressed, but with five minutes of Tai Chi and my kata practice, I am in a better mood and ready to embrace the day."

Elements of Higher-Consciousness Spirituality that I Find Challenging

To me, its openness and consumerist tendencies may make Higher-Consciousness spirituality vulnerable to emotional manipulation. I've encountered many Higher-Consciousness leaders who exhibited great integrity and spiritual depth; however, the "pay to play" procedures, and the tendency to steadily increase demands on participants, can cause participants to suffer isolation from family and friends who are unwilling to become involved with the group or critical of their relative's or friend's involvement, as well as impede the participant's own growth and fulfillment.

I'm also concerned about the strongly privileged ethos of some Higher-Consciousness spirituality. Spiritual depth can't be bought. Its emphasis on convenience can make some of its practices spiritually shallow. I'm convinced that every human being has spiritual experiences, but I believe that to successfully live a spiritual life requires conscientious discipline and practice, as well as enduring commitments beyond self and "in-group."

I don't believe that humanity will become spiritually higher, more conscious, or more loving just because they are concentrating their efforts on individual growth, just as I don't believe that blind commitment to hierarchical and authoritarian faiths will bring salvation to anyone. Individual growth is unlikely to change the world without consistent efforts to build organizations and institutions for global betterment. Only when individuals actually begin to invest a significant portion of their time, energy, and wealth in the betterment of humanity, rather than maximizing personal gains, can a New Age as envisioned truly become a reality.

Elements of Higher-Consciousness Spirituality that I Find Particularly Relevant

For most of my adult life, I've been interested in but skeptical about Higher-Consciousness or new age spirituality. In the congregations I served, many members were curious about it; and they challenged me to address the topic, which I did in worship services and adult-ed classes. I have had three significant periods of therapy; coincidentally, the three therapists I had were associated in some way with Higher-Consciousness spirituality. The first was my gestalt therapist friend in Bloomington, Indiana, with whom I also pursued several gestalt training workshops. He knew Fritz Perls and had made pilgrimages to Esalen. My second therapist was a Jungian in Bergen County, New Jersey, who became temporarily fascinated by Unitarian Universalism. The third was a UU therapist in New Jersey, who combined humanistic and transpersonal therapeutic methods. I also benefitted greatly from several Higher-Consciousness-related workshops, including a weeklong workshop for helping professionals with Ram Dass; another with engaged Buddhist Thich Nhat Hanh; a weekend with Jungian therapist Jean Shinoda Bolen; and a workshop on the martial art of Aikido as a spiritual discipline.

Mysticism is central to enabling spiritual experiences. Higher-Consciousness spiritual methods have provided many people with life-changing spiritual experiences and afford access to many who are alienated from traditional religions or are dissatisfied with secularized scientism. Since seminary, I've read about many scientific studies that had spiritual and ethical implications, and I found them invaluable adjuncts to my spiritual beliefs and practices. As a karma-yogin and activist, I perceive myself as on that branch of the Higher-Consciousness spectrum that emphasizes its social, community, and ethical involvements. So, while Higher-Consciousness spirituality has often not seemed central to my spiritual life, a significant part of my reading, and several of my most influential spiritual teachers and central spiritual experiences, have been in the embrace of Higher-Consciousness spirituality, and have blessed me with life-changing benefits.

Neal Vahle and Ted Scott have been central to my spiritual growth in the last decade. I agree with Neal Vahle that anyone can be helped by positive thinking, affirmations, and living in the present. We do need to work hard to avoid getting caught in past disappointments, anger, and resentment. Neal's athletic, disciplined, joyful-warrior mentality inspired me. Like Ted Scott, "I don't care much about labels.... I care what happens to human beings when they are connected to a larger consciousness within themselves and between themselves." I agree with Ted that consciousness "needs to rest within the best human rational standards of justice, compassion, and love." Like Ted, I have been primarily a spiritual practitioner in my life. By being privileged to listen and help others find their ways, I have been encouraged to become more deeply spiritual.

Japanese rock garden, Portland, Oregon.

Israeli children and Islamic prayer tower, Haifa, Israel.

Section IV

Chapter 19
The Sacred:
From Transcendent to Community

What do people most hold sacred? To answer this question requires categories. The sacred comprises: *the cosmic-transcendent*—powers beyond humanity; *Earth-centered intermediaries*—individuals and institutions that act as spiritual specialists; *immanency*—individuals' own spiritual experiences (including their practices and ethical choices); *between*—the sacred intimacies in collegiality; friendship, and love; and *among*—we experience the sacred when we mingle in spiritual groups and religious communities.

Cosmic-Transcendent

I believe in the Cosmic Divine as the creative energies of the multiverse, particularly its Earthly, human, and benevolent forces—somewhat analogous to "the Force" of *Star Wars* fame. Transcendent God is not a being, but a process, largely implicit in its cosmic and Earthly natural laws and orders, but also creative energies capable of intervention, evolution, and change. Like process theologian Alfred North Whitehead, I believe there is a *primordial nature*—the cosmic laws of the universe, some of which may remain inscrutable. Quite like Teilhard de Chardin's evolutionary vision in *The Divine Milieu,* Creation is a vector that challenges us to move in positive cosmic directions. I treasure concrete images. My favorite is the Hindu god Vishnu because it returns in evolving forms as the cosmos, nature, and history requires Creation's help to regain equilibrium. My preferred natural symbols for Creation are our sun, waterfalls, mountains, and ancient trees.

Earth-Centered

The Earth too has its sacredness. Like Whitehead, I believe that the divine has both a *primordial* nature, discernable in cosmic and natural laws, and a *consequent* divine nature in which the divine is dependent, changing, and in process. God is enriched by the Earth and by humanity. The scholarly term is "pantheism." From our human perspective, Creation is neither all-powerful nor all-good. On Earth, however, God's work must surely be our own, for Creation has expectations of us. Humanity and every individual have responsibilities.

Many contemporary physicists are as much in awe of the cosmos as were their ancestors, though the wonder is now based more on empirical evidence, yet 85 percent of the cosmos remains mysterious. Early 20th-century Hindu Srinivasan Ramanujan's mathematical breakthroughs are just now being used to help astrophysicists grapple with dark energy, dark matter, and black holes, yet this math genius from a century ago believed his formulas were given to him by his Hindu god. One of my seminary professors, Ralph Burhoe, a recipient of the Templeton Prize for Religion in an Age of Science, revered natural selection. A member of my Florida congregation with PhDs in engineering and physics was a theist because he felt that the periodic table confirmed cosmic laws. Dr. Francis S. Collins, the geneticist who led the Human Genome Project as director of the U.S. National institutes for Health, combines his science with a strong Christian faith. He wrote:

> At its most fundamental level, it's a miracle that there's a universe at all. It's a miracle that it has order, fine-tuning that allows the possibility of complexity and laws that follow precise mathematical formulas. Contemplating this, an open-minded observer is almost forced to conclude that there must be a 'mind' behind all this. To me, that qualifies as a miracle, a profound truth that lies outside of scientific explanation.[1]

There are those who choose to argue that there is no transcendent, that the cosmos is a chance creation without purpose or direction, and certainly without benevolence; however, every single atheist, agnostic, skeptic, and anarchist I've known has acted daily as if life had meaning, and people had value, and that the world was rich with benevolent intentions. A person's spirituality is primarily what they do—how they act, not their tenacious creeds or their professed cynicism, skepticism, or disbelief.

The cosmic realm remained mysterious for eons while early humans studied the Earth intensely in order to survive. Humanity has only become aware that its own greed and disregard for the physical environment could jeopardize the planet, and that the Earth's bounty is not inexhaustible. These insights are producing synergies with, and renewed respect for, aspects of the faiths and ethics of indigenous peoples, who realized eons ago that in order to flourish they must find a balance with nature and protect the Earth's vulnerable resources. Scientists have helped us realize that if creation had evolved slightly differently, our cosmos would be chaotic, and that if Earth's evolution had been marginally different, humanity almost certainly could not have emerged. Our present state as a species results from an almost endless series of improbabilities, so it's practical to believe that we are here for purposes that include respecting and revering the good Earth, and serving it as patiently and nobly as it serves us.

At the end of his book, *The Gene: An Intimate History* (2016), Dr. Siddhartha Mukherjee, Columbia University professor and Pulitzer Prize-winning author, writes:

> Scientists divide, discriminate.... We break the world into its constituent parts—genes, atoms, bytes—before making it whole again. We know no other mechanism to understand the world: to create the sum of the parts, we must begin by dividing it into the parts of the sum....(However) the (reassembly) of the parts is different from the whole before it was broken into parts.[2]

Mukherjee recognizes that people must continue to distinguish between what can and cannot be divided. Like the rest of us, scientists should remain humble so as not to forget "that genes may be more connected than we think, and that understanding genes have a significant role in human destiny does not imply that the human genome is itself manifest destiny."[3]

Because my childhood faith developed from my parents' nature mysticism and nonviolent-justice humanism, I never believed that scientific efforts and empirical investigations of nature conflicted with spirituality or religion. Faith deserves to stand the best tests of our experience, and investigation and scientific method are among the best ways to test the truth and value of them. There are, however, secularists as rigid in their disbelief or in their commitments to ideologies such as capitalism, communism, or scientism as religious fundamentalists are to their too-narrow faiths. Like them, they discredit others' experiences—or even their own—when those experiences don't fit within their inflexible ideological boundaries. Technological, corporate, and institutional actions now often have more negative global consequences than earlier human errors and produce greater catastrophes.

We must make peace with the Earth and find ways to live in balance with natural systems. It is now essential for humanity's survival for us to realize that we are but a portion of the Earth's interdependent web of living ecological systems. We can't do what we please with no concern for the health and sustainability of the natural world. Technology must not become our new religion; neither should convenience or expedience remain our predominant human practices. If we want there to be a sustainable future for the Earth and any future for our descendants, the world's peoples must work together, with shared goals that require mutual understanding and respect for one another and for nature's living systems.

Intermediaries: Spiritual Specialists and Religious Institutions

Every historic religion and ideology still tends to focus on intermediaries between cosmic and Earth-centered powers and individual human beings and societies. Most people with religious affiliations invest a few scriptural passages with great personal significance and adopt one or more historic figures as role models or foci of their reverence. They support them with images and rituals that hold mythic importance for them. Secular individuals generally adopt a "replacement ideology" that explains the meaning and purpose of their lives, invest certain personalities with respect, and practice rituals and revere images from their adopted ideologies.

An objective in considering various religious traditions has been to understand how worthy beliefs and practices have evolved, though grievous errors in judgment and practice also occurred during their histories. People deserve prophets—admirable figures, models to follow and try to emulate in character and virtue. These prophets usually had valuable things to say, and perhaps some traits worthy of emulation, while they passionately hoped not to be seen as perfect beings, and certainly not as saviors. Moses didn't consider himself a leader or public speaker. Jesus wished to model a relationship he felt everyone could have with God. Muhammad claimed to be only a reciter of holy words. Mahavira hoped to demonstrate self-conquest. Buddha wanted people to wake up and realize that most of our suffering arises from our needless craving, and that we can accomplish much good by becoming compassionate. Lao Tzu hoped to reveal how to follow nature's ways. Confucius wanted to save societies from chaos, and to teach his students how to practice mutually beneficial social relationships.

Once religious figures take on political power or develop military, territorial, or material aims, their spiritual claims ought to be challenged, whether they lived centuries ago or today. Some of their actions or character traits remain admirable, but without exception, made selfish, shortsighted decisions, and they sometimes proclaimed beliefs and practices that have had immensely negative, enduring consequences. In this sense, I remain an active Protestant, *protesting* that each individual must take personal responsibility for her or his spirituality, and that every tradition must continue to evolve so as to remain suited to its time and circumstances. I honor many spiritual seers and religious movements, but I consider no person or organization sacrosanct. Institutions can empower us, spiritual guides can help us, but we must do our spirituality ourselves.

The Immanent Divine: Aspects Within

The 21st century presents amazing opportunities for people to fully explore their evolving spirituality, and many choose to devote time and effort to doing so. There have always been spiritual mystics and seekers who concentrated on experiencing the divine themselves, and on learning to make their discoveries worthy of widespread reverence. Many committed members of religious and ideological groups combine their individual spiritual experience with their jointly practiced convictions. It is essential, however, as Joseph Campbell suggested, not to get lost, and eat the menu, the spiritual intermediaries, thinking that by depending upon these intermediaries alone they can receive spiritual sufficiency. Nor should people try to extricate themselves from personal responsibility for their actions. Belief alone can't save anyone; no one can undo a life of selfishness, shortsightedness, or violation through a single sacrament, a guru's blessing, or martyrdom. Images, myths, prophets, and scriptures are tools to help us interpret our spiritual experiences, but they aren't what the divine wishes or life expects from us. Seekers and mystics provide core insights into the appropriate paths for 21st-century people of faith.

Increasingly, I believe humanity will shift its spiritual emphasis from the worship of transcendent cosmic deities, their focus on the cosmos, or trying to manipulate or replace natural laws, and will instead seek partnership relations with the laws of nature and the awesome wonders of the natural world. I gladly pay daily reverence to Creation, to the cosmic transcendent, and to the bountiful Earth and its beauty and amazing intricacy. I revere the good Earth; however, my reverence and my spirituality are primarily focused on our individual insights into, and spiritual experiences with, the immanent aspects of the sacred within and the sacred between and among other people.

These social forms of the sacred are discovered in our intimacies within collegiality, friendship, and love, and in the sacred among, that sacred discovered by responsible members within spiritual groups, religious communities, and civic institutions that nurture humanity and our shared future. I believe people will grow more alike in their religious choices, spiritual practices, and ethical choices as individuals within an increasingly global society. The future of religious practices will be focused on the divinity within, between, and among human beings.

The Sacred Between: Intimacy in Collegiality, Friendship, and Love

Most people get closest to the sacred and to their own spirituality through fulfilling experiences of human intimacy. These most often happen in our love relationships with a spouse, children, parents, siblings, and dear friends. During our lives, many of us are fortunate to have a variety of friends with whom we develop intimate relationships, and some of us are blessed with collegial relationships that become intimate.

Martin Buber expressed this as *I-Thou* relationships of mutual intimacy rather than *I-It* relationships in which we only make use of others. Hindus say that intimates perceive the *atman* in each other; other religions might view it as the Divine or the Spirit at work. Intimacy proposes that intimates belong to our deepest natures and we belong to theirs. Intimates believe in us, enable our spirits, ennoble our souls, raise our consciousness, and help us become and remain the people we wish to be. The ancient Greeks divided intimacy into *philia, eros,* and *agape,* for love comes not only through sexual or sensual intimacy but also in ways that provide expressions of every aspect of love. In genuine intimacies, individuals regularly risk being fully honest and constructively critical within a context of deep admiration and respect. No one can expect a single person to meet all their intimate needs, for this diminishes both individuals as they cling to some illusion of perfection.

My collegial intimacies have sometimes been with other clergy, but as a pastor, I became intimate in various ways with many congregants, and some became intimate friends. I also experienced collegial intimacies with volunteer civic activists. Friendships have been crucial to me; they've helped me grow in ways I could never have foreseen. My beloveds and my wives, in sensual as well as other forms of intimacy, have often saved me from my worst impulses or rescued me when I stumbled, while also helping me mature and deepen in love and spirit.

Sacred Among: Members Mingling in Spiritual Groups and Religious Communities

I'm convinced that people want groups in which to intentionally nurture and strengthen their spirits, or souls, and deserve religious communities where they can participate in shared expression of their faith. Increasingly, people want to live their spirituality freely, and to practice their faith as responsible, well-intended individuals. I've found the sacred in causes and meditation halls, as well as in congregations. We all need to stretch ourselves by living among diverse groups who share faith elements but are different from each other. Sometimes, there will be spiritual specialists, as I was as a pastor, professor of religious studies, activist leader, and meditation instructor, but such relationships need to be equitable. I never viewed myself as spiritually superior, as having had a higher consciousness, or as having been more ethically advanced. Intermediaries, like clergy, should be perceived as practical tools for religious growth, as helpful steps in our spiritual journeys, but not as authoritarian prophets, saviors, or leaders who can't be questioned. In the 21st century, all our relationships deserve to be mutual ones, in which we grow together through dialogue and negotiation.

When I retired from active UU ministry in 2009, and became a parishioner in a congregation, and a grandparent, it took adjustment because I was no longer the focus of attention. I think that many people of color, women, and other non-dominant individuals, feel this way much of the time, as do most of us when we leave our jobs and are again simply people, without a clearly defined position in some organizational structure. For far too long, arbitrary divisions have allowed some people to feel superior and entitled to a range of built-in advantages. Higher-caste Hindus are not spiritually superior to lower-caste or non-caste Indians; lighter-skinned people in almost every culture in the world are not inherently superior to their darker-hued sisters and brothers. Boys and men are not inherently superior to girls and women; Arabs and Saudi Arabians are not inherently better Muslims, nor are denominations within each of our global religious traditions superior to their religious relatives.

To become spiritually liberated and to access the revered, we must treat everyone as spiritually equal. We need to discover the sacred around us, but to accomplish this, our groups and communities need to be egalitarian, democratic, pluralistic, and activist. Twenty-first-century spirituality, and the heart and soul of religion, will be our internal discoveries, but at least equally our experiences with intimates and in our spiritual groups, religious communities, and civic commitments when they aspire to reach beyond their current selfish interests.

Sharing My Personal Theology and Spiritual Practices

My personal theology and the spiritual practices that arose from it developed over many decades and reflect the multitude of experiences I've had since the beginning of my spiritual journey. Your journey has been different and will inspire unique practices that reflect how you responded to your own life experiences. I hope my examples lead to ideas that help you create practices that express your gratitude for all you've been given during your life on this Earth.

My Theology

God is Creation, a process, largely independent of humanity yet partly dependent on humanity in some very modest ways, on each of us. Nature proceeds by evolutionary laws that we need to cooperate with in order to endure and flourish. My favorite religious concept for divinity is Hinduism's Brahman-atman, the transcendent, Earthly, and immanent in a single integrated term. I am a Jesusian rather than a Christian because I revere Jesus as a human ethical model who understood that every person is a portion of the image of God, that we are all children of God. The *saved* are not a minority of believers in a particular religion or life ideology, or a sect or denomination within a religion or ideology. I strive to be loving and humble, as I believe Jesus tried to be. With Jainism, I face reality as probabilistic and truth as circumstantial and contextual and strive to be disciplined and nonviolent. I agree with Buddha that people need to awaken from obsessive craving and realize that we create our egos. We need to practice empathy with, compassion for, and forgiveness of others and of ourselves.

I agree with Lao Tzu that we need to live more in tune with nature, and with Confucius that we need to concentrate on our human relationships and social organizations. I'm in tune with the Shinto sense that the divine permeates all aspects of reality and that beauty remains encompassing. I agree with the Judaic realization that we must live responsible lives and do our part to heal the world. I wish to be as loving and as filled with hope as the most exemplary Christians. With Muslims, I feel a daily need to realize that I am dependent on Creation and the Earth, and submit to that reality, but also to live in peace with all people of goodwill, whatever their faith, and to dedicate myself to remaining hospitable to strangers, generous to the needy, and open to new truths discovered by science and scholarship. I cherish the Sikhs' work ethic and combination of mystical worship and neighborly activism. As a humanist, I want to use the tests of reason and experience, of science and intuition, and to concentrate on a healthy future for humanity and sustainability with the Earth.

People tend to integrate their past with their present. My mother was a nature mystic, as am I, but I've become more scientifically informed, environmentally active, and ecologically aware than my mother could be. My father set me on a global course, but his globalism was infused with elements of white colonialism, racism, and male chauvinism. As I became increasingly conscious of the inequities of white male privilege, my choices became more inclusive. My maternal grandfather was a kind and generous man and a civic activist but remained a racist and doctrinaire capitalist. One important aspect of my maturation was to make different choices than my father's and grandfather's about race, colonialism and foreign affairs, about capitalism's alleged inevitable superiority, and to openly differ with them about these issues while I remained their intimate.

As I proceeded through adulthood, I continued to learn from others. I usually remained respectful, but also spoke up honestly and acted differently when I disagreed. Like everyone else, I continue to evolve, and my beliefs and practices adapt. Now, I'm learning from my adult children and from my grandchildren as I continue to grow, and from my contacts with friends, neighbors, activist colleagues, fellow congregants, and from strangers.

Spiritual Practices

Spiritual practices are what individuals do alone that connects them with and helps them live their ultimate beliefs and understanding of reality. Spiritual practices are best understood as a spectrum of understanding and practices. I don't necessarily distinguish between a philosopher's reflections and a monk's meditations. When a person is silent, still, and focused on what's most important to her, it's on the *meditation spectrum,* and it's unfair to brand one type as more respectful of truth or more spiritual than another. When an individual uses words or concepts and addresses them to powers beyond his selfish, shortsighted ego, those are on the *prayer spectrum*. Why would a conscientious atheist's pleas to the universe be less likely to be "answered" than the prayers of a devoted believer?

For most people, music, movement, and art are central to their beliefs and spiritual practice. I rarely get through a day without playing piano, singing, or listening to music, which often speaks more directly about what's sacred than spoken words do. People deserve to dance or move in any way that helps them connect viscerally with what they revere and value most, and to express the awe, love, fear, and hope they feel. People deserve to celebrate holidays and invest their lives' transitions with meaning and value. I urge everyone to set aside minutes daily to be in focused, silent meditation. I advocate that each expresses gratitude and hope every day, whether we believe these prayers will be answered or not. I urge everyone to be musical and artistic and to move rhythmically, not just as consumers or spectators but as participants, and to involve themselves in the cultural holidays and vital transitional moments of the people in their lives.

I urge you to have a personal or family altar in your home, whether it's a wall of photos of treasured relatives and honored mentors, paintings or magazine clippings of historical heroes or current heroines, or traditional images from your chosen religion or ideology. I suggest that each of us also keep a loose-leaf scripture, a collection of admonitions that we've found most profound and meaningful. These words may be from scriptures or philosophers, poets, scientists, or neighbors. Don't shut yourself off from the words and ideas that have touched your heart and changed your life. For 21st-century humans, spiritual practice should be as much a part of daily life as their family responsibilities, vocations, and quests to do justice and heal the world.

Our empirical research and our intuitive syntheses and commitments should not remain estranged from each other. We live our lives striving to make choices that we hope will succeed or satisfy; then we access the results and adapt our beliefs accordingly given those new experiences; and then we make renewed or different commitments and act on the basis of them. Our actions are our most public expressions of faith. I'm convinced that everyone deserves a continuing combination of focused and disciplined individual spiritual practice, dedicated participation in some religious or life-affirming groups, and ethical actions with intimates, strangers, and our global siblings.

My Current Spiritual Practices

Each of us needs to choose, practice, and evolve his or her own spiritual practices. I begin my days with my face against a yoga mat like a Muslim at prayer: I submit to the universe and the Earth to remind myself that most of life is beyond my control. Then, I silently pray to Creation, the powers that exist: "Creation, I am grateful for my life, for the miraculous continuing evolution of the Earth, for people's positivity, creativity, ingenuity, and courage, and for the progress humanity has made." Most of my prayers are in gratitude for the countless gifts of love and caring I've received. Sometimes I focus on a person or experience from my past or present. I consider what I hope to accomplish that day, and my hopes for those whom I'm especially concerned about.

I'm under no illusion that these hopes will automatically be granted; however, to focus on them allows me to feel that I'm concentrating on what's important, that I'm stretching beyond myself, and sometimes beyond my intimates. Details change from day to day and through the years. It took over a year after my divorce before I was again ready to express the deep gratitude I feel daily for what Madhavi shared with me. I added the word "positive" to my general affirmation about humanity because 9/11 renewed my awareness that evil practitioners can be creative, ingenious, and determined. Many of my New Jersey congregation's families were directly impacted by its devastation, including a wonderful young man, whom I'd watched grow up and whose family were partly of Arab ancestry, who was not able to escape one of the Trade Center towers where he worked.

Seated in a half-lotus yoga position, I begin and end by ringing a little Buddhist bell, which connects me directly with the world at that moment. The sound lasts; it radiates outward like ripples on a lake, and reminds me that my good works may endure, and, because the sound does disappear into silence, that I will die, and need to do what I can before then. Quietly chanting Om, I consider the spiritual mentors whom I've embraced through the years: Gandhi, Jesus, Buddha, Martin Luther King Jr., Moses, the Dalai Lama, Thich

Nhat Hanh, Martin Buber, Mother Teresa, several poets like Rumi, Mary Oliver, and Pablo Neruda, and some political figures. In each case, I've chosen three of their character traits that I hope to occasionally approximate. With Gandhi, for instance: nonviolence, selfless service, and politics with integrity. With Buddha: to grow beyond ego, to foster compassion and interdependence. With Mother Theresa: to care for the dying, to be courageous in the face of spiritual doubt, and to manifest the will to organize.

I proceed to our bedroom, where there's a group of images of personal mentors or spiritual prophets, each represented by a statue, plaque, or photo. I ring a larger bell, and greet each of these inspirations: Vishnu, Jesus, Sarasvati, and Buddha, my wife, my parents, Mary Magdalene, Kwan Yin, two Chinese Bodhisattvas, Krishna, Mahavira, and Ganesh. These morning devotions take about ten minutes and help make my day whole.

I urge you to take a few minutes at the beginning of your day to focus on what's most important, true, and dear to you; to express your hopes and concerns in that moment, to express gratitude, and to honor the figures from your life, and from the history or myths you most respect. I suggest you have some images or photos of those you consider exemplary; these can become your personal altar. I suggest also that you have some musical object, like my Buddhist bells, to help you celebrate and to set apart your chosen acts of reverence, and help you be in tune with the rhythms of Creation.

Historical and mythic figures aren't perfect; in fact, it's much better if you can recognize that they, like you and all of us, are only exemplary in certain ways and contexts. Saviors without blemish or sin are ultimately unbelievable. This is an advantage of including people you've known, as well as mythic or historical persons that you've studied enough to understand their frailties and failures as well as their splendid traits and actions. They too were imperfect, fallible, even somewhat broken, but they discovered wisdom, and did well not only for themselves but for many others. Gandhi was not an exemplary husband or father. Mother Teresa was full of spiritual doubt. Martin Luther King was not always faithful to his wife.

Thich Nhat Hanh taught me that a desirable goal of meditation is to consider every worthy activity as a possible form of meditation. I clean up after meals, and that has become one of my periodic concentrated silences. Gardening is my wife's most reliable spiritual practice. Meditation has two primary goals. First, the meditator needs to clear out the trash in her mind, to get beyond the monkey mind that darts in a thousand directions and struggles to focus or become centered. The easiest way to do that is to focus on each breath and gradually relax any area of physical or mental tension, such as feeling stuck on a problem you can't presently solve, so let it go, gradually relax, and get centered.

Now, you're ready for the second goal of meditation: To concentrate on some subject of importance. Chants or songs, memorized poems, verses of scripture, and philosophical wisdom now come in handy. Pick something that fits with where you are or where you feel you need to get to and do your best to focus on that one idea. No one consistently succeeds. Don't let anxiety overwhelm you or tempt you to give up just because your mind is monkeying with you again. Just return to your breath and then get back to your chosen focus for that meditation. It takes practice, and it never gets easy, but just to make the effort regularly will brighten your days and energize your life. On most days I meditate for several periods, often including thirty minutes in silence; I let my mind empty and then watch the flow. Other times, I chant, remember treasured words, sing a few world religious songs. I usually do this while actually "sitting," but sometimes lie down or stare into space.

A good prayerful beginning is Reinhold Niebuhr's aphorism, popularized by the 12 Step Programs: "Help me to change the things I can, bear the things I cannot change, and learn to know the difference." I would invite you to concentrate on gratitude *and* hope. There is much available beauty in the shabbiest of lives; someone to thank in the grimmest contexts. A much greater proportion of humankind is now blessed almost beyond imagination in comparison to most people in history's earlier eons. There are days when I'm uncomfortable, confused, or angry; then, my prayers just feel like I'm just going through the motions, but I've discovered that going through those motions affects how I feel, how I respond to people, and what I do, so I persevere with my daily routine, and sometimes encounter transcendence, bliss, or fulfillment. My prayers are sometimes answered, often not exactly as I'd initially hoped, but that's probably part of what spiritual learning and wisdom are all about.

Before I get into bed, I routinely kneel, not because I believe Creation expects it, but because, like my Muslim position of submission in the morning, being on my knees helps me feel connected with the powers greater, humbles me, and pushes me beyond my narrow ego. Those short prayers are mostly of gratitude for experiences of that day; sometimes hopes for an intimate's health, safe travels, or success in some upcoming crucial challenge; occasionally for world peace, environmental sustainability, or some desired political change.

It might seem ironic that a retired clergyperson would appear to separate individual spiritual beliefs and practices from shared experiences and religions. What I'm saying is that 21st-century people deserve to have their own spiritual lives and practices. These may differ from their surrounding cultural identities or childhood ideological or religious affiliations. I advocate that everyone make space and time in their lives to ponder spirituality and to develop and try to consistently practice spiritual actions. I suggest that your choices include interactions with different, even challenging, beliefs and practices beyond your previous experience. Don't miss out on life's abundance and the unique opportunities that being alive in this century affords.

I've attended spiritual retreats and professional religious workshops, and led ecumenical, denominational, and congregational events that combined, empowered, and challenged my personal spiritual practices. Also, I had three important periods of individual therapy that stimulated spiritual growth by challenging my actions and assumptions during times of turmoil. I've counseled more than a thousand congregants; often, I was able to provide some spiritual help or insight, almost always, at least a caring presence. I often received invaluable spiritual challenges or insights, particularly from people who were going through experiences I hadn't yet had or was unlikely ever to have. In recent years, my meetings every few weeks with several friends in spiritual search, and my attendance at UU services and events, as well as other activist events, have continued to help me grow in ways that wouldn't have happened if I practiced all of my spirituality alone. As in my youth, I'm again now more often a recipient than an inspiration.

When my children were young, I provided them some spiritual insights, but even then, they also challenged my spiritual assumptions and opened new vistas for me. Now, as accomplished adults, they're more often my guides, and I have the incredible blessing of sharing regularly in our grandchildren's growth. Like music, their thoughts, questions, and actions often make me feel as though Creation is cutting through my emotional defenses to help me embrace spiritual truths. My late wife, Madhavi, suggested that I involve myself directly in our grandchildren's spiritual education, and I do so now whenever I'm with them, and occasionally also by correspondence.

My Community Celebrations

As a Unitarian Universalist minister, I had the freedom to adapt the traditional Judeo-Christian ceremonies, sacraments, and worship forms to fit congregants' needs and hopes, and to reflect my own understanding. UUs don't "wash away babies' sins" with our infant dedications because we don't believe that children inherit sin; we think people learn and practice their sins themselves. Our death ceremonies aren't an opportunity to teach dogmas, but instead a-once-in-a-lifetime opportunity to celebrate the deceased individual's entire life. In the many weddings I've performed, I never decreed that one person was the dominant partner or insinuated that producing children was required within that union or that they accept other arbitrary cultural expectations. Each Valentine's Day Sunday for the last twenty years of my ministry, I celebrated a marriage reconfirmation ceremony that included all who wanted to rejoice in their relationships, including the spouses of soldiers on active duty abroad, same-sex couples who couldn't yet get a marriage license, and committed couples who hadn't sought legal sanction for their love.

In each year, I held services that celebrated most of the world's primary historic religions as relevant. Often, I adapted their messages to reach the congregants, while maintaining the essence of their historic wisdom. Our Easter bread was a celebration of the Earthly, our wine or grape juice a celebration of spirit. Our Seder was not the freedom of escape but the liberty of dedication, as the Jews earned liberty by accepting the yoke of the Ten Commandments, and we sang not only Jewish songs but the old spiritual *Go Down Moses*, for, as you've discovered in reading this book, each of the historic religions was built on and enriched by many of the others.

You have done and will each do similar things with your own religious commitments and spiritual choices. I do not expect others to adopt mine, but simply to be free and courageous enough to create and nurture your own, enriched by your background and earlier experiences, but also created, nurtured and embodied by your unique and very personal present and future choices, practices, and commitments.

Chapter 20
Ethics

The word "ethics" means how people should relate to one another and behave within groups and societies. Many believe morals relate to how an individual acts during intimacies, while ethics refers to interactions within organized groups and institutions, like rules for negotiating disagreements. Generally, people agree that we should be respectful and fair, hospitable to guests, and civil to strangers. Ethics relates directly to right and wrong, good and evil, sin and virtue. Most people are prepared to forgive wrongs done out of ignorance or confusion, but expect us all to learn from our mistakes and adopt appropriate behavior.

A further subdivision includes ethics of custom, conduct, or character. *Custom ethics* make culture or community the foundation of ethics; *conduct ethics* focus on situations and roles, while *character ethics* are based on conscience, i.e., personal standards. Conscience may be an inborn tendency toward altruism and the greater good, and/or behavior learned through education and experiences that develop character, nurture self-discipline, and are tested by faith. Today, most would argue that aspects of ethics fit into each of these categories. Every religion contains various ethical ideas, conceptual frameworks, and processes. Here's a selection I found helpful.

Religious Ethical Foundations

Hinduism

The ethical foundation of Hinduism is for everyone to fulfill his or her individual dharma, or spiritual vocation, by learning to transform cravings into understanding, empathy into loving enthusiasm, and greed into graciousness and generosity. The *Katha Upanishad* states: Do not choose the short-sighted path of pleasure, instead pursue the wise path of joy. That path provides rest from untamed sensuality, which allows people to focus on their responsibilities and find peace in their hearts. Gandhi's nonviolent activism, which calls on us to serve those most in need and practice negotiation with care for all concerned, is my primary Hindu ethical model.

Jainism and Buddhism

The ethical perspective of Jainism is based on the realization that existence is relative and transient, and the recognition that everyone is a microcosm of the macrocosm. Nonviolence (ahimsa) is a necessary foundation for ethical behavior. As Gurudev Chitrabhanu suggested, we need to move beyond categories and labels to discern our true self. The foundational Buddhist ethic is to choose occupations and activities that promote life and sustain the future; to live without impudence, and without greedy attachments. Kwan Yin provides an image of compassion; she applies tough love as she strives to resolve the problems of others. The Dalai Lama asks us to acknowledge life's limitations and to approach equanimity by embracing scientific method and spiritual practices that transform our anger into compassion. Joanna Macy reminds us: "There is no self to defend. We can help to empower reality's evolution. Power is not a zero sum game but win-win—the energy found in synergy, a neural net, a computer web, or ecosystem."[1]

Taoism, Confucianism, Shintoism, and Zoroastrianism

In Taoism, the foundation of ethics is to learn the wisdom of nature, which Lao Tzu summed up in the Tao Te Ching #10: "Creative endeavor without possession, action without aggression, and development without domination." Confucians believe that people should keep heaven, earth, and humanity in balance, which is achieved through deft practice of the primary intimate societal relationships. "Be fair to people when they err, when good your pleasure show; their faults be quick to understand, in judging them be slow." I admire the Shinto concept of amae: to develop mature forms of dependence with family, colleagues, and chosen communities, and to become other-centered rather than I-centered. The Zoroastrians with whom I became acquainted enthusiastically engaged with and affirmed life, while they also resisted the powers of evil in themselves, among their intimates, friends, or loose in the world.

Judaism

I honor and strive to approximate Judaism's ethical goal of tikkun olam—to heal our broken but worthy world. Like Job, we need to assert our integrity yet remain humble before the ultimate; patiently do the justice we understand, and live the love we feel, while we respect others and have the courage to intervene on their behalf. I admire Martin Buber, who perceived evil as separation from the essential self and God and who viewed sins as choices that separate us from our own intuitions of divinity, other people, and human institutions. Wickedness can become a habitual giving-in to separateness, which leads people to treat others as *Its* rather than as *Thous*. Humanity tends to empower evildoers by tolerating or even abetting their wickedness—whether that was most Germans' treatment of their Jewish neighbors as Hitler's forces executed the Holocaust, Israelis when they dispossess, exile or ghettoize Palestinians, any of us when we "It" our neighbors.

Christianity, Islam, and Sikhism

Christianity urges us not to give in to anger or disrespect, to practice reconciliation, help others willingly and circumspectly, worship humbly, and even to love your enemies. I have been particularly guided by Martin Luther King, Jr.'s words and public ministry in this regard and tempered by Reinhold Niebuhr's Christian realism. I celebrate the Qur'an admonitions, "God has given to everyone a path and a way; so let there be no compulsion in religion.... And that God hates an aggressor." Sikhs I've known have been exemplary in sharing with others and earning an honest living. They strive to keep their minds and souls above life's tensions and divisions while taking personal responsibility to serve the larger community and the future.

Good and Evil

Good intentions can't make up for what we do or fail to do. Christian theologian Paul Tillich said: We experience freedom as responsibility and destiny as tragic. Religions often distinguish among different kinds of evil: as sins against oneself, against others, or against God. A great many people occasionally like to be wicked, to do something unwise for themselves or sinful according to their professed values, but hope that these actions will have few negative consequences for others. They confess to occasionally being disagreeable, even to elements of bad character; however, few believe that they regularly act reprehensibly or are malevolent. Social practices, norms, laws, and traditions that promote virtuous behavior while they minimize temptations toward evil are important tools in our efforts to be good.

Values that promote good behavior include mutual respect, empathy, democracy, just laws, compassion, negotiation, cooperation, fairness, truth-telling, restitution, and reconciliation. The practical steps urged during the Jewish High Holy Days are a useful model in confronting misdeeds: confess to sins committed against others, make amends, and then focus your future efforts on learning how not to repeat past errors. Concentrate on helping to heal the world. When you can't make amends directly because of death or absence, take analogous actions with people in similar situations. Doing no evil is not by itself being good. Neutrality is simply the zero point on the ethical spectrum between good and evil. Life's apparent cosmic neutrality as well as the prevalent selfishness and lack of concern of many other people are difficult for people to accept because we want to matter to the powers that be and to be cared about by others. Scientific and natural laws provide some guidelines for behavior, but we cannot base adequate ethical choices on physics, genetics, biology, or ecology alone. As human experiences have become universal, people are trying to develop more global and timeless expressions of morals and ethics.

Most people resist evil's worst expressions, but all have impulses toward evil. Paths to power such as conquest, domination, even violence, seem instinctual. It appears "natural" to act selfishly, and shortsightedly violate others rather than empower them. For some, to nurture is less instinctive than impulsive violence. Conquest feels easier than persuasion, domination easier than collaboration. Love takes more patience than selfish apathy.

Contexts of Consent and Routines of Decency

Since the emergence of humanity, most cultures claimed that their behaviors were appropriate while other groups exhibited "unacceptable"' behavior. Within a culture, many categories of people were thought unworthy of respect or consideration: women, children, subservient groups such as slaves, serfs, lower castes or classes, illegal immigrants, and the poor were not treated equally or even humanely by custom or law. Unfortunately, that is still true for many millions of people throughout the world.

Much of what people call evil may be caused by accidents or through stupidity. If we pay attention, prioritize appropriately, and reject deceptive information, we can avoid many accidents, but the only way to eliminate stupidity is to become better educated to understand the realities of life. At the same time, it's appropriate to enact policies that can minimize both accidents and stupidity, such as limiting access to murder weapons, and control of addictive or poisonous substances to reduce bad outcomes.

Two central foundations for evil actions arise when societies classify entire groups of people as beyond concern, and allow those with power to harm such groups, or they treat the natural world as an inexhaustible or expendable resource that can be used with impunity. To understand systematic evil, such as genocide, extinction, or individuals randomly killing large numbers of people, we need to focus our attention on the *cultures of consent* that engendered these heinous acts by enabling them. The media seems obsessed with flagrant evil acts, and deluge us with crime and horror programs, murder mysteries, and blood-and-mayhem news reports. The public and the media rush to explain away violent crime as the acts of aberrant individuals or the insane deviations of a tiny minority, while virtue is undermined by this chronic repetition of horrible evils or by the associated propaganda of fear, distrust, or impending Armageddon. We do need to remember and seek justice for evils committed, while focusing primarily on what communities can do to diminish contexts of consent that enable evil.

Good behavior is based on and fostered by *routine habits of decency*. Nonviolent activists, nurturers, and expert negotiators will help us learn habits of cooperation and fairness, processes of truth-telling, restitution, and reconciliation. We need to join in discovering the contentment that collaboration and peacefulness provide. We need to build museums modeling virtue, provide instructions in the skills and rhythms of decency to counter-balance our obsessions with the "banalities of evil" (Hannah Arendt's phrase).

Religious Evil and Disreputable Religious Institutions, or Cults

In *Fields of Blood: Religion and the History of Violence.* Karen Armstrong maintains that all religions have participated in violence. Ideological terrorists, religious or secular, believe their violations are sanctified on behalf of their God or cause (ideology, nation, or ethnic group). Cults can be identified by their authoritarian or absolute leaders, required member compliance within a totalitarian or manipulative organizational framework, exploitative demands for service and financial support, requirements for secrecy and deception, the regular use of mind-control techniques, devaluation of outsiders, and punishment for dissent. Cultish religiosity or ideology is maintained primarily by ignorance reinforced by false information, which promotes feelings of persecution, fanaticism, disconnection from ordinary living, or visions of apocalypse.

Guilt

We are all guilty of sins of commission and sins of omission, deeds that we shouldn't have done, and deeds we left undone that we should have done. We need to recognize our guilt when it really is ours; when we've personally committed a misdeed or have earned a portion of collective responsibility for social misbehaviors, injustices, or violations during adulthood. However, people feel misplaced guilt for much that's not their fault or was unavoidable. Some things happen by chance or are inevitable. Such things are abuses of guilt that continue to lay unjust burdens on humanity. Religions, cultures, and various groups are all blameworthy for inflicting such abuses, which magnify human tragedies.

Five common abuses of guilt are original sin, inherited guilt, inappropriate cultural stereotypes, perfectionism, and equating our feelings or thoughts with our deeds. Original sin is the concept that people are guilty simply because they are born: "In Adam's fall, we sinned all." People are imperfect and incomplete, but those aren't sins. I don't believe in original sin, and Unitarian Universalists don't commit the travesty of washing it away from infants that haven't learned how to sin and have committed no sin by being born. Inherited guilt is the idea that we inherit our ancestors' misdeeds and remain responsible for the mistakes they committed long ago. I don't believe that people inherit either a perpetrator's guilt or their ancestors' victim status because of their forebears' behavior or suffering. To try to impose inappropriate cultural stereotypes is an unfortunate tendency of religions and cultures that wish to force others to adopt their way of doing things as the only acceptable model for universal behavior. Perfectionism is the idea that people should become perfect, as Jesus, Buddha, or Muhammad are considered by some as perfect. No one, including our spiritual mentors, is perfect. Perfectionism makes good behavior unattainable. Guilt's fifth abuse is to equate feelings or thoughts with deeds. Occasionally, everyone has frightening feelings, terrible thoughts, and shameful fantasies, but most of the time, most of us control ourselves and don't turn these into harmful actions. This distinction between thoughts and feelings, and deeds remains central to any viable ethic. Today, people can increasingly concentrate on becoming responsible human beings, strive to be fair to everyone, do justice in our collective actions, reach deeper with compassion, and stretch our love beyond our intimate circles.

Sins and Virtues

Discussions of sin and virtue remain pervasive in identifying objectionable or desirable behavior. In the Western world, three primary categorizations persist: 1) The seven Roman Catholic sins are pride, anger, greed, lust, envy, gluttony, and sloth; 2) The ancient Greeks identified four primary virtues: wisdom, courage, being temperate, and doing justice; and 3) The three virtues found in the New Testament are faith, hope, and love. If the term "sin" offends, perceive sins as conscious mistakes, and virtues as wise choices. Few people abstain from all conscious mistakes, and every virtue can be overdone.

Augustine called pride the origin of all evils. The ancient Greeks' word for pride was *hubris,* which inevitably led to tragedies. Hindus think pride makes people overreach, and tragedy follows. East Asians perceive pride as losing right relationships within society, or causing imbalance among heaven, earth, and humanity. Many people today equate pride with uncontrolled egotism. This can take many forms: wealth, power, knowledge, ideology, ethnicity, class, or faith—for some, even arrogance about their ignorance. People have the right to self-respecting pride. Aristotle called this a golden mean between arrogance and self-deprecation. A temperate person does not keep bad company, credit herself for achievements not of her own making, or continue to consume products or participate in activities that she cannot wisely control, but temperance doesn't mean being anti-sensual. Most people's achievements and virtues are largely dependent on others and were enabled by their communities. Idolatry is displaced reverence. The ultimate spiritual pride is to worship yourself as a being who always deserves to be in charge, dominate, and win. Optimists think that everything will always come out right, while hopeful people simply try to make the most of their resources and opportunities, even amidst tragedy and disappointment, and find useful lessons in setbacks while they continue to savor life's many gifts even in the most challenging circumstances.

Sloth is a prevalent vice; people tend toward apathy, inactivity, and indolence. Humans are inevitably affected by natural-cosmic trends toward entropy, while love and faith allow us to persevere and remain energetic. *Hesed* is the popular Hebrew term for love or lovingkindness. Lovingkindness and compassion are also common Buddhist terms for the practice of empathy and love. The Golden Rule is a pervasive standard among world religions: If you want respect, cooperation, equity, and kindness from others, then you need to practice those behaviors yourself. The ancient Greeks divided love into eros (romantic love), philia (brotherly-sisterly love), and agape (love willing to make sacrifices for others). In the New Testament, Paul wrote: "Love suffers long, envies not, does not boast, is not selfish or easily provoked ... .and bears all" (1 Corinthians, 13). Faith and love provide understanding of how to treat others and counter our tendencies toward sloth and entropy.

The four remaining traditional sins, *gluttony, greed, lust, and envy,* are associated with excess. An appetite, a desire to own, sexual needs, and hopes of achieving successes aren't inherently bad, but each can easily grow beyond our control and become a bad habit that leads to poor health or can diminish or ruin our relationships. I'm an enthusiastic disciplined sensualist, but for most of us, most of the time, moderation in all sensual things is the wisest path. At seventy-eight, I have neither the appetite nor ability to pursue some earlier experiences I craved. As I matured, I've learned to more fully savor the pleasures that I still appreciate. We all have foods we can no longer digest and desires we can't fulfill, while social media tempts us to "satisfy" our sensual weaknesses. A worthwhile discipline for living well is to learn healthy substitutes that are both personally fulfilling and socially acceptable.

To possess *wisdom* has long been considered a worthy goal—to understand what's true, good, and feasible. We continue to adjust our understanding, which often entails making new choices. As Confucius said, wisdom lies in using knowledge to make good choices. The Bhagavad Gita, 4:38: the wise person is: "one not troubled in sorrow and not caught in craving, fear, or anger." Despite devastation, Job preserved his integrity while he remained faithful to his God, friends, and family. Ecclesiastes taught that there is an appropriate time for every kind of mood and action. *A Rosary of Islamic Readings* (2:56) states: "Reflection is an ocean, and wisdom the pearl you find in it." For me, wisdom means understanding based on experience, self-knowledge, empathy, a disciplined and balanced life, kindness, and social usefulness.

Anger is the most extreme and impactful sin because it often leads to despair, hatred, violation, and violence. The contrasting virtue is *courage,* but *justice* is also a powerful virtue by which to balance anger and occasionally transform it into a virtue. Anger is grounded in fear and lack of self-assurance, which makes those caught in anger volatile and unpredictable, sometimes so fearful that they despair or so enraged that they hate and despise. Anger reinforced by others easily escalates into violation, and violators consciously inflict lasting harm, whether by child molestation, adult rape, bodily harm, or murder. Violators are cowards, ready to become indignant, with compulsions to dominate and control their worlds.

Anger can also become a positive force, a powerful motivator. How does this transformation occur, and what does it motivate people to do? When we learn to channel our anger into actions that resolve problems rather than multiply them, anger can be transformed into appropriate self-assertion and involve actions that solve problems without violating others or betraying our own best qualities and intentions. We must be brave enough to do what needs to be done despite our fears and apprehensions. We need to treat people as worthy individuals, not as things, and concentrate on means that create proper ends.

How do we face up to life's complications? Gestalt therapist Fritz Perls said that when people resolve their internal and interpersonal conflicts and become reintegrated, they regain energy and vitality. Learn to avoid or minimize social contexts that suppress, oppress, or pervert your good intentions. Take responsibility for your choices; otherwise you remain a passive, dependent victim, drift into antisocial behavior, or become violent. Nonviolent activism is the most powerful way to become lastingly courageous. Don't persist in bad means toward good ends, stick to your principles, and use only forces that persuade rather than coerce. Refuse to follow bad policies, choose to join boycotts and strikes, discover solutions, and participate in institutions that exemplify your hopes.

Inspirations I've Drawn from Ethicists and Ethical Systems

In the fourth century BC, Aristotle wrote in his *Nicomachean Ethics* that nature equips individuals to receive virtue, but habits bring this ability to fulfillment. People need to learn and practice moral conflict. It is their task to aim at advantages for the whole of life, not just their selfish, short-term impulses. People must discover their own consuming vocations and devote their powers to their service. Excellence is destroyed by either excess or deficiency. Wisdom is the exclusion of whatever cannot be brought into subjection to our chosen ends. People need to use careful examination, logic, and reason, but must also refuse to become enslaved by them. People are made good by nature, habit, and law. Ignorance in moral choice is no excuse when individuals are responsible for their ignorance. Aristotle's intellectual descendant, Epicurus, wrote that the pursuit of pleasure should be guided both by the sobriety of reason and by transparency, and that it is wise to commit no act that you want to hide.

Spinoza held that to be rational, people had to make their reasoning, appetites, and environments compatible. Virtuous habits require a lifetime of experiential learning. People need to understand their desires, or they will become their slaves. Piety is simply doing justice and living with charity toward one's neighbors. Effective altruism requires societies to enforce unselfish norms. Reason stimulates creative effort, and creative efforts succeed through social cooperation, that allow us to nurture communities of friendship and kindness.

Hobbes postulated a social contract, a set of rules that rational people agreed on and accepted for their mutual benefit, on the condition that others in the group also followed these rules because it was in their mutual interest. Locke provided benchmarks for individual liberty and democratic institutions. Their shared understanding of 'inborn senses' remained based on peoples' evaluations of their experiences. The categorical imperatives of 17th-century German philosopher Kant were: act as if your moral principles might become universal, and never treat people only as means to an end. Combinations of empiricism and idealism liberated large swaths of humanity, stimulated political revolutions, and provided principles and foundations for democracies, more inclusive communities, and cooperation.

In the 19th century, more classes of people received the right to vote and to participate as citizens, and *utilitarian* ethics advocated the greatest good for the greatest number. American *pragmatist* William James held that ethics involves trust or faith because people cannot always determine proof before they make ethical decisions. Ethics requires that people learn to cooperate. Twentieth-century American pragmatist John Dewey believed that ethics inevitably remains experiential and experimental, so people need to focus on means that create such ends as education, and upon their chosen spiritual vocations. Ethics remain fallible because people can never be sure their choices will satisfy or fulfill them. Spiritual experiences remain important but must be tested to see whether they work for all and accomplish their intended results. Pragmatism connected ideas with practical experience and creative action.

Contemporary ethics usually tries to avoid extremes of either sacred or universal assumptions, the constraints of traditional customs, and rules or obligations that cannot be questioned. They want to look at each situation and at the various participants' roles in it. In the 1960s, Joseph Fletcher, a Christian *situational utilitarian,* proposed: do what you can, where you can, when you can, without falling into anarchy or impulsive choices, and without unbending principles. When I was a Harvard Fellow, I studied the *responsibility ethics* of H. Richard Niebuhr, James Gustafson, and Stanley

Hauerwas, whose ethical rule is: to discover the most fitting thing to do in a given set of circumstances. All three encourage us to take responsibility for our actions and to develop ethical dispositions that guide us intuitively. They believe that religious beliefs provide special ethical sensitivities and helpful ways to apprehend and intuit the right thing to do in any given situation. John Rawls proposed *contractual ethics,* by which we can develop procedures that best sustain life in a social context and best develop standards of freedom, equity, and fairness that are separable from religion and cultural traditions. His basic question is: what do people owe each other? Individuals choose their plan of life to regulate their actions to assert their sense of justice.

In *A Feminist Ethic of Risk,* Sharon Welch proposed that a lone person can't be moral. We need relationships and communities; we have no choice but to embrace our differences and cultural diversity. *Communal ethics* that propose that one group's ideas and actions are the only way must be replaced by *communicative ethics,* which combine pluralism and social responsibility. We can't eliminate human conflict or nature's limitations, but by realizing that divinity is simply a quality of relational power, we can replace false notions of perfection with grace—the resilient healing powers of everyday living. A self-realized person is fundamentally a history of those caring relationships with others that nurture love of life in relatedness, enables us to accept accountability, and to discover a larger self.

Martin Seligman's and Christopher Peterson's *character ethics* is explained in *Character, Strengths, and Virtues.* It lists and describes the richness in virtuous character traits including wisdom (creativity, open-mindedness), humanity (love, social intelligence), justice (fairness, leadership), temperance (self-control, forgiveness), transcendence (gratitude, humor), and courage (perseverance, vitality). We must learn when to give up, and to know ourselves we need to be known by others.

A particularly important ethics book for me is Peter Singer's *One World: The Ethics of Globalization.* A bioethics professor at Princeton, he believes different interests warrant different treatment: a starving person's interest should be given more weight than someone with only a minimal desire; a poor person who steals food should be treated more leniently than a corporate executive who stole millions from thousands for years. We need to balance all the interests in a situation, and then maximize the legitimate interests of those most adversely affected. People are self-interested and competitive, yet, if society provides the right conditions, people often act ethically together, using reason to do the good they understand with substantial capacities for cooperation, empathy, and self-sacrifice.

In our global, world no single entity is really in charge; however, international corporations have too much power and put their profits ahead of individual rights and environmental sustainability. Widespread incentives have deregulated the private sector too much, which has hurt a growing proportion of the world's population and seriously degraded the global environment. In 1985, the world responded to the crisis of refrigerants that caused depletion of atmospheric ozone by implementing the Montreal Protocol; by 1999, the hole in the ozone layer had stopped growing. We humans don't lack the capacity to face our problems, but often lack sufficient attention, education, and the prompt international actions that are needed.

Singer proposes that global authorities set minimum standards for environmental protection, worker safety, union rights, and animal rights; pursue a renewable energy policy with tools such as carbon credits, and help developing economies move directly into 21st-century technologies. Rich nations need to cut tariffs, particularly agricultural tariffs. Globally, nations need to cooperate, the most progressive international bodies need to realistically be strengthened, the UN Security Council should be expanded, the ability of any nation to veto international agreements and actions should end, and representation in all international legislative bodies should be based on national population. Singer believes that if all economically developed nations gave just one percent of their annual national wealth for programs for the less-developed nations, global poverty could be eliminated in a generation.

My Ethical Views

I believe that continuing adult development transforms ethical growth into lifelong ethical maturation. This progresses from a sense of what we like and want, to autonomy, then initiative, and on to skills and achievements. Eventually, we develop a strong identity within a social order, and as young adults a growing mastery. In middle-age, people search for truth and intimacy built on social contracts and higher laws. In maturity, our ethics can either stagnate or evolve into concern for the future as we seek personal integrity and universal justice through service to others. In old age, we can either fall into despair or maintain our integrity, largely determined by whether we can focus beyond ourselves to a future beyond our own lives.

I believe in a spirituality judged by our deeds. I don't blame demonic powers for my bad actions. I am responsible, and when we're part of a group or society, we bear a portion of responsibility for that group's or society's actions during our lifetimes. The more privileged we are, the more responsibility we have for what occurs during our adulthood. In society, it's often what we haven't done that we could and should have done, our cultures of consent, that allow evil to flourish. We need to face up to reality, spread our justice-doing toward everyone in a global society, with emphasis on those most in need, if our species is to endure and thrive.

To do justice combines justice and mercy, standing by principles, and being fair. It involves appropriate anger for bad behavior and the will to inflict justified punishment for those who break laws, act unfairly, or create harm. People tend to believe that others ought to live by the rules, but too often exempt themselves and their intimates from the constraints of those rules, or believe that their nation, ethnicity, or class can be excused from appropriate behavior—as in American exceptionalism, being lighter in skin color, or higher in class, caste, or power. To be faithful, we all need to play by rules that guide us so we do not violate others.

I agree with the Old Testament prophet Micah: "What the Lord requires is to do justice, love mercy, and walk humbly with your God" (Micah 6:8). We should do justice both in individual interactions and by supporting groups that do justice in their collective actions. To be merciful is to give people the benefit of the doubt and treat them generously and kindly even when we feel they haven't earned such treatment. We need to err on the side of mercy and kindness because our feelings and judgments may be wrong, biased, or unduly affected by experiences that are no longer applicable. We can't choose which laws we're going to apply to ourselves, our friends, or members of our identity groups while we hold others to a different standard; nor do I believe that we should give people a pass for bad behavior because their ancestors were oppressed.

Obsessing on individual choice and group autonomy as signs of liberation and acts of freedom appear, at times, to have diluted evil into transgression and turned responsibility into experiment. I do not believe that ethical behavior can be replaced by psychological diagnoses or sociological excuses for antisocial behavior. Most mentally unstable people don't become serious criminals, and most people with miserable life histories still function lawfully in society. Elements of modernity have tended to universalize victimhood and use historic injustices, poverty, or failed parenting to excuse lawbreaking and bad behavior. Forms of individual excess and antisocial choices have historical roots, but most of those who suffer from these historic and/or current inequities do not break laws, become addicts, remain homeless, or reject the viable alternatives offered by civic institutions and community groups.

It's appropriate to punish people who break the law, and to insist on treatment and, when socially necessary, institutionalization of the mentally ill and addicted for their antisocial acts. It's fair to expect impoverished people as well as the privileged to be law-abiding. It would be wise to isolate and control people who can't or won't become responsible for their own behavior, and to tax and penalize all who continue to burden society by behaving irresponsibly, whether they're individuals, groups, corporations, or institutions. Justice needs to be as fair as possible, but like all virtues, it's always a work in progress.

Individuals may be virtuous at certain moments or courageous in a particular context. Character is demonstrated throughout our lifetimes and is usually judged by demonstrating some consistency. To an ethicist's perennial question about the value of people doing good acts for inadequate reasons, I believe that's still usually preferable because desirable behavior helps people who've done good things for bad reasons acquire the habit of acting responsibly. When we experience kindness, mercy, love, or forgiveness, we're more likely to practice them. The central disciplines of ethical growth are our gradually developed ability to become more altruistic, less narcissistic, have objectives broader than merely satisfying our own egos or our immediate appetites. For ethical groups and governments, the reduction of violent, cruel, greedy, and oppressive acts, and the cultures of consent that enable them need to remain primary goals, whether the practitioners are dictators, soldiers, terrorists, suicidal murderers, or greedy or violent parents, spouses, neighbors, friends, or colleagues.

Relationships are normally built upon reciprocity; however, when confronted with violations of self, intimates, institutions or values that we hold dear, we often focus opposition on these opponents to protect ourselves and our interests. When we feel secure and/or are emotionally connected with others, we're more likely to be merciful, but when we feel most threatened and/or least connected, we're more likely to inflict harsh justice in thoughts, words, and/or deeds. I agree with Carol Gilligan that a superior ethics is an effective synthesis of an ethics of rules, rights, and equal treatment with an ethics of relationships, care, and nurture.

Societies can't maximize all positive values simultaneously. Who benefits most from the decisions being made? If we increase profits and other economic advantages for wealthy individuals and businesses, as most of the world presently does with their tax, regulation, and power arrangements, then workers' rights, economic fairness, and public funds sufficient to support the most vulnerable will not receive their due. If we broaden individual liberty, as the U.S. and several other nations presently do, then those societies make themselves especially vulnerable to bad individual choices and disruptive and vicious social behaviors. If a medical system makes every possible effort to keep the elderly alive, even when only a few more months of marginal existence remain for them, then it's unlikely that such societies will also have the resources needed for the preventive care and medical attention that the rest of their populations deserve. Individuals, groups, societies, and nations must choose and prioritize; the already privileged need to make genuine sacrifices for justice to be done. We must face conflicts by constantly negotiating so we understand one another and proceed nonviolently, since violence inevitably causes more problems than it resolves. Our objectives should be: to strive to do justice, be fair, and whenever feasible to act with compassion and love.

I am a utilitarian who practices situational ethics based upon acting responsibly, as much as possible with empathy and fairness for everyone involved. Effective ethics is a synthesis of good habits and social justice practiced with care and fairness. Love, genuine social equity, and universal justice remain worthy ideals, but for most people, being tolerant, trying to act fairly, and hoping to do justice are what they can manage. A modicum of internal peace and joy, combined with stretching themselves to love a few intimates, be trustworthy with friends, and fair with colleagues, is what most people set as their standards for good behavior. As a 21st-century ethical goal, I urge that we steadily shift the balance of our lives, as individuals and as societies, toward the realizable goal of investing 25 percent of our time, energy, talent, and wealth: in our own best long-term interests, those of our intimates, of our chosen groups (from family to nation), and the essential needs of humanity and the Earth.

The desirable goal is not I win, you lose, we both lose, or you win and I lose, but rather that all of us experience a net gain from our interactions. Such results routinely require negotiation, compromise, and cooperation, and are abetted by patience and maturity. Institutions that function effectively make positive outcomes much more likely. These attitudes and methods challenge us to understand ourselves and each other and ask us to nurture our communities and the sustainability of our environment. They thrive when people and groups can work together to achieve visions beyond their immediate desires. They become effective as people work together to nurture mutual understanding so they can respond to life's challenges with actions that embody soul force, compassion, and deeper intimacy. Our planet has grown into a global village in which everyone can potentially become a worthy neighbor. Our friendship circles and sense of community must begin to approximate a global embrace.

Chapter 21
From Experiences to Conceptual Systems and Back

P eople have experiences, process them through varied forms of thought, and test their interpretations with later experiences. Consider this hierarchy for the reliability of experience, with data, information, knowledge, and wisdom as its ascending levels. It keeps only data that have proven reliable, holds on to information that remains relevant for the future, continues to credit knowledge that still shapes our thinking, and considers wise only knowledge that continues to explain our choices. People embrace different styles of primary attachment: secure, anxious, or avoidant. About half are primarily secure and remain open to new ideas. Another quarter is anxious, wants to work with others, but still feels disrespected. The remaining quarter leave conflicts unresolved and reject others' attempts at intimacy. Formed in childhood, attachment styles can evolve with effort. There are also various forms of intelligence; everyone has aspects of each, and particular situations bring certain forms of intelligence into intense development. Forms of intelligence include verbal, logic-mathematical, practical, kinesthetic, musical, interpersonal, intrapersonal, and naturalist-scientist.

Thinking combines fast intuitive decisions grounded in memory, and slow, deliberate thinking that requires training and repetitive practice. Both are necessary, desirable, and inevitably continue. Expert intuitives are experienced people who've developed abilities in their specialties that allow them to recognize relevant patterns and quickly produce wise responses. Formal education or status aren't necessary to be wise or effective. Many people are dependably effective within their chosen areas of experience. My occasional childhood companion, Annie, the African American caretaker of my maternal grandfather's Georgia farm, had no formal education, but knew that farm intimately, understood each of its cows, accurately predicted the weather, and most of the time held the place together singlehandedly. In her venue, she was an expert intuitive and a woman of great character who had a lasting influence on my life.

Be wary of efforts to manipulate you toward your most selfish or short-term impulses—particularly electronic media, which does this so successfully. Mastery requires many experiences, persistent effort, and lots of practice. No one is instantly good at anything important. We need also to learn how to do a better job with our unconscious rapid thinking. Expert intuitives can better account for their judgments because they learn from their mistakes and adjust their opinions accordingly. We need to discard our prejudices and narrow-mindedness so we're able to think as wisely with our intuitive hearts as we try to do with our logical analysis and scientific inquiries; to become as wise and loving with our intuitive thinking as we hope to be accurate and honest in our logical analysis. Without spiritual practices that require learning, nurturing, and control of both our intuitions and our reasoning, it becomes impossible to realize a responsible search for truth or a wise and loving ethical life.

To realize any goal, we must suppress other goals. Maturity requires us to accept the reality of diminished powers, restricted freedom, and imperfect connections with the people we love. We need to discover socially acceptable substitutes for unacceptable impulses. Negotiation is the basis for social interchange because it gives each partner some power to bargain and compromise until we find acceptable outcomes. Say *We* instead of *I*, ask questions, and reveal what you don't know.

Becoming a victim may often be out of our control, but remaining a victim is always a choice. We need to take responsibility for our own recoveries. Most grownups learn to accommodate their needs to the greater good of loving relationships, to delegate authority, and sometimes to surrender rather than resist. Different categories of thinking about thinking vary, but the underlying point is that we think and act in a variety of ways over time, even in our interactions with the same people or in similar situations. Those differences may confuse or challenge others, so it helps to remember that we've used many ways of thinking ourselves, and that each can be useful and effective. We need to take responsibility for our actions, remain able to change, and sustain both hopeful enthusiasm and humble realism. These insights can become a basis for a 21st-century ethics that combines responsibility, altruism, and compassion.

Your level of comfort in groups, relative dependence on data or imagination in making choices, the relative weight you give to feelings or analysis, and whether you like to keep options open or make up your mind varies greatly. I tend to be a "both-and" instead of an "either-or" person: I prefer to use both my intuitive-imaginative faculties and my logical-analytic faculties, to make use of the great myths and rituals of traditions, but not to mistake them for spiritual sustenance. I want people to read scriptures and other great literature as useful tools to understand and make the most of their own experiences, but never to forsake the need to find their own individual paths and practice their personal spiritual disciplines.

Erik Erikson's adult stages of development, and those of Maslow, Kohlberg, Fowler, Gilligan, and other developmental psychologists, have been crucial to my life, ministry, and conceptual thinking because they perceive truth as probable and life as evolving. They provide both direction beyond the egoistic and short-term, and hope for maturation and continual progress as individuals, in communities, and globally. Erikson explored varied psychological developments in distinct cultures and wrote developmental psychological biographies of Martin Luther and Mahatma Gandhi. One of his students, Robert Coles wrote *The Spiritual Life of Children*, which explored how children of different religions coped with life in spiritual terms.

> Each child is a pilgrim, with a spirit and a spiritual life that grows, changes, and responds constantly to other lives that make up the individual we call by a name and know by a story that is all his or hers. All of us are wanderers, explorers, adventurers, stragglers, and sometimes tramps, vagabonds, even fugitives. All are travelers on a road with some spiritual purpose in mind.[1]

As parents, teachers and child-care workers know, children vary incredibly. My children were and are quite different, as are my four grandchildren. A child's brain is literally growing. At age seven, the brain has only 10 percent of its adult volume; by age sixteen, brain volume has grown to 90 percent of its adult size. I'm eternally grateful for the adults and older youth who treated me as a credible learner and challenged me to stretch my capacities as I grew. I've done my best to act similarly with my own children and grandchildren and the hundreds of children I've known. Each person we encounter is worthy of our attention and respect. Each will take in and use what they can, and sometimes, what they find most challenging in the moment may later inspire them to breakthroughs previously unimagined.

Approaching life and the world with awe is the foundation for gratitude, and respect is the foundation on which gratitude is built in our communities. Three gifts of maturity are the courage to live with an *attitude of abundance*—whatever your circumstances, the ability to decide that you have *enough,* and a continual willingness to find practical *balances* in your living. These enable us to be sustainable creators, responsible workers, and effective citizens instead of egotistical competitors, greedy consumers, or self-satisfied narcissists. Emotions remain stronger than thoughts, for we are social-emotional creatures from start to finish, so we need to foster positive emotions, reach out to others, and create mutually nurturing environments.

Consciousness always feels like something. Psychologists say we're in flow when we're aware of the impermanence of reality, able to tune into our deeper selves and the futures beyond our individual lives. We're truly focused, can allow feelings to arise without rejecting them, and make wiser choices about whether to act on them. We are being conscientious while being fully conscious. We need to learn to postpone gratification, continue being responsible, maintain internal emotional control, and keep a hopeful outlook, particularly in the face of adversity. Learn to relax when anxiety arises, then actively challenge your worrisome thoughts. As the Dalai Lama explained: Stop fighting inevitabilities, in yourself or the world. Solitude is chosen time-outs so that you can connect with and be responsive to others, while loneliness endures by remaining disconnected because you are angry, frightened or have avoided responsibilities, and makes you think that you can flourish alone.

Spiritual Pluralism

Because my family encouraged me to mingle with a variety of people, I learned early that there were many individuals who were ignored but were truly wise people of good character. These experiences trained me to become a pluralist; we need to balance our thinking between rational, analytical thought and imaginative, intuitive, meditative practices. Meditation can free the mind—tune us into the rhythms of nature, music, and other people, and focus our attention on what is useful for the larger self and the future beyond our existence.

I've participated in ecumenical efforts including the International Association for Religious Freedom, Interfaith Councils in Bergen County, New Jersey, Sacramento, California, Jacksonville, Florida, and San Francisco. For many clergy and lay leaders, ecumenical organizations offer the deepest encounters with other faiths, interfaith dialogues, and civic efforts for society's progress.

My model for spiritual pluralism is Professor Diana Eck, who was also much influenced by Erik Erikson. At Harvard in 1987, I audited her course on Gandhi. As I became better acquainted with Eck's written works, I realized that she was an exemplary model of the spiritual pluralism that I was trying to live and to share with others. Her creation and leadership of Harvard's Pluralism Project (carrythevision.org) and her book, *A New Religious America: How a "Christian Country" Has Become the World's Most Religiously Diverse Nation* awoke the American public to the fact that, since the 1965 Immigration Act, the U.S. has become the world's most religiously pluralistic nation. The United States is not a Christian nation, but both by law and by custom, a religiously diverse nation whose highest principles are individual liberty and religious freedom. A majority of nonchurchgoing Americans do identify as Christians; however, we rarely view people as employed simply because they approve of working or as college graduates because they occasionally read a book.

Harvard's Pluralism Project website summarizes Eck's four principles of religious pluralism: it entails energetic engagement with diversity; actively seeks understanding across boundaries of difference; is an encounter of commitments; and is based on dialogue. Pluralism doesn't mean anything goes; it also doesn't mean giving up one's own truth in favor of some

413

unconvincing spiritual correctness. It doesn't presume that all religious truth is the same, or that all good people believe all the same things. Instead, it tries to discover shared beliefs and practical ways in which people can work actively and effectively together. It holds that differences needn't be only sources of anxiety and tension but can also provide powerful impetus toward a fuller truth, deeper personal practices, and a more neighborly and loving global community. Effective pluralism must continue to be earned, as it requires continued participation in and attunement with the lives and energies of those who are different. It is much more than "being tolerant." Spiritual pluralism inspires us to become inter-religiously literate, self-conscious about our own spiritual contexts by learning to question our own visions in dialogue with global "others." At the Installation of my UU colleague, Galen Guengerich, at All Souls in New York City, Eck's said:

> In a world divided by race and religion, the very presence of a church like this, committed to the oneness of God, the love of God and neighbor, and of service to humanity is a beacon for the world. UU theology does not reduce the mystery of the divine but broadens it to include the many, many ways in which the divine is known and yet unknown. The world is in need of your theology.[2]

My passion is to help these principles become practical realities. Most Unitarian Universalists still have quite a bit more work to do to actualize them. The vision is there, but we need to deepen our own personal spiritual developments, grow beyond our anxieties about becoming fervently religious, and be willing to fully engage with our spiritual neighbors.

Krista Tippett is the creator and host of the public radio/podcast *On Being* and the author of *Becoming Wise: An Inquiry into the Mystery and Art of Living*. She says Christianity is her mother tongue and homeland, but that her yoga practice and the nourishment she gets from Buddhist and other spiritual texts are now as important in her life. She calls her audience seekers with serious spiritual and religious practices, along with others still searching for their spiritual paths. They grow as much through questions as answers, and that non-Judeo-Christian practices are transforming millions of lives.

We are the first generation who have not mostly inherited our spiritual identities, are without much religious baggage, and are committed to uniting our inner and outer lives. We need to be faithful in ways that can be lived today, with a broader and deeper collective consciousness. We need the wisdom of spiritual traditions to deal with suffering and merge our spiritual and civic lives.[3]

Michael Krasny was co-host of *Forum,* San Francisco's preeminent interview program on KQED radio, wrote a touching argument for theological agnosticism entitled *Spiritual Envy.* He grew up Jewish but decided that he wanted to understand religion in a spiritual and mystical way, arguing that people often make choices based on an intuitive-emotional sense that there is a higher meaning which provides ways to fulfillment and peace. Having interviewed prominent atheists, he discovered they resembled fundamentalists. He urges us to abandon scientism without either curtailing science or forsaking transcendence and immanence.

The United Religions Initiative (URI) is a leading global grassroots peacebuilding network with more than 850 members in over ninety-five countries. Begun by San Francisco Episcopal Bishop William Swing in 2000, and now led by Episcopal Canon Charles Gibbs in San Francisco, URI cultivates changemakers across religious, cultural, and geographic boundaries. It harnesses their collective power to take on religion-motivated violence and social, economic, and environmental crises that destabilize regions and contribute to poverty. Its basic organizational unit is interfaith cooperative circles made up of at least seven individuals, from at least three different religions or spiritual traditions, who meet regularly. There are 207 cooperative circles in Africa, 314 in Asia, fifty-four in Europe, forty-eight in Latin America, seventy-seven in the Middle East and North Africa, seventy-six in North America, fifty-three in Southeast Asia, and fifty-three that communicate only electronically. Their primary activity varies from interfaith dialogue to peacebuilding, human rights, health, ecological imperatives, and sustainable, just economies.

Eboo Patel is the founder and executive director of the Interfaith Youth Core (IYC), which organizes interfaith groups of young adults to carry out volunteer projects. Patel grew up in a Chicago suburb, received his doctorate in sociology of religion at Oxford, and is an Ismaili Shia Muslim. He writes *Faith Divide,* a blog for *The Washington Post,* and wrote *Acts of Faith: The Story of an American Muslim, the Struggle for the Soul of a Generation.* The IYC combines volunteer cooperation with a vision of large-scale transformation; it takes spiritual diversity seriously, by bringing varied faiths' young adults together for the common good. Patel believes the Qur'an assumes that each reader brings his own experience to its interpretation, that Islam's central message is to establish an ethical, egalitarian order on Earth, and that God has given every person an inner light. Patel opposes all religious totalitarianisms and is concerned that tremendous resources are being invested into reactionary schools and websites. As Archbishop Desmond Tutu said: "Religion is like a knife: you can either use it to cut bread or stick it in someone's back."

All of us spend our lives having experiences and then trying to make sense of them. My own life as well as my vicarious experiences through education and relationships with many congregants, activist colleagues, and students has convinced me that there are natural progressions through increasingly complex and nuanced conceptual systems. We have experiences, judge them to be successes or failures, and if we are wise, we learn from both and make progress during our lives. As it is natural to progress from your birth family and friends to your chosen and nurtured family and friends, so in the modern world it's also natural to progress from relying solely on the traditions and beliefs of your childhood and to take progressive steps to nurture the traditions that remain effective for you, while you continue to test and evolve your beliefs to fit your experiences.

Chapter 22
Spiritual Evolution

S piritual evolution is pervasive and continuous because individuals continue changing and groups and traditions react, develop, and adapt. In this final chapter, we consider how global spiritualities have evolved during the last seventy years.

In *After Heaven: Spirituality in America Since the 1950s*, Princeton Professor Robert Wuthnow discusses three spiritual modes. In his sacred-place spirituality, God creates a fixed sacred space wherein people may dwell with God within clear religious traditions represented by their local congregation, which provides boundaries, exclusion, and security. Wuthnow believes that habitation spiritualities fail to provide people the individual freedom or dignity they deserve and inadequately respond to a global society's needs. In his "seeking" mode, individuals seek sacred moments that reinforce their conviction that the divine exists, continue to explore new spiritual vistas, and negotiate among complex and confusing meanings to guide their contemplations or occupations. He believes seeker spirituality lacks boundaries and constraints and remains unfocused upon any particular objective, so these faiths remain too fluid to provide the needed social support, and fail to encourage the stability or dedication required for individuals to mature either spiritually or in character. His preferred mode is spiritual-practice religion, which puts spiritual responsibility squarely upon everyone to regularly spend time in worship, in communion with, and trying to understand the ultimate sources of sacredness in their lives. It normally contains community elements and is embedded in existing religious traditions, but requires individuals to continue to engage reflectively, develop moral and ethical dimensions that instruct on how they should behave, while they remain hopeful and aware of the finitude and partiality of their own faith so they become increasingly aware of the mysterious and transcendent within the sacred.

For a generation, Elizabeth Lesser was the organizer behind the Omega Institute, the Hudson River valley retreat center that I attended in the 1980s. To become spiritually mature, she believes that we must use psychology to resolve our childhood issues and unrealistic expectations, and mature into disciplined love that blends healthy aspects of both masculinity and femininity while we challenge patriarchal obsessions with power and control, proceeding slowly and patiently with a persistent sense of humor and compassion. Her book *The Seeker's Guide* divides spiritual terrain into four landscapes: mind, heart, body, and soul. Landscape of the mind focuses on meeting life on its own terms; we choose curiosity instead of control, move where events are flowing instead of constantly struggling against life's dominant currents, and discover ways to proceed outside of our own limited perspectives. Her landscape of the heart focuses on finding your own true voice, stay open to your feelings without the need to always act upon them, become less judgmental or unforgiving, and more spontaneously filled with wonder and love. Her landscape of the body focuses on letting your energy flow, accepting support, and giving up control while taking responsibility. Her landscape of the soul focuses on attention to simple pleasures, and since hatred, annoyance, and grudges block the soul's energy, instead concentrate on forgiveness, kindness, and generosity.

Leigh Eric Schmidt, also at Princeton, wrote *Restless Souls: The Making of American Spirituality from Emerson to Oprah*, which proposes that transcendentalist Ralph Waldo Emerson, with his combination of spiritual mysticism, scientific naturalism, cosmopolitan religion, and progressive social activism, represents both the foundation and future of American religion. Schmidt also believes that religious freedom requires regularly practiced spiritual discipline, quiet reflection, focused meditation, patient communication, and an activist social conscience that eventuates in effective actions. People need to be in communities that enable their spiritual practices and empower them to put good intentions into action. Freedom needs to be tested through effective social action; mysticism tempered by rationality, and tolerance empowered by spiritual democracy and a clear-eyed spiritual universalism.

Schmidt agrees with Robert Bellah and his coauthors who in *Habits of the Heart* declared that U.S. individualism had grown cancerous and was laying waste to civic institutions and religious traditions. Schmidt is critical of the prosperity gospel popularized first by Norman Vincent Peale and maintained by many others. Schmidt calls this the "Oprah-fication of religion," and claims that it rests too casually on feel-good experiences and a shopping mall-consumerist mentality. Spectator-based spiritual experiences can only empower individuals when they proceed with canny self-awareness and self-criticism and a genuine acquaintance with the evolution of religions and ideologies. People must recognize that their prosperity gospels usually remain soaked in unresolved conflicts and unrealized perfectionism.

Many Americans have a high degree of religious identification accompanied by a low level of religious literacy, even about their own religion. This is often as true for people who believe they are devout as for those who identify as irreligious or are filled with doubts. In *Religious Literacy: What Every American Needs to Know—And Doesn't*, Stephen Prothero points out that while two thirds of Americans say they believe that the Bible holds the answers to most of life's basic questions, only one third even know that Jesus delivered the Sermon on the Mount, and 10 percent thought Joan of Arc was Noah's wife! As *New York Times* writer Nicholas Kristof, a Roman Catholic, reminded us in his Dec. 13, 2015, column: religions are a tangle of contradictory teachings; the Bible has twice as many violent-cruel passages as the Qur'an, and we continue to dangerously "otherize" those outside of our own groups, making them seem perilous (i.e. in 1944, 44 percent of U.S. citizens believed we should kill our Japanese citizens). *The Week* magazine (11/6/09) reported that a majority of Americans who chose no religious identity, nevertheless believed in God, and one third of them prayed at least weekly.[1] In *American Grace: How Religion Divides and Unites Us*, sociologists David Campbell and Robert Putnam noted that Americans have become a nation of religious changelings, unabashed religious entrepreneurs who often go church shopping.

In his Dec. 22, 2013 column, *New York Times* writer and Roman Catholic Ross Douthat proposed that there are three spiritual Americas: devout Biblical—with a vertical link between God and their tradition; the spiritual are connected horizontally with Earth and believe the divine is active in human affairs; and the secular are comfortable seeing the sacred as simply liberty, fraternity, and human rights, but represent only a small proportion of Americans, though are predominant among the intelligentsia.[2] Then, in his April 6, 2017, column, Douthat had decided that although liberal mainline churches had suffered institutional decline, they had triumphed culturally. Their most distinctive features: ecumenical spirituality and a progressive social gospel now permeate academia, the media, pop culture, and the Democratic Party. As a Republican, he feared that U.S. plurality would lose its liberalism and become an illiberal cult of "victimology" willing to condemn dissenters, and that this progressive majority needed to discover a non-transactional organizing principle because spiritual impulses without religious institutions are unable to bind families together or deter personal despair.[3]

There's a growing tendency to think we have a right to believe whatever we want, regardless of the evidence. This cultural inclination has been enabled by philosophical relativism and consumerist-materialist narcissism. We need to remain aware of our own frailty, continue to have visceral interactions with nature and direct experience and respectful dialogue with other people who think and act differently, and remain systematically involved in working cooperatively with these "others." We need to continue to improve our ability to listen to and heed our inner wisdom while also stretching beyond ideological comfort food into purposeful ethical actions, empathy with "others," and effective caregiving that enable us to energize humanity and sustain the future.

Spiritual Practices

A primary intent of this book has been to help you understand that your spiritual practices can lead to satisfactory maturity, lasting happiness, fulfillment, and peace of mind and spirit. No one reaches a point of perfection. Particular actions during one life stage may not work well later, so we all continue to learn, change, adapt, and find what works now with our own and others' evolving personalities and circumstances.

Spiritual practices continue to evolve throughout our lives. As a youth I did not consciously pray; now I pray often. As a teenager, I began to spend time in quiet reflection, but didn't consciously adopt specific meditation methods until I was a minister. My meditation practices continue to change, not only from one year to another but occasionally from one week to another. My relationship with religious scriptures began as intellectual curiosity; then I worked at understanding them, and eventually integrated many scriptural passages from various traditions as vital references for my spiritual life. As a young minister, I rewrote basic elements of the Christian scriptures and creeds, and have continued to reinterpret central elements of other world scriptures throughout my life.

In my thirties, I wrote versions of all 150 Old Testament Psalms (published as *Creation Songs*). The Psalms are foundational in Jewish and Christian liturgies. Yet, I found many psalms to be violent, hateful, or bigoted. Seven years later, when I had completed *Creation Songs*, I had a deeper understanding of and respect for the psalmists' intent; the relevance of many psalms was saved for me by a phrase or two, or even a single idea found in a particular psalm, that made spiritual sense to me. For instance, my version of Psalm 97 was vital for some—including several congregants who requested that it be included at their death services:

We are a multitude of islands adrift in the blissful ocean of God. Darkness and complexity surround us, yet goodness and truth remain the essence of life. Some of us serve idols. Others boast of themselves. Each person must decide what is to be served and do those things. God seems far away, so preserve us with caring friends. Light spreads from righteous action, gladness glows from the upright heart. Rejoice and give thanks for the common grace of our days.

I tried throughout my active ministry to develop and share rituals, holidays, and sacraments not only from traditional Christian and Jewish traditions and Native American cultural practices but from the other great historic religions, including the contemporary African American holiday Kwanzaa. You have your own experiences, which are the foundation for your understanding, beliefs, and hopefully for your life practices.

You will benefit if you develop a home altar with images, photos, and mementos, and pay attention to it daily. A weekly tour of your residence can connect you with loved ones, treasured friends, and special places or times in your life. A monthly pilgrimage to a place or event that nurtures and renews your soul can be as valuable for your spirit as a physical workout is for your body. Many of us participate in a spiritual community or other group organized to further certain beliefs and practices—friendship or activist groups, professional or labor associations, or issue-related events all can become essential tools for your life's fulfillment. Find an opportunity, at least yearly, to retreat from your ordinary existence, perhaps at a retreat center, workshop, or vacation, that sweeps you clear of electronic media, work and routines, and recharges your life and spiritual batteries. Keep a loose-leaf notebook of your favorite scriptural passages, poems, and sayings that helps you review your beliefs and hopes. It's also useful to try to summarize what you believe as your circumstances change and you proceed through life.

Spiritual practices cover a broad spectrum of activities. As a teen, I found weekly solace in walking quietly alone for an hour or two around my little town's outskirts, observing nature, people, buildings, and myself. Now, in my seventies, I find myself again able to quietly sit and observe for renewal periods—sometimes even amidst crowds of people. You might find spiritual renewal in dancing with friends, attending a concert, reading a poem, or carefully observing a human scene, a work of art, or a moment in nature.

Many of my own intense spiritual experiences were in friendly discussions with people I respected. Years of repetition sometimes prove invaluable. I can be repeating something I've thought or said a thousand times, and in a particular moment, it can break open my heart and connect me with the enduring, so I meditate every day, at least for moments, sometimes for an hour or two, and I pray every day, that is, I address the universe or Creation and express gratitude for events that have occurred and hopes for actions I wish to take. Sometimes my meditations appear to come up empty, and certainly my wishes aren't always fulfilled, but these practices nonetheless remain central to my happiness and fulfillment. I urge you to remember each day to breathe deeply, sit in silence, and express gratitude and hope. I don't care what you call these practices—just do them, whether you feel like it or not, because eventually they'll provide abundant harvests.

The basic test for any life is whether you've developed practices that help you fulfill what you understand and believe, that keep you sane in an often confusing world, and give you peace in your spirit, given life's inevitable tragedies, disappointments, and triumphs. You fail yourself when you don't regularly find time to nurture your spirit, pause in quiet to weigh what's most important so you can continue to make wise choices. It matters what we do.

Your vocations are important, your paid employment and volunteer work, but also your leisure. There's so much beauty and worth in the world that I advocate focusing on them while not being blind to the ugliness. It remains tempting to be seduced by the ugly, violent, or awful, but why waste time on behaviors and activities we're ashamed of ourselves? Confront life's realities, including the ugliest and most repugnant, but don't degrade your life by giving them sustained attention. Choose issues that you can do something about and make progress in resolving them. If activities serve you and yours well and benefit others, keep doing them.

Growing Up Spiritually

Our world today lends itself to a "consumerist-please-yourself" mentality, which fools us into believing that we can be good without sacrifices on behalf of the greater good. To embrace this prosperity gospel can easily fall into naïve self-indulgence. To grow up spiritually means to accept life realistically, to seek a form of happiness that embraces the world and the future, accepts imperfection, grace, the need for forgiveness, and a continual process of practice, assessment, growth, and negotiation with everyone affected by our actions.

Integrity has no meaning unless we take personal and community responsibility for our actions and inactions. The impulse for faith can free us from idolatrous forms of communal loyalty, or it can reinforce negative impulses toward pride, dogma, bigotry, or violation. We need the help of other people and participation in communities to correct the residual egotism and shortsightedness of even the most effective person or most rational or intuitively wise faith. The common grace of love relationships, friendships, and community activism carry most of the weight in human existence. Common grace provides the pull of responsibility and the joy of exercising our innate creative potential, but I agree with Reinhold Niebuhr that saving grace can add a deeper awareness of human finitude, genuine unity within our responsibilities, and faith in and hope for benevolence beyond our personal lives.

Our spiritual homes are not just the places we go to in crisis but much more, they're the places where we regularly participate. When we return to our ordinary lives, we are renewed, refreshed, and reassured, yet have also been challenged to get on with and live up to what our beliefs are all about. At their best, they make us face up to life's hardest truths, take responsibility for our choices, and help us evolve as spiritual citizens who continue to find opportunities and take responsibility, and practice shared values that challenge us to remain exuberant but humble co-creators with the good Earth and Creation.

We reach what is larger and more enduring than ourselves through our relationships and dialogue with others in our communities, by our negotiations and cooperation, and through our imaginations during artistic, literary, musical, and physical activities. We need to face our fears, hurts, failures, and losses and learn from them, work hard to stretch our capacities and use our talents, choose what we read, see, listen to, participate in, say, and do carefully and thoughtfully, critically and respectfully. Choose companions with character, integrity, and compassion; then take time to listen to and respond to them. In all our social activities, we need to strive for inclusive justice and nurturing and joyful attention to all participants. Balance care, activism, and celebration with adequate time alone to grieve, sleep well, consume modestly, breathe deeply, and engage in your own spiritual practices.

People cannot be good alone. We can't maintain moral purity by staying separated from the world or out of the action. We must become involved where the action is and the moral choices are being made. In doing so, we will fail sometimes, be disappointed, and won't always live up to our own principles or ideals, but the alternative is to fail to live your life and never become the child of Creation that you are uniquely able to be. Each of us makes ethical and moral choices from the beginning to the end of life. The most effective ethical activists turn each choice into a thoughtful moral calculus and, simultaneously, a playful game or interesting experiment. They find a life balance in which they care for themselves, have an intimate and satisfying personal life, and help nurture and transform the world. That's what the world, Creation, the Divine asks of us—that is our human task, and what faith demands.

The proof of any faith is what good it does in the world. Some faiths are more helpful than others; some may become destructive to their practitioners or to the world. As humanity has grown capable of destroying both itself and our planet, it's become necessary to develop a post-national world in which a global humanity lives by social laws and customs that serve most of the world with fairness and helps our species find sustainable solutions to our planetary problems. We need to significantly change the balance of our lives from obsessive concentration on ourselves or our intimates to greater investments of time, energy, and talent in global solutions. This will require us to give up ethnic chauvinism and nationalism as forms of idolatry, and instead create international institutions and global solutions for our increasingly global problems.

As ethicist Sissela Bok said in *Secrets: On the Ethics of Concealment and Revelation,* human maturation is the realization that while complete intimacy or omniscient power are not possible, self-transcendence, growth, and closeness to others are within everyone's reach. When Jesus, the humble carpenter, became a prophet at age thirty, he had a mythic encounter with three major temptations: to turn stones into bread because of his hunger; to risk his life to prove his faith in God; and to worship idols instead of saving his reverence for what is worthy. His responses were: to live by his spirit and not merely in response to his hungers; to realize that it is inappropriate to test God or the universe, and to take personal responsibility for his existence by revering only what is worthy of reverence. Other historic religions have similar temptation stories. Get beyond your short-term desires; risk your life on what you're able to take responsibility for, and spend your life doing what's worthy of respect.

Useful Insights from World Religions

Another primary aim of this book has been to persuade readers that just as we can learn useful things from different people because of their varied experiences, talents, and insights, so we can learn much from the different world religions and ideologies. Consider them for yourself; try ideas and practices that interest you to see whether they prove helpful. Only those that continue to be of enduring value stand the test of time. This book has demonstrated that each of the world's religions has itself learned from and benefitted from other historic religious traditions. They have emerged from one another and will continue to grow more interrelated. In the 21st century, none can stand alone, and no individual can realistically depend on one single conceptual system or faith. Consider the contributions of each of the world's great religions to cope with our global dilemmas.

Hinduism focuses on the individual's lifelong spiritual journey, attentive to personality differences and stark variations in human experience, life's progressive stages, its many options for spiritual practices, and urges each individual to have his or her own direct spiritual experiences. Many of Hinduism's ideas and practices have spread widely beyond its ancestral believers. Deepak Chopra summarized his Hindu practices: Meditate twice daily to witness intelligence in all beings and practice being nonjudgmental; consider each encounter as a gift, for every action generates a return force in kind; allow yourself and others to be who they are; permit solutions to emerge, and seek your own best ways to serve humanity. Understand what Gandhi called seven worldly blunders: wealth without work; pleasure without conscience; knowledge without character; commerce without morality; science without humanity; worship without sacrifice; and politics without principle. As medieval Hindu seer Kalidasa urged:

> Look to this day for it is life, the very life of life; in its brief course lie all the verities and realities of your existence: the bliss of growth, the glory of action and the splendor of beauty. For yesterday is but a dream and tomorrow is only a vision, but today well lived makes every yesterday a dream of happiness and every tomorrow a vision of hope. Look well, therefore, to this day!

Jainism is the humblest of the world's historic religions. It reminds us that truth is only probable and life inevitably transient. It proposes the central aim of self-conquest and emphasizes that nonviolence must become the foundation of our interactions with nature and other people. India's first prime minister, Jawaharlal Nehru, transformed Jainism's pancasila doctrine into an intention toward international peaceful coexistence.

Buddhism asks us to awaken to the impermanence of our egos. If we outgrow our obsessive cravings, we become not only freed of our self-imposed suffering but empowered to spend our energies on effective compassion with others in a needy world—to be in the world without being caught by the world. Meditation and practical kindness help us live with benevolence. Every human act needs to approximate loving-kindness, joy, and equanimity.

Taoism points out that if we can tune in to nature's ways, become like water, in harmony with the evolving Earth, then we can find our balance between the cosmic powers and our human dilemmas. By practicing wu wei, we can learn to avoid aggression, self-defeating behaviors, and fruitless attempts to conquer nature or resist the inevitable. We can practice the Way, ride the boundless energy and delight of Creation itself. What the caterpillar calls the end, the world calls a butterfly.

In our 21st-century world, where so many people perceive themselves primarily as humanists, Confucians offer us several useful lessons. Confucian truth is relational truth; it urges individuals to take responsibility within their primary relationships and strive to develop ways that broaden and deepen their communities. Choose our friends wisely, employ our days prudently, and while we understand the errors and faults of others, act as we wish they would act with us. Do justice; act at least reciprocally but stretch toward the global and the future since the universe is essentially energy governed by dynamic and evolving laws of rationality, centered in a Great Ultimate and thus mutually interdependent with humanity and nature.

Japanese spirituality has combined its Shinto roots with its Buddhist learning and practices. Everyday life becomes the spiritual path. We are here on Earth because of our ancestors' efforts, so we need to live with gratitude for the past and transmit what's worthy to the future. Since human life is full of conflict and disappointment, we need to live careful, disciplined lives within society's laws. Life contains contexts for shame, self-purification, and self-restraint. Life is a combination of fate and purpose, destiny and chance, but chance often appears to reveal opportunities. For life existed long before us, interacts with us, and continues long after we die. As a Zen Buddhist monk I encountered in 2017 said: Get beyond your ego, stand with all of humanity, and work to create the future.

When in October 2017 I met with the patriarch of the Neo-Shintoist group Konkokyo, a man whom I'd last spoken with in 1970, we had both grown old, and he, like any wise Japanese, was striving to discover how he could best communicate with me after so many years' absence and with only a short time together and the need for translation. After formal greetings, he excused himself and returned with a drawing his five-year-old granddaughter had made that showed his wife and him as jolly elders—a little like Mr. and Mrs. Santa. Then, he introduced his family. In so doing, the patriarch cut through the many years since we had last met to the heart of our hearts: both of us now face futures beyond ourselves yet related to our lives.

As this book shifted west, its first historical stop was in Persia, one of the most ancient civilizations. Its early religious flowering was Zoroastrianism, iconic in the Christian story as the Magi, or three kings, who followed the star and visited Jesus at his birth in the stable. The Zoroastrians revere natural substances: water, air, soil, and fire, and eventually turned them into idols that they could not blemish with their deceased bodies. They conceive of this world as a continuing battle between two gods, and that humanity's task is to ally itself with the good god and to oppose the evil god. After Islamic forces conquered Persia, Zoroastrians were increasingly attacked, and though there are still Zoroastrians in modern Iran, most of the few hundred thousand remaining Zoroastrians live in India.

Zoroastrian concepts remain potent because they significantly changed Judaism, and some Zoroastrian ideas were integrated into Christian and Islamic theologies. Millions of people still perceive the world as two eternally warring camps: one is faithful, righteous, and good, and the other tempting, evil, and bad. This is true not only within the religions of the Book (Judaism, Christianity, and Islam) but also among many who espouse contemporary secular ideologies, and among some practitioners of other global faiths. This is a seductive view because it makes you and your side the true believers who represent goodness and ethical behavior, while those not of your faith are heretics. A cancerous aspect of this pernicious worldview is that its practitioners soon expand their fears and opposition not only to the "heathen" of other religions but may begin to include those among their own faith who fail purity tests. Islamic militants justify killing not only non-Muslims but also Shia Muslims, Sufi Muslims, any non-Wahhabi Muslims, or even those Wahhabi who dare to question self-appointed religious, political, or military authorities. Examples abound: Myanmar's Buddhist majority "cleansing" their nation of their Rohingya Muslim citizens; Hindu militants excusing violence against Muslims or lower-caste Hindus; Jewish expropriation of Palestinian property and ghettoizing of their Palestinian citizens; or anti-LGBT violence by evangelical Christians in Africa and elsewhere. This behavior represents true evil, for it undermines the foundations of faith, ethics, happiness, and fulfilled lives by making life easier than it is or can be. No person ever becomes so rational, scientific, faithful, or pure that they are incapable of violence and violation. No one deserves to be treated as a thing. Everyone deserves fairness and justice and remains capable of giving and receiving love.

Judaism contains much wisdom and many lessons. I agree with medieval scholar Bahya Ben Joseph Ibn Pakuda that worship is whatever recognizes life's benefits and does beneficial acts, and that religious practice is an exercise of self-control. Maimonides said: Evil arises when good is absent, and he described three kinds of evil: that caused by nature; the evil that people bring upon others; and the evil they bring upon themselves. Everyone has merits and everyone practices iniquities; what matters is which one predominates. With Spinoza, I believe that God, nature, and reality are largely one and the same. To nurture happiness, we must make our reasoning, appetites, and environments compatible. Understand your desires so you don't become a slave to them. Like Martin Buber, I find the spiritual and worthy most often in the *between and among us* as people in communities, determined to discover the spirit at work in our friendships and love relationships, negotiations, compromises, and collaborations.

Christianity clasps firmly to a central human truth. Every human being is a potential co-Creator with Creation itself. The sacred Kingdom is here among us now, if we only had eyes to see, hearts to love, and hands to help each other. I am a Jesusian, not a Christian, because I do not believe in Christ but in Jesus, in the Gospels of Mary and Thomas much more than the Gospel of John or the Book of Revelations. With Augustine, I believe that divinity is a circle whose center is everywhere and whose circumference is nowhere. With Martin Luther, I urge humanity to continue evolving and reforming. As he suggested in his *An Argument in Defense of all Articles*: Life is not righteousness but growth in righteousness, not health but healing, not being but becoming, not rest but exercise, we are not yet finished, but growing toward it. I believe in *metanoia*, a Christian's change of heart, mind, and character engendered by love and community, the long, slow turning of the world itself toward justice and peace. I hope, like Teilhard de Chardin, that someday we will harness for Creation the energies of love; then, for a second time, we will have discovered fire.

A growing majority of Muslims are modern people—literate, scientific, and technological—who wish to combine their faith with the blessings of modernity. Millions of Muslim men genuinely wish to accord the women in their lives the respect and equal treatment they deserve. Often, the most progressive and effective practices of Islam have been and are now practiced in nations where a variety of religions flourish in mutual respect and understanding, both in some nations with Muslim majorities and in many with significant Muslim minorities. It is time for an Islamic reformation, and I believe it will be led by women and men unafraid of truly living in the 21st century—probably not by Saudis or Iranians, and certainly not by violent terrorists.

There is so much good about Islam. People do need to submit to reality; we do need to act fairly with one another. Daily prayers based on peace, hospitality, fairness, and mercy are beneficial. To regularly set aside 2.5 percent of your wealth for the truly needy would be a worthy aim for the entire human race. I'm an enthusiastic fan of spiritual pilgrimage, but I wonder whether it isn't time to get past Mecca as the inevitable center of the Islamic world. After all, the Kaaba was a pagan shrine for centuries before Muhammad. Perhaps each Islamic community could develop its own pilgrimage site, and thus truly reflect the wealth and variety of Islamic history. Islam has already liberated worship from confinement to specific places, for wherever people might be, they can turn to God and enter into communion with God. The Qur'an made clear that Allah does not favor certain individuals, peoples, or nations because Allah created all as spiritual equals. Gratitude is the heart of worship, and faith resides in all persons' hearts and is proved by their deeds. Islam asserts that our lifelong struggle is not to forget every human's relationship with God, but to know daily that the true jihad is each individual's battle within himself to live up to his own life of peace, mercy, and helpfulness. As Pakistani Muhammad Iqbal said: Only democracy is truly consistent with Islam's spirit.

Sikhism and Judaism have interesting parallels and similar dilemmas. There are 23 million Sikhs, concentrated in India's state of Punjab, but also spread worldwide. There are 14 million Jews, the majority of whom live in the U.S. and Israel, but there are Jewish communities worldwide. Both religions regard their scriptures as the sacred centers of their faiths and recite them in worship, yet only a minority in either faith can confidently analyze their sacred writings. Both have set high ethical standards for their behavior, and urge their members to be active citizens, be very hospitable in their religious communities, perceive good deeds as effective prayers, and advocate sympathy and compassion for others. Both have a sense of being chosen peoples with threatened histories, both became ferociously militarized when they were most politically powerful, and both have a strong sense of "their" sacred land, which has often not been under their political control. These facts have made many non-Sikhs and non-Jews feel, rightly or wrongly, that they may not be welcomed as their neighbors. I deeply respect both Sikhism and Judaism, use their teachings, and continue to draw from their wise models of ethical and community behavior. I believe, however, that both traditions have idolatrized their scriptures, ancient languages, and historic homelands, and are mistaken to perceive themselves as chosen, except that with advantages come extra responsibilities to help unchosen others.

The Future of Spiritual Evolution

If your faith is built on what divides us, and has basically become a way to justify oppression of and unfairness for most of humanity, then I believe your faith has lost its religion and abandoned its spirituality, and neither seeks truth nor does justice—whether that faith is Fox News evangelism, a form of ethnic or national chauvinism, racist, religious, or ideological tribalism, or anti-spiritual scientism. In the 21st century, we must overcome both tribalism and authoritarianism. Anarchistic individual liberty and autocracy both lead to chaos and degradation. We need to embrace the spiritual dignity of every person, and learn to live democratically, from our intimacies with partners and friends, through our families, groups, businesses, and nations, in order to deal with our global problems. No person and no group ever outgrows a capacity for evil, so we must systematically overcome contexts of consent that enable much of the world's evil. We need to remain pluralistic and humble.

Twenty-first-century identities based on ethnicity, race, gender, age, or class are no longer viable. Faced with so many fake truths and profit-and-power-based propaganda machines, we cannot continue to let our illusions become so persuasive that we end up living within them. Twenty-first-century spirituality needs to adopt an experimental and self-correcting spirit. Checks and balances are as necessary in science, technology, ideological presumptions, and religious beliefs as they are within effective political, economic, and ethical systems. Religion deserves our best standards of rationality and decency. We need to continue to test our spirituality by what works in our lives and lives up to our best thoughts and actions. Twenty-first-century spirituality deserves a continuing utilitarian calculus, focused institutional passions, and our best intuitive wisdom. In the 21st century, we need many overlapping identities to help us remain open to new insights and keep our most savage and self-defeating passions in check. The Divine, that which is worthy of reverence, often remains unseen but felt, not clearly factual or evident, yet it determines our critical choices and destiny. So, we need to remain open, with many ways to wander, lest we become blind to the miracles, beauty, and wholeness that surround and permeate us all. Like Robert Bly's poem, "The Third Body," (1999) obeying a third body that humans have in common, that we do not know, yet know of, and may never have seen, yet have promised to love. Our immortality is surely built upon our work well done and through our continuing efforts toward friendship, intimacy, and love.

I try to live guided by ideas like Bertrand Russell's—that the good life is one inspired by love and guided by knowledge, and UU James Luther Adams's principles: revelation is continuous, nothing is exempt from criticism; relationships rest on mutual consent; faith must be activated by direct efforts to nurture a just and loving community; effective goodness is inconceivable without constructive institutions; and though life inevitably remains tragic, we need to live in hope. With Martin Luther King, Jr., I believe people should remain maladjusted to injustice, violence, and hate. Like the Sisters of Charity, we should take time to think which is the source of power; to play because it is the secret of perpetual youth; to sing because music reflects transparent soul; to live in spirit for grace surrounds us, and gratitude and hope keep us going.

The human future needs to be based on sharing, cooperation, nonviolence, and partnership. We need to become religious pluralists and remain spiritual seekers who develop global spiritualities and learn to view the Earth as our home and the human future as our time; to progressively become active members in larger and more enduring human families. Most of these future spiritual institutions won't be based on past hierarchies or narrowly circumscribed areas, but on chosen associations in often far-flung networks that work together because they genuinely share similar values. We will likely discover the divine primarily in *the between:* between intimates, among chosen and nurtured families, in collaborative organizations that seek to meet the needs of everyone, and that proceed in ways that serve the future. We will learn to live lucid lives; we will be resolute and energetic, and do our best to minimize our arrogance or despair by filling our lives with celebration, hope, love, and service to the future and the globe. We will then be doing our best to fulfill our spiritual potential and most effectively serve Creation.

Endnotes

Section II

Chapter 6: Jainism
1. Heinrich Zimmer, *Philosophies of India.* Joseph Campbell, ed. (Princeton: Princeton University Press, 1951), 507.
2. Peter Heehs, ed. *Indian Religions.* (New York: New York University Press, 2002.), 93, 97, 100–102, 91

Chapter 7: Buddhism
1. Walpola Rahula, *What the Buddha Taught.* (Bedford, GB: Gordon Fraser Gallery Ltd, 1967), 72.
2. Ibid., 2–3.
3. Joanna Macy, "In Indra's Net: Sarvodaya and Our Mutual Efforts for Peace" (pp. 17–180) and "Taking Heart," (pp. 203–216). In *Path of Compassion*, Fred Eppsteiner, ed., (Berkeley, Ca: Parallax Press and the Buddhist Peace Fellowship, 1988).

Chapter 8: Taoism
1. Lao Tsu, Tao Te Ching, translated by Gia-Feng and Jane English, (New York: Vintage Books, 1972), Nos. 24, 28, 30, 48, 52, 61, 66–68, 72, 79, 81.
2. Ibid., 513.
3. Ibid., 516.
4. Ibid., 527.

5. Ibid., 532.
6. Ibid., 552.
7. Ibid., 554–56.

Chapter 9: Confucians
1. Tu Wei Ming, interviewed by Bill Moyers on *A World of Ideas: On Faith and Reason*, (Public Broadcasting Corp. October 7, 1990).
2. Robert Ballou, Horace Friess, Frederic Spiegelberg. *The Bible of the World.* (New York: Viking Press, 1939), *Analects*, 379–80.
3. Ibid., Book of Poetry, 387, 390.
4. *The Economist* magazine, February 3, 2007.
5. *Chicago Tribune.* June 5, 2007.
6. Confucius, "Words from Sacred Traditions," in *Singing the Living Tradition.* (Boston: Beacon Press, 1993), #186.

Chapter 10: Shinto and Japanese Spirituality
1. William De Bary and Ryusaku Tsunoda, eds., "Chronicle of Ancient Events," in *Sources of Japanese Tradition, Volume I.* (New York: Columbia University Press, 1964) 32–33.
2. John B. Noss, *Man's Religions.* (London: Macmillan & Company, 1963) 443.

Chapter 11: Zoroastrianism
1. Ballou, Robert, ed., *The Bible of the World,* 561, 563, 565–570.
2. Ibid., 574–99.
3. Ibid., 618–19.
4. Ibid., 618–22, 636.
5. Lawrence H. Mills, *Avesta Eschatology.* (Chicago: Open Court, 1908), 1–2, 36, 45, 69–84.

Chapter 12: Judaism
1. Martin Buber, *I and Thou.* (New York: Charles Scribner's Sons, 1958) 66–67.

Chapter 13: Christianity

1. Reinhold Niebuhr, *The Irony of American History.* (New York: Scribner, 1952), 63.

Chapter 14: Islam

1. Kitagawa, *Religions of the East*, 230–40, 261.

Chapter 15: Sikhism

1. Noss, *Man's Religions*, 317.

Section III

Chapter 16: Liberal Religions in an Increasingly Secular World

1. Stephen Hay, ed. *Sources of Indian Tradition: Volume Two: Modern India and Pakistan.* (New York: Columbia University Press, 1988) 71.

Chapter 17: Contemporary Indigenous, Neo-pagan, and Feminist Spiritualities

1. Rev. Joan Goodwin, "To the Four Directions," in *Singing the Living Tradition*, Boston: Beacon Press, 1993, #446.

Chapter 18: New Age or Higher Consciousness Spirituality

1. B. L. Walls, "Spirituality According to Oprah," in *AARP Bulletin*, October 2015.
2. Frances E. Vaughan, *Awakening Intuition*. (New York: Anchor Press, 1979) 180–99, 45.

Section IV

Chapter 19: The Sacred from Transcendent to Community

1. Francis S. Collins, *The National Geographic*, April 2013.
2. Siddhartha Mukherjee, *The Gene: An Intimate History*. (New York: Scribner, 2016) 485–86.
3. Ibid., 490, 492.

Chapter 20: Ethics
1. Macy, Joanna, (In "Indra's Net: Sarvodaya and Our Mutual Efforts for Peace"), Fred Eppsteiner, ed. (Berkeley: Parallax Press and the Buddhist Peace Fellowship, 1988), 203–213.

Chapter 21: Conceptual Systems
1. Robert Coles, *The Spiritual Life of Children*. (Boston: Houghton Mifflin Harcourt, 1991) 308–335.
2. Eck, Diana, Installation of Galen Guengerich, All Souls Church, New York City, 1993.
3. Krista Tippett, "Voice of America's Spiritual Journey," *Lion's Roar*, January 2017.

Chapter 22: Spiritual Evolution
1. *The Week,* Nov. 6, 2009.
2. Ross Douthat, "The Real but Overstated Decline of American Christianity," *New York Times*, May 13, 2015, https://douthat. blogs.nytimes.com/2015/05/13/the-real-but-overstated-decline-of-american-christianity/.
3. Ibid., April 6, 2017.

Bibliography

A Rosary of Islamic Readings, 7th to 20th Century. Jaipur: National Publishing House, 1973.

Abdu'l-Bahá. *The Secret of Divine Civilization.* Translated by Marzieh Gail. Willamette, IL: Baha'i Publishing, 2007.

Adams, James Luther. *On Being Human Religiously: Selected Essays in Religion and Society.* Boston: Beacon Press, 1986.

Adler, Margot. *Drawing Down the Moon: Witches, Druids, Goddess-Worshippers and Other Pagans in America.* New York: Penguin Books, 1979.

Al-Ghazali, Abu Hamid Muhammad. Edited and translated by Richard Joseph McCarthy, *Deliverance from Error: An Annotated Translation of Al-Munqidh Min Al-Dalal and Other Relevant Works of Al-Ghazali.* Louisville, KY: Fons Vitae, 1999.

The Arabian Nights. London: Ward, Lock & Company Limited, 1940.

Aristotle. *Nicomachean Ethics.* Translated by Robert Williams. London: Longmans, Green & Co., 1869.

Armstrong, Karen. *A History of God: The 4000-Year Quest of Judaism, Christianity and Islam.* New York: Random House, 1993.

Armstrong, Karen. *The Battle for God.* New York: Ballantine Books, 2011.

Armstrong, Karen. *Fields of Blood: Religion and the History of Violence.* Toronto: Knopf Doubleday Publishing Group, 2014.

Arthur, Max. *The Sikh Religion: Its Gurus, Sacred Writings and Authors.* Oxford: Oxford University Press, 1909.

Aslan, Reza. "Islam's Long War Within," *Harvard Divinity Bulletin,* Vol. 33, No. 2, (Autumn 2005). https://bulletin-archive.hds.harvard.edu/issues/autumn2005.

Atlas, James. *New York Times Magazine.* June 17, 2012.

Ballou, Robert, Horace Friess, Frederic Spiegelberg. *The Bible of the World.* New York: Viking Press, 1939.

Barks, Coleman, trns. *The Essential Rumi.* Edison, New Jersey: Castle Books, 1995.

Bellah, Robert, Richard Madsen, William Sullivan, Steven Tipton, Ann Swidler. *Habits of the Heart: Individualism and Commitment in American Life.* Berkeley: University of California Press, 1985.

Bellah, Robert and Joas Hans. *Religion in Human Evolution from Paleolithic to the Axial Age.* Boston: Belknap Press, 2011.

Bly, Robert. *Eating the Honey of Words: New and Selected Poems.* London: HarperCollins e-books, 2009.

Bok, Sissela. *Secrets: On the Ethics of Concealment and Revelation.* New York: Vintage Books, 1989.

Boulton, Matthew. "Cross Purposes," *Harvard Divinity Bulletin.* Vol. 34, No. 3 (Autumn 2006). https://bulletin-archive.hds.harvard.edu/issues/autumn2006.

Braun, Erik. "The Many Lives of Insight: The Abhidhamma and Transformations in Theravada Meditation," *Harvard Divinity Bulletin.* (Winter/Spring 2016). https://bulletin.hds.harvard.edu/the-many-lives-of-insight/.

Brock, Ann Graham. *Mary Magdalene, First Apostle: The Struggle for Authority.* Boston: Harvard Divinity School, 2003.

Brock, Rita Nakashima., Parker, Rebecca Ann. *Proverbs of Ashes: Violence, Redemptive Suffering, and the Search for What Saves Us.* Boston: Beacon Press, 2002.

Brock, Rita Nakashima, Parker, Rebecca Ann. *Saving Paradise: How Christianity Traded Love of This World for Crucifixion and Empire.* Boston: Beacon Press, 2008.

Buber, Martin. *I and Thou.* New York: Charles Scribner's Sons, 1958.

Buber, Martin. *Between Man and Man.* New York: Macmillan, 1968.

Bunjiro, Kawate. *Konko Daijin.* Japan: Konkokyo Honbu, 1981.

Campbell, David E., Shaylyn Garrett, Robert D. Putnam, *American Grace: How Religion Divides and Unites Us.* New York: Simon & Schuster, 2010.

Campbell, Joseph. Interviewed by Bill Moyers. *The Power of Myth.* Public Broadcasting System Television Series, 1988.

Capra, Fritjof. *The Tao of Physics.* London: Shambhala, 1975.

Carruthers, Susan L. *The Good Occupation: American Soldiers and the Hazards of Peace.* Cambridge, MA: Harvard University Press, 2016.

Charfi, Mohamed. *Islam and Liberty: The Historical Misunderstanding.* London: Zed Books, 2005.

Chicago Tribune. June 5, 2007.

Chitrabhanu, Gurudev. *Realize What You Are: The Dynamics of Jain Meditation,* edited by Leonard Marks. New York: Dodd, Mead & Co.,1978.

Coles, Robert. *The Spiritual Life of Children.* Boston: Houghton Mifflin Harcourt, 1991.

Collier, John. *Indians of the Americas: The Long Hope.* New York: New American Library, 1964.

Confucius. *The Complete Confucius: The Analects (Book 2, Book 4, Book 5, Book 15, Book 17, Book 19), The Doctrine of the Mean, and The Great Learning.* Translated by James Legge. Mineola, NY: Dover Publications, 2013.

Confucius. "Words from Sacred Traditions." In *Singing the Living Tradition.* Boston: Beacon Press, 1993.

Daly, Mary. *Beyond God the Father: Toward a Philosophy of Women's Liberation.* Boston: Beacon Press, 1973.

Darwin, Charles. *The Descent of Man, Part I and II.* Charleston, SC: BiblioBazaar, 2009.

Darwin, Charles. *On the Origin of Species.* Ottawa: East India Publishing, 2019.

Dewey, John. *Experience and Nature.* United Kingdom: Open Court Publishing Company, 1929.

Dewey, John. *The Quest for Certainty: A Study of the Relation of Knowledge and Action; Gifford Lectures,* 1929. New York: Putnam 1960.

Dewey, John. *A Common Faith.* New Haven: Yale University Press, 1947.

Dickerson, John S. *The Great Evangelical Recession: 6 Factors That Will Crash the American Church… and How to Prepare.* Grand Rapids: Baker Publishing Group, 2013.

Donner, Fred M. *Muhammad and the Believers: At the Origins of Islam.* Cambridge, MA: Harvard University Press, 2012.

Dosick, Wayne. *Living Judaism: The Complete Guide to Jewish Belief, Tradition, and Practice.* New York: HarperCollins Publishers, 1995.

Douthat, Ross. "Ideas from a Manger," in *New York Times.* December 21, 2013, https://www.nytimes.com/2013/12/22/opinion/sunday/douthat-ideas-from-a-manger.html.

Douthat, Ross. *New York Times,* April 6, 2017.

Douthat, Ross. "The Real but Overstated Decline of American Christianity," *New York Times*, May 13, 2015, https://douthat.blogs.nytimes.com/2015/05/13/the-real-but-overstated-decline-of-american-christianity/.

Dower, John W. *Embracing Defeat: Japan in the Wake of World War II*. New York: W.W. Norton & Co., 1999.

Eck, Diana L. *A New Religious America: How a "Christian Country" Has Now Become the World's Most Religiously Diverse Nation*. San Francisco: HarperSanFrancisco, 2001.

Eck, Diana L. *On Common Ground: World Religions in America*. New York: Columbia University Press, 2001.

Eck, Diana L. Speaking at Rev. Galen Guengerich's installation, All Souls Church, New York City, 1993.

Economist Magazine, February 3, 2007.

Eisler, Riane. *The Chalice and the Blade*. San Francisco: HarperSanFrancisco, 1988.

Eisler, Riane, David Loye. *The Partnership Way: New Tools for Living & Learning*. San Francisco: Harper San Francisco, 1990.

Eliade, Mircea. *History of Religious Ideas: Volumes I - III*. Chicago: University of Chicago Press, 1978 – 1985.

Eltahawy, Mona. *Headscarves and Hymens: Why the Middle East Needs a Sexual Revolution*. New York: Farrar, Straus and Giroux, 2015.

Engle, Stephen. "Zhu Xi's Breakthrough" in *Harvard Divinity Bulletin*. (Autumn-Winter, 2017).

Eppsteiner, Fred, ed. *The Path of Compassion*. Berkeley: Parallax Press and the Buddhist Peace Fellowship, 1988.

Erikson, Erik H. *Childhood and Society*. New York: W.W. Norton & Co, 1950.

Ferguson, Marilyn, John Naisbitt, *The Aquarian Conspiracy: Personal and Social Transformation in the 1980s.* London: J.P. Tarcher, 1987.

Financial Times, February 2017

Fletcher, Joseph. *Situation Ethics: The New Morality.* London: Westminster John Knox Press, 1997.

Fowler, James. *Stages of Faith: The Psychology of Human Development and the Quest for Meaning.* San Francisco: HarperCollins, 1981.

Frazer, James G. *The Golden Bough.* London: Macmillan & Company, 1890.

Friedman, Maurice S., *Martin Buber: The Life of Dialogue.* New York: Harper & Row, 1960.

Giles, Herbert Allen, trans. *Chuang Tzü: Mystic, Moralist, and Social Reformer.* The Project Gutenberg eBook, 2019.

Gilligan, Carol. *In a Different Voice: Psychological Theory and Women's Development.* Cambridge, MA: Harvard University Press, 1982.

Gleanings from the Writings of Baha'u'llah. Translated by Shoghi Effendi. Willamette, IL: Baha'i Publishing, 2005.

Goodwin, Rev. Jane. "To the Four Directions," in *Singing the Living Tradition*, Boston: Beacon Press, 1993, #446.

Goldstein, Joseph. *Shambhala Sun.* November 2007.

Gross-Loh, Christine, Puett, Michael. *The Path: What Chinese Philosophers Can Teach Us About the Good Life.* New York: Simon & Schuster, 2016.

Gustafson, James. *Ethics from a Theocentric Perspective: Theology and Ethics.* Chicago: University of Chicago Press, 1983.

Guttierrez, Gustavo. *A Theology of Liberation: History, Politics, and Salvation.* Translated by Sister Inda Caridad and John Eagleson. Maryknoll, NY: Orbis Books, 1988.

Hanh, Thich Nhat. *True Love: A Practice for Awakening the Heart*. Boston: Shambhala Publications, 2004.

Hanh, Thich Nhat. *Being Peace*. Berkeley: Parallax Press, 2005.

Hanegraaff, Wouter J. *New Age Religion and Western Culture: Esotericism in the Mirror of Secular Thought*. Leiden: E.J. Brill, 1996.

Hauerwas, Stanley. *A Community of Character: Toward a Constructive Christian Social Ethic*. Notre Dame: University of Notre Dame Press, 1981.

Hauerwas, Stanley, Jean Vanier. *Living Gently in a Violent World: The Prophetic Witness of Weakness*. Downers Grove: InterVarsity Press, 2018.

Hay, Stephen, ed. Sources of Indian Tradition: Volume Two: Modern India and Pakistan. New York: Columbia University Press, 1988.

Heehs, Peter, ed. *Indian Religions*. New York: New York University Press, 2002.

Heelas, Paul. *The New Age Movement: Celebrating the Self and the Sacralization of Modernity*. Cambridge: Wiley, 1996.

Herzl, Theodor. *The Jewish State*. Scotts Valley: CreateSpace, 2018.

Hirsi Ali, Ayaan. *Heretic: Why Islam Needs a Reformation Now*. New York: Harper, 2015.

Hobbes, Thomas. *Hobbes's Leviathan*. W. G. Pogson Smith, ed. Oxford: Clarendon Press, 1967.

Hoover, Roy, Robert Funk, *The Five Gospels: The Search for the Authentic Words of Jesus*. New York: Polebridge Press, 1993.

Huxley, Aldous. *The Perennial Philosophy*. London: Chatto & Windus, 1947.

ibn Gabirol, Solomon. *The Fountain of Life, Fons Vitae*. Translated by Harry Wedeck. Azafran Books, 2017.

ibn Pakuda, Bahya ben Joseph. *Duties of the Heart.* Jacksonville, FL: Bloch Publishing Co., 1925.

Iqbal, Muhammad. *The Reconstruction of Religious Thought in Islam.* London: Humphrey Milford, 1934.

James, William. *The Principles of Psychology, Vol 1.* New York: H. Holt, 1890.

James, William. *The Varieties of Religious Experience: A Study in Human Nature.* London: Modern Library, 1902.

Jaspers, Karl. *The Origins and Goal of History.* Translated by Michael Bullock. New York: Taylor & Francis Group, 1949.

Jung, Carl G. *Memories, Dreams, Reflections,* edited by Aniela Jaffe, translated by Richard and Clara Winston. New York: Vintage Books, 1965.

Jung, Carl Gustav, Jolande Jacobi, Joseph Lewis Henderson, Marie-Louise von Franz, Aniela Jaffé. *Man and His Symbols.* New York: Doubleday, 1964.

Kabir, Robert Bly. *The Kabir Book: Forty-four of the Ecstatic Poems of Kabir.* Boston: Beacon Press, 1977.

Kadri, Sadakat. *Heaven on Earth: A Journey Through Shari'a Law.* New York: Farrar, Straus and Giroux, 2012.

Kant, Immanuel. *Groundwork of the Metaphysics of Morals.* Mary Gregor, ed. Cambridge: Cambridge University Press, 1998.

Kant, Immanuel. *Critique of Practical Reason.* New York: Dover Publications, 2012.

Kennedy, Hugh N. *The Great Arab Conquests: How the Spread of Islam Changed the World We Live In.* Philadelphia: First Da Capo Press, 2007.

Khayyam, Omar. *Rubaiyat of Omar Khayyam.* Translated by Edward Fitzgerald. New York: Random House, 1947.

King, Karen. *Gospel of Mary of Magdala.* Santa Rosa, CA: Polebridge Press, 2003.

Kitagawa, Joseph M., ed. *Religions of the East*. Philadelphia: The Westminster Press, 1960.

Kohlberg, Lawrence. *Psychology of Moral Development*. New York: Harper & Row, 1984.

Konko Daijin. *Kyoten Gorikai: Teachings II*. Japan: Konkokyo Honbu, 1987.

Konkokyo Kyoten, (Konkokyo scriptures in 5 volumes–Revelations, Memoirs, and Gorikai I, II, III), Konko-cho, Japan: Konko-machi, 1983.

The Koran. Translated by N.J. Dawood. New York: Penguin Books, 1990.

Kornfield, Jack. "The Path of Compassion," *The Path of Compassion*, edited by Fred Eppsteiner, 24–30. Berkeley: Parallax Press and the Buddhist Peace Fellowship, 1988.

Kornfield, Jack. "Walking the Talk," *Lion's Roar*, May 2016.

Krasny, Michael. *Spiritual Envy: An Agnostic's Quest*. Novato: New World Library, 2010.

Kristof, Nicholas. New York Times, Dec. 12, 2015, https://www.nytimes.com/2011/05/22/opinion/22kristof.html

Kruse, Kevin. *One Nation Under God: How Corporate America Invented Christian America*. New York: Perseus Books Group, 2015.

Lao Tzu. *Tao Te Ching*. Translated by Gia-Fu Feng and Jane English. New York: Vintage Books, 1972.

Lesser, Elizabeth. *The New American Spirituality: A Seeker's Guide*. New York: Random House, 1999.

Lewis James R. and J. Gordon Melton, eds. *Perspectives on the New Age*. Albany, NY: State University of New York Press, 1992.

Locke, John. *Locke: Two Treatises of Government*. Cambridge: Cambridge University Press, 1967.

Luther, Martin. *The Essential Luther*. Indianapolis, IN: Hackett Publishing Company, 2018.

Macauliffe, Max. *The Sikh Religion: Its Gurus, Sacred Writings and Authors*. Oxford: Clarendon Press, 1909.

Macy, Joanna. "In Indra's Net: Sarvodaya and Our Mutual Efforts for Peace" and "Taking Heart," Fred Eppsteiner, ed. (Berkeley, Ca: Parallax Press and the Buddhist Peace Fellowship, 1988).

Maimonides, Moses, ed. Michael Friedlander. *The Guide for the Perplexed*. Mineola, NY: Dover Publications, 1956.

Manji, Irsjad. *The Trouble with Islam Today: A Muslim's Call for Reform in Her Faith*, New York: St. Martin's Press, 2003.

Mascaro, Juan. *The Upanishads*. Translated by Juan Mascaro. London: Penguin Group, 1965.

McLaughlin, Corinne, Gordon Davidson. *Spiritual Politics: Changing the World from the Inside Out*. New York: Ballentine Books, 1994.

Miller, Barbara. *The Bhagavad Gita*. Translated by Barbara Miller. Toronto: Bantam Books, 1986.

Mills, Lawrence H. *Avesta Eschatology*. Chicago: Open Court, 1908.

Mishra, Pankaj. "The Last Dalai Lama?" *New York Times Magazine*. December 6, 2015.

Moyers, Bill and Betty Flowers. Tu Wei-Ming quoted in *A World of Ideas: Conversations with Thoughtful Men and Women about American Life Today and the Ideas Shaping Our Future*. New York: Doubleday, 1989.

Murphy, Michael, George Leonard. *The Life We are Given: A Long-term Program for Realizing the Potential of Body, Mind, Heart, and Soul*. New York: Putnam, 1995.

Murphy, Michael. *Golf in the Kingdom*. New York: Penguin Group, 1972.

Murphy, Michael. *The Future of the Body: Explorations into the Further Evolution of Human Nature.* New York: J.P. Tarcher, 1992.

The National Geographic, April 2013.

Niebuhr, H. Richard. *The Responsible Self.* New York: Harper & Row, 1963.

Niebuhr, Reinhold. *The Irony of American History.* New York: Scribner, 1952.

Niebuhr, Reinhold. *Man's Nature and His Communities: Essays on the Dynamics and Enigmas of Man's Personal and Social Existence.* New York: Charles Scribner's Sons, 1965.

Nishi Hongwonji pamphlet. Kyoto, Japan, 2017. (John contacting denomination)

Noss, John B. *Man's Religions.* London: Macmillan & Company, 1963.

Otto, Rudolph. *Mysticism East and West.* Translated by Bertha Bracey and Richenda Payne. London: Macmillan & Company, 1932.

Pagels, Elaine. *Adam, Eve and the Serpent: Sex and Politics in Early Christianity.* New York: Vintage Books, 1988.

Pagels, Elaine. *Beyond Belief: The Secret Gospel of Thomas.* New York: Vintage Books, 2004.

Paine, Mabel Hyde. *The Divine Art of Living: Selections from the Writings of Bahá'u'lláh, the Báb and 'Abdu'l-Bahá.* Willamette, IL: Bahá'í Pub., 2006.

Patel, Eboo. "Faith Divide" blog, *The Washington Post.* October 2008. https://www.npr.org/templates/story/story.php?storyId=95286690

Patel, Eboo. *Acts of Faith: The Story of an American Muslim, in the Struggle for the Soul of a Generation.* Boston: Beacon Press, 2010

Peale, Norman Vincent. *The Power of Positive Thinking.* New York: Touchstone, 2015.

Prothero, Stephen. *American Jesus: How the Son of God Became a National Icon.* New York: Farrar, Straus and Giroux, 2003.

Prothero, Stephen. *Religious Literacy: What Every American Needs to Know—And Doesn't.* New York: HarperOne, 2009.

Quṭb, Sayyid. *Milestones.* India: SIME Journal, 2005.

Rahula, Walpola. *What the Buddha Taught.* Bedford, GB: Gordon Fraser Gallery Ltd, 1967.

Ramadan, Tariq. *Islam, The West and the Challenges of Modernity.* Leicester: The Islamic Foundation, 2009.

Rawls, John. Erin Kelly, ed. *Justice as Fairness: A Restatement.* Cambridge: Harvard University Press, 1981.

Rawls, John. *Theory of Justice.* Cambridge: Harvard University Press, 2009.

Reich, Charles A. *The Greening of America: How the Youth Revolution is Trying to Make America Livable.* NY: Random House, 1970.

Rodriguez, Robert. Interviewed by Bill Moyers on *A World of Ideas: On Faith and Reason*, Public Broadcasting Corp. October 7, 1990.

Rūmī, Jalāl al-Dīn. *The Essential Rumi.* Coleman Barks, ed. Translated with John Moyne. Edison: Castle Books, 1997.

Rubaiyat of Omar Khayyam. New York: Random House, 1947.

Rushdie, Salman. *The Satanic Verses: Novel.* London: St. Martin's Press, 2000.

The Sacred Scriptures of Konkokyo. Okayame-ken: Konko-cho, 1973.

Salzburg, Sharon. Speech delivered at the Unitarian Universalist General Assembly, June 2006.

Sayadaw, Ven Ledi. *The Manual of Insight and the Noble Eightfold Path and Its Factors Explained.* Onalaska, WA: Pariyatti Publishing, 2017.

Schmidt, Leigh Eric. *Restless Souls: The Making of American Spirituality.* San Francisco: HarperCollins, 2005.

Schucman, Helen. *A Course in Miracles: Original Edition Text.* Mill Valley, CA: Course in Miracles Society, 2009.

Schweitzer, Albert. *The Quest of the Historical Jesus: A Critical Study of its Progress from Reimarus to Wrede.* Baltimore, MD: Johns Hopkins University Press, 1998.

Searle, John. *The Construction of Social Reality.* New York: The Free Press, 1995.

Searle, John. *Rationality of Action.* Cambridge: MIT Press, 2001.

Searle, John. *Making of the Social World: The Structure of Human Civilization,* Oxford: Oxford University Press. 2010.

Seligman, Martin, Christopher Peterson. *Character Strengths and Virtues: A Handbook and Classification.* New York: Oxford University Press, 2004.

Singer, Peter. *One World: The Ethics of Globalization.* New Haven: Yale University Press, 2002.

Smith, Huston. *The World Religions.* New York: Harper Collins Publishers, 1958.

Spinoza, Benedictus de. *Ethics: Including the Improvement of the Understanding.* Amherst: Prometheus Books, 1989.

Starhawk. *The Spiral Dance: A Rebirth of the Ancient Religion of the Great Goddess.* San Francisco: Harper San Francisco, 1979.

Stark, Rodney. *The Rise of Christianity: How the Obscure, Marginal Jesus Movement Became the Dominant Religious Force in the Western World in a Few Centuries.* San Francisco: HarperCollins, 1997.

Stefan, V. Alexander. *Thus Spoke Einstein on Life and Living: Wisdom of Albert Einstein.* La Jolla, CA: Stefan University Press, 2011.

Streiker, Lowell D. *The Promise of Buber: Desultory Philippics and Irenic Affirmations.* Philadelphia, PA: Lippincott, 1969.

Suzuki, D.T. *Mysticism: Christian and Buddhist.* New York: Harper, 1957.

Surma, M.S. *Guru Nanak–The Apostle of Love.* Riverside, CA: United Sikh Mission, 1974.

Teilhard de Chardin, Pierre. *The Phenomenon of Man.* New York: Harper and Brothers, 1959.

Teilhard de Chardin, Pierre. *The Divine Milieu.* New York: Harper and Row, 1960.

Tillich, Paul. *The Courage to Be.* New Haven: Yale University, 1952.

Tippett, Krista. *Einstein's God: Conversations About Science and the Human Spirit.* New York: Penguin Publishing Group, 2010.

Tippett, Krista. *Becoming Wise: An Inquiry into the Mystery and Art of Living.* New York: Penguin Publishing Group, 2016.

Tippett, Krista. "Voice of America's Spiritual Journey," in *Lion's Roar,* January 2017.

Toffler, Alvin and Heidi. *Future Shock.* New York: Bantam Books, 1970.

Toffler, Alvin. *The Third Wave.* New York: Bantam Books, 1981.

Tolle, Eckhart. *The Power of Now: A Guide to Spiritual Enlightenment.* Novato: New World Library, 1999.

Tolle, Eckhart. *A New Earth: Awakening to Your Life's Purpose.* London: Penguin, 2006.

Tse-Tung, Mao. *Quotations from Chairman Mao Tse-tung.* Beijing: Foreign Languages Press, 1966.

Underhill, Evelyn. *Mysticism: A Study in the Nature and Development of Spiritual Consciousness.* New York: E.P. Dutton, 1930.

von Franz, Marie-Louise. *Man and His Symbols.* London: Aldus Books Limited, 1964.

Walls, B.L. "Spirituality According to Oprah," in *AARP Bulletin,* October 2015.

Welch, Sharon. *A Feminist Ethic of Risk.* Minneapolis: Fortress Press, 1990.

Whitehead, Alfred North. *Process and Reality.* New York: Free Press, 2010.

Wieman, Henry Nelson. *The Source of Human Good.* Chicago: University of Chicago Press, 1946.

Wieman, Henry Nelson. *Man's Ultimate Commitment.* Carbondale: Southern Illinois University Press, 1958.

Williamson, Marianne. *A Return to Love: Reflections on the Principles of A Course in Miracles.* San Francisco: HarperOne, 2009.

Wuthnow, Robert. *After Heaven: Spirituality in America Since the 1950s.* Berkeley: University of California Press, 1998.

York, Michael. *The Emerging Network: A Sociology of the New Age and Neo-pagan Movements.* London: Rowman & Littlefield, 1995.

Young, John L. *A Graceful Minority.* Paramus, NJ: Central Unitarian Church, 1984.

Young, John L. *Our Faith.* Paramus, NJ: Central Unitarian Church, 1984.

Young, John L. *Creation Songs: Interpretations of the Psalms.* Bloomington, IN: Xlibris Publishing, 2004.

Young, John L. (Autobiography of Frederick H. Schultz as told to). *The Gift of Public Service.* Jacksonville, FL: Jacksonville Historical Society, 2011.

Zimmer, Heinrich. *Philosophies of India.* Edited by Joseph Campbell. Princeton: Princeton University Press, 1951.

About the Author

John Young is a retired Unitarian Universalist minister and professor. He grew up in Kansas, earned a BA at Wichita State University, completed his doctoral coursework in political science at Washington University in St. Louis, and received his Doctorate of Ministry degree from Meadville/ Lombard Seminary at the University of Chicago. In mid-career, he was a Harvard Fellow.

John served churches in Chicago; New York City; Bloomington, Indiana; Paramus, New Jersey; Sacramento, California; and Jacksonville, Florida. He was also an adjunct professor at the University of North Florida where he taught courses in nonviolence, the religions of India, the truth and reconciliation process (with Archbishop Desmond Tutu), liberal religion, and combining activism with personal spiritual practices.

John has been an active advocate for civil rights, disarmament, mental health, LGBTQ rights, and overcoming poverty, racism, and homelessness. He has served as president: of the U.S. Chapter of International Association for Religious Freedom and the UU-UN Office, was chair of the UU Society of San Francisco's social justice council, and presently serves on the U.S. chapter board and the international Council of IARF. John is married to Kathleen Moran, a retired editor and technical writer. John and Kathleen hike, bike, play piano, and savor the Bay Area's cultural offerings.

CPSIA information can be obtained
at www.ICGtesting.com
Printed in the USA
BVHW040244040422
633072BV00001B/3